THE LAMPS WENT OUT
IN EUROPE

Ludwig Reiners

THE
LAMPS WENT OUT
IN EUROPE

TRANSLATED FROM THE GERMAN

BY RICHARD AND CLARA WINSTON

Meridian Books

THE WORLD PUBLISHING COMPANY

CLEVELAND AND NEW YORK

TITLE OF THE GERMAN ORIGINAL EDITION:
In Europa gehen die Lichter aus

A Meridian Book
Published by The World Publishing Company
2231 West 110th Street, Cleveland, Ohio 44102

Published simultaneously in Canada by Nelson, Foster & Scott Ltd.

First Meridian Printing 1966

Library of Congress Catalog Card Number: 55-10282

Printed in the United States of America.

CONTENTS

Chapter

The lamps are going out all over Europe; we shall not see them lit again in our life-time.

—GREY

The mistakes that have been committed in foreign policy are not, as a rule, apparent to the public until a generation afterwards.

—BISMARCK

World history is not the soil of our happiness.

—HEGEL

CHAPTER ONE

Bismarck's Heritage

This man was one of those who always come
When an age about to die draws up the sum
Of everything that it has been and meant.
Then one man, under the whole weight unbent,
Casts all into the cavern of his heart.
The others took their good and bad apart,
But he can feel nothing but life's great mass,
And that he holds all things in one embrace.

—RILKE

I

German history has been a sad affair ever since the middle of the thirteenth century, when the last of the Hohenstaufens died. The authority of the empire disintegrated; there was no longer a recognized capital; Germany splintered into hundreds upon hundreds of petty states and fragments of states. The political, economic and cultural barriers between these states were raised higher and higher. Finally the religious dissension of the Reformation split the German people into two hostile camps. Once upon a time the German Empire had shielded the western world against Arabs, Normans, Hungarians, and Mongols. Now Germany became the threshing-floor upon which foreign nations flailed their bloody harvests. They profited mightily. The coastline of Germany was not her own. Poland, Sweden, Denmark, and France held much of German soil. In the turmoil of the Religious Wars Germany was caught in a Franco-Swedish pincers; then the Turks replaced the Swedes, but the steel pinched just as hard. The Germans deeply felt the danger of their position in the heart of Europe. While other nations were reaching out across the seas, the Germans retreated into dusty libraries where no sea-breezes penetrated. That the Germans are abnormally deficient in any gift for politics is both cause and effect of this history. But the power vacuum in the heart of Europe was no blessing to other nations either. Had Germany not been divided, Louis XIV would never have been able to set the Continent blazing for forty years; Napoleon would never have begun his parades to Madrid and Moscow. In all the battles of those centuries German blood was shed on both sides.

Within Germany herself, the powerful rivalry between two German powers, Austria and Prussia, while making for a tremendous enrichment of her culture, had the direst political consequences. The Holy Roman Empire of the German Nation was a medieval phantasm which Napoleon dispelled with a kick. The Confederation of the Rhine seemed to the French the last word of history, and the German coast as far as Lübeck became part of the French Empire. In Aachen all German newspapers were banned; in the Palatinate recruits were loaded aboard the French vessels which Nelson was to send to the bottom at Trafalgar; on the snowy plains of Russia tens of thousands of German soldiers bled under the banners of Napoleon. It was only a fortunate accident that a power had risen in northern Germany which was able, with the support of Russia, to check Napoleon's presumption.

But the powerless German Confederation remained the laughing-stock of Europe. The "parliament of professors" at Frankfurt imagined that its decree on "fundamental rights" would be sufficient to bring in the dawn of a new era; it did not suspect how German unity would be opposed by Europe. This parliament decided to build a navy, and England coldly retorted that she would treat the German flag as a pirate flag. In 1863 Denmark, in open breach of the London Treaty, annexed Schleswig. In reply to a German protest, England's subsequent prime minister, Salisbury, wrote that Schleswig-Holstein was needed only as a naval base—and Germany did not need a fleet. Her claim to Schleswig, he declared self-righteously, was like Ahab's claim upon Naboth's vineyard—an attempt at outright theft unparalleled in history. He continued cynically that France might, "without undue pangs of conscience," tear up the treaties which barred her from the left bank of the Rhine and absorb those "half-French" districts—the Rhine Province, the Rhine Palatinate, and Rhine-Hesse. Only by such a move, he maintained, would Napoleon III regain the wavering affections of his people.

Thus a man of Salisbury's standing wished to see prolonged the fragmentation of Germany which had obtained over the centuries. Such was the situation in Europe when there appeared on the stage of history the man who was to bring Germany out of her six-hundred-year-old misery—though only for a few short decades.

II

Bismarck did not follow any preconceived plan for creating a German Empire. In politics he was never a system-monger. It was his way to keep in view a variety of goals and to exploit the many opportunities which offered themselves at any given moment. Or as he himself expressed it in one of his magnificent images: "We can do no more than wait until we hear the footsteps of God in history; then we must leap forward and try to hang on to His coat-tails."

The annexation of Schleswig-Holstein by Prussia was only the prelude to German unification, but even in taking this first step Bismarck had the entire world against him. England, France, Russia, and Austria opposed this action, but so did the German people, so did King Wilhelm of Prussia. Bismarck first secured Russia's friendship by helping the Czar to suppress a Polish uprising. Members of the Prussian *Landtag* who were innocent of the realities of politics upbraided him; he would do better, they said, if he persuaded the Czar to treat the Poles with less severity. Bismarck replied sharply: "It is always perilous to give advice to foreign states on their internal affairs. It leads easily to responses in kind. The advice His Majesty the Czar would give me on how to handle the Prussian *Landtag* I would not dare mention in your presence." He then kept Napoleon III in check by dangling before him vague promises of territory in Belgium or the Rhineland; rightly calculated that he had nothing to fear from England because of Gladstone's indecisiveness; and lured Austria into the game on his own side. Proceeding toward his goal with the greatest circumspection, he offered Denmark a compromise: let Schleswig-Holstein return to its former status of union with Denmark and he would be content. Denmark, deceived by all the talk in the British press of England's surely coming to her aid, rejected this suggestion. Only then did Bismarck unleash the Prussian and Austrian troops.

His initial solution for the German question was also conceived in modest terms. Prussia was to become the predominant power in North Germany, Austria in South Germany. Austria would not accept this compromise. Realizing then that his ideal of German unity would have to be imposed by force on the German states, Bismarck faced the necessity of war against a brother nation. Once he had made up his mind, he did not hesitate, even when the Prussian *Landtag* assured him that he would not be able to get the recruits into the troop trains. Always flexible in pursuit of his aims, he tried to win over Bavaria by offering her hegemony in South Germany, but in vain. Ruthless toward his own past, this notorious reactionary proposed the election of an all-German parliament by universal suffrage; at that time not a single great power in Europe had gone this far in the direction of democracy. Even August Bebel, the great socialist leader, thought the German people not yet ripe for it.

When Austria committed the folly of mobilizing the troops of the German Confederation against Prussia, Bismarck insisted that King Wilhelm declare war. The King refused. Bismarck retired from his audience with the King, and burst into tears in the anteroom. Fifteen minutes later he returned to the fray and forced Wilhelm to sign the declaration of war—this time leaving the King in tears. We can feel only admiration for the monarch who found this decision so hard to make, and admiration for the statesman who was willing to take the burden of responsibility upon his own conscience for Germany's sake.

A few weeks later, after the Austrians were decisively defeated at Sadowa, this same man opposed his own generals and demanded extreme moderation. By threats of resignation he made King Wilhelm accept the "disgraceful" peace settlement by which Austria lost not a foot of territory and paid not a penny in reparations. He was not above using the methods of spy thrillers to attain his ends: during the negotiations with Bavaria he had a note smuggled into the coat pocket of Count Bray, the Bavarian minister. The note read: "Reject all territorial claims; offer instead a military alliance with the North German Confederation." On this basis he came to terms with South Germany.

It was this incredible flexibility of his, this plethora of new ideas, this constant shift from hard to soft policy, that kept France from intervening during this Austro-Prussian war of 1866. Such intervention would probably have meant a world war, for before the war Austria had made a treaty with France agreeing to the formation of an "independent" Rhenish state. After Prussia's victory France promptly demanded Luxemburg, the Saar, the Palatinate, Rhine-Hesse, and Mainz as "compensation" for the unification of North Germany. But by then it was too late. Count Benedetti, the French ambassador, wrote anxiously to Napoleon III that he did not dare deliver such demands orally to the hot-tempered prime minister of Prussia. He sent a note, which Bismarck simply ignored. He could afford to do so now that he was again at peace with Austria and South Germany.

Bismarck again employed the greatest delicacy in bringing about unification with the South Germans. As late as 1868 he assured the war minister of Württemberg that the formation of a united Germany in the nineteenth century would be unlooked-for good fortune; that if anything of the sort should happen in ten or even five years it would be an outright miracle. He suspected that France, Austria and Italy had formed a triple alliance to oppose German unification. That alliance had at its disposal more than one hundred million people and nearly three million bayonets. France and Austria had agreed that, if it came to war, they would not lay down their arms until Germany had been converted into a confederation consisting "insofar as possible of equally powerful states." Austria was to receive Silesia; France the left bank of the Rhine. The French, Austrian, and Italian armies would meet in the neighborhood of Leipzig.

Bismarck had no intention of provoking this triple alliance. He therefore rejected Baden's offer to enter the North German Confederation, preferring not to give the French any pretext for war. Meanwhile he waited for God's footstep. When it came, he leaped. Napoleon III, tormented by an ambitious wife, gallstones, and waning popularity at home, was lured into forcing the issue of the Spanish succession after the Hohenzollern aspirant had solemnly renounced his candidature. He demanded further guarantees and an apology from King Wilhelm. Prussia rudely rejected the demand, and France declared war. Because Bismarck had the support of Russia, Austria played a waiting game, and after the first Prussian victories she held to her neutrality. South Germany marched at Prussia's side; Italy did not lift a finger; and France was beaten.

But even now the building of a German Reich called for super-human tact. Bismarck granted the South German states every special privilege they desired. He did not stop at bribes. King Louis II of Bavaria and his intimate associate, Count Holnstein, were awarded large pensions in return for offering the imperial crown to King Wilhelm of Prussia; the letter King Louis sent to the hated Prussian King was written by Bismarck. With a margin of just two votes above the necessary two-thirds majority, the Bavarian *Landtag* gave its approval. Bismarck shrugged off Wilhelm's protest that he wanted to be titled "Emperor of Germany," not the "German Emperor." After the procla-mation containing the offensive phrase was read out, the new Kaiser strode past the creator of his Reich without a word and went on to greet the princes and generals.

III

But the German Reich had been founded. "Under the guns of all of Europe" Germany was at last a nation-state—centuries later than her neighbors. Profiting by the situation beyond her borders—a friendly Russia, a beaten France, an intimidated Austria, and an England benevolently waiting to see—the most helpless country in Europe had become at one magic stroke the most powerful state in the world. All the statesmen of Europe kept a wary eye on Berlin. They felt certain that after such tremendous triumphs Bismarck would reach out for further booty—like Louis XIV or the two Napoleons.

But nothing of the sort happened. What followed was a development unique in history: a statesman at the summit of success renounced all further efforts to extend his country's power and bent every effort to preserve peace. In a note intended only for Kaiser Wilhelm's guidance —not for publication—Bismarck wrote that German unification was the most Europe could be expected to brook from the Germans; Germany must therefore attempt no further expansion and must keep herself within bounds her neighbors would not resent. When Randolph Churchill, Winston Churchill's father, said to the chancellor's son,

Herbert Bismarck, that Germany and England together might rule the world, the chancellor noted quietly: "Not enough." More than once the German generals urged a preventive war against France or Russia. Each time Bismarck replied that so long as he remained in charge no preventive war would ever be fought; in such a venture one could never foresee the ways of divine Providence. He also asked his Austrian opposite numbers to make sure that the general staff never became political advisers to the Emperor—government ministers would naturally be more peacefully inclined than military men. And he was so strong in his own eyes and in those of the world that he felt he need not be anxious over the prestige of Germany. During the Egyptian crisis of the eighties Germany demanded nothing for herself. "We are no prestige-mad fools," the chancellor wrote to his Foreign Office. And the *London Times* testified that no European power had behaved with such great modesty and wisdom as Germany; that Germany was really the great moderating and restraining influence in Europe and had employed her tremendous military strength consistently to frustrate every attempt to disturb European peace.

As Bismarck saw it, Germany's geographical position and small size made a policy of expansionism a ridiculous luxury for her. Colonies, he had declared bitingly in the seventies, reminded him of the sable coats of certain Polish noblemen who did not have a shirt to their name. Ten years later he was still of this opinion, although special reasons prompted him to acquire certain colonial areas.

All the details of his policies sprang from this basic attitude. In 1871 he had reluctantly yielded to the insistence of the generals and annexed Alsace and a fifth of Lorraine. He dubbed as "an idea of schoolmasters" the argument that these areas were really German; he took full cognizance of the fact that no one in those provinces wanted to "come home to the Reich" and that all the delegates from Alsace-Lorraine had objected to the annexation. Military considerations prompted Bismarck to make this one great diplomatic mistake of his life. At the time, he was not sure he could rely upon the South German governments and he was afraid that if the French were in Alsace they might, in case of war, arrive in Karlsruhe and Stuttgart sooner than the Prussian troops. But he proposed to the general staff that Metz at least be left to the French. Instead of the city, he recommended, the thing was to demand an extra billion francs in reparations and use the money to build another fort. The general staff would not hear of this proposal and Bismarck barely succeeded in having Belfort left to the French. Later he refused, and according to the thinking of his time had to refuse, to return any of the annexed territory. When it was suggested to him that he restore Metz to the French, he snapped instantly, in the words of Schiller's King Philip: "Hand the knife to my murderer?" He felt certain that the French would not abandon thoughts of revenge, no matter what concessions were made to them. Had they not demanded *revanche* for the Prussian victory over Austria?

Nevertheless, he instructed Field Marshal Manteuffel, commander of the occupation troops in France, to "deal generously" in all matters; a victor could not be civil enough, he said. Let Manteuffel act in the spirit that he, Bismarck, had shown during the peace negotiations when he made a point of seeing Monsieur Thiers to the front door after each conversation. The field marshal followed the suggestion; when the occupation troops withdrew, the President of the French Republic wrote to him to express gratitude for his "justice and impartiality."

What was more, Bismarck did everything to obtain for France tenfold compensation overseas for the loss of Alsace-Lorraine. Thanks to his backing, the French were able to build up their colonial empire in Africa and Asia. The chancellor repeatedly assured France that Germany's support throughout the world was certainly worth more than the two provinces to them. And in fact French President Grévy declared in 1883 that he was well aware of how amicably Bismarck had treated France in the thirteen years following the war. When Bismarck acted as mediator in the Franco-Chinese war, the French ambassador in Berlin told him that the French people, who understood nobility and gratitude, would never forget this service of his. For a while Bismarck was called the *Grand Electeur* of France.

But for all his wooing of France, Bismarck never succeeded in banishing entirely the idea of *revanche*. He therefore did everything in his power to make Germany secure against France. France by herself could never attack Germany. Everything therefore depended upon preventing her from winning allies. War, Bismarck thought, would be certain the day France felt she could count upon Russia's assistance.

Throughout his chancellorship, therefore, Bismarck took pains to maintain good relations with St. Petersburg. He was, however, well aware that to comply with all the Czar's wishes would be the worst method of retaining Russia's friendship. Russia would consider a docile ally no more than a vassal. Two years after the establishment of the Reich, the Czar—still thinking in terms of the politics of 1813—demanded that Germany cede North Schleswig to him as recompense for his neutrality. Six years later he asked for a free hand to attack Austria. These incidents were instructive. So long as Germany had no ally but Russia, she would be unable to influence Russia. The only way to remain on a good footing with Russia was to form still closer ties with Russia's rival, Austria.

But Kaiser Wilhelm, from the bottom of his heart, rejected an alliance with Austria. Such a tie struck him as betrayal of his friend and nephew, Czar Alexander; rather than commit such a foul act of disloyalty, he declared, he would abdicate in favor of his son. Bismarck, vacationing in Bad Gastein at the time, sent a long letter in his own hand to the Kaiser. Wilhelm refused to yield. The chancellor's idea that an Austro-German defense alliance would isolate Russia and therefore force her closer to Germany was too subtle for the Kaiser's uncomplicated mind. He agreed only after Bismarck consented to Wilhelm's informing Czar Alexander of the general nature of the treaty.

The result of this treaty was a balance of power in which every slightest nuance might be decisive. Bismarck therefore carefully avoided interfering with Russia's drive to obtain ice-free ports. If the huge empire were going to insist upon harbors in Constantinople or East Asia, Germany would not say nay. Rather than becloud his good relations with Russia, Bismarck refused a Japanese offer of an alliance. He also saw to it that Germany was not dragged into needless adventures by her alliance with Austria. Several times he declared in plain language that all the Balkans were "not worth the bones of a single German grenadier." The alliance did not cover Austria's Balkan ambitions—"for that would mean encouragement for her to look for trouble." The pact was not intended to forward aggression and expansion, but to insure the *status quo*. When the Austrians sent a note stating that, if the situation called for it, a declaration of war upon Russia should be issued by Austria and Germany on the same day, Bismarck wrote on the margin of this dispatch: "Nonsense. We will declare war on Russia only after she has attacked Austria or has declared war upon Austria, in which case Austria will already be at war." When the Viennese ambassador reported that Emperor Franz Josef's mood was distinctly depressed, Bismarck wrote: "Better than if it were enterprising." He urged the Austrians to let Russia push to Constantinople. Russia, he argued, would only be weakened by such an undertaking, and England would stop any further advance—England in any case had a real interest in keeping Russia far from the Suez Canal. The naive Austrian statesmen thought to assure themselves England's friendship by maintaining an anti-Russian posture. Bismarck explained to them that they must give England the impression that they could always make a deal with Russia. He gave short shrift to a Russian proposal which meant in effect: "The devil with Austria. She must disappear from the map. You take the German provinces."

Bismarck's idea that an Austro-German alliance would lead Russia back into the German fold turned out to be absolutely right; within a year the Three Emperors' Alliance was formed. It lasted for six years; then Russia refused to extend it because of her anger over Austria's Balkan policy. At the same time she proposed continuation of the Russo-German alliance. Bismarck then concluded the famous Reinsurance Treaty providing that both powers should remain neutral if the other were attacked. He did not fear Austrian suspicions; on the contrary, he wanted some knowledge of the treaty's contents to trickle through to Austria so that Austria, knowing she would not have Germany's backing in a war of aggression, would look before she leaped.

Italy had earlier asked to be admitted to the Austro-German alliance. The result was the Triple Alliance which was then joined by Rumania, and for a time by Serbia. The King of Spain personally assured Bismarck of his aid in case of a Franco-German war.

Still not content, Bismarck created a Mediterranean triple alliance among England, Austria and Italy which guaranteed the territorial *status quo* in the Mediterranean. Spain joined this alliance. Had France tried to take Morocco at this time, these four powers would have interfered. When England proposed that Germany also join the Mediterranean pact, Bismarck refused, since such an alliance was incompatible with his Reinsurance Treaty with Russia. His diplomacy depended upon keeping the friendship of Russia, but at the same time so balancing the scales of power that the Czar also urgently needed a friendly Germany.

He never would have succeeded in keeping his understanding with Russia had he not simultaneously kept the English card in his deck, ready to play at any time. The chief threat to the peace of the world at this time were the tensions between England and Russia; the two empires were clashing in Constantinople, in the Far East, and on the borders of India. Bismarck kept out of the quarrel, but he was on such excellent terms with London that Prime Minister Salisbury hailed news of the Austro-German alliance as "glad tidings of great joy." Some British newspapers protested this abuse of a Biblical expression. Salisbury had indeed come a long way from "Naboth's vineyard." During the eighties England was often referred to as "the sea power of the Triple Alliance," and the Triple Alliance was called "England's land army." London considered the members of the Triple Alliance a group of contented and peace-loving powers, whereas France and Russia were the troublemakers. But to England also Bismarck never committed himself entirely. He never let the British become overconfident of their hold on Germany; he contrived to remind them skillfully that it was better to have Germany as a friend than as a foe. He was far from being naive enough to think continual good behavior would assure British friendship. "Given the ruthlessness of British policy, timidity is a poor way to maintain good relations with England," he said.

When Gladstone treated him badly, he whipped up a German colonial policy out of nothing, and to the amazement of Europe made Germany the master of a million square kilometers of African soil. Probably Bismarck's colonial policy had another purpose as well. Crown Prince Friedrich was married to the daughter of Queen Victoria. If Friedrich succeeded to the throne, there would be a danger of Germany's becoming so intimate with England that the ties with Russia would be broken. For that eventuality Bismarck wished to keep a few areas of friction with England in readiness.

As soon as Bismarck put his back up, Gladstone became conciliatory. His associate Chamberlain declared that Prince Bismarck had performed such great services for England that he felt sure there was no power in the world England would so gladly oblige as Germany. He profoundly regretted it if awkwardness on the part of a British statesman had aroused temporary ill-feeling. Salisbury, too, repeatedly hailed the chancellor as a good and reliable friend of England. At one time, when a conflict arose between France and England, he went so far as to plant in a newspaper the statement that, in case of a war between Germany and France, England would have nothing to say against Germany's marching through Belgium. At that time Bismarck could have smashed France so thoroughly she would not have recovered for many years. Not for a moment did he dream of doing so.

Finally Bismarck offered Salisbury an alliance. He proposed that England and Germany enter an open defensive alliance, agreeing to help one another if either should be attacked by France. This alliance, he pointed out, would make war in Europe completely impossible. France would never dare to attack either England or Germany if it were clear that she would have both powers to contend with, and Russia would never attack England unless she could count upon aid from France. Salisbury replied that he too would consider an Anglo-German alliance a blessing, but that he would be unable to win a majority for it in the House of Commons. Unfortunately they were no longer living in the age of Pitt when the aristocracy ruled and it was possible to pursue an active foreign policy. Now democracy ruled, he went on to say, and along with it party government which made every minister dependent upon popular favor. He thanked Bismarck for the proposal and expressed the hope that such a pact would be forged within his lifetime. "Meanwhile we leave it on the table without saying yes nor no. That is unfortunately all I can do at present."

These negotiations nevertheless proved useful in a way Bismarck had anticipated. Word of them trickled through to St. Petersburg, and a mistrustful inquiry came from the Russian capital: why was Bismarck's son Herbert in London? Bismarck replied that he was negotiating the Samoa question. Furious, the Czar wrote on the margin of Bismarck's letter: "This knave has something up his sleeve again and is trying to throw dust in our eyes." Had the chancellor learned of this comment he would only have smiled; anxiety and respect were just the feelings he wished the Czar to have toward him. It only secured his hold on Russia. About this same time the Russian ambassador in Berlin told Bismarck that "that filthy little sow Serbia" might as well be left to Austrian influence.

In his *The Diplomacy of Imperialism* the Harvard historian William L. Langer has said:

"Pivoting upon the alliance between Germany and Austria-Hungary, the great chancellor had succeeded, during the last decade of his regime, in building up the Triple Alliance and at the same time in maintaining intact the wire to St. Petersburg. Through the Mediterranean Agreements of 1887 he had established the connexion with England by way of Rome and Vienna. The Bismarckian fold was a veritable menagerie; the Russian bear and the British lion lay down together with the imperial eagles. Only the Gallic cock was missing."

IV

The aim of Bismarck's policy was simple: the peace of Europe. Its methods were complicated, for only by constant shifts of strategy could Bismarck quell the aggressive ambitions of the other powers. A rigid system, fixed principles, would have handicapped him in meeting the ever-changing demands of the day. He was no hidebound programmaker; rather he was an opportunist who acted in accordance with the pressures of any given time. Later Kaiser Wilhelm II was to reckon in terms of fixed world antagonisms. Bismarck never made this mistake. He considered politics a fluid element; that alone explains his tacking between the two actual world powers of this time, England and Russia; it explains his emphatic lack of interest in the Orient, his friendly but never soft attitude toward Austria. In policy of this sort, of course, every single chess-move was deliberate; there was no room in Bismarck's brand of diplomacy for temperamental outbursts such as Wilhelm II loved. Bismarck never acted emotionally. "The point is not to proclaim feelings, no matter how justified, but to practice politics. The word *indignation* has no place in politics."

Bismarck has frequently been pictured as one of those men of action who go their way ruthlessly. In reality he was nothing of the kind. To be sure, he did not know the meaning of fear; at the age of seventy-four, for the reception of the Sultan of Zanzibar, he galloped his horse up the steps of a railroad station in order to dispose of the rumors that his health was failing. Sentimentality was unknown to him. Threats only hardened his determination. He was capable of passionate furies. But in politics he was circumspect and prudent; aside from the annexation of Alsace-Lorraine, he never violated the honor of foreign countries; instead he always acted like a gentleman, so long as German interests were not endangered. With infallible sensitivity he knew how far nations could be expected to go. When Germany fell out with Spain over the Carolines, a group of Pacific islands, Bismarck said: "We shall have to yield because Spain is too weak to make concessions." He knew that at home and abroad the Spanish government was not strong enough to be able to afford compromises. At the same time he knew how to wring an advantage from his own concessions: he proposed that the Pope arbitrate the dispute and thereby solidified his amicable relations with the Vatican, which had been shattered during the *Kulturkampf*. Leo XIII became an admirer of Bismarck and conferred the Order of Christ upon him.

This alleged country squire was in speech and in writing wittier and more brilliant than most of the writers of his era; next to Goethe and Lessing he was Germany's greatest prose stylist. The finest of satirists might envy him the pithy irony of his utterances. The "iron" chancellor was a man of shades and nuances; his policy was reared upon a foundation of fantastically delicate balances. Thus he joined weird contradictions: he expelled Austria from Germany and then made Austria an ally; he collaborated harmoniously with Napoleon and then waged war upon him; he founded the Reich with Russia's backing, assiduously courted Russia's favor, and at the same time kept her in fear of Germany. He made England swallow the annexation of Hanover and his transformation of Germany into a mighty Continental power. In spite of this he could always count on London's friendship. He was the very opposite of methodical; he was a creative personality.

Bismarck has been called the prime minister of Europe. The British ambassador, originally one of his opponents, wrote to London that Bismarck's word was gospel in St. Petersburg, Paris, and Rome; his statements evoked awe and his silence fear. In the eighties, Waddington, then French ambassador to London, later French premier, declared that he considered Bismarck the guarantor of world peace. The German chancellor, he said, held the position of arbiter in Europe; after him there would be no one to fill a similar position. "It is my firm conviction that as long as Bismarck remains at the rudder we can count unconditionally upon Germany's good faith. Once the chancellor lays down his office, stormy times will descend upon Europe. Only then will we realize how precious present German policy has been for the peace and prosperity of the nations." When the German diplomatic papers were published after World War I, the great British historian Gooch wrote: "Our belief is confirmed, that from 1871 till his fall in 1890 Bismarck was the pillar of European peace." Since pacifism consists not in demands and declamations, but in the art of finding ways to keep the peace, Bismarck was a great pacifist from the day the Reich was established.

CHAPTER TWO

The Wire to St. Petersburg Is Severed

It may take fifty years before political blunders become obvious and produce their ultimate consequences, but in the end History presents her reckoning for every mistake; she is more exacting about that than our Prussian Bureau of the Budget. Only when the figures lie before the public is it possible to see the line of fracture where the thing went wrong.

—BISMARCK

I

On March 20, 1890, Wilhelm II, by God's wrath German Emperor and King of Prussia, dismissed Prince Bismarck from office. It was just a few days before the chancellor's seventy-fifth birthday. The reasons Wilhelm gave for this action were of the flimsiest. The plain fact was that he wanted to rule the Reich alone. The greatest statesman in German history was, as he himself described it, "fired on a day's notice" and in terms which no decent draper's shop would have used toward a clerk of many years' service. Bismarck was asked to return his salary for the last eleven days of the quarter, which had already been paid out to him. The new chancellor, General von Caprivi, was instructed not to go to Bismarck for a briefing on the world situation. The general took the post simply as a soldier obeying orders. The Kaiser had said to him: "There are no mysteries about diplomacy. The responsibility will be all mine."

All the capitals of Europe were alarmed. Government bonds fell on the Paris bourse. Everywhere people feared for peace. In London, *Punch* published the famous cartoon: "Dropping the pilot." The powers must be prepared to change their policy toward Germany, the Belgian ambassador wrote home; moreover, the Triple Alliance would miss the towering prestige of Bismarck. "The hopes of Germany's enemies may revive when they see themselves no longer confronted by an adversary whose superiority was incontestable and uncontested."

Only one nation learned of Bismarck's dismissal with equanimity: Germany herself. The *Reichstag* was triumphant. The Left was pleased, and with low bows to the young monarch the entire Right accepted the fall of the man of the century. In Paris Paul de Cassagnac wrote: "No, the Germans are not a good people. For us Frenchmen the sky itself would not be high enough to raise our praises for a Bismarck." In Germany there were only a few people wise enough to be anxious; Bismarck's old enemy Windhorst, leader of the Center, begged the prince to stay in spite of the Kaiser, and the intelligent democrat Ludwig Bamberger wrote in concern: "His opponents as well as his disciples have been struck with a terror of the Unknown, to which the doors have been thrown open unnecessarily. They wonder at the senselessness of taking the man who commanded the greatest political authority in the world, an authority which he used in the service of world peace, and throwing his living body into the charnel-house."

The rudder of the Reich was taken over by Wilhelm himself—a young man whose father had written to Bismarck a few years earlier to say that because of the Crown Prince's lack of maturity and his tendency toward arrogance it would be dangerous to let him get in contact with foreign policy. This young man failed to see that Bismarck's prestige in the world was worth more to Germany than ten army corps; that Bismarck, and Bismarck alone, could pursue a policy of moderation without giving either the world or his people the impression that it was motivated by fear; that Bismarck, and he alone, possessed that combination of originality and subtlety which make the statesman. Ignorant of what he was losing, Wilhelm received in the gayest spirits the resignation he had forced. When the letter was handed to him he went on turning the pages of music for his friend Eulenburg, who was singing sentimental songs. "The course remains the same: full steam ahead!" he telegraphed to the world. But Bismarck had never sailed full steam ahead. And it was only a matter of a few days before Wilhelm had steered the ship of state straight into a deadly reef.

II

A few days before Bismarck's fall the Russian ambassador, Shuvalov, had proposed a six-year renewal of the Russo-German neutrality pact. We will recall that in this Reinsurance Treaty Germany and Russia had agreed to remain neutral if either partner became involved in a war, though an exception was made if Russia attacked Austria or Germany attacked France. Both powers further agreed that territorial changes in the Balkans were to be undertaken only by mutual agreement. Germany promised diplomatic support if Russia should occupy the entrance to the Black Sea.

In concluding this treaty Bismarck had had three purposes. First, he wanted to prevent a Russo-French alliance; that in itself would safeguard Germany, for France could not attack Germany unless she were certain of Russian aid. Second, he wanted to show the British, traditionally opposed to Russia, that Germany's friendship was of value to England. Third, he wanted to restrain Vienna; the security of the German position vis-à-vis Austria depended upon the possibility of a German understanding with Russia. "Once this possibility disappears, Austria will become a far more demanding ally!" Bismarck warned. For that reason he would have preferred to publish his treaty with Russia, but the Czar had the Pan-Slavists to consider and wanted to maintain his pose of a strong man with a free hand.

Nevertheless, the terms of the treaty were known in London and Rome, probably also in Vienna. That the treaty lent support to Russia's aggressive attitude toward Turkey was precisely what Bismarck wanted; fear of a Russian attempt to seize Constantinople helped to keep the cabinets in London and Rome friendly toward Germany. At the same time, Russian designs on Constantinople were a wedge between St. Petersburg and Paris. It seemed unlikely to Bismarck that Russia would actually make the attempt, or that if she did she could carry it off, for the Mediterranean Triple Alliance stood in her way. For Bismarck, the Reinsurance Treaty and the Mediterranean Triple Alliance formed a seesaw of which Germany was the pivot. Fear of Russian expansion prevented the other countries from entering into an alliance with St. Petersburg; at the same time Russia was effectively held in bounds, at least as far as Europe was concerned. As Bismarck said, the treaty put a premium upon peaceful conduct.

For Russia, on the other hand, the treaty represented the realization of her dearest wish: in case of a war with England she need not fear German and Austrian divisions on her western frontiers. For the Czar the Balkan question was not urgent; he preferred to continue pushing forward into Central and East Asia. Alexander III was peaceable; his foreign minister, Giers, was a timid old gentleman, a Swedish Finn definitely not inclined toward Pan-Slavism. Bismarck treated him with great respect and cordiality; he wanted to strengthen Giers's self-assurance and his position with the Czar.

Shuvalov, the Russian ambassador, was in despair when Bismarck, replying to his request for extension of the treaty, said that he was about to be dismissed and therefore could no longer make any policy decisions. Bismarck's son Herbert, who was then foreign secretary, also referred the ambassador to his as yet unknown successor. Shuvalov replied that his instructions called for negotiating only with the Bismarcks, father and son, and that he would have to obtain new instructions. Everything now depended upon the Kaiser. The chief persons influencing Wilhelm's decision were his chief of the general staff, Count Waldersee, and Privy Councillor Holstein.

Waldersee hated Bismarck's peace policy. An old hand at intrigue, he hoped by crude flattery of the young Kaiser to win the post of chancellor some day. It was he who had persuaded the Kaiser that Bismarck was incompetent and must go. At the same time he was capable of writing in his diary: "God alone knows that I have done nothing whatsoever to push myself forward into such a career. I am well aware that I cannot cope with such tasks and would be grateful could I remain in my proper profession. . . . I consider anyone who would wish to assume the succession right now extremely reckless. It may be worth considering after one or two successors have broken their necks." This hero was wont to say that nothing remained for Germany but "to kill somebody to the left or to the right." A campaign in alliance with Austria against Russia seemed to him the more tempting homicide. That nations cannot be killed, and that a victory would gain Germany nothing but a second vengeful neighbor, never occurred to him; these ideas were too complicated for a mind like his. Three years earlier, before Wilhelm came to the throne, Waldersee had persuaded the young prince to come out privately for a preventive war "in order to smash the Russian power."

Since that time, it is true, Wilhelm changed his mind more than once. Five days before Bismarck's dismissal he announced his intention of visiting the Czar. The next day, in order to be able to cast blame on Bismarck, he chose to believe unfounded rumors and declared that Russia was mobilizing against Germany. It was imperative that Vienna be warned. The day of Bismarck's dismissal he shifted ground again— thanks to a clever move by Herbert Bismarck. The foreign secretary wrote to the Kaiser giving an exaggerated version of Shuvalov's remarks; in view of the change of chancellors Russia preferred to let the treaty lapse. Herbert Bismarck was well aware that there was no better way to make Wilhelm favor the renewal.

The Kaiser was dumbfounded. Was this the first consequence of Bismarck's dismissal? Was he, Wilhelm, less trustworthy than his chancellor had been? Were foreign difficulties to come of this domestic decision? Had Bismarck turned the Russians against him? At one o'clock in the morning he sent a military policeman to waken Shuvalov and ask him to come to the palace next morning. Shuvalov took this to mean that there was bad news concerning the Czar. Instead, the Kaiser assured the Russian ambassador that he had no intention of changing Bismarck's policy; for his part he was eager to renew the treaty.

St. Petersburg was content. Although the Czar informed the Kaiser that he hoped Bismarck would soon return to office, he simultaneously issued orders that new instructions, and the necessary authorization to negotiate with the new chancellor, be sent to Shuvalov. He went still further and left it to Germany's discretion to decide whether the supplementary clause about the Straits should be retained. Everything seemed to be going well, and Waldersee wrote irritably in his diary: "We are now changing décor fast and frequently." But before the papers for Shuvalov arrived there came a counterstroke that decided the fate of Europe. It came from Holstein.

III

Fritz von Holstein held the post of privy councillor in the Foreign Office. At this time he was fifty-five years old, with a somber life behind him. His youth had been solitary. He had lost his mother while still a young child; his father was killed in a fire before his eyes. He never attended school, never had playmates. The sweetheart of his youth married some other man; throughout his life he wrote her endless letters, signing them, "Your brother Fritz." He was eccentric from boyhood; he used to force himself to break his sleep in the middle of the night and sit for a time in an uncomfortable position in accordance with his strange theory that it was effeminate and debilitating to get a full night's rest. By the age of twenty-six he was troubled by rheumatism and stomach cramps. In St. Petersburg this awkward young official was the butt of much mild ridicule—a thing which he never forgot. He lost his next post, at Washington, because he had become too intimate with the wife of a high American official. He took leave of the diplomatic service for several years and hoped to get rich by running a tugboat company. As might have been expected, it was a losing proposition. Returning to government service he was employed by Bismarck when the chancellor had to do—as he used to say in English—"evil things in this evil world." In 1870 Bismarck sent Holstein to Florence to contact Italian revolutionaries and organize an uprising in Italy in case the Italians attempted to come to the aid of the French. When difficulties arose between Crown Prince Friedrich and Bismarck, Holstein is supposed to have suggested that the chancellor have the Crown Prince poisoned. Holstein was next attached to the embassy in Paris and was employed by Bismarck to spy on Arnim, the intriguing ambassador to France. The story goes that he lay under a sofa, eavesdropping, while his superior conducted negotiations. When Arnim was brought to trial in Germany, Holstein was the chief witness against him. This cost him the little popularity he might have had. He was boycotted by his peers. When he went to any of the noblemen's clubs, a yawning emptiness formed around him. The numerous kin of the Arnims had enough power socially to more than outweigh Bismarck's benevolent backing. Holstein would have liked to challenge his snubbers to a duel; he had never been cowardly. But how could he take on an entire club?

"Useful only below stairs," Bismarck said concisely, and he called Holstein the man with the hyena eyes. Holstein repaid him and the world for their contempt with bitter hatred. He went about with a loaded revolver in his coat pocket. He compiled lists of homosexuals, adulterers, alcoholics, sadists and bankrupts. He "had something" on everybody. He lived in a three-room apartment, tyrannized by an aging housekeeper. When the Kaiser sent him an invitation to an official luncheon, he replied that he had no dress suit. Using his knowledge of government secrets, he speculated on the stock exchange and lost the rest of his fortune. "If I don't trip him, he will trip me," was his guiding principle in all his relations with others. Calculation ruled his every thought. With superiors he stressed a footing of equality, proving to himself that he need not be servile. For years he was on terms of close friendship with one of his associates; suddenly, without even telling the man the reason, he refused to see him again. On a Sunday evening at Bismarck's home he would pay court to a lady so tempestuously that Bismarck's wife would smilingly have to intervene; on Monday when he met the same lady on *Unter den Linden* he would not even raise his hat to her. Bismarck said later: "I was the only one who could handle Holstein because he knew that if necessary I would slash his face." Holstein soon collided with Herbert Bismarck. Shortly before Bismarck's fall the two men were close to the breaking point. Both Bismarcks bluntly said he was unbalanced; in spite of his superior abilities he was employable only under supervision.

IV

Holstein had long ago realized that under Bismarck he could never hope for power. Therefore Bismarck had to go. Consequently he joined the group who were constantly urging the Kaiser that he must no longer tolerate the "Bismarck dynasty." It was Holstein who supplied Waldersee with material against Bismarck. Was the Kaiser to go on travelling around the world for the "firm of Bismarck and son"? The old prince was, he alleged, a drug addict, servile to Russia, senile, and ready to sacrifice the Triple Alliance to the Russians. All of Holstein's thinking circled around a single point: how to win power for himself. In that light alone he regarded the problem of the Reinsurance Treaty. If the treaty were extended, the Czar might possibly persuade the Kaiser to recall Bismarck. Once the mighty prince again mounted the steps of the *Wilhelmstrasse* with thunderous tread, Holstein would promptly find himself back home with a slender pension. The Czar might even blackmail the Kaiser; he would threaten to publish the secret terms of the treaty unless Bismarck returned to office. In fact Bismarck himself could force his reinstatement by this same threat—

and what a revenge the chancellor would then take! Obviously the Bismarcks were insisting on extension of the treaty only for these personal reasons, Holstein decided. In frantic haste he wrote to Count Eulenburg, the middleman through whom he sent information to the Kaiser: "If the agreement goes through, our reputations and our social positions will depend upon the discretion of R. [Russia]. It is to R.'s interest to be indiscreet, for as soon as that affair is even suspected, everybody, that is, our other friends, will break with us. We will then be dependent upon our association with R. alone, whose social position as against the others will rise as ours falls. R. can then impose conditions upon us for continued association. The first condition would be: 'I want to deal with my former business associate B., and with him alone!' Do you understand the affair now?" Such was Holstein's mad reasoning!

But how could he poison the minds of the young Kaiser and the new chancellor against a treaty which was in fact so greatly to Germany's advantage? Holstein first asserted that the neutrality treaty went against the spirit—if not the letter—of the Triple Alliance treaty. He himself did not believe this argument; the Triple Alliance treaty obligated Germany to come to the aid of Austria if she were attacked, and the neutrality treaty with Russia did not deal with such a case. The Triple Alliance was, as Bismarck had repeatedly stressed, not designed for aggressive purposes, but to secure the *status quo*. This was precisely the aim of the neutrality treaty with Russia.

Holstein also argued that if this treaty were made known to the public, Germany would be exposed before the whole world. He craftily concealed the fact that Bismarck had desired rather than feared Russian indiscretion. Respect for Germany in London and Vienna would only be increased if it were known there that the wire between Berlin and St. Petersburg was intact. For Vienna, a German-Russian understanding would not be pleasant, but salutary.

Holstein also pointed out that the Reinsurance Treaty violated the German alliance with Rumania. (His resorting to so paltry an argument—for the German-Rumanian treaty could easily have been amended, if necessary—should have alerted his audience to his insincerity.) Finally, Holstein declared, the whole treaty was unnecessary; the possibility that Russia might switch to the French camp had only been one of Bismarck's silly notions; an alliance between the Czar and a republic was simply inconceivable.

There was, of course, still the new chancellor to take all these empty arguments under consideration. And now it became clear just how terrible a blunder the Kaiser had made in entrusting the destiny of the Reich to a man for whom politics was an alien land. Germany's unfortunate position in Europe, the fact that she was exposed on all

sides, necessitated subtle diplomacy. To deal mechanically in political
abstractions and bureaucratic acrobatics was not enough. But the
world of abstractions and bureaucracy was the only world that either
Caprivi or Holstein knew. Caprivi resembled a capable corporal who
one day is entrusted with the command of a division and then suddenly
discovers how different things look from up on top. He declared flatly
that he could not juggle five balls at once and keep three of them in
the air like Bismarck. Perhaps Bismarck had been strong and clever
enough to manage such an act, but he was a general and would have
to "simplify" politics. He simplified by eliminating from his juggling act
the key ball.

Confronted with so fateful a question, it did not occur to Caprivi to
apply for advice to the foremost diplomatist in the world, Prince Bismarck, who had generously invited him to lunch with him daily. Caprivi did not go, alleging as a reason that Bismarck's wife had made
critical remarks about the Kaiser. Folly is seldom free of cunning; Caprivi violated the policy of his own department by holding conferences
with his other officials behind the back of Herbert Bismarck, who at
this time was still foreign secretary. Some of these gentlemen unfortunately agreed with Holstein. Wilhelm promptly shifted his position
again; probably it gave him pleasure to be able to destroy a part of
Bismarck's work. He said to Waldersee: "Last year I swore loyalty to
the Emperor of Austria, and I shall keep that oath." On such adolescent principles he thought he could govern the Reich. It did not
occur to him that he was under no obligation to further Austria's aggressive projects in the Balkans, and that in fact he could serve Austria
best by preventing her from committing follies.

A week after Bismarck's dismissal, Germany refused to extend the
Reinsurance Treaty.

The following day Wilhelm changed his mind again. Shuvalov had
an audience with him, and in the face of the Russian's calm exposition
of the situation all of Holstein's arguments dissolved into mist. But
this intermezzo lasted only a few hours. Holstein and his followers informed the Russian ambassador that rejection had already been decided upon; the Kaiser shifted ground once more; and Shuvalov wired
the decision to St. Petersburg. Full steam ahead Wilhelm II had sailed
the German ship of state into the most dangerous reef of all.

Shuvalov's dispatch arrived in St. Petersburg at the very moment the
instructions for him to sign the treaty were going out. The Russians had
even decided to be obliging and eliminate the clause about Constantinople, since their interest had turned to East Asia rather than the
Balkans.

When the Russians heard of the German refusal, they were as-
tounded. Was it not only a week since this same Kaiser had routed

their ambassador out of bed at night in order to be assured that the treaty would be renewed? Was an emperor's word meaningless in Berlin? Moreover, when a great power declined to renew a treaty, the universal custom was for it to make counter-proposals, either in order to win more favorable conditions, or in order to escape the odium of being alone responsible for rejection. Apparently the new men in Germany did not think the Czar worth such a courtesy! Had not this same Wilhelm written to his grandmother, Queen Victoria, to say that he was agreeable to the British fleet's being strong enough to force an entry into the Dardanelles if need be—that is, to bombard the Black Sea ports in violation of international treaties! This compromising letter ran directly counter to Bismarck's entire Straits policy, and the British had naturally allowed news of it to leak to St. Petersburg. Now an old general was informing the Czar that a ruler who thought he could do without Bismarck also thought he could do without Russia. "There can be no doubt," the Czar noted on a report from his foreign minister, "that a political change has taken place in Germany." Obviously the young Kaiser, son of a British princess, had changed his course and was now sailing in the English wake.

This interpretation was immediately reinforced. The day after Bismarck's departure the Kaiser attended a dinner in honor of the British Crown Prince, his Uncle Edward, and delivered a speech hailing the German-British brotherhood in arms at Waterloo! Russia felt she was up against a plain Anglo-German coalition. In addition she had to be prepared for an aggressive Balkan policy on the part of Austria. For, as Giers noted anxiously, "as a result of the ending of our treaty Austria is freed from the wise and well-meaning, but strict control of Prince Bismarck."

Alexander and Giers were peaceable by nature. But Russia seemed to them most vulnerable in her isolation. In order to carry out her plans for colonization in Asia, Russia needed secure frontiers in Europe. Russia therefore decided to make an energetic attempt to clear the air. If the Germans were really troubled at the prospect of disloyalty to Austria, the Czar would put their minds at rest on this score. Giers offered renewal of the Three Emperors Alliance as it had existed at the beginning of the eighties when it had guaranteed the peace of Europe. This alliance had been the crowning achievement of Bismarckian bargaining; now the Germans could have it again without lifting a finger. Russia's one stipulation was that she and Germany settle the Bulgarian question together. But she no longer demanded—as she had a few years ago—the appointment of Russian generals and a Russian Crown Prince in Bulgaria. She asked only that Prince Ferdinand should abdicate. Ferdinand's position in Bulgaria was thought illegal by the Germans also, and he was soon to become anathema to the Kaiser

as he already was to the Czar. In place of Ferdinand, Russia suggested that the German Kaiser propose a German Protestant prince for
Bulgaria. The Russians would recognize him without more ado.

V

But meanwhile the sorcerer's apprentices in the *Wilhelmstrasse* had
committed another fateful blunder. They had informed Vienna that
they were severing the wire to St. Petersburg and were now united
with Austria in closer friendship than ever before. No concessions to
Russia would be made on the Straits question without Austrian approval. In other words, the Kaiser and his new chancellor were telling
the Austrians, with disarming naïveté, that they no longer held any
trump cards. In vain Bismarck had written: "If the Austrians think the
bridges between Russia and Germany have been shattered, they will
try to make Germany Austria's pawn. German lives and German
wealth will be squandered on the Viennese Balkan policy." His words
had been prophetic; the Austrians now decided that Germany was se-
curely in their hands. Count Kalnoky, the Hungarian who directed the
Hapsburg foreign policy, was neither a bureaucrat like Caprivi nor a
psychopath like Holstein. But he correctly read the characters of those
wretches in Berlin, saw the way clear for Austrian expansion in the
Balkans, and flatly rejected the proposed Three Emperors Alliance.

Caprivi had in any case come to the conclusion—probably under
Holstein's influence—that the alliance would be superfluous and harm-
ful. Caprivi's memorandum on the question advances the argument
that rapprochement with Russia would not be to the liking of the German people—a remark singular in its folly, presuming as it does that
foreign policy must be guided by the feelings of the people when in
fact those feelings must be molded to the necessities of foreign policy.
Aside from which, Caprivi was confounding the German people with
a few deputies. Schlözer, a disciple of Bismarck who was at the time
ambassador to the Vatican, wrote: "Caprivi's ignorance in non-military
questions is simply stupendous; consequently we have little to say to
one another. He does not understand one because he has hardly ever
emerged from the Berlin circle and has no knowledge of human nature. Any battalion commander would do just as well for a chancellor."

Giers made up his mind to have the situation fully clarified. He sum-
moned the German ambassador in St. Petersburg, Schweinitz, and
read aloud to him the first telegram the Kaiser had sent, agreeing to
extension of the Reinsurance Treaty. For his own part, he was ready
to drop all clauses which Germany considered objectionable, including
Russian hegemony in Bulgaria. He was even willing to go along with

Germany's decision not to renew the treaty. But he wished to see an exchange of diplomatic notes, or even an exchange of personal letters between the two monarchs conveying assurances that Russia would be guaranteed security from German attack, Germany security from Russian aggression.

Schweinitz warned Caprivi that "if only in view of France's position he should not ignore the hand which the Czar was amicably holding out." But Holstein was immovable; he did not want Russian friendship even as a gift. It might all too easily lead to a return of Bismarck. Caprivi therefore returned the ironical reply that Prince Bismarck's prestige at home and abroad "would perhaps have enabled him to make plausible to public opinion in Europe the compatibility of the various obligations he had undertaken." But he himself had no talent for duplicity—he found it necessary to consider public opinion in Germany where so complicated a system would not be understood.

In the fall the Kaiser and the chancellor visited Russia. They met with a cool reception. The exchange of ideas between the Czar and the Kaiser threatened—as Waldersee noted—"to freeze up in spite of the summery heat." The treaty was not discussed at all. Giers stressed that both empires had peaceful intentions and would adhere to the existing international treaties on Bulgaria and Constantinople. Caprivi agreed. He did not sense that negotiations were already under way between Russia and France. Giers, however, hated the prospect of an alliance with France, and his feelings were shared by Czar Alexander. Only a few years before he had called the members of the French government "canaille" and had all but refused to receive a French ambassador. Only three months earlier he had put his foot down against dancing with the French ambassador's wife, thus turning the whole order of a ball topsy-turvy.

Giers therefore made a fourth attempt to preserve Russo-German amity. When Caprivi was back in Berlin, the Russian ambassador, Muraviev, read him a brief memorandum summarizing the contents of the discussions in St. Petersburg. Caprivi agreed that the memorandum was a faithful account of these discussions. Whereupon Muraviev asked the chancellor to give him just a single sentence in writing, endorsing this memorandum. Caprivi was terrified. Nervously he replied that although the paper Muraviev had read to him was quite accurate, he could give only an oral confirmation; he was not in a position to commit anything to writing. With a naive attempt to placate the ambassador he added: "I do not possess Bismarck's political power, but I am honest and you can rely upon our good faith; we will never leave you in the lurch." He was unaware that such well-meaning avowals only fostered the Russians' suspicions. Muraviev gave him a long, searching look. Then he replied politely that he had made his request only as a personal matter, and took his leave of the unhappy chancellor.

Then, as though Caprivi was determined to leave the Russians in not the slightest doubt as to Germany's hostile intentions, he concluded a treaty with England whereby Germany exchanged part of her African possessions for the island of Helgoland. Bismarck had wanted Helgoland only if he could have it for nothing; as he saw it, the island would be safest in British hands if Germany and France should become involved in another war. In Bismarck's day a war between England and Germany was as inconceivable as a war against the moon. Now—as the explorer Stanley remarked—Germany received "a trousers button for a suit of clothes." Nobody in Europe could believe that such a bad bargain had actually been made in good faith; everyone assumed that England had secretly agreed to join the Triple Alliance.

VI

Now at last Alexander realized that nothing could save Russia from isolation but an alliance with those "canaille" in Paris. He had to endure the experience of greeting a visiting French fleet at Kronstadt and standing at attention while the Marseillaise was played—which a Russian had only to whistle to earn three years in Siberia. The new Franco-Russian alliance began by being quite loose, but the German chancellor contrived to strengthen it by, for example, his pro-Polish domestic policy. His friendliness toward the Poles helped him to keep his majority in the *Reichstag*. But to the Russians the parliamentary and humanitarian considerations seemed mere pretense; if Germany was pro-Polish, it was because she was anti-Russian. France's days as Cinderella were past.

For twenty-five years Bismarck had prevented a Franco-Russian alliance. The mere idea of it had been a nightmare to him. Only a few months after the pilot went, the landlubber captains in the *Wilhelmstrasse* made the nightmare reality. That single stone wrenched out of the foundation of his building destroyed everything. England complacently noted that she was now the tongue of the balance between the Triple Alliance and the Dual Alliance, and that the leadership of Europe had passed from Berlin to London. In France the hope of vengeance burst into full flower.

As for Russia, the distrust aroused by Wilhelm's fantastic policy remained permanent. Italy calculated that Germany, with a Russian enemy at her back, could not offer her much help against France and therefore demanded large concessions in return for renewal of the Triple Alliance. To their delight the Austrians were informed by the Kaiser that the main reason for Bismarck's dismissal had been his false-hearted bias toward Russia—a statement which was not only wildly untrue but also fatal to the welfare of his country, for Austria now knew that henceforth Berlin would be dependent upon Vienna. Like a cautious man to his mistress, Caprivi had told the Russians: "Nothing in writing." But to Vienna he had committed himself blindly.

CHAPTER THREE

Weltpolitik

*World-politics! If only I knew what that means;
at present it is only a slogan.*

—WALDERSEE

I

For centuries now the Union Jack had been
hoisted over greater and greater portions of the globe. But in the last
third of the nineteenth century the other great powers had gradually
settled their differences. Their hands freed, they too began experimenting in colonial policy. The supply of available lands was rapidly
shrinking; statesmen were seized by a panicky desire to get their share
before the curfew. Rivalry stimulated their hunger for power; newly
discovered national pride blinded them more and more to realities.
It was the age of imperialism, of *Weltpolitik*.

The patient newspaper reader was fed with economic rationaliza-
tions: industry needed raw materials and markets. There was nothing
to these arguments. In those happy days a German manufacturer in
Augsburg could buy raw textiles from foreign colonies just as cheaply
as his competitor in Lancashire. As for markets: industry at that time
was bent on supplying knives and forks even to the cannibals. But
those hotly contested overseas territories figured little in the total of
economic life; all the European colonies put together never absorbed
as much as one twentieth of the production of the advanced countries.
In 1910, after twenty-five years of careful nurturing, the German protectorates abroad accounted for only one per cent of German foreign
trade, and in return for one hundred million marks' worth of exports
Germany had to contribute an almost equal sum in government sub-
sidies. A poorer business proposition could not be had anywhere else
in the world.

Could surplus population be settled in these colonies? Germany,
like England and France, was an immigration country; the number
of Polish migratory laborers in Germany was growing to alarming
proportions. In 1914 only two thousand Germans lived in all the German protectorates. Colonies, unless they were as sizable and wealthy as
England's, were an economic burden. European flags were rising above

palms and deserts all over the world; but the reason for that was politics, not economics. The men who stood cheering beneath those banners were in part crackpot idealists, in part adventurers who used national interest as a blind for the pursuit of their own fortunes. In modern economic life imperialism was an anachronism, a hangover of feudal instincts for aggrandizement; imperialism was not the legitimate heir of capitalism, but at best a bastard; it was not the product of cold economic calculation, but of blind, irrational yearning for power. It is worth noting that in Bismarck's *Thoughts and Memories,* his political testament, colonies are not mentioned.

Any such criticisms were nevertheless unpopular in Germany. Did not France own colonies twenty times, England ninety times, the extent of the motherland—whereas Germany's colonial possessions were only twice the size of Germany herself? Was it not essential to raise the colors of Germany over far greater portions of the globe?

Such thoughts came to every German. But people with a modicum of common sense immediately saw the difficulty: Germany's geographical position was far more unfavorable than that of the other great powers. England was protected by the sea, Russia by the vastness of her land, Italy by the Alps, and France on at least three sides by the seas and the impotency of Spain. Germany alone was everywhere exposed to aggression. Moreover, on the west an unhappy history, on the east the folly of her government, had made enemies of her neighbors. The best colonial lands had long ago been distributed, and for the remaining booty—China, Morocco, Persia, Siam—many contenders were standing in wait with guns in hand. Given this world situation, how could Germany ever hope to hold colonies in case of war? In addition, to pursue policy on a global basis, a cosmopolitan mind was needed. The Germans, with their political naïveté, had neither the geographical foundation nor the innate talent for imperialism. Germany was like a gambler ready to enter a game whose rules he did not know. With accurate insight, though far too great candor, Caprivi declared that nothing worse could happen to Germany than that someone should present her with the whole of Africa.

It was obvious to every unbiased observer that new overseas territories would benefit Germany only if they could be had without endangering her security in Europe. In other words, she could acquire colonies only in league with England, the great sea power. Any other kind of imperialism was dangerous in the extreme, for it would drive the British into the camp of Germany's enemies. Perhaps Germany might have embarked on some such modest type of imperialism if the unimaginative Caprivi had remained at the helm. But the Kaiser dismissed him summarily; Caprivi had not been supple enough in following Wilhelm's sudden inspirations.

II

Caprivi's successor, Prince Chlodwig Hohenlohe, was a clever *grand seigneur* who surveyed the world from aristocratic heights. He had already held other posts with great success—he had been premier in Bavaria, ambassador to Paris, governor in Alsace—and knew how to handle most kinds of people, whether they happened to be bothersome parliamentarians, crooks attempting to blackmail him on the score of his numerous amorous escapades in Paris, or the Kaiser himself. To the latter's objections to a speech of his he replied curtly by telegram: "I am not a chancellery clerk, but the chancellor and must know whereof I speak." But Chlodwig was seventy-five years old when he became chancellor. His memory was not all it should be—he could no longer make speeches extemporaneously, but had to write them out to the last word. His wife, a sturdy Russian princess and renowned bear huntress, begged Wilhelm's wife, who was a relative of hers, to prevent the appointment which would appreciably shorten her husband's life. But Wilhelm thought old "Uncle Chlodwig" would make an agreeable associate and replied by telegram: "The prince is sacrificing himself for Kaiser and Reich." After a year in office Hohenlohe was a sadder and a wiser man. "I have firmly resolved," he said, "not to be upset by anything, and to let things take their course. If I were to take any other attitude, I should have to hand in my resignation at least once a week." His function in the chancellery had come to be merely to postpone precipitous decisions; and he did not succeed in doing even that much. The history of German imperialism became a history of German blunders.

Shortly before the turn of the century the United States trumped up some slender pretexts to declare war on Spain, her major purpose being to seize Spain's colony of Cuba. Kaiser Wilhelm came out with this bold statement: "The Hildalgo will pound Uncle Sam black and blue, for the Spanish fleet is the stronger." Actually, Spain was beaten on all fronts, and a revolution broke out in the Philippines—at the time under Spanish government. Admiral Tirpitz promptly informed the Kaiser that Germany absolutely must take over the Philippines. He recommended that the German East Asian squadron occupy the Filipino capital of Manila as soon as the revolutionists freed it from Spain. An American squadron was already lying in Manila harbor and the Americans had no desire to turn their war booty over to Germany—but that did not trouble Wilhelm. The East Asian squadron steamed for Manila and went to no trouble to disguise its intentions. Washington promptly telegraphed the admiral of the American fleet at Cuba: "Do not risk another ship; war with Germany impending." But the Kaiser did not want war; he abandoned the idea of taking the Philippines; again he had earned the reputation of troublemaker without obtaining the slightest advantage.

III

Germany was now on unfriendly terms with France and Russia. But what about Japan? The German government contrived to acquire there too an enemy who was to prove most potent when the hour of decision arrived.

In the nineties the Japanese had defeated the Chinese in war, and at the peace of Shimonoseki had appropriated small coastal strips of China. The Russian Bear became concerned. Russia was reaching for ice-free ports on the Yellow Sea; a strong Japan was a dangerous rival. Accordingly, Russia and her ally France decided to protest to Tokyo against the terms of the peace treaty, their object being to keep Japan off the Asiatic mainland. England refused to participate in the protest. Germany was in the happy position of being a disinterested observer. But Holstein was hit by the weirdly romantic notion that a war of France and Russia against Japan would "weld in blood" the alliance between the two countries. The idea was preposterously naive. A war over the issue was improbable, and even if it should come about—a victorious war does not generally seal an alliance; on the contrary, the disputes which arise over the sharing of the booty generally promote hostility. Holstein, however, offered to participate in the protest to Tokyo. As if that were not enough, while Russia and France were making their complaints with moderation, the German ambassador threatened armed intervention. "My language apparently made an impression," he reported to Berlin. It made such an impression that twenty-three years later, at the beginning of World War I, when the Japanese demanded Kiaochow from Germany they employed the phrases of Holstein's note word for word. Soon afterwards the Kaiser sent to the Czar an oil-painting of the "Yellow Peril" made after a sketch of his: fierce Asiatics were storming forward under Buddha's leadership while a heavily armed Michael, patron saint of Germany, blocked their way, supported by other European states. The picture, the artistic merit of which was on a par with its political sagacity, bore the motto: "Peoples of Europe, guard your most sacred goods!" It aroused the ridicule of Europeans and the fury of Asiatics.

The Kaiser soon found an opportunity to defend those most sacred goods. The murder of two missionaries supplied Germany with a pretext for occupying the Chinese port of Kiaochow. "The area is large enough for us to commit plenty of follies," Bismarck growled. The Kaiser promptly made this prophecy come true; to his brother Heinrich, who was leaving for peaceful East Asia with a number of German warships, he gave the parting instructions: "If anyone at all should try encroaching on our rights, go at him with a mailed fist!"

Two years later he was to hear a good deal more about "fists." The Chinese had been watching with growing bitterness the penetration of their country by foreign nations. Now a nationalistic movement sprang up among them, and as easily happens with such movements, it attracted a good many of the criminal elements. These anti-foreign extremists called themselves, with obvious symbolism, "fists," and the word was translated into European languages as "Boxers." In Peking they seized power and killed the German ambassador, Ketteler. The Europeans took refuge in their embassies, whereupon the insurgents cut the telegraph wires. For two months Europe waited anxiously to learn their fate.

What a chance for Kaiser Wilhelm to vent his chaotic feelings. When word came that Ketteler had been killed—oddly enough, a false report of it arrived two days before the actual murder—he telegraphed Bülow: "Peking must be stormed and levelled to the ground." As the German troopships left on their grim mission, the Kaiser sent a parting command: "No quarter will be given. No prisoners will be taken. Whoever falls into your hands, let his life be forfeit! The Huns under King Attila a thousand years ago made a name for themselves that has remained mighty in tradition and tale to this day; may you make the name of the Germans a thing to conjure with in China for a thousand years so that never again will a Chinese dare to so much as look askance at a German." It was on the basis of this speech that the Germans were called "Huns" during World War I.

The China War gave Wilhelm an opportunity to put through one of his pet ideas: that a German field marshal should hold the supreme command of an international army. The obvious candidate by rank, age, diplomatic talent, and knowledge of languages was Count Waldersee. The Kaiser secured the consent of the Czar—afterwards claiming that the Czar had himself proposed the appointment. He made Waldersee a field marshal and prevailed on the other powers to accept his plan. Everything seemed to be going well. Then, a week before Waldersee's departure, came the terrible news: Peking had been liberated and the foreign colony found unharmed. Wilhelm was outraged. Waldersee had to leave nevertheless—though it was difficult to see what military operations he could lead. Nevertheless he remained "supreme commander" for seven months; if he himself had not been clever enough to point out that the harsh climate was literally endangering his life, the Kaiser might never have recalled him. He returned home and died three years later.

IV

With his military boldness and his diplomatic acumen, Waldersee had been one of the outstanding talents of his age. But that talent had been mortgaged by a restless ambition coupled with a habitual untruthfulness excessive even in a courtier. So strong was his bent for deception that he had no clear grasp either of the world or of himself. First he had caused the fall of Bismarck by shamelessly exploiting the Kaiser's vanity; he had expected that Caprivi would fill the chancellor's post only temporarily, and nursed the pious wish that he would soon come a cropper. Consequently he described Caprivi in his diary as a "profoundly honorable man of solid character." But within little more than a year the "honorable" Caprivi had maneuvered Count Waldersee out of office and out of the Kaiser's favor. For all that he was such a good soul, Caprivi was not altogether a fool. As a military man he knew enough to set a few booby traps for obvious rivals. For ally he had Waldersee's old friend Holstein who considered any established favorite of the Kaiser's an enemy of his. In vain Waldersee lamented in his diary that he had been too innocent, that Holstein was a scoundrel, "as many people had always thought him."

The Kaiser offered Waldersee demotion from chief of the general staff to commanding general in Stuttgart; Waldersee would also be, he added, a kind of governor for South Germany. When Wilhelm II made such remarks, no irony was intended; he was the sort of man who believed anything he said as soon as he pronounced it. Chief of the General Staff Waldersee turned down the proposition, but this helped him little; he had already lost the Kaiser's favor. He was then offered command of the army corps in Altona, this time with the injunction: "You must keep an eye on Prince Bismarck who has lately been acting very suspiciously again and intriguing against me." In vain poor Waldersee objected that such surveillance was the business of the police, not of a commanding general, and that an officer could not accept such a degrading duty: "Your Majesty should not allow to remain in the army officers of such inclinations." But there was no help for it; he was ordered to Altona.

At this point Waldersee renounced the vanities of this world much as the Hindus in the desert vouch to eat no fish. His diary notes: "Advent. With Marie I went to the garrison church to take communion, having found some time beforehand for quiet self-examination and meditation. How vain at such times seems the increasingly restless and hollow bustle of the world. As a human being and as a Christian I ought to have made far more progress by now, and would have done so were I not so fettered by stupid politics. At any rate my motive is not ambition or anything of the sort, but pure love of country." He visited Bismarck in Friedrichsruh—in order, as the aged prince remarked, to see whether the time had come to order an appropriate wreath.

But "self-examination and meditation" go by the board when new hopes beckon. Soon Waldersee was writing: "The impression grows upon me that the Kaiser is really entertaining the idea of appointing me chancellor if circumstances warrant. . . . God grant that this cup may pass from me. Although several acquaintances have told me that men of principle are persistently counting on me." But once more the ardently desired cup passed by those thirsting lips. At this point he became resigned; in fact, his bitterness toward the Kaiser made him suddenly aware of Bismarck's greatness. He quite forgot that he had helped bring about Bismarck's fall, and opined that with Bismarck in the chancellery Germany's prestige would still be at a high point. He even held that the Kaiser himself now regretted Bismarck's dismissal. A few days before his death he made the following entry in his diary: "God grant I may not live to endure what I see coming."

V

Germany was experimenting with *Weltpolitik* in the Near as well as the Far East. Bismarck's position on the Orient had had the advantage of great simplicity: he held Germany aloof from all Oriental questions. He knew that Russia wanted to take possession of the key to the Bosporus, through which a large part of her exports passed. Bismarck had felt that it was not Germany's business to prevent Russia from appropriating territory so vulnerable—neither was it Germany's lookout that the gulf between England and Russia would be thereby widened. Three years before his dismissal he told the Russians: "If you overthrow the Sultan, we will be very sorry, for he is really a good friend of ours, but we will not take up arms for his sake." Bismarck was also convinced that the moment Germany and Russia quarrelled over the Orient, Germany's friendship with England would be impaired rather than solidified—for then England could use Germany to pull her chestnuts out of the fire. When the Deutsche Bank financed railroads in Asia Minor, he refused to "guarantee notes connected with such risky undertakings." Unlike his successor, he did not identify the interests of the German Reich with those of the German Bank. A year after his dismissal he prophesied that world war would start in the Orient.

The young Kaiser took a quite different view of the matter. He was allured by the romanticism of the Orient, allured by every seeming extension of Germany's power, and he could never resist a chance for fancy oratory. In Damascus one day he announced that he was a good friend of the three hundred million Mohammedans—whereupon England, France, and Russia warily pricked up their ears, for more than half of these new protégés of Wilhelm lived under their flags. Soon afterwards the Germans began construction of a railroad from Constantinople to Bagdad.

In the eyes of England such a railroad represented a strategic threat to Persia and India; in the eyes of Russia it was good medicine for the Sick Man of Europe, whose health would undoubtedly pick up dangerously as a result of the railroad. About a billion marks were poured into Turkey; the Turkish war minister became the fattest man in his country. Count Muraviev, the Russian foreign minister, proposed that the Germans give the Russians a free hand on the Bosporus, in return for which Germany would be given a free hand in Asia Minor. Wilhelm considered this offer a threat; he scribbled on his ambassador's report: "Nicholas I and Friedrich Wilhelm IV must have talked in such terms with one another, but under my reign things are damned different, if you please! Let Herr Muraviev click his heels and stand at attention when he talks to the German Emperor!" Muraviev did nothing of the kind; instead he strengthened his ties with England. A few years later, when Germany invited Russia, England, and France to participate in the Bagdad Railroad, Russia talked both her friends into declining the favor. Objectively, the railroad—"my railroad," Wilhelm called it—did not result in German occupation of Asia Minor. In the days of the Reinsurance Treaty and Anglo-German amity, the railroad might have been made palatable to the other powers. But within the context of Germany's many other blunders, Wilhelm's railroad only contributed to the breakdown of Bismarck's structure. The Mediterranean Alliance was not renewed by England.

CHAPTER FOUR

British Overtures

Fortune has a pretty forelock but a bald pate.
—LATIN PROVERB

I

The attitude of Wilhelm toward his mother Victoria was one of deep dislike. He thought he had good reasons for such feelings. His left arm dangled almost useless at his side; he, the heir to the Prussian throne, was unfit for military duty. He suspected that at his birth his mother, out of puritanism, had not allowed a doctor to be called in time. And had not his mother given him to understand that his brother Heinrich would have made a more imposing sovereign? Had she not always played the superior Briton, vaunting her contempt for the coarse-grained Prussians?

Victoria made no bones about returning this dislike. "If you think Wilhelm will ever do anything for other than personal reasons, you are mistaken," she assured her friends. As a boy Wilhelm had been humiliated, as a man praised to the skies by the sycophants who surrounded him. When he visited the country of his mother and grandmother, the British received him with measured courtesy. They thought of him as a foreigner weighed down by complexes. But Wilhelm wanted much more from the British. He wanted open admiration, a commodity the English deal in sparingly.

Such were the origins of Wilhelm's ambivalent hate-love for England, and out of that hate-love arose his hope of uniting all the peoples of Europe against the English so that those prideful islanders would owe their lives only to his imperial generosity. He did not want to destroy them; he wanted only to impress them. But how could he intimidate them and bring them round to amazed admiration? There was only one way he saw: by Germany's becoming a great sea power. And so he began building a fleet. "Our future lies on the water." "The trident belongs in our hand." With such phrases Wilhelm trumpeted his plans to the world. "The ocean also proves," he declared with weird logic, "that upon it and in the distant lands beyond it no great decisions shall henceforth be made without Germany, without the German Emperor."

One man raised his bushy eyebrows in wrath: Bismarck. Was Wilhelm hoping to avert attacks from the sea? "I should like to know who is supposed to be the aggressor. Not, I should hope, the one country that might be driven into a coalition against Germany by an un-German mania for prestige and by hasty naval rearmament which would be interpreted as a sign of hostility on our part." But against Wilhelm's ambitions the views of the old-fashioned former chancellor carried no weight. Nor did Moltke's advice that Germany was England's natural ally precisely because Germany had never been much of a sea power. What did it matter that every pfennig put into the fleet was being taken from the army. "Let the dogs pay until they're blue," Wilhelm said to the *Reichstag*.

Without any fleet at all, Bismarck had contrived to preserve German overseas interests against England. For in the background he always had his tie with St. Petersburg, and the potential threat to England of a Russo-German combination. But Wilhelm ignored such considerations. When a man ardently desires a thing, he never lacks for arguments. The great argument for building a fleet was: world politics. That slogan and Wilhelm's ambivalence toward England were the forces behind the flurry of activity that sent the keels of so many German warships sliding down the ways.

Germany, the imperialists insisted, needed a strong fleet if only to protect her overseas trade. The theory seemed sensible, but it had not been thought through. Germany's trade was in no danger if she went to war either with France or Russia; so long as England remained neutral she would not permit a blockade of all Europe aimed at isolating Germany. On the other hand, if England took part in the war German overseas trade was lost in any case, for the Germans could not possibly build a navy as large as Britain's. England was committed to a powerful fleet because she had to dominate the seaways—without imports she would starve. And she was able to keep her lead over Germany because Germany—no richer than Great Britain—also had to finance a mighty army. In view of this unequivocal situation, a large German fleet would only make for trouble between Berlin and London without affecting relative strength. England would be forced into an accelerated shipbuilding program. The gray squadrons of new German warships lying in the harbor at Kiel might look magnificent under their waving flags; but the truth was that they blocked Germany's way to her overseas territories and to free trade. Wilhelm's imperialism won Germany no new territories of any consequence; his only acquisitions were the lease on Kiaochow, an item which was paid for in 1914 by war with Japan, and a few minute South Sea islands which provided homes for forty German settlers and the title of count for Bülow, who was chancellor at the time.

The accomplishments of shipbuilders, officers, and sailors in so rapidly creating a navy out of virtually nothing were indeed brilliant. But admiration for their achievements does not detract from the fact that such a huge fleet was a political burden to Germany. Having already made enemies of France and Russia, Germany could not afford the hostility of England also. Wilhelm never dreamed that his imperialist policy lost Germany her role of arbiter among the powers which Bismarck had built up precisely by keeping Germany out of overseas conflicts. To be sure, imperialism was not Wilhelm's brain child. But while the other great powers practiced imperialism with cannon whose roar shook Africa and Asia, Germany only talked imperialism. But she did her talking in so shrill a voice that the whole world grew suspicious of her.

In 1898 Otto von Bismarck died. His was a lingering death. "The dying man," his family reported, "kept calling out: 'Help, help!' In his delirium he named England, Turkey, Russia, Serbia. Then he cried again and again: 'But alas, Germany, Germany, Germany!'"

II

He had good reason to fear for Germany. The Helgoland treaty had fostered friendship with England; friction over Africa opened fresh sores. The German government sent a stream of notes to London the tone of which, as Salisbury remarked, might have been right for dealings with Monaco. And worse was to follow.

One day the Scotch physician Leander Starr Jameson led a few hundred volunteers—with the knowledge and consent of Colonial Minister Chamberlain—in an attack upon the two Boer republics of South Africa. He was to be thoroughly beaten by the Boers and taken prisoner. Practically, Germany was in no way affected by the incident. But Kaiser Wilhelm saw it as a wonderful chance to jump in and vent his hostility feelings toward his English cousins. His first idea was to land German marines in South Africa. Then he proposed proclamation of a German protectorate over the Boer republics.

Chancellor Hohenlohe passed over these brilliant inspirations, but he considered some concession to His Majesty's mood necessary. He therefore suggested that the Kaiser telegraph President Kruger congratulating him on having repulsed the attack without calling upon outside aid.

It has never been determined just what the German government intended to accomplish by this telegram. Germany could not have sent actual aid to the Boers. Could Wilhelm II really have considered going to war with England for the Boer cause? "To fight England without fighting the British Navy" was one of the Kaiser's favorite notions at the time, Holstein later remarked sarcastically. Or was the Kaiser's belligerent attitude designed to bully the English into a friendship he now desired? That can hardly be assumed; the grandson of Queen Victoria knew the English too well to imagine they could be bullied. Improbable as it sounds, the only explanation seems to be that the authors of that telegram merely wanted to air their emotional reactions to the world, and gave no thought to the possible consequences.

The telegram to Kruger hit the British on their sorest spot, for their self-assurance was already dreadfully shaken by Jameson's defeat—an invasion, if unsuccessful, is immoral. And now Queen Victoria's grandson twisted the knife in the wound. Three years later, when a Prussian prince went to London for Victoria's Diamond Jubilee, the crowds kept shouting at him: "If you want to send a telegram to Kruger, the post office is just around the corner." In Germany, however, the Kruger telegram had won the Kaiser enormous popularity, for his people were filled with enthusiasm for the Boers and understood no more about the exigencies of foreign policy than he did.

Many Englishmen never forgot that telegram. But there were also other bones of contention. German trade was giving England stiff competition in many parts of the world. If Germany were to vanish from the world, every Englishman would be richer on the following day, the *Saturday Review* wrote. This comment was abysmally stupid, for Germany was England's best customer; her downfall would have made every Englishman poorer. But the argument nevertheless made an impression upon the British; trade rivalry, illogical as it is for the nation as a whole to care, stiffened the popular antagonism toward Germany.

III

Luckily the Salisbury government did not customarily shape its policies according to popular sentiment. There were two objective factors which prompted the British to regard the German government with greater favor. These were the Russian penetration in East Asia and the French advance in Central Africa. When Cossacks rode into Manchuria and French troops appeared on the Upper Nile, the Kruger telegram no longer seemed so unforgivable. After all, not even the British Empire could make its way alone in the world—especially when it wanted to annex both the Boer republics. Queen Victoria was unable to take her customary trip to the Riviera because England's grab for India had embittered the French. In Brussels, shots were fired at Edward, the Prince of Wales; and if he had dared to go to Holland he would have been greeted by crowds singing the Boer anthem. Russia rudely rejected the most tempting offers—though Salisbury was even willing to discuss the question of Constantinople—because she had frozen the situation in the Balkans and was reaching out toward Manchuria and Korea. English novels dealing with things to come drew a frightening picture of a Russo-French invasion of England.

Under such conditions Wilhelm, that boor of a cousin across the North Sea, seemed a good deal more tolerable. During the last years of the nineteenth century Germany was enjoying unprecedented good fortune. For with Russia occupied in the Far East, France in Africa, and England in all corners of the world, all were dependent upon Germany's good will. But Germany was incapable of seizing her opportunities, not even when England cautiously made overtures to her, tentatively proposing an alliance.

England offered a good deal—although everything she offered was the property of other countries. She talked of West Morocco, Northern Asia Minor, Northern China. The trouble was, of course, that there was a dose of poison in all these tasty morsels, since to swallow any of them meant incurring the hostility of the French and the Russians. She also suggested that both countries should stand together if they were attacked by two great powers; there was good reason to believe that no one power would venture an attack, which would in any case be not too formidable.

None of these offers were ever made outright. London merely hinted at her plans and waited to see what Germany would reply. Prime Minister Salisbury had admired Bismarck; he considered the Kaiser spiteful and mentally disturbed. Therefore he held his cards close. In any case Salisbury despised the type of diplomacy which niggled over exact commitments and precise terms; far more important, he felt, was a general understanding and a settlement of individual questions as they came up. That was how England was to manage with France and Russia several years later, without any treaty of alliance. It was an hour of fateful decision—just as it had been ten years earlier when the Czar fled from the terrors of isolation to the arms of Germany, and was rudely repulsed.

As always, the Kaiser wavered. At the bottom of his heart he wanted friendship with the proud British more than anything else. But it was a different kind of friendship he hoped for. His feelings toward the British were like those of a rebuffed lover who wants to humiliate the proud beauty before he generously takes her into his embrace. A loose alliance would give him no sense of triumph; moreover, it would be a reason for the *Reichstag* to refuse him his big fleet. And how otherwise was he to impress the British? So he swayed like a straw in the wind; the same Wilhelm who had sent the Kruger telegram conferred the highest of German decorations, the Black Eagle, upon Lord Roberts, the conqueror of the Boers!

IV

Aged Hohenlohe had meanwhile been succeeded by Bernhard von Bülow. If Bismarck merited the name of Iron Chancellor, von Bülow might well have been called the Rubber Chancellor. Gay as a May morning, unburdened by convictions or principles, brilliantly culti-vated, with a breadth of reading that could be considered almost sus-pect in a man of his class, a *causeur* in four languages, possessor of an extensive collection of anecdotes, a sizable fortune, and an Italian wife descended from a princely house who was his intellectual superior—he was a poor choice for the post of chancellor. In fact his wife begged the Kaiser to reconsider the appointment. Von Bülow's ever-smiling countenance and his highly groomed appearance radiated so much charm that even his grossest falsehoods carried a certain plausibility. Like Demosthenes he practiced speaking against obstacles, but instead of outshouting the thunder of the Aegean Sea he tried to be heard above the rush of bathwater in his apartment in the Bucharest Embassy; his servant stood in the adjoining room to make sure the speech was audi-ble.

Chancellor Bülow's favorite technique was flattery. It rarely missed fire. On one occasion, however, he told *Reichstag* Deputy Naumann that Naumann's *Letters on Religion* lay on his night table and that he read them aloud to his wife in the evening. Naumann replied tartly: "Your Excellency must think me very stupid if you expect me to be-lieve that!" The Kaiser, however, was far more susceptible to even the crudest flattery. Shortly after taking office Bülow wrote to their mutual friend Eulenburg—with the obvious intention of having the letter passed on: "He stands so high! Along with Frederick the Great and the Great Elector he is far and away the most eminent Hohenzollern who has ever lived. He combines uniquely genius, the most genuine and original genius, with the clearest common sense. He possesses an im-agination that carries me as if on the pinions of an eagle above all trivialities, and at the same time he has an utterly practical eye for what is possible and attainable. And along with all this, what vigor! What a memory! What swiftness and sureness of understanding!" The Kaiser found nothing cloying in this overflowing honey; instead he as-sured Eulenburg that he worshipped Bülow.

Bülow had a shrewd knowledge of human nature, an extraordinary cleverness in finding crooked ways; he was a thoroughgoing opportun-ist, agile, subtle in his handling of details, not a bureaucrat, not an ivory-tower scholar; under the guidance of a real statesman he would have made a first-rate assistant secretary. But leadership was beyond him; he had no aims and no weight. He danced like a cork on the waves. Since he kept one eye peeled for the Kaiser's smiles and another for the approval of the crowd, his whole policy necessarily consisted in *laissez-aller*. Come what may, Bülow held, the important thing was to "take it easy."

He took the British overtures easily also. The cleverest thing to do, he reasoned, was to "behave like an utter sphinx," to "wait with patience and composure for the further development of elemental events." Given time, the British would undoubtedly raise their bids. With the Boer War on, an Anglo-German alliance would be unpopular in Germany, and the chancellor never did anything unpopular. He was so eager to please that Holstein called him an old whore. Completely indecisive as he was, the best policy seemed to him to "squirm through with a bow to the British Lion on the one side, a curtsy to the Russian Bear on the other."

Perhaps the chancellor might have spoken more sensibly had he not succumbed so often to the promptings of Holstein. Holstein, still anxiously avoiding promotions, was now directing foreign policy. In private letters he sent instructions to the ambassadors and occasionally prescribed what they should say in their reports on the declarations of foreign statesmen. To Holstein every offer was suspect, British proposals doubly so, offers of an alliance triply. The thing to do was to "see through them" and wait. The best course to follow would be to snub England—which would make her turn to Paris and St. Petersburg, be rejected there, and then come back to Berlin wagging her tail. There were also, it must be admitted, some sound reasons against the British proposals, as there were against any new combinations. For in this world even the best arrangements have some disadvantages. An alliance with England might cause further deterioration in Germany's relations with Russia—and in a crisis the alliance might collapse.

Holstein overlooked the crucial point: that if Germany were allied with the most powerful country on the globe, in fact, if she only had "an understanding" with the British Empire, she would be far more powerful than if she tried to remain the tongue of the balance or joined the opposite side. Holstein was certain that the Whale and the Bear could never unite—just as he had thought ten years before that France and Russia could never join hands. Germany's only practical choice was to accept England's proposals or find herself totally isolated along with Austria. England, on the other hand, had an alternative; she could throw her lot in with Paris and St. Petersburg. Even if an Anglo-German entente meant no more than England's benevolent neutrality, it could still protect Germany from a war; the Franco-Russian Dual Alliance would hardly venture a war against the Triple Alliance if it were faced with the alarming prospect that England might meanwhile arrange things to suit herself in all parts of the world. To be sure, the skill of a Bismarck was needed to arrange an "entente" with England, given her suspicions of Germany. Holstein certainly was not the man to carry it off. His conduct of the negotiations was procrastinating, full of intrigues, surprises, threats, and counterdemands, so that all prospects of agreement faded away without his even noticing.

V

During these negotiations the British had not so much as mentioned the German fleet; at that time it was planned to be of middling size and did not impress England as anything to worry about. But in the first years of the new century it grew rapidly, for it was Germany's misfortune that her new navy was headed by a man who combined a penetrating mind with great adroitness and unshakable will, one of the few politically gifted men of Wilhelmine Germany. In another post he might have been a savior. As it was, he now turned his talents toward a task which far from guarding Germany's security, gravely imperilled it.

Alfred von Tirpitz, the ennobled son of a civil servant, created the German navy. He was a fighter to the core, a man to whom obstacles meant nothing. When he stood up in the *Reichstag*, a heavy-bodied man with a long beard, and presented his budget, the delegates looked aghast and voted him the funds. In popular humor he was known as the "father of lies"; it was said that when he took a cab home at night, he gave the driver a wrong address because he could not bring himself to utter an honest numeral. Writing his memoirs in his old age he unequivocally stated that Germany could not have won England as a friend unless she were willing to go back to the status of an impoverished agricultural country; the fact that Bismarck's Germany had been friendly with England without taking such a humble role he simply wiped out of his memory. In answer to the obvious argument that Germany could never build a fleet equal to England's, he invented the concept of the "risk fleet." That is, the German navy had to be big enough so that in case of war England would have to risk severe losses and would therefore be unable to cope with the fleets of other powers; hence England would not be able to afford a war with Germany. That argument simply would not hold water. England's wealth was such that she could keep as much ahead of Germany as she deemed necessary. Soon she would be able to count upon the French navy as an ally, and Italy could be relied on for at least neutrality. Germany's fleet was too small to assure victory in a war with England, and big enough to make the British suspicious. With naive glee, Wilhelm showed off his battleships to Uncle Edward, Victoria's successor. He did not realize that this vivid argument was bound to drive his uncle

into the French camp. So much went into the building of the fleet
that the army had to make economies—and when the curtain went up
on the international conflict, the fleet dared not play a part. All of
Tirpitz's assurances that the fleet would save Germany from a blockade
proved vain. As Churchill wrote, the hammers that rang in the ship-
yards of Kiel and Wilhelmshaven forged the coalition that ultimately
defeated Germany.

Back in England, the building of the fleet was grist for the mill of
the Germanophobes. First Sea Lord Sir John Fisher suggested that the
British "Copenhagen" the German fleet, that is, destroy it in peacetime as Nelson had once done to the Danish fleet. Fisher was a person
who prided himself on being a man of violence. "Hit first, hit hard,
keep on hitting," was his watchword. "Merciless, hard and pitiless"—
these words were forever on his lips. Not everybody took them seriously. But even more moderate personalities than Fisher said that the
big German navy and German bad manners were more than England
could tolerate.

Germany's manners, in fact, were those of a sheep in wolf's clothing.
The Kaiser had no desire to draw his saber, but to his mind a strong
policy involved rattling it continually. The noise gradually got on other
peoples' nerves. The result was that Germany, which under Wilhelm's
government hardly increased her territory, was considered furiously
belligerent, while the other great powers quietly tucked away country
after country and nevertheless preserved a reputation for harmlessness.

VI

The Anglo-German negotiations for an alliance had come to nothing.
Six months later, in January 1902, England concluded a different alliance with Japan. Both powers undertook to help one another if either
were attacked by two great powers. For a long time the Japanese had
been watching with bitterness the Russian advance into Manchuria.
The treaty with England gave them the assurance that in case of war
France would give Russia no aid. The tensions between Russia and
Japan sharpened. "Willy" cordially advised his dear "Nicky" to undertake a "crusade"; a show of weakness undermined the monarchic principle, he said. Bülow finally had to explain to the Kaiser that such talk
was no good. Either it would make the Russians cool off or prompt
them to invite German participation. Wilhelm replied that the Czar's
weak-kneed behavior was damaging to all monarchs and especially to
the German Emperor.

Russia asked England to mediate, but after a long struggle with his
conscience Prime Minister Balfour refused. Although England was always against war, he said, this war "would not be an unmixed curse,"

since Russia would certainly come out of it weaker than she had gone in.

The Russo-Japanese war broke out. The experts were all agreed on the outcome. Sea Lord Fisher indicated the point on the map where the Japanese would be beaten, and the German general staff issued similar prophecies. Faithful to her alliance, England helped the Japanese; she refused to let the Russian Baltic fleet through the Suez Canal. The captains of this fleet were overwrought and thought they saw Japanese torpedo boats already in the English Channel. They shelled some British fishing vessels. Balfour was on the point of urging drastic steps against these criminals; the Russians however quickly paid the compensation England demanded. The Kaiser, sorry that an Anglo-Russian war had not come off, recommended that the Czar carry out military demonstrations on the Persian-Indian border. But poor Nicholas had other worries; the Russians were being thoroughly beaten by the Japanese.

Now Wilhelm wooed Russian friendship by guaranteeing the Czar peace in Europe and by supplying the Russian fleet with coal. But after the war, when he expected St. Petersburg to give him something for his timely aid, he found that in the end acts count less than manner. The Russian ruling group did not turn against England—without whose support Japan would never have dared to go to war, let alone been able to win it—but against the hated Germans whose assistance was now completely forgotten. Had not this noisy, arrogant, loud-mouthed Kaiser set the snare? Was not he responsible for the whole disaster? If a person is unpleasant, a bad construction is placed upon his actions, no matter what he does.

CHAPTER FIVE

The Morocco Crisis

*I must admit that everything has turned out
differently from what I expected and desired.*
—HOLSTEIN

I

At the beginning of the twentieth century one of the European powers occupied a huge African territory whose independence had been guaranteed by all the countries of Europe. Another great power protested, refused the bribe designed to placate her, and insisted that a European conference be held over the matter. A tremendous storm of hatred for the disturber of the peace rose up.

But strangely enough, Europe did not regard France as the disturber of the peace, for all that France had occupied Morocco. The blame was laid at the door of Germany who submitted the dispute to international arbitration. When the quarrelling simmered down, the German Reich had suffered damage and humiliation and stood branded as an aggressor. It had taken a great deal of talent to cut so miserable a figure after starting out from so strong a position.

Morocco, with a coastline on both the Atlantic and the Mediterranean, was like a corner store in a fine business location. As large as France, rich in minerals, with five million inhabitants, the country represented the most prosperous part of as-yet-undivided Africa. During their recent negotiations London had offered the Germans the Atlantic coast of Morocco; some time afterward Paris had hinted at a division of the country between Germany and France. In their first agreement with Spain, the French had made provision for Germany's sharing in the swag. Bülow had taken the whole matter too "easy," and done nothing.

But the stone the builders had rejected was to become the cornerstone of the Anglo-French alliance. At the turn of the century the dispute over Egypt had stirred bad feeling between England and France. At that time Lord Northcliffe, the newspaper king, wrote that the British admired the Germans and despised the French. When King Edward visited Paris, the populace sent cheers up for the Boers; his adjutant said irritably: "They don't like us here." "Why should they?"

he replied, and with all the charm of an aristocratic commercial trav-
eller he began suing for their affections. Certain spiteful people have
called Edward the greatest German statesman after Bismarck—allud-
ing to his German family tree. He was not that, but a first-rate diplomat
possessing the charm of an ingenuous playboy.

When London turned toward Paris after the negotiations with Germany had petered out, French Foreign Minister Delcassé was delighted. A former schoolteacher of utterly unprepossessing appearance,
Delcassé regarded amity with England as the goal of his dreams. He
did not insist on any formal alliance; he was content to see a few old
points of dispute wiped out. The core of the agreement was simple:
France gave the British a free hand in Egypt; England gave the French
a free hand in Morocco. As usual the agreement was divided into two
parts, one public and one secret. Publicly the two powers guaranteed
not to alter the *status quo* in Egypt and Morocco; secretly they agreed
to the precise opposite. (British Foreign Minister Grey, who had a
talent for self-deception incredible to a Continental, asserts in his memoirs that only one or two minor clauses were kept secret—although by
the time he wrote this, the text of the secret treaty had been published
for all the world to see.)

But even though the secret clauses were unknown at the time, everyone in Europe realized that the Anglo-French treaty was handing
Morocco over to the French. What was Germany to do? In Berlin there
were differences of opinion. Kaiser Wilhelm wanted to make an alliance with France; Schlieffen, the chief of the general staff, wanted to
declare war on France. The same reason underlay these two opposing
views: Russia's hands were tied by her unfortunate war with Japan.
Therefore France was for the moment without an ally. Both the Kaiser
and Schlieffen wanted to seize the opportune moment, though in opposite senses. Insanely, German policy pursued both aims simultaneously.

II

Schlieffen was Waldersee's successor. The cunning intriguer Waldersee had been succeeded by a man whose whole character structure had
frozen in a pattern of impersonal objectivity. Extreme near-sightedness
had nearly kept him out of military service. After sowing wild oats
during his years as a young lieutenant, he had made a very happy
marriage, but lost his wife after only four years. He found consolation
in the pietism of the Moravian Brethren and in the fanaticism of the
specialist. A hard man himself, he wanted to raise up a generation of
hard men. "Be more than you seem," and "general staff officers have
no names" were the mottoes he held out for his subordinates. On

Christmas Eve he would present his associates with a military problem which had to be worked out over Christmas Day. As a young man Moltke had written verse and short stories; in his social contacts he showed genuine kindness. Schlieffen wrote nothing but historical studies in beautifully polished style; in society he was haughtily sarcastic. When his adjutant once pointed out a lovely view, a valley smiling in the morning sunlight, Schlieffen said cuttingly: "An insignificant obstacle for trained troops."

Schlieffen groaned beneath the weight of a tremendous and unremitting responsibility: the fear that he might some day have to defend Germany against France and Russia, and perhaps against England also. Now, in the midst of the Russo-Japanese War, Russia was *hors de combat* and the Anglo-French alliance was not yet definitely concluded; should not this sterling opportunity to "settle" with France be seized? To a soldier the idea was appealing; Russia, Austria, Italy, and England might well have remained neutral at this time. Schlieffen was too limited to realize that even a complete victory would only paralyze France for a few years, and would produce a more intense thirst for vengeance. A British periodical published an article pointing out that the situation was so favorable for Germany that even so peace-loving a monarch as Wilhelm II would hardly be able to resist the temptation. Schlieffen had the article shown to the Kaiser, but Wilhelm noted on the margin: "No, I could never be capable of such an act!"

III

Instead of attacking France the Kaiser wanted to carry out his pet idea: to unite the Triple Alliance and the Dual Alliance in one great entente of the five Continental powers, in order to triumph at last over England. He hoped to be rewarded for his acts of friendship during the Russo-Japanese war by an alliance with Russia. Next on the agenda was to effect a *rapprochement* with France (whom he usually called Marianne). Next was to shake off all ties with England. A draft of the alliance was sent to St. Petersburg, and Willy wrote to his dear Nicky that although Marianne was obligated "to lie in bed with Nicholas, she ought to give me a caress or a kiss now and then and not go creeping right into the bedroom of that eternally intriguing *touche-à-tout* on the island." The embarrassing imagery reflects the wildness of Wilhelm's plan. Marianne had not the slightest intention of giving a kiss to the hated cousin of her friend Nicholas; France would not enter an alliance with Germany when such an alliance could be directed only against England. She had settled her accounts with England, whereas Alsace-Lorraine was still a festering wound. Wilhelm, infatuated by this idea of a great Continental alliance, did not take Morocco seriously.

Meanwhile all kinds of weird notions were simmering in Holstein's fantastic mind. As he later admitted, he had never believed an Anglo-French agreement possible. It took several months before he grasped the new situation. Then he decided to "break the encirclement"—by war, if need be. He wanted to start his new action with a roll of drums; Kaiser Wilhelm was to take a Mediterranean trip, land in Tangier, and recognize the independence of Morocco. The idea was a fresh blunder. Germany would be playing her best card right off, although it was obvious that this card was no trump. It was absurd to imagine that at this time Wilhelm II could be persuaded to go to war with Marianne.

With disrelish the Kaiser listened to Holstein's plan for his landing in Morocco. The idea of riding on an unfamiliar horse through an Oriental city which was known to be the refuge of innumerable Spanish anarchists did not attract him. But Bülow skillfully appealed to his vanity and the Kaiser conditionally agreed. Luckily, there was a rough sea on the day set for the landing; it seemed impossible to go ashore at Tangier. Wilhelm was relieved. But while his yacht lay at anchor in the roadstead at Tangier the German chargé d'affaires, von Kühlmann, in a soaking-wet Uhlan's uniform, climbed up a rope ladder and swung himself aboard. The Kaiser, chagrined at this apparition, declared that he would grant him a lifetime post as instructor in acrobatics. Undaunted, Kühlmann reported that the Sultan's uncle was expecting the Kaiser, that everything had been prepared for his reception, the Spanish anarchists won over by sizable bribes to form a claque of cheering demonstrators; the horse had been tried out and was extremely gentle; everywhere portable wooden steps for Wilhelm to use while mounting and dismounting were ready. In short, there was no excuse for not going ashore. And so the Kaiser landed; the Moroccans howled with enthusiasm; and Wilhelm, all his theatrical instincts fired by the careful staging, assured the people that Germany would demand Morocco's independence.

One thing Holstein had accomplished: Europe was alarmed. "What do the Germans want?" the French asked themselves. Bülow and Holstein enjoyed their superiority. "If the diplomats ask about our policy toward Morocco, do not tell them anything and maintain a grave and impassive expression. For the present our attitude on this subject must resemble that of the Sphinx who, though besieged by curious tourists, betrays nothing." In Paris the Rouvier government grew worried. It was made up largely of business men—"it is a board of directors, not a government," the most belligerent journalist in France, Georges Clemenceau, had sneered. For years the French army had been deliberately neglected; ever since the Dreyfus scandal the government feared sedition on the part of the generals.

For the annexation of Morocco the French needed Germany's consent, since in the Treaty of Madrid all the great powers had assured one another equal rights in Morocco. France also knew that without Russian aid she would not be Germany's match if it came to war. She was therefore inclined to make sacrifices in order to preserve peace. Delcassé let Bülow know this; he was willing to concede to Germany either a port on the Atlantic coast of Morocco, or a share in the French Congo, or perhaps a claim upon the Belgian Congo. Best of all he would have liked to settle all disputed colonial questions at once in the spirit of the Franco-British treaty. It accorded with European tradition that, when one great power acquired such vast new territories as were in question here, the other great powers would receive "compensation" in order to prevent a total shift in the balance of power. Thus, in compensation for Morocco, England had demanded and been assured Egypt; Italy was to take Tripoli. But Bülow and Holstein would not hear of compensation. When an Italian diplomat attempted to mediate, they were not ashamed to advance the idiotic argument that overthrowing the Sultan of Morocco would impair the institution of monarchy. They wanted something better than the Congo or a port on the Atlantic; they wanted a conference.

They could have wished for nothing more foolish. To be sure, the status of Morocco had been guaranteed by the international Treaty of Madrid and could therefore be changed only by another international treaty. Germany therefore had international law on her side. But surely Bülow should have been aware that international law was mere ornament when the interests of the chief powers were opposed to it. France had paid honestly for Morocco by giving Egypt to the British, Tripoli to the Italians, and a share of the booty to the Spaniards; she could depend upon her ally Russia in any case. But Holstein, who all his life infallibly predicted the opposite of what actually happened, declared that this unity among the great powers was a mere smoke screen. Holstein was counting upon President Roosevelt, who had called Delcassé a scoundrel. He did not suspect that the Senate and American public opinion would never hear of war against France and England, and on the side of Germany, for the sake of Morocco. Roosevelt had something in common with Kaiser Wilhelm; as a witty diplomat remarked at the time, the President would always want to be the child at a baptism, the bride at a wedding, and the corpse at a funeral. But a fondness for playing the lead and for vigorous phrases had no practical effects.

Delcassé took umbrage at the idea of any such conference. He claimed that the British had promised, in case of war with Germany, to land a hundred thousand men at the mouth of the Elbe. But Premier Rouvier recoiled from any such suggestion. "May my hand wither before I sign such an alliance," he cried, and informed the German ambassador that he would drop this troublesome Monsieur Delcassé as soon as possible, but would prefer to wait for a domestic pretext. Holstein was delighted. To hang Delcassé's scalp on his belt tempted him far more than the Congo. Was he going to succeed at last in reading the law to a great power?

Delcassé resigned, and the same day the Kaiser conferred the title of prince upon Bülow. Then—heaping one blunder upon its opposite— he remarked that same day to a French general that now all was well; he would be glad to let the French have Morocco.

Delcassé's fall was a misfortune for Germany. It brought no advantage to the Germans, but it ignited French nationalism and irritated every government minister in Europe. Six years later it had still not been forgotten, for Lloyd George remarked that in case of dispute between England and Germany the Germans would probably demand his resignation. Rouvier had hoped that Delcassé's dismissal would clear the way for direct negotiations, but Holstein obstinately insisted on his conference.

The conference met at Algeciras. On every motion Germany and Austria stood alone; not even Italy went along with them, for she had been sufficiently bribed by the promise of Tripoli. International law proved elastic enough for the powers on the one hand to guarantee solemnly the independence of Morocco, and on the other hand to open the doors to the French. Holstein was indignant and considered resorting to arms. However, Bülow was wiser this time; he shut Holstein off from access to the documents, and himself supervised the negotiations on Morocco. But neither Bülow's smoothness nor Holstein's aggressiveness could change the fact that the Germans remained totally isolated; the conference granted the French and Spanish the rights they needed in order to begin a "peaceful penetration" of Morocco. Meanwhile Rouvier, in the eyes of his ambitious countrymen compromised by his dismissal of Delcassé, had to step down to a rival; Georges Clemenceau became French premier.

Germany had engendered a crisis and had got nothing out of it— neither the Congo nor a portion of Morocco. She had won the reputation of backing her friends—first President Kruger, then the Sultan of Morocco—only to let them down, and of interfering in the internal affairs of other powers. Moreover, she had firmly welded the Anglo-French entente and helped bring to power the champion of intense French nationalism.

IV

In the midst of the Morocco crisis a weird episode took place: Willy and Nicky concluded an alliance. Meeting with the Czar at the Baltic

island of Björkö, Wilhelm brought the negotiations between Germany
and Russia to a "successful" conclusion. We will do best to let Wilhelm
tell the story in his own words:

"I now felt that the moment had come! How would it be, I suggested,
if we two also made up a 'little agreement.' I reminded him that we
had discussed the matter once before during the winter, and said I
happened to have a copy in my pocket. The Czar took me by the arm,
led me from the salon to the imperial cabin of his father, and himself
closed all the doors. 'Show it me, please!' [Conversation between Wilhelm and Nicholas was conducted in English.] As he spoke his dreamy
eyes sparkled brightly. I took the envelope out of my pocket. Once,
twice, three times he read through the text which I have already communicated to you. Meanwhile I sent up a fervent prayer to God to be
with us and guide the young ruler. All was utterly still except for the
swish of the waves; the sun shone bright and gay into the pleasant
cabin, and through the porthole I could see the gleaming white *Hohenzollern,* the imperial standard fluttering high in the morning breeze.
As I was reading the words, *Gott mit uns,* upon the black cross of the
flag, I heard the Czar's voice beside me, saying, 'That is quite excellent; I quite agree!' My heart beat so loudly I could hear it, but I
pulled myself together and said quite casually: 'Should you like to sign
it? It would be a very nice souvenir of our entrevue.' He skimmed
through the paper once more; then he said: 'Yes, I will.' I opened the
ink stand, handed him the pen, and he wrote in a firm hand, 'Nicholas.'
Then he handed me the pen and I signed. My eyes were filled with
bright tears of joy—although perspiration was also trickling down my
forehead and back. And I thought: Friedrich Wilhelm III, Queen
Luise, Grandpa and Nicholas I must be close by at this moment. Certainly they looked down upon us and they must all have rejoiced!"

Since these illustrious predecessors would not do for earthly witnesses, two members of the entourage also had to sign the agreement.
"That morning of July 24, 1905 at Björkö has been a turning point in
the history of Europe, thanks to the Grace of God; and it has meant a
great alleviation in the plight of my dear Fatherland, which at last is
set free from the abominable pincers formed by Gaul and Russia."
The paper that Willy happened to have in his pocket was a declaration
that the two powers would aid one another with all their forces if
either were attacked by a European great power. The dreamy Czar
added the words "in Europe"; thus if Germany became embroiled in a
conflict with England, the Czar was not required to help by attacking
India. His hands were tied against the island in any case, since the
Japanese had sent his whole fleet to the bottom of the sea. The agreement further provided that Russia should induce France to join the
alliance. Wilhelm's brilliant achievement was a form of repentance for

having refused to renew the Reinsurance Treaty. Bismarck had been virtually charged with selling out his fatherland in making that treaty, yet all the blame unjustly heaped upon it could justly be heaped on the Björkö Treaty. For under the Reinsurance Treaty Germany would have remained neutral if Austria attacked Russia, whereas under the Björkö Treaty she would have to march upon Vienna.

But Wilhelm's repentance came too late. When he returned home, beaming with pride, two dreadful disappointments lay in store for him. Bülow declared that the two added words "in Europe" made the treaty valueless for Germany, and asked permission to submit his resignation. Bülow's behavior was incomprehensible to the Kaiser; even with the addendum he thought the treaty a triumph.

From his heaven of unreasoned delight Wilhelm promptly plummeted into a hell of undignified despair. "You will permit me not to describe to you my state of mind, my dear Bülow. To be treated in this way by the best, the most intimate friend I possess without being given a cogent reason has been so frightful a blow to me that I have completely collapsed and fear I may succumb to a nervous breakdown. . . . Do not forget that you used me against my will in Tangier in order to assure the success of your Moroccan policy. For your sake, because the Fatherland demanded it of me, I landed, mounted a strange horse in spite of the difficulty I have with riding because of my crippled left arm, and the horse came within a hair of killing me, a risk you let me take. I rode right through the midst of the Spanish anarchists, since you had assured me this act would advance your policy. And now, when I have done all that for you, and as I confidently believe a great deal more, you want to leave me in the lurch because you think I am in grave trouble! Bülow, I have not deserved such treatment from you. No, my friend. You must stay in office and at my side, and together you will work with me *ad majorem Germaniæ gloriam.* You cannot and must not fail me; if you did so, the policy you have pursued all this year would in effect be disavowed by you yourself, and I should be shamed forever. I could not survive that! I appeal to your friendship for me and will not permit you to say another word about your intention to resign. After you receive this letter send me a telegram saying, 'All's well'; then I will know that you are going to remain. For the morning after your request for resignation arrives your Emperor will no longer be among the living. Think of my poor wife and children!"

All the agitation was needless. The Russian government informed the Czar that the treaty was incompatible with the spirit of the Russo-French Dual Alliance; that it was out of the question to "include" France in the Björkö agreement. In vain Willy reminded his poor cousin Nicky: "We shook hands and signed the agreement before God, who heard our oath. It is therefore my opinion that the treaty can very well come into force. . . . What is signed, is signed. And God is our witness!" Unfortunately this witness could not be haled into any court of international law; the treaty never was ratified.

V

Uncle Edward succeeded where Wilhelm failed; England achieved an understanding with Russia. In many respects it was harder for her to do so, since during the Russo-Japanese War she had helped the Japanese; all of Europe had considered Japan merely England's Asian sword. Moreover, England had many areas of friction with Russia. On the other hand she was not an enemy of Russia's ally, France, as Germany was. England and France were now on the best of terms.

The British started their campaign much more wisely. Instead of preparing a treaty of alliance with cleverly devised clauses, they simply settled several points of conflict in Tibet, Afghanistan, and above all in Persia, which was divided into three "spheres of influence." In practice the agreement was far from working out perfectly. The Emir of Afghanistan never recognized it; as for Persia, *Punch* published a cartoon showing the Russian Bear and the British Lion engaged in a tug-of-war over the Persian Cat. Nevertheless, the pact created a new world situation, forging a decisive link in the Triple Entente that henceforth would encircle Germany. It proved that the letter of treaties is not what decides history, but the spirit back of an agreement. The creator of this entente was the British ambassador to St. Petersburg, Arthur Nicolson, a man who had been suffering from the "German nightmare" ever since the Morocco crisis. He feared that Germany, already possessing the biggest army in Europe, would also build up the biggest fleet and suddenly fall upon England.

The Anglo-Russian entente was an indication of how much Germany had thrown away in 1900. If Bülow at that time had arranged a similar loose pact with England, and if Germany had continued for the next few years to pursue a quiet, adroit foreign policy, she would now be in the same fortunate situation as France; without necessarily having formal treaties to fall back upon, she would have bonds of friendship with England and Russia.

But what had once been rejected was now irrevocably lost. France could relax, confident in the friendship of England and Russia, and could without risk tear to shreds the formal decisions of the Algeciras Conference. She completed her peaceful penetration of Morocco by bombarding the coastal cities, landing policing forces and installing a new sultan. Finally she decided to march upon the capital city of Fez in order to "restore order" in Morocco. Once more Germany was faced with the question: How could she allow this?

VI

Germany now had a new foreign minister, von Kiderlen-Wächter. Kiderlen, a Swabian of recently ennobled family, had the appearance of an intelligent doorman. He had two ways of gaining his ends. Sometimes he would amuse people with the gabble for which Swabians are famous and then, when he had them in an amiable mood, would put something over on them. At other times he would intimidate them by extreme rudeness. He had decided to pose as a particular type, and he played the part to perfection. For a while he was one of Holstein's intimates and had aided him in bringing about the fall of Bismarck. Eight years later, when Bismarck was already fatally ill, Kiderlen had to pay an official call on the old prince. Suspicion of Bismarck among the Holstein clique was still so exaggerated that Kiderlen's mistress warned him to eat nothing unless Bismarck tasted it first. He had no occasion to be embarrassed, however, for—as he wrote—"nothing was offered to me, not so much as a glass of beer or a cigar."

Thanks to his brilliant repertory of anecdotes, Kiderlen for a time was a favorite of the Kaiser and his regular companion on summer trips. But when eager busybodies discovered in letters of his that his broad humor did not stop at His Majesty, he fell into disfavor for a good ten years. His letters to his mistress, with whom he preserved intimacy in the face of various social difficulties, remained brashly cheerful. "So far I have seen very little of Rome; the only antiques I have encountered are the Queen's ladies in waiting, but they are as ancient as anything Rome has to offer. . . ." While he was ambassador in Copenhagen there was trouble between Germany and Denmark. A mob gathered in front of his apartment, threatening to smash the windows. At this moment Kiderlen himself came down the street. Promptly he stooped, picked up the first stone and threw it himself—not as his apartment on the second floor, but at the ground-floor flat where his landlord lived. Delighted, the mob followed his example and smashed every window on the ground floor. Kiderlen's presence of mind had averted the far more serious international incident that would have resulted had the German ambassador's windows been broken.

But when Kiderlen returned to Berlin at the age of fifty-eight, he was only a shadow of his former self; wine, women, and tobacco had consumed his powers.

VII

When French Ambassador Cambon informed Kiderlen of France's latest plans for Morocco, the artful foreign minister pointed out that such high-handed actions were not permissible under the Algeciras Treaty, and would probably tend to agitate the natives rather than to restore order in Morocco. Although he fully understood France's concern, Kiderlen declared, he hoped that the occupation of Fez would be postponed until the Moroccan question had been satisfactorily settled between Germany and France. Translated from the language of diplomacy into plain speech, that meant he was demanding traditional adjustments. A power that did not add to its strength when a neighbor did so, automatically suffered a relative decline in strength. For compensation Kiderlen wanted the French Congo. He thought France would meet this demand only if she realized that Germany was prepared to prevent an uncompensated occupation of Morocco by force of arms. With some difficulty he persuaded the reluctant Kaiser to send the gunboat *Panther* to Agadir.

The "Panther's spring" aroused great enthusiasm in Germany, especially among the "Pan-Germans," a small association of retired army officers, idealistic schoolmasters and jingoistic Main Streeters who manifested an amazing ignorance of the real world, and constantly advocated a policy of force and violence which they expected would increase the power and add to the territory of Germany. This association was a plaster lion; its imperialism was a hollow carcass.

But the storm of applause enhanced Kiderlen's appetite; for a while he considered demanding a share in Morocco also. When Cambon, through an intermediary, offered a part of the Congo colony which included a considerable stretch of coastline, Kiderlen declared that he must insist upon the entire Congo. The Kaiser informed him, however, that he would not dream of fighting over Morocco. Kiderlen replied with a memorandum in which he argued that yielding on this point would make Germany's enemies so arrogant that sooner or later she would have to fight. If the Kaiser did not see it this way, the foreign minister wished to hand in his resignation. He concluded his memorandum with a statement of the obvious: "Anyone who declares in advance that he will not fight can accomplish nothing in politics." But when he put his demands to Cambon in his customary rough tone, the ambassador replied: "Keep your temper, your Excellency. Your Kaiser himself has told me: 'I will not wage a war over Morocco.'"

France was not only counting on the Kaiser's love of peace; she was also relying on England's readiness for war. When the German ambassador in London, Count Metternich, asked what England would do if France violated the Algeciras Treaty by occupying Morocco, Grey replied that if complications ensued, all of England's obligations would come into force at once. That was an amazing reply when we consider that the treaty in question had been signed by fourteen states, including England. But on the other hand it was an understandable reply, since Morocco was the plum England had offered the French in return for France's renouncing all claims to Egypt. *France militaire,* the official military journal, wrote: "With her peculiar lack of finesse Germany thought she was making a master stroke when she ordered the *Panther* to stretch her claws toward Agadir. She has been grievously disappointed, and we are now witnessing the sad spectacle of a braggart whose illusions are falling like leaves from the trees in an autumn wind. . . . It is essential that Germany retreat, and if it requires force to make her do so, why not apply it?" French Premier Caillaux, a rich and clever person who like most millionaires was fond of peace, decided to take advantage of the Kaiser's anxiety and Grey's courage by bluffing; he threatened to send British and French warships to Agadir. At this point the Kaiser, who for so long had yearned for Marianne's kisses, lost his temper. "This is colossal impudence upon the part of the French; on top of all our patience and forbearance it is like a slap in the face." He declared that unless France apologized the negotiations were to be broken off.

Luckily Kiderlen remained calm. He silently ignored the Kaiser's instructions, though he suspended negotiations for several weeks, to prove the stoutness of his nervous system. In so doing he was combining business with pleasure, for he took his mistress Marina, the wife of a Russian diplomat, to a French spa. His letters to this lady were always marked by the greatest candor, in both erotic and diplomatic matters. Among other things he had written to her that he did not want a war because of war's inevitable democratizing effect. Kiderlen did not suspect that his dear Marina was a French spy who promptly sent his letters on to Premier Caillaux; ten years later Caillaux included Kiderlen's love letters in his memoirs, admitting that they had stiffened France's backbone.

The final result of the negotiations was as sorry as might have been expected under the circumstances. France ceded 275,000 square kilometers of hinterland in the Congo colony to Germany, but the territory was so infested with sleeping sickness that it was virtually worthless. Lindequist, the German colonial minister, resigned in protest. Cambon sent a photograph of himself to Kiderlen with the inscription: "*A mon terrible ami.*" The German replied wittily with his own picture inscribed: "*A mon aimable ennemi.*" The Moroccan apple of discord had been divided; Germany had received the stem. In Paris there arose a sense of superiority to Germany that boded no good for world peace. Those who had called Kiderlen the "Swabian Bismarck" were insulting both Bismarck and the Swabians.

CHAPTER SIX

Austria-Hungary

This is the curse upon our noble house:
To strive half-heartedly, by half measures,
To bring about half of what must be done.
—GRILLPARZER

I

Germany now had only one friend left in the world: Austria-Hungary. This dual monarchy was a strange creation. Ten nations lived inside her borders. One fourth of the population consisted of Germans who led the other peoples in wealth and education but lagged far behind the others in influence, since the government counted upon German support in any case. Key posts were therefore reserved for peoples of the other nations; the State Council which decided for war in 1914 consisted of two Hungarians, a Pole, a Croat, and only one German.

Hungarians possessed the preponderance of political power. They were the toughest of the ten nations. Their romantic history had not made visionaries of them; they sometimes lost sight of reality, but never of their own advantage. Theirs was the vitality of uncomplicated souls whose capacity for action is never sicklied over with the pale cast of thought. In the Hungarian nobility the strong natural patriotism of the Magyars reached such a pitch of intensity that for them Hungary alone mattered on the entire globe. The upper class was infatuated with the glorious past. Until the middle of the nineteenth century the official language of the Hungarian parliament had been Latin, which every educated Hungarian of the time spoke fluently. Questions of form were of paramount importance. Open revolution almost broke out in Budapest over the problem of whether the Austro-Hungarian army should be called *kaiserlich-königlich* (imperial-royal) or *kaiserlich und königlich* (imperial *and* royal). Hungarian experts on constitutional law wrote weighty books arguing that since the King of Hungary included in his title the crowns of Rumania, Bulgaria, Serbia, Galicia, and Bosnia, those countries by rights belonged to Hungary and must be restored to her. Three hundred landed proprietors owned one fifth of the soil; the average estate was one hundred and seventy square kilometers, and some were more than two thousand square kilometers. In private life the ruling caste preserved a rigid etiquette; Hungarian hospitality was proverbial, and the slightest insult made a duel mandatory. The Hungarian nobility provided the state with leaders of great vigor, but these leaders could not be bothered listening when the interests of non-Hungarians were being discussed. When the Hungarian minister of trade went to Vienna, his Austrian opposite number usually played sick; negotiations with Hungarians always meant giving, never receiving.

The Germans and the Hungarians were the actual pillars of the dual monarchy, but they could usually count upon a third nation, the Poles, who constituted a tenth of the population. The Polish nation had been divided up among Russia, Germany, and Austria. Neither the Russian knout nor Prussian order appealed to the Poles; therefore they gave the Empire their loyalty.

The Czechs, who together with the Slovaks made up a seventh of the population, were a good deal less reliable. The upper class among the Czechs desired complete autonomy within the Austrian Empire. This urge for independence sprang from a slowly growing consciousness of their own culture. But not even the leaders wanted separation from the monarchy. The father of Czech nationalism, Palacky, feared St. Petersburg far more than Vienna.

The most difficult national group in the monarchy were the six and one-half million South Slavs. They comprised three groups: Serbs, Croats and Slovenes. The three million Croats were Roman Catholic, divided along sharp caste lines, with an ancient nobility proud of its traditions, and a cultivated middle class. The majority of the Croats were loyal to the imperial family and had always supplied the emperors with their finest soldiers. The Croats were suspicious and full of scorn for the two million Serbs who inhabited Austria-Hungary. The two nations spoke almost the same language, but as the result of three hundred years of subjugation by the Turks the Serbs had developed in a different direction. In religion they were Greek Orthodox. They were an undifferentiated peasant folk without a nobility, without traditions. For the most part they were illiterate, and the few who could write used the Russian script which Croats could not read. Should street names be written first in the Roman alphabet and then in the Russian, or vice versa, in Serbian-Croat districts? Over this world-shaking question the two related peoples were ready to knife each other. The leaders of the Croats and the Serbs had solemnly proclaimed their undying fraternity, but declarations did not close the gap. The Croats were certain that they were the finer and nobler nation. Alongside these two groups were the one and a half million Slovenes, an impoverished and modest nation who inclined toward the Croats in political matters. The Croats and Slovenes looked to the West, the Serbs to the East. It was the ancient antinomy between Roman and Byzantine culture.

Along with these seven groups—Germans, Hungarians, Poles, Czechs, Croats, Serbs and Slovenes—there were three other minorities, splinters from neighboring states: three million Rumanians, two million Ukrainians and eight hundred thousand Italians. Most of the Italians pined for a reunion with Italy, although it was said that Austrian bureaucracy was a race horse compared to Italian administration. Hungarian oppression impelled the Rumanians to look toward Bucharest; however, Rumanian misgovernment was such that they looked without leaping. The Ukrainians, who were called Ruthenians, were mostly loyal to the Empire, for if Austria-Hungary broke up they could be taken over by Russia. That was going from the frying pan into the fire, and therefore they clung to the Hapsburgs.

II

It was not easy to govern this ten-nation empire. In addition to twenty-four *Landtage* (provincial parliaments) there was a Hungarian parliament and an Austrian *Reichsrat*. Not counting the splinter groups there were twenty-four parties in the *Reichsrat;* the Czechs, for example, were split into Old Czechs, Young Czechs, Czech Agrarians, Czech Clericals, and Czech National Socialists. No bill could be passed unless the government bribed some of the parties by offering concessions in linguistic and economic matters. Legislation opened up bottomless depths of complexity. Each party saw black schemes in the motions of the other parties. Should a rival second a motion, the party that proposed it took fright; it could only think that it was being tricked and anxiously tried to discover wherein it had been deceived.

Austrian government was therefore a system of eternal tacking back and forth. This process was rendered easier by the peculiar nature of the Viennese upper classes. The educated bourgeoisie had adopted the attitudes of the nobility whom it naively worshipped. The nobility were extremely numerous, since every higher army officer and government official was raised to the nobility upon his retirement. The high aristocracy did not take this professional nobility seriously, but the exclusiveness of the aristocracy was ameliorated by a cheerful resignation. The old families were so sure of their superiority that they smilingly forgot about it. The life of the nobility was an endless round of party-going, hunting, and love affairs. Military service they could tolerate; but high posts in government service were simply a burden. To be a minister of state was to make the supreme sacrifice. The Austrian nobility was newer, but also richer than that of Germany, was linked to the crown with unquestioning devotion, was too soft and fond of comfort to be a match for the Hungarian nobility. On the whole the Empire was hurt more by Hungarian narrow-mindedness than by the Austrian tendency to let things drift.

In the middle of the nineteenth century the government declared its intention to work gradually toward autonomy of the various nationalities. This declaration brought forth the ironic comment:

All parts of the land will henceforth be independent,
But centralized bayonets will keep the army in the ascendant.
Favoritism in government used to be the accusation;
Now the hand of oppression weighs alike on every nation.
All the nationalities will now be treated equally, like brothers,
And if necessary each will be whipped up against the others.

Later Premier Taaffe, whose support derived mainly from the Slavs, came out with the statement that the aim was to go on "muddling through" and keeping all the nationalities in "an equilibrium of well-tempered dissatisfaction." One of the secrets of the Austrian art of government is contained within the smiling irony of these phrases.

North Germans regarded the Austrians with feelings of exasperated arrogance. Austria was the Prater, lanterns, *heuriger* wine, zithers twanging mournfully, a Strauss waltz, a coffee shop with a hundred newspapers, people forever friendly, charming, amiable, who never said no to your face, who were always grumbling, griping and mocking but never had the resolution to change anything: "Oh, let the government worry about it; that's what it's there for. . . . You can never get the Viennese down." Everything there was soft pastry, nothing of steel and stone. Here was a nation that made fun of itself: "Austria's future is dark but certain." And the essence of this Austrianism was Vienna, at whose gates Asia began—or perhaps Asia began inside its coffee shops, flea markets, and in the people's Slavic craving to be liked.

But to judge Austria by such Prussian standards is a cardinal sin. Historical reality proved the workability of this way of life. For four hundred years this same Austria had been the heart of the Holy Roman Empire of the German nation. It had raised up an imperial house over whose realm the sun never set. It had saved Europe again and again from the flood tide of Turkish power. These Austrians, more gracious, flexible and joyous than any other Germans, had introduced into German art, German science and the German way of living an element of gaiety and lightness that was balm to the souls of all but the most austere and puritanical northerners. It was an un-teutonic Germanism, without vast nostalgias and titanic grandeurs, impregnated with sweet Slavic melancholy, illuminated by the ardent glow of the

Italian spirit, with a touch of the enchantment of Oriental fairy tales—
a musical and unmathematical Germanism, historically unique and of
the highest quality. And the Danube state which emerged from this
mingling of nations had been for centuries a secure and comfortable
home for its inhabitants. There everyone could speak his own language
as he pleased. The state's prosperity far surpassed that of its neighbors,
and it gave to its people a far happier life than they were ever to enjoy
in the decades after its collapse. We cannot estimate the achievements
of the dual monarchy by the standards of an ideal state—for no country has ever attained those standards. Rather, we must base our judgment on the almost insuperable difficulties that flow out of the inter-
mingling of so many races in the valley of the Danube. That Empire
could not have been governed without sly negligence, a wilful obscur-
ing of issues, a shunning of crises, and a sovereign sense of irony toward
self and everyone else.

During World War I, a Berliner in Vienna remarked that the mood
of people in Prussia was grave, but optimistic. He received the answer:
"Just the opposite here. We're pessimistic, but cheerful." Everybody
railed at Austria-Hungary; a German deputy stated publicly in the
Reichsrat that nobody would shed a tear if the monster kicked the
bucket. But in 1914 Austria had enough confidence in her people to
place Serbian and Rumanian regiments in the field against Serbs and
Rumanians, and during the very last days of the war, when the Empire
was falling apart, the army communiqué praised the bravery of the
Ruthenian and Croatian units. When Austria-Hungary went under,
many a tear was shed.

Only those who knew what life was like in old Austria-Hungary can
judge the country fairly. To sit in the Mirabell Gardens and look up at
the castle of Salzburg, to saunter down the *Stradone* in Ragusa, to see
the *Goldmacherhäusl*, the alchemist's cottage, gleaming on the Hrad-
schin at Prague, to hear the tolling of the bells of the Stefansdom at
Vienna, to admire the frowning castle in Budapest, the mosque in
Mostar, the Mickiewicz memorial in Cracow, and the Dante memorial
in Trient—is to realize that tradition and selfishness, geographical necessity and the play of chance, had collaborated here to build a structure supremely individual, of which three men so different in outlook
as Palacky, Bismarck, and Disraeli remarked that if it did not exist, for
the sake of European peace it would have had to be invented.

III

The ruler of that Empire, Emperor Franz Joseph, had been wearing
his crown for more than sixty years. For more than sixty years, summer
and winter he was at his desk every morning at half past four. If he

were returning from some social function so late at night that it was hardly worth going to sleep, he had a cup of coffee, rode his horse in the Prater, and turned to his duties. To one of his ministers he remarked: "I know you are a late sleeper and I mean to be considerate; you need not come to me with your daily report until six o'clock." He studied documents and listened to reports until evening; his sparse lunch was brought on a tray and set down among his papers. No work was ever postponed. The ministers reckoned that bills submitted to His Majesty would be attended to within one day; no department head ever worked that hard. If there were decisions which required haste, he insisted that he be awakened during the night. Although he suffered from constant bronchial catarrh, he disobeyed the warnings of his doctors and went on with his daily cold sponge baths, which he took upon rising from his iron army cot. His health was fundamentally unassailable; at the age of eighty he went galloping across fields in the course of army maneuvers. He was always dressed in uniform; while working at his desk he wore army greatcoats that had been made over into dressing gowns. Under his uniform he wore nothing but a shirt; he never used underwear. One day a valet by mistake gave him a brand-new tunic to wear on a journey; he sat shivering with cold, at four in the morning, in the open carriage, but refused to put on his coat—"because the embroidery on the collar would be damaged by the rubbing of the coat." He needed nothing for himself; his personal expenditures came to no more than the expenses of a middling civil servant. He was anything but a man of the world. When he wanted to give a birthday present to his mistress, Katharina von Schratt, he told her to choose something she liked and charge it to him. When she showed him the pearl necklace she had bought and asked him how much he thought it had cost, he guessed 500 gulden. "It cost 30,000 gulden," she told him. "Not too expensive either," the Emperor replied politely. He took no notice whatsoever of the invention of the telephone, the automobile, and the elevator.

Everything he did was done thoroughly. He spoke fluently the languages of the peoples of his Empire—Hungarian, Czech, Croat, Polish, Italian. In questions of detail his judgment was sure; but when it came to formulating general views, making comprehensive decisions, planning or even tolerating new approaches—these were not within his range. All that could be accomplished by common sense, he accomplished; courage, enthusiasm, or imagination were not among his gifts. It was impossible to influence his emotions because he had none. When he was informed of the assassination of his prime minister, Count Stürgkh, he replied—he was at this time eighty-six—without any sign of alarm: "And who is to take his place?" He hated sentimentality as any other form of self-indulgence. No one was as un-Austrian as the

Emperor of Austria. It was impossible to imagine him giving way to his inclinations or to temperament. He was completely matter-of-fact, entirely without whims. The dignity of his position was so ingrained in him that all vanity, all desire to shine, all self-display and self-love were put aside. Loud talk, loud laughter, effervescent merriment, even lively gestures were unthinkable in his presence; his only reproof would be a look, but such behavior was never forgotten. No one would ever have dared to tell him a joke. When reasons of state forced him to tell a lie, the old man blushed. He kept the circle of his intimates small; people with strong convictions were a burden to him. He was a devout Catholic, but forcefully guarded the interests of the State against encroachments by the Church. He had no bias against non-Catholics. Every year he received the greetings and blessings of Catholic archbishops, Lutheran pastors, Jewish rabbis, Orthodox priests and Mohammedan muftis. He thought of all as too far beneath him for him to notice the differences. Of all his peoples he had the most regard for the Hungarians; he regarded the Slavs as adolescent sons; of the Germans he demanded obedience, since they were of his own blood.

By nature he was no soldier, but he was unquestionably a first-rate military administrator. He ordered a careful survey to determine how far apart buttons should be placed on the military blouses of Austrian officers, and he knew more about the style of tunic of the ten foreign countries whose uniforms he was entitled to wear than did their own monarchs. Books he never read; he did attend occasional performances of the court theater because he considered an inspection of its work among his duties.

For minor errors he had a keen eye, but his attitude toward the frailties of his country was one of majestic resignation. When an electoral reform was to be undertaken, he asked one of his ministers: "Do you think it will work out?" "Certainly, your Majesty." "I don't; nothing ever works out in Austria." At the outbreak of the war he told Frau Schratt: "I shall be content if we get out of this with nothing worse than a black eye." In the second year of the war he declared: "The struggle is proving beyond our strength."

His resignation sprang from personal sorrows. His wife was assassinated; his only son, Crown Prince Rudolf, took his own life and that of his sweetheart; his brother, Emperor Maximilian of Mexico, was condemned to death by court martial, and shot. Maximilian's wife went mad; another of his sisters-in-law was burned to death in a charity-bazaar fire; one of the archdukes died of a fall from a horse, another by the accidental discharge of his own gun, and a third in an Atlantic storm. When Franz Joseph became Emperor at the age of eighteen, Austria was the leading German power; the Double Eagle fluttered above Milan and Venice, and Hungary was a secure part of the Empire. Twenty years later all was lost; he had been forced to concede the Hungarians virtual independence.

His marriage was unhappy from the very beginning. The radiant beauty of his seventeen-year-old Bavarian princess Elizabeth was insufficient to break the power of a domineering mother over this dutiful pedant. As the years went on, he was tolerant of the whims and extravagance of his restive, highly imaginative wife, but he could not win her strange heart. "What can you expect from Franz Joseph? He is nothing but a sergeant!" said Elizabeth in despair. When at the age of fifty-six he formed an intimacy with an actress, his wife promoted this friendship with genuine warmth. Nor was this hard for her. Katharina von Schratt, twenty-three and separated from her husband, a petty Hungarian noble, was a bright, simple child of nature. Elizabeth called her "my chosen sister." Franz Joseph treated Katharina with the shyness of a high-school boy and the solicitude of a grandfather. When he asked her friendship, he apologized for being importunate; when he sent her money, he assured her that he often sent his children money for their birthdays. He asked her not to write to him more often than she had time and inclination. When a few days passed without a letter from her, he thanked her "most fervently and heartily in particular for your having responded to my plea and, what with the incredible demands upon you these past few days, having not troubled yourself over a reply any sooner. . . . And would you believe it, in spite of all I was still so foolish that my not hearing from you since a week ago yesterday gave me the greatest anxiety. I tormented myself with the thought that you might be unwell, and with even gloomier imaginings, and so received your letter with great rejoicing, for it was a true deliverance." In his letters to her he used the formal personal pronoun.

One day when she passed by the palace later than agreed, so that he was not standing at the window, he wrote humbly: "I must indeed beg your pardon for not having come later to our particular window, and I felt deep regret when from a window in the Empress' salon I saw you walking across the palace square and—for this I thank you most cordially—look up several times at the curtained window. In apology I can only say that since you had told me you would be crossing the square earlier than usual I waited until after eight o'clock in my room. Then I decided you must have gone straight home after church, and since the Empress had called me to join her at breakfast some time before, and earlier than usual, I went to her apartment, and as the result of this haste missed the joy of being able to greet you from the distance." Katharina was the only person with whom he could drop his dignity; he went so far as to write her that he would not have his corns cut away "because of the danger involved," and continued:

"How fortunate you are not to have corns!" When he was seventy and she forty-seven, he could still write to her: "I thank you for having smiled once more at me through the peephole in the carriage after we had already said goodbye." She visited him frequently to the day of his death and survived him by twenty-four years.

IV

Austria's most pressing problem was her relationship with Serbia. Both countries had originally been good friends. An Austrian field marshal, Prince Eugen, had freed Serbia from the Turkish yoke. Later the land had been lost again, but individual Serbs continually sought refuge from Turkish oppression in the neighboring monarchy; in this way Serbian settlements in Hungary were formed. Then, in Napoleonic times, the son of a Serbian peasant and former Austrian corporal, "Black George," organized a revolt against the Turks. He repeatedly asked the Austrian monarchy to annex the liberated areas. But the Viennese chancellor was "momentarily overburdened" by the Napoleonic wars and never got around to answering George's letters. Thus Serbia became an independent kingdom.

Seventy years later the Congress of Berlin assigned a restive part of Turkey, the provinces of Bosnia and Herzegovina, to the Austrians. Disraeli remarked that only Austria could establish order in that area. Two years before, Russia had consented to Austrian annexation of Bosnia and Herzegovina in compensation for her own recent conquests. In order to compensate Serbia also, Austria obtained for her the Turkish districts around Nish, which by rights should have been ceded to Bulgaria. Thereupon Serbia concluded a voluntary treaty of friendship with Austria, virtually accepting the protectorship of her big neighbor. A few years later King Milan of Serbia offered to abdicate at any time in favor of the House of Hapsburg if he were assured Austrian citizenship and the hereditary title of Royal Highness for himself and his son Alexander. The Austrian foreign minister declined this offer rather sharply, saying that he had only too many Slavs in the monarchy already.

Of the seven kings who ruled Serbia until World War I, not a single one succeeded in dying in his bed. They were all assassinated or driven into exile, except for those who avoided the occupational hazard of their position by timely abdication. In vain Serbia at the beginning of the new century repeated her offer to become a part of the Austrian Empire. Somewhat later General Staff Officer Dimitriyevitch had King Alexander—who admittedly was a thoroughly objectionable person—stabbed during the night, together with the Queen and the King's ministers. The church bells rang, Belgrade was decked with flags, and the parliament unanimously voted its thanks to the assassins. Whereupon the foreign ambassadors left the city—all except the French envoy.

The new king, Peter, was a descendant of Black George and a former officer in Gambetta's army. He appointed Pashitch, the leader of the radical party, to the post of premier. Pashitch promptly issued a memorandum declaring that the prime purpose of Serbia was to rescue the South Slavs from Austria-Hungary; Belgrade must be for the South Slavs what Piedmont had been for the Italians. Pashitch liked hearing himself called the Serbian Bismarck. The destruction of Austria-Hungary was inevitable, he maintained. Austria's reply was a typical half-hearted measure: the Pig War. The Austrian public health inspectors put difficulties in the way of Serbia's exports of pigs. The campaign was a failure; Belgrade's pigs were sold to other countries, primarily to Germany. When Austria offered to call off the Pig War in return for political rapprochement, Serbia refused; she preferred to pour salt on the wound. Then something else happened that exacerbated the sore.

V

In Constantinople the reformist party of the Young Turks had come to the helm. With the immature nationalism of young democracies they announced their intention of reconquering all one-time Turkish lands: Egypt, Algeria, Caucasia. They intended to hold Turkish elections in Bosnia, which Austria had occupied for thirty years. The Austrian foreign minister at this time was Baron von Aehrenthal. Descended from an ancient family of grain dealers, this big, heavy man with pronounced, melancholy jowls, bristly hair and mournful fish eyes, was fired with the ambition to prove himself a great statesman. The Turkish maneuver was easy to parry; he would call for elections to a Bosnian provincial parliament. But then why not go a step further and transform the mere occupation of Bosnia into annexation? That would once and for all put the Serbs in their place. In Bosnia the Catholic Croats and the Moslems—who together constituted a good half of the population—favored annexation. Living under Austrian bureaucrats was no pleasure, but to exist under Serbian or Turkish officials was perpetual punishment.

Unfortunately for Europe, another ambitious parvenu had become foreign minister in St. Petersburg: Izvolsky. A small, rotund man, he affected a monocle, patent-leather shoes, white gaiters, a white ribbon on his vest and a pearl-headed tie-pin. His hair and mustache were always carefully groomed; his short neck stuck stiffly over a high collar. When shaking hands with someone he never looked him in the face. But all these mannerisms, including the fragrance of Parma violets that emanated from him, could not confer upon that puffy face with its slack lips the slightest trace of elegance. In St. Petersburg society, Izvolsky was familiarly known as Prince Bosporus—he was determined to settle the Black Sea question.

Such an ambition fitted in very neatly with Aehrenthal's plans. He arranged a conference at the Palace of Buchlau in Moravia, which belonged to Count Berchtold, the Austrian ambassador to St. Petersburg. Aehrenthal declared that he wanted to proclaim the annexation of Bosnia in about three weeks. Izvolsky was willing to maintain an attitude of benevolent neutrality toward the annexation if Austria agreed that Russian warships—and Russian ships alone—would be allowed to use the passage through the Bosporus from the Black Sea to the Mediterranean. By this he thought to convert the entire Black Sea into an impregnable Mediterranean harbor for Russia. Aehrenthal acquiesced and the two men parted on a note of cordial understanding. Izvolsky went on to Paris and London to secure the agreement of the French and British governments. Germany, of course, would agree to whatever suited Austria.

Izvolsky had committed an unforgivable folly. When he gave Austria carte blanche in Bosnia, he was giving away something final, for Russia was the only power seriously interested in that territory. What Izvolsky was getting, on the other hand, was highly uncertain; if Paris and London were not complaisant, Vienna's go-ahead was worthless. It has been said that Izvolsky's conversation with Aehrenthal was interrupted by the planned entrance of several pretty ladies of the Austrian aristocracy who asked him to join them. The roly-poly Russian, for whom the beautiful countesses held the enormous attractiveness of the socially unattainable, could hardly wait to take up their invitation; consequently he neglected to consider the deal carefully. He was to regret his haste bitterly; he ruined his career, and his animosity on this account helped to destroy Europe.

VI

France agreed to Russia's plans for the Straits. While in Paris, Izvolsky received a message from Aehrenthal that the annexation would take place in the course of the following week. He promptly informed the Serbian ambassador that Serbia would really be gaining by the deal, since Bosnia was lost to Serbia anyhow. But three days later the whole picture changed fundamentally; England flatly refused to countenance the opening of the Straits. Izvolsky declared that this obstinacy would endanger the Anglo-Russian Entente. He even tried to talk to Grey in English—"it was touching," Grey recounts. The British foreign minister could not be intimidated. Izvolsky's Straits plan had failed.

Meanwhile Aehrenthal—over the head of his German ally—had announced the annexation of Bosnia.

Now a storm broke loose, not in Bosnia, where all remained calm, but in Serbia and in Russia. Izvolsky was bitterly attacked. What was he to do? First he rushed to Berlin to denounce Aehrenthal, whom he called an "adventurer." "He cheated me, the dirty Jew!" he declared to Bülow. The chancellor clapped his hands to his ears, saying: "If you speak ill of my friend Aehrenthal, I must close my ears. But I promise you that if Aehrenthal should employ similar language in talking about my friend Izvolsky, I will do the same." The Russian insisted, with British backing, that the Bosnian question must be placed before a European conference, since Aehrenthal had repudiated one of the decisions of the Congress of Berlin. Serbia and Montenegro would have to receive territorial compensation. Bülow declared that he would participate in a conference only if the powers had come to an agreement beforehand. In any case, he said, Izvolsky could not expect any support from Berlin; was he not a great proponent of the Anglo-Russian Entente?

"Was it Russia or Germany who repudiated the Reinsurance Treaty?" Izvolsky replied pointedly. But the argument was ineffective, as are all arguments in a struggle for power. Izvolsky returned to St. Petersburg empty-handed. The Czar, who knew nothing about Izvolsky's agreement with Aehrenthal, assured Pashitch that Russia would not tolerate the annexation of Bosnia.

Meanwhile Aehrenthal—or Count Aehrenthal, as he had recently become—was nursing dreams of using this occasion to "settle" with Serbia. Such a settlement by force of arms could only have worsened, never solved, the monarchy's South Slav problem. Bülow was ready to stand at his side with "the loyalty of the ancient Germans." He declared: "I know that doubts have entered your mind as to whether the present unsavory conditions in Serbia will in the long run be endurable. I have confidence in your judgment. . . . I shall regard the decision you ultimately reach as the one demanded by the circumstances." That letter is a milestone on Germany's road to ruin. Bismarck had stated frankly in the *Reichstag:* "No one is going to throw a lasso around our necks over the Oriental question." His successor went ahead and gave the Austrians a written promise that henceforth he would trot meekly along led by the Austrian rope. He did so, moreover, in terms of sneering contempt for Serbia, taking an attitude of superior arrogance that did not allow him to see the depths of the problem. It was not his "whore's nature" alone which made Bülow kowtow to the newly made count. He wanted to impress Europe by a demonstration of force. Moreover he feared—unreasonably—that Austria, too, might break away from her alliance with Germany. "It might be said," he noted nervously, "that our policy after the resignation of Prince Bismarck resulted in the lapsing first of our alliance with Russia, then of our good relations with England, and finally of the Triple Alliance." That in view of Germany's present isolation, the Triple Alliance could only be a defensive league, that it could not be used for purposes of aggrandizement, was something he would not perceive. All he could see was that at the moment Russia was in no position to fight; this was an opportunity which had to be exploited. He had forgotten Bismarck's warning: "If peace is preserved at the expense of the pride of a great nation such as Russia, a virus remains active in that nation's system which earlier or later will seek healing at the cost of the peace of Europe." This warning was to prove prophetic.

For the present Austria came to an agreement with the parties primarily concerned. For two and a half million Turkish pounds Istanbul surrendered its claim to Bosnia. Now it was simple for Austria and Germany to reject the Russian proposal for a conference, and Izvolsky's personal predicament became desperate. He had removed from the state records all the notes on his journey, with their damning evidence that he had accepted Aehrenthal's plan. But even this did not do the trick; the Austrian foreign minister threatened to make public the whole story. Poor Izvolsky pleaded with Berlin to intercede and prevent publication. On the one hand he used the threat of similar indiscretions on his part; on the other hand he offered renewal of the League of the Three Emperors, or Russian aid in case of a French attack. Simultaneously he ordered Belgrade to come to terms with Vienna. Luckily Aehrenthal had meanwhile realized that a war with Serbia "had no object"—in other words, that the advantages would not be worth a general deterioration of European relations.

In Berlin Kiderlen-Wächter had taken over the Foreign Office. He thought the affair had to be resolved. He therefore proposed to St. Petersburg that Austria ask all the participants in the Treaty of Berlin for their consent—provided this consent was assured beforehand. He wanted a definite yes or no on this, he said; if the reply were vague, Germany would "let things take their course." The "things" in question were publication of the details of the Buchlau discussions, and perhaps also an Austrian invasion of Serbia. Chancellor Bülow signed this note, but without bothering to read it; Kiderlen himself was somewhat worried about his "impudence." England, however, delivered virtually the same proposal to St. Petersburg. Izvolsky said yes, and the Czar telegraphed the Kaiser to express his gratitude for having found a peaceful solution. Soon afterwards, however, Izvolsky maintained that this "ultimatum" had been humiliating to Russia. He stepped down as foreign minister and was sent to Paris as Russian ambassador.

Deserted by Russia, Serbia now had no choice but to recognize the annexation of Bosnia. She solemnly agreed to change her ways and to support no movements aimed at breaking away parts of Austria-Hungary. However, Serbia made this declaration only after Izvolsky had privately given her assurances in precisely the opposite sense; he told the Serbs that their country's misfortunes would end when Austria-Hungary fell apart. The annexation of Bosnia had brought the moment closer, and when the time of reckoning came Russia would reopen and solve the Serbian question. He, Izvolsky, was well aware that a struggle with the Teutons was inevitable; Russia's policy would always be pro-Slav. Encouraged by these promises, Serbia—a few days after her solemn declaration of amity with Austria—sent her ambassador in Vienna instructions "concerning continuance of the Greater Serbia propaganda campaign in Austria-Hungary." These instructions reported the establishment of a propaganda center in Prague, and concluded with the sentence: "Insofar as revolutionary political propaganda appears to be necessary, it will from now on be directed from St. Petersburg and from golden Prague. We will promote this activity through our connections, which in the future also will be helped and supervised by the Serbian general staff."

Bülow and Aehrenthal were triumphant, but wrongly so. The annexation would have made sense only as a first step toward the transformation of the Austrian monarchy into a genuine federal union. A federal union would have been the salvation of Austria-Hungary, and it was blocked by the obstinacy of the Hungarians and the laziness of the Austrians.

CHAPTER SEVEN

Kaiser Wilhelm II

*Vanity is a mortgage which must be deducted
from the abilities of the man who is burdened
with it in order to arrive at the capital which
remains as the usable sum of his talent.*

—BISMARCK

I

When Wilhelm II ascended the throne, it
was with the resolve to make his people happy. He wanted to preserve
peace, improve the condition of the poor and promote the arts and
sciences. He was an idealist whose ideal was—as Bismarck put it—
"popular absolutism." He was convinced that he could accomplish this
great and sacred task, since he knew for a certainty that he was smarter
than most other monarchs and statesmen.

In this opinion he was not mistaken. Nature had been more than
generous to him. He possessed a mind that grasped things immediately, and an ever-ready memory of extraordinary reach. When the
Casino in Wiesbaden was to be dedicated, the architect, Thiersch, was
to deliver a speech. An hour before, the Kaiser came to him and asked
to hear the talk. Then he told the startled creator of the building: "I
will make the speech." To the amazement and enthusiasm of the festive
crowd, he mounted the platform and delivered a quite respectable
lecture on the technical aspects of the building. His excellent memory
carried him through, so that he made very few mistakes.

The Kaiser's talent for inspiring phrases was equally remarkable. He
was a born rabble-rouser; when he spoke off the cuff, he let himself
be carried away by the mood of his audience.

But he was not just an orator and a man with a singular memory. He
was often wiser than his advisers. His interest in art and science,
especially archeology, was no mere pose; it was really part of his lively,
indefatigable mind. In his official dealings with people he had few
social prejudices. Although he was occasionally fond of summoning up
the traditions of his country or his family, he had made up his mind
to be the most modern monarch of his age. In thinking up ways to
express his favor to someone, he could be quite ingenious. On Menzel's

seventieth birthday he went to enormous trouble to have his entourage reproduce in tableau Menzel's famous painting, "Flute Concert in Sanssouci." He himself greeted Menzel as an officer of Frederick the Great. On Moltke's ninetieth birthday he sent the old general the victory flags of his various great campaigns. When French President Carnot was assassinated, he indicated his sympathy by pardoning some French officers who had been condemned to death as spies.

He had a lively sense of humor. He was having a holiday on the Norwegian coast when his first grandson was born. Through an oversight of the German consul, the news of this great event did not reach the Kaiser. He found out two days later when the telegrams of congratulation began arriving. They were heaped on his desk in alphabetical order, that of Sultan Abdu-l-Hamid on top. The Kaiser promptly telegraphed his son: "Have just heard from the Sultan that a son has been born unto you."

The Kaiser's love of peace was quite genuine. He saw himself in the idealized image of a monarch who would bring happiness to his people. Moreover, he had not inherited his grandfather's tough nervous system and he shrank from any thoughts of violence. His dream was to reconcile all nations, just as he hoped to be the impartial mediator among all the classes of his own nation.

In short, if mental endowment and good will sufficed to make a statesman, Wilhelm II would really have led his people toward "those splendid times" he had expressly promised them. But since talent is dependent on character, the history of the German people under his rule once again became a sad affair.

II

The strong and weak points of his character were largely the product of his childhood. At his birth a midwife made a slip; the shoulder joint of his left arm was injured. As a result arm and hand were permanently crippled; when he was full grown his hand reached only to his coat pocket. All his life he had to eat with a special utensil for one hand; his left arm could neither hold a rifle nor throw a tennis ball.

But a Prussian prince must be a soldier—a good soldier. Hinzpeter, the Kaiser's tutor, undertook to overcome Wilhelm's timidity, the natural result of his physical defect. He mounted the frightened boy on a horse and started it trotting. Wilhelm's lack of balance, his overdeveloped right side, pulled him off. Instantly the weeping child was mounted anew, fell off again, and had to mount again. This Spartan education was continued until his riding skill was perfected and his spirit damaged forever. He learned to drive a four-in-hand; he learned to ride the thoroughbred mare Ecstasy; and he learned to pretend courage in all situations. A worse education for a monarch can scarcely be conceived. He was trained to keep check over his own behavior all the time. All his natural impulses, all simple and spontaneous actions, were bound to wither in this inferno of his youth. He remained insecure. One of the few women to whom the Kaiser was drawn, the pretty Princess Daisy of Pless, a descendant of the British high aristocracy, was later to say of him: "Great areas in his soul had, like his arm, simply not grown. . . . As a man he is impossible. He is so dreadfully tactless, loud and theatrical; he has no manners; he does not know how to choose his friends. In small things, that often does not matter— but in for a penny, in for a pound. He is bourgeois and loud—and yet he sometimes has the charm of youthfulness."

By dint of constant deception he eventually developed the outward presence of a man of great force and sturdiness—but this did not win him his parents' love. It was a grief to them to see their son so clumsy, so psychologically ill-balanced. On the occasion of the Prince's coming of age, his father said to the Rector of Berlin University: "You congratulate me—you, a psychiatrist?"

Uncle Edward said soberly of his sister's son that his nephew Wilhelm always had to be flaunting himself like a peacock; if he could not do so, he felt inferior and unhappy. That was an accurate judgment. Physical disability and an unhappy childhood had produced in this prince a sense of great insecurity which resulted in an unlimited craving for applause. Soon after Bismarck's dismissal the Kaiser's former admirer, Waldersee, noted: "A single idea governs all his actions: the desire to be popular. . . . Since he is very conceited about his own abilities (which conceit unfortunately is based upon gross self-delusion), he delights in flattery." Like many men hungry for status, he was a dilettante in numerous fields. He wrote verses, set them to music, and conducted bands at defenseless officers' clubs. He painted and sculpted; at evening parties he talked uninterruptedly for hours about all the sciences; he drew plans for palaces, cathedrals, or warships; he outdid all farmers in the excellence of his rye and all industrialists in the perfection of the porcelain made at his model factory in Kadin; he delivered recommendations to theater directors and engineers; he was an authority on religion, art, and military uniforms; he solved with sovereign ease the most difficult general staff problems —after the solution had been given to him. To the naive minds of his generals and court officials he must have seemed a genius. Was it not amazing that a monarch, when an Orientalist was invited to luncheon, should recite between hors d'oeuvres and roast the names of all the Assyrian kings without a hitch and in the correct sequence? Or that aboard his yacht, the *Hohenzollern*, he should hold a religious service as competently as any chaplain and deliver a sermon scarcely a bit more boring than that of an average clergyman.

His vanity increased so that he succumbed to a feminine craving for ornament. He loaded his fingers with rings. He owned more than a thousand different uniforms and on some days would change twelve times. When he went to hear Wagner's *Flying Dutchman* he wore an admiral's uniform. Noting that the Czar was wearing an adjutant's aiglets, he learned on inquiry that Nicky had been his father's aide. Promptly he betook himself alone to the tomb of Wilhelm I, emerged adorned with an aide-de-camp's aiglets, and explained to his alarmed entourage that he had just appointed himself aide-de-camp to his late grandfather. Stubbornly he would always refer to this grandfather as "Wilhelm the Great" and spoke of his being "an almost sacred figure." The fact is that his grandfather had once remarked that he considered modesty a necessity since he could never be sure whether his personal valet might not be assigned a higher place in the Hereafter than himself, for more ably doing his duty.

How different the grandson was! Only by considering himself an emissary of God could he keep up the tremendous conceit which was necessary to him in order to offset his tormenting inferiority feelings. "How the Kaiser has found out what the will of God is no one can say," Bismarck sneered. But Wilhelm himself was certain that he had, as it were, a direct wire to Heaven. In his heart he remained an absolute ruler. When he suddenly put the brakes on the social reforms he had announced, his ministers felt he had left them high and dry. Whereupon they had to swallow the following: "After discussion with the President of the State Ministry, it is *I* who prescribe to him the procedures by which *I* wish to see My Policy executed. Not vice versa! And whether I choose to drive the carriage of State at a walk or a trot it is for Me and not for the passengers to make up my mind about. . . . Respect for parliament and country evidently plays a major role! We seem to have caught the constitutional virus. That I am satisfied is enough and of far more importance than anything else." When dissenting views were reported to him, he said crossly: "Yes, that's it, my subjects ought simply to do what I tell them, but they always want to think for themselves and that is what gives rise to all difficulties."

He considered himself infallible and felt that any attempt to influence him was *lèse-majesté,* even if it came from his peers. When Czar Nicholas was on the point of suggesting some pact to stop the arms race, Wilhelm declared: "If he makes such an offer to me, I'll paddle him!" This arrogance was typical of his relationship to Nicky. We need only glance at a picture of the two men together to see how the shy Romanov must have hated this eternally swaggering cousin of his.

While the plump Czar of Bulgaria was leaning out the window of the palace to watch a parade, Wilhelm gave him a resounding slap on the behind—in the presence of the entire court. When the tiny King of Italy came to visit, Wilhelm assigned a six-foot-six aide to shepherd him around.

But Wilhelm remained unaware of the dislike everyone felt for him. Vanity blinded him. He thought Nicky an obedient disciple of his, was certain he could handle the Social Democrats by himself. Gradually this conceit grew so monstrous that it became funny. After the suppression of the uprising in Southwest Africa a colonel remarked modestly to him: "I owe these successes entirely to my officers." Wilhelm immediately retorted: "Those are My officers."

He took everything personally, and because he did so his conduct in politics was extremely fickle. While he was still crown prince and in command of a brigade of guards, his best friend and adviser was Waldersee. One day the general pointed out to him that he was really no longer bound to carry out all the orders of his dying father. Wilhelm considered this an insult to the imperial dignity; moreover, he could not resist the opportunity to deliver a snub. Drawing himself up, he made this reply: "I shall carry out every order of my father's. If one of them should read: 'General Count Waldersee, having attempted to mislead the Commander of the Second Infantry Guards Brigade into disobeying his Emperor and violating his oath to the flag, is to be put up against the wall and shot,' I would carry out that command to the letter—with pleasure." The general took his helmet and stalked out.

The Kaiser lived only in extremes; he knew no middle roads. During the conflict with Bismarck over the labor laws there was a miners' strike. Wilhelm wanted to withdraw the troops from the area. "Then when the homes of the rich owners and directors are set afire and their gardens trampled, they'll give in!" But shortly afterwards, when there was a strike of streetcar workers in Berlin, he telegraphed the commanding general: "I expect that at least five hundred people will bite the dust when the troops intervene." Shortly before the war the great Russian statesman, Count Witte, characterized him as "unbalanced and not normal"; the American diplomat Colonel House declared that he was close to the brink of mental illness.

III

Vanity could never have so dreadfully taken possession of his whole being if it had not been fed by the flatteries of his courtiers. "The Kaiser is surrounded by a jellylike mass; whichever way he moves it gives way," remarked Bismarck from his retirement in Friedrichsruh. Wilhelm's grandfather was the type of man whom no one would ever have presumed to praise to his face. The grandson, on the other hand, kept about him a claque of toadies who chorused at every boastful word of his: "Just like Frederick the Great." On every occasion they assured him: "Your Majesty has deigned to create something for the ages by this act." "No flattery has ever been too much for him," Waldersee declared. A court chaplain delivered so sycophantic a sermon that even a blind worshipper of the Kaiser, Admiral Müller, spoke out against it. Thereupon the Kaiser came forward and said radiantly: "It's a long time since I've heard so splendid a sermon."

When he took vacation trips on the *Hohenzollern* he would insist on his generals and ambassadors doing knee bends for the morning gymnastics. Then he would knock them off balance by poking them in the ribs, and they had to grin gratefully at this token of intimacy. He was as discreet as a cannon shot. His idea of fun was to pour a glass of champagne from the bridge of the *Hohenzollern* upon the gala uniforms of the members of his entourage. To say something embarrassing was, to his mind, a sign of robust wit. At a hunting party, Wilhelm greeted the owner of a large estate and member of the Prussian House of Lords, a man aged fifty-seven, with the words: "What, you old pig, have they invited you too?"

Did none of the proud men of the Prussian nobility ever flare up at such treatment? Did none of them ever throw to the winds the career of their sons and their own advancement and answer rudeness with rudeness? None did! A good many avoided the court as much as possible, but that was as far as they dared go. Behind his back, however, his closest associates began murmuring that a mental disturbance seemed to be developing in connection with some ear trouble. The people in his entourage would be bitterly annoyed with him one day, only to be disarmed the next. Upon casual acquaintance he could be completely charming. "He wins all hearts wherever he goes—if he does not stay long," remarked Waldersee.

When Tirpitz, one of the few self-respecting men in the Kaiser's retinue, asked permission to submit his resignation because he had been bawled out for no good reason, Wilhelm declared jovially that he threw far worse insults at the heads of the other ministers; where would things be if they all wanted to resign?

Wilhelm was not absolutely intractable. If spoken to privately and diplomatically, with due consideration for his autocratic make-up, he could be made to see the point—but only for the moment. A day later he might change course entirely, under the influence of someone else or some new event. His instability made him the football of his impressions of the moment. His lack of solid substance made him appear profoundly, if unconsciously, false. His best friend, Eulenburg, said of him that he lied as naturally as a bird sings.

IV

But in spite of his impulsive energy and his resolution to be a magnificent ruler, Wilhelm II never held the reins of the Reich in his hands for long—for the simple reason that he was lazy. The very year that Bismarck was dismissed, Waldersee wrote in his diary: "Everyone who has to do with him is gravely worried because he himself no longer has the slightest inclination to work. Distractions, such as trifling with army and especially navy affairs, travelling, or hunting, are more important to him than anything else, so that he scarcely has any time for real work. He reads very little—perhaps regularly only newspaper clippings, scarcely writes anything more than marginal notes on memoranda. He thinks the best report is the one that is the shortest." The Kaiser had dismissed Bismarck because he wanted to deal with each of his ministers personally, without Bismarck's intervention. But soon it became difficult for any minister to obtain an audience with him.

What did he do with his day? According to his marshal of the court, he rose between nine and ten, breakfasted heartily, went for a drive or a walk with his chancellor and then—reluctantly—devoted an hour or two to receiving reports, often seizing the opportunity to deliver a lecture to his advisers. Around one o'clock he lunched, rode out again, signed documents. Then came tea, an afternoon nap of two or three hours, dinner with guests about eight. Evenings he frequently went to the theater, after which there would be entertainment until twelve or one at night. There was no room in this day for carefully scheduled work, for composing himself inwardly, for allowing ideas to mature quietly. This unfortunate man required incessant stimulation from without: flattery, pomp, festivals. He was the kind of person who would have liked to have a birthday every day.

His favorite trick for escaping from work was travelling. Two hundred days out of the year he was moving around. He spent more than one fifth of his entire reign aboard his yacht, the *Hohenzollern*. The purpose of these trips was not rest and meditation, but distraction. Puns dominated conversation and noise ruled the day since—as his best friend reports—"the Kaiser is the kind of person to whom noise is an agreeable sensation."

Aside from travelling, his principal amusement was hunting. But his hunts consisted merely in shooting down the game as it was driven past his stand; to true sportsmen he was just a "butcher." When he killed his two-hundredth stag, he had a stone weighing more than a ton erected as a memorial. In archaic German it bore the inscription: "Our moste noble Margrave and Lord Emperour Wilhelm II Alle Highest felled here on Septembre 19, 1902 his 200th noble stagge upon Grimnitz Heath." At the age of thirty-four he had a similar stone erected to celebrate the killing of "his 50,000th creature, a white pheasant."

Quite incidentally, this way of life consumed a great deal of money. The very first year of his reign he demanded and received a salary increase of six million marks—an embarrassing request, for everyone knew that the former Kaiser had saved considerable sums from his civil list. (As a matter of fact, Wilhelm himself put aside four million in two years.) He was capable of ridiculously naive demands. At maneuvers one time the hot-water heater in the imperial barracks was out of order; thereafter the Kaiser insisted that a company of engineers must always take part in the maneuvers.

Oratory he loved even more than travel. But his rhetorical gifts were a danger to the state. Carried away by the mood of the crowd and his insatiable need for applause, he would produce the most unfortunate turns of phrase. Rapped out in a harsh voice, these flights of his would convey the impression of a brutal saber-rattler—when in fact the speaker was only a poor, ill-balanced, timid soul drowning out his insecurity with thunderous oratory, like a child whistling in the dark. When Uncle Edward had him sounded out on the possibility of Germany's coming to an agreement with France over Alsace-Lorraine, he replied in a public speech: "I believe we will answer that with one voice: that we would leave all our eighteen army corps and forty-two million inhabitants lying upon the field of honor rather than cede one single stone of the territory my father acquired!" He declared that "the party of revolution must be exterminated to the last member." To the soldiers he said: "If your Emperor commands, you must fire upon your own fathers and mothers." To the world in general: "Whoever opposes me I shall smash." Referring to his grandfather's advisers, he said that they had all been lackeys. "Boys will be boys," commented Bismarck. He used telegrams and marginal notes to let off steam. When the Social Democrats gained more seats in the *Reichstag,* Wilhelm's reaction to the election was an uncoded telegram in which he said that he did not give a hang whether red, black, or yellow monkeys were swinging around in the *Reichstag* cage.

But it would be unjust to take these emotional outbursts seriously. "People must not hold me to my casual remarks," he himself declared. And in fact his ministers usually paid no attention to them. When it came to action, the Kaiser was on the whole far more prudent than he was in his speeches. But an emperor's speeches often have consequences.

V

In one matter Wilhelm II acted as unfortunately as he spoke. That was on the naval question. England's liberal government wanted social reforms. Such reforms cost money, and money could be saved only on armaments. But how could England save on armaments if Germany went on building more and more warships? Consequently, England cautiously proposed that both countries cut down on ship construction. Lloyd George, then Chancellor of the Exchequer, pointed out to the Britons that Germany after all did not keep an army twice the size of any other powers—the ratio of naval strength England had hitherto insisted on. Therefore, he said, a ratio of three to two in naval power seemed to him sufficient; England ought to come to an agreement with Germany.

But here he touched Wilhelm's sorest spot. Was he to reduce his fleet on orders from Britain—that fleet which was the symbol of his hate-love for England. In his rash style he declared: "If England intends to hold out her hand graciously to us only to remark that we must limit our navy, she is behaving with colossal impudence. Such remarks comprise a grave insult to the German people and to their Emperor!" An official note on the limitation of German armaments would be equivalent to a declaration of war, he stated. Germany did not desire good relations with England at the price of sacrificing her fleet. "The Navy Law will be carried out to the last jot and tittle, whether the British like it or not! If they want war, let them begin it; we are not afraid of it."

Bülow was more open to reason; he demanded that Tirpitz tell him straight out whether there was any chance for an agreement, since Germany's present naval program was arousing in England misconceptions of Germany's intentions and thereby increasing the danger of war. "Should the consequences be of a grave and undesirable nature," he wrote to Tirpitz, "I should have to place the responsibility—in the eyes of His Majesty, the country and history—upon your Excellency alone." The chancellor then proposed building more submarines and coastal fortifications. But Tirpitz reminded the Kaiser that he, and he alone, was commander in chief of the armed forces. The admiral knew how to handle the Kaiser. He had heard from a most reliable source, he recounted, stroking his long beard, that during the Morocco crisis, while His Majesty was aboard his yacht in Norwegian waters, British torpedo boats had received orders to send the imperial yacht to the bottom if war broke out. The Kaiser exclaimed indignantly: "And they want me to come to an agreement with such people!"

No wonder he wrote the following comment on a report from his ambassador, Metternich, concerning Lloyd George's proposals: "One of these days he must give those gentlemen who object to our 'wanton aggressive ambitions' a coarse answer like 'Kiss my . . . ,' to knock some sense into their heads. Metternich ought to get a good kick in his behind. He is too soft." Count Metternich, however, wrote calmly:

"I should be falsifying history if I couched my reports otherwise. I cannot sell my convictions, not even for the favor of my sovereign. What is more, I doubt that I should be serving Your Majesty properly if I continued to send smooth and pleasant reports until we suddenly found ourselves facing war with England."

CHAPTER EIGHT

Intrigues

Whoever wishes to hit a target must occasionally hit the men behind it.

—TREITSCHKE

I

For twenty long years the German Emperor had led Germany on the downhill path. Flattered and hated by his entourage, wondered at and admired by an unsuspecting middle class, he had been regarded with careless benevolence by the broad masses of the people. Then, when he was almost fifty, two scandals suddenly descended upon his head. And as luck would have it, he was innocent in both cases.

At the age of twenty-seven Wilhelm had met a man twelve years his senior into whose heart he had looked—as the man himself put it— "as into a cup filled with a drink whose ingredients were ideally suited to his taste." The man was an East Prussian count, a retired guards officer, a diplomat, a poet who could improvise witty verses at the drop of a hat, a singer and pianist, a composer who set his own songs to music. He had an inexhaustible supply of brilliant anecdotes, revelled in romantic fantasies, dabbled in mysticism, saw ghosts—no wonder the young prince "was afire with friendship" for him. "It did not take me long to see that you are a warmly emotional person, a person wholly congenial to me," he wrote. Forty years later the dethroned monarch would still declare: "When he entered our home, it was always as if sunshine were coming into our everyday dullness."

Philipp Eulenburg certainly was one of the most charming persons who ever strode across the harsh soil of Prussia—a man of warm feelings, or at least very weak nerves. Compared to other members of his class and generation he was offensively well educated, and perfumed in soul and body like a successful cocotte. What distinguished him from others was the perfect smoothness of his nature; incredibly flexible, he had never been roughed up by friction with other persons. His muted voice never spoke a harsh word; his veiled eyes never sent forth a wrathful look. Friendship was the world in which he lived; he possessed a warm feeling for other men, a nostalgia for Greek beauty and romantic chivalry. There was nothing dense, angular or coarse in his character. And nothing altogether genuine. He was an actor down to the fingertips of his soft white hands; but his mask of overflowing cordiality had grown to be a part of his face. Old Bismarck alone had not succumbed to the charm of this man, and had remarked laconically: "Eyes that can spoil the best of breakfasts for you." As Bismarck saw it, romantic visionaries of homosexual leanings were dangerous company for an unstable monarch.

The Kaiser suspected nothing of his one friend's abnormal tendencies; he never knew that Phil and his fellows among themselves referred to him as "the darling." He appointed Eulenburg ambassador to Vienna, made him a hereditary member of the Prussian House of Lords, and finally elevated him to the rank of prince. Eulenburg very nearly became vice-chancellor.

For fifteen years Eulenburg was the liaison man between the Foreign Office and the monarch, "Germany's ambassador to the Kaiser's court," as some people jeered. He undermined Bismarck, helped topple Caprivi, invented stature for Bülow, was appealed to by all and sundry to save the situation whenever the Kaiser had committed some new folly. This he did to the best of his ability. On the whole he spoke up for peace and common sense and exerted a salutary influence, insofar as so weak a person could wield influence at all. On the other hand, any overt attack on the Kaisers' prestige aroused his indignation. The following passage, on account by Eulenburg of a meeting with Holstein, Kiderlen and the chancellor's son, Alexander Hohenlohe, indicates on what side his loyalty lay: "Reeking of wine and in from a drinking bout, there followed a malicious concentrated attack by this foul-hearted triumvirate upon His Majesty and me. Holstein said . . . His Majesty must be treated like the child or the fool he is. Alexander seconded, and Kiderlen spurted venom like a skunk. Disgusting. The Kaiser would either have to back down completely or his chancellor would resign. And if it came to that, the press would soon take up the matter in a tone that would force His Majesty to realize his insane folly (!!!). I have seldom felt such a deep sense of offended loyalty and love for our noble, good lord, who rose up before my mind's eye like a veritable Siegfried."

The recipient of this letter was Eulenburg's protégé, bosom friend, and nemesis, Bernhard von Bülow. The "Eel," as Kiderlen called Bülow, had made use of Eulenburg's influence upon the Kaiser to further his own career. When Bülow was still ambassador to Rome and needed Philipp's good will, he wrote the most lyrical letters to his sponsor: "As sisters our souls rose in days gone by out of the mysterious wellspring of all existence; we differed only in being given other wrappings and wings of different colors. If the gods have given to you the magical gift and the shining talent, yet I can still . . . hand to you many a stone for the edifice which you are building with a hand both light and sure. Against your own inclinations, but for the good of our Emperor and our country, you have thrown yourself into the political arena. You perhaps are more Germanic and Hellenic, like the Second Part of Faust; I more Prussian and Roman; you more chivalrous; I more military. . . . With your infinitely fine sensibility you are a handsome falcon in a forest filled with foxes, wild boars and geese. . . . May the Eternal Power which guides you keep you, my Philipp!" Soon afterwards Bülow wrote in this style: "Nothing, no one, will ever part us from each other. God protect, bless and guide you, dearest, in the new as in the old year, and forevermore. I embrace you in deepest love." By means of such effusions, Bülow rose to the office of chancellor.

The friendship lasted for a few years more, until Bülow began to regard his "sister soul" as a rival for the Kaiser's favor—and moreover as a person in a dangerous situation, and therefore dangerous to know. For if ever Friend Philipp's game should be up, Friend Bernhard would be ruined with him. Poor Phil quite understood this and assured the younger man that he would no longer burden him with his friendship; he was retiring from public life. "Before this decision, office, politics, the life of the world fade into insignificance. . . . Like a lovely dream I see before me, my music, my quiet Liebenberg Palace, my family restored to me. How few persons have been graced by God with the chance to take up life anew, to return to what is truly and properly one's own!" He retired to his Liebenberg Palace where he maintained an honorable family existence with his wife and eight children, and began devoting himself to what was "truly and properly his own"— well-meaning verses and musical compositions. But he could not separate himself entirely from his past; he remained the friend and counselor in foreign policy of the Kaiser. And now his nemesis caught up with him. It bore—again!—the countenance of Holstein.

II

For many long years Bülow had tolerated Holstein. As time passed the man became more and more difficult to deal with. To a British correspondent he declared that the Kaiser would end either in a madhouse or by destroying the Reich. When Holstein's mismanagement of the Morocco crisis led to Germany's making enemies of the whole world, Bülow decided to get rid of him. But he had to proceed cautiously, for he knew Holstein as a blackmailer who could make such a fuss that the interests of Germany would be seriously damaged. Perhaps he had personal reasons for fearing Holstein. The story went that

Holstein had in his possession youthful love letters of Bülow's wife to the pianist Tausig. The Eel however hit on an ingenious way to secure himself against Holstein's possible vengeance; not only would he force out the old intriguer but he would destroy his rival Eulenburg in the process. Bülow's scheme was something out of a French comedy.

During the Morocco crisis a new foreign secretary had been appointed, a Herr von Tschirschky. The good fellow had become unnerved at Holstein's habit of popping in and out of the office through the connecting door. He therefore locked the door and instructed Privy Councillor Holstein to announce himself in the usual manner. Holstein's reply was a letter of resignation—his twelfth. He added in unmistakable language that after his resignation he would be no respecter of persons. Bülow filed the resignation in a drawer and waited for the end of the Morocco crisis. He then had Tschirschky present it to the Kaiser, who approved it. Upon which Bülow went to attend a big debate in the *Reichstag* and there, worn out by overwork, suffered a collapse before the eyes of all Europe.

As soon as Holstein heard of Bülow's breakdown he wanted his letter of resignation back. There was always the danger that it might be approved, and he now had reason to hope for Bülow's death or withdrawal from active political life. In either case the successor might be more pliable. But the letter of resignation could not be found anywhere; twenty-four hours later it returned to its author, approved, accompanied by the diamonds of the Order of the Red Eagle as a parting decoration from the Kaiser. This could only be a bad dream; Holstein rushed to the chancellor's sickbed. Profoundly distressed, Bülow told him that that fool Tschirschky must have submitted the letter to the Kaiser while he, Bülow, was stricken sick. Even the suspicious Holstein could not but believe in the authenticity of an illness which had overcome the chancellor before the eyes of the assembled representatives of the German people. (Bülow was quite capable of having induced a real fainting spell when he needed one.) To play it safe Bülow assured his sorely tried friend that he would continue to call upon him for counsel in the future.

But the battle was by no means won. Knowing Holstein, the chancellor knew that he must provide him with both an occupation and an enemy against whom he could vent his lust for revenge. Therefore he crowned his master stroke with another; he indicated—we are guessing here—that it was not Tschirschky who was really responsible for Holstein's fall, but someone who had the ear of the Kaiser. Eulenburg, of course! There is no record of Bülow's saying this to Holstein, but the course of events is comprehensible only if we fill in this missing link.

Bülow badly needed a lightning rod to divert Holstein's fury; he could not be sure that the arch-intriguer would continue to credit his sudden illness. Moreover, Eulenburg would serve splendidly as a target, for by striking him, one struck the Kaiser. And if the Kaiser's position were weakened, Bülow's would be strengthened. What was more, Bülow suspected Eulenburg of intriguing against him, and of telling the Kaiser that Bülow was too ill to continue in office. Whether Eulenburg had really done so we do not know; perhaps the Kaiser invented the whole thing in order to make bad blood between the two men. In his memoirs Bülow maintained that Eulenburg tried to persuade Bülow's doctor that the chancellor must resign for the sake of his health, that he, as a devoted friend, had a deeper understanding of the true state of affairs than the detached mind of a doctor. Bülow even suggests that Philipp, in his own peculiar manner, had convinced himself about this. But this tale of Bülow's represents Eulenburg as more stupid than he really was; it sounds rather as if Bülow were making excuses for his treachery toward Eulenburg.

Did Holstein believe Bülow's fable about Eulenburg? Did he really think it plausible that the dilettante who all his life had trembled in fear of exposure could have dared to unseat the most vindictive intriguer in Germany? No matter. Innocent or guilty, Eulenburg was going to pay for Holstein's downfall. Holstein wrote a letter to Eulenburg full of the nastiest and most vulgar vituperation. For thirty years Holstein had swallowed his hatred for the world; now he spewed it forth all at once. Eulenburg sent his seconds. He was very firm about the conditions of the duel; shots would be exchanged until one of the parties was hit. But at the same time he negotiated. He assured Holstein that he had had no part in his dismissal. The negotiations bore fruit; Holstein issued an involved statement to the effect that he withdrew the insulting expressions. However, he did not take back the assertions he had made in his letter, and he did not promise to keep silent. On the contrary, he promptly went to see the journalist Maximilian Harden.

Harden, originally an actor, had founded the weekly magazine *Zukunft* (The Future) and at the time of Bismarck's resignation had written pro-Bismarck articles in one publication and anti-Bismarck articles in another. The old prince had received him at Friedrichsruh several times—Bismarck was not very choosy about people who worked for him. Later, however, because of a breach of confidence he had banished Harden from his house. Harden went in for a cranky kind of jingoism preached in a pompous, highfalutin style. Germany, he maintained, needed vast new territories; otherwise she would soon be "dwarfed down" to a second Belgium. He praised war as "a bracing educational experience," called it "the noblest ornament of the Germans' soul that they do not belong among the oily swarm of peaceful nations," sneered at those "despisers of war" who in "the syrupy language of humanitarianism" were wont to call him to account. It infuriated him that the Morocco dispute had ended peacefully. When Holstein now produced his evidence against Eulenburg, Harden decided to give the scandal a twist suggesting that a group of effeminate homosexuals had been seducing the Kaiser into a policy of weakness.

Harden's charges were published in several issues of the *Zukunft*. Eulenburg and several high army officers, including the commandant of the Berlin garrison, were described in the most vulgar terms. The Crown Prince showed these issues of the *Zukunft* to his father.

Wilhelm was outraged. He promptly decided that Eulenburg must clear himself by suing for libel, or else resign and go abroad. The unhappy man knew that even if he fled abroad the persecution would continue; in addition, everyone would interpret flight as a confession of guilt. He therefore stayed, and there followed a number of court trials which Harden turned into horrible farces. Harden back-tracked in the case of the garrison commandant, declaring that he had never accused him of inversion. When the state prosecuting attorney nevertheless foolishly continued the libel suit, the journalist declared in court that although he had not charged the general with homosexuality, he would nevertheless prove it unless the case were dropped. The circulation of the *Zukunft* rose sharply.

In the trial involving the commandant, Eulenburg had sworn under oath that he was innocent. Harden promptly paid the venal editor of a small Munich newspaper to publish an assertion that Harden had dropped his charges against Eulenburg in return for a million-mark bribe. Harden then sued the Munich newspaperman for libel and—this was the purpose of the maneuver—during this sham trial brought into court, to testify under oath, several men who were rumored to have had relationships with Eulenburg. The testimony of two of the witnesses was such that the state prosecuting attorney entered perjury charges against Prince Eulenburg—and Bernhard Bülow approved the order for the arrest of his "sister soul." The trial had to be dropped, however, because Eulenburg's health broke down—although he lived for eighteen years afterwards in the solitude of his palace of Lieben-berg.

III

But Bülow, too, did not come through the mess unscathed. Perhaps the Kaiser suspected who had started the ball rolling. A coolness arose between him and Bülow. Chance, or rather Bülow's basic trait, frivolity, put the chill of death upon their relationship.

Wilhelm had again made an attempt to convince the British of his fondness for them. To this end he told a British colonel that in truth he was England's only friend in Germany. During the Boer War, he said, when Russia and France wanted to unite with Germany against England, he had refused to enter the conspiracy and had informed London of it. He had even, he claimed, supplied the British with a plan of campaign against the Boers which he had first had checked over by his own general staff. Furthermore, the operations undertaken by the British commander, Lord Roberts, had followed this plan closely. He had not built up his navy for use against England, he maintained, but in order to have a say in Far Eastern affairs.

Europeans read these words and shook their heads. The British, far from being pleased by all this good will on the part of the Kaiser, were outraged at the implication that they had won the Boer War with Wilhelm's assistance. Fortunately the British minister of war declared, while the House of Commons roared with laughter, that the ministry knew nothing of the plan of campaign of which Wilhelm was supposed to have made them a present. Wilhelm had actually sent to his uncle nothing but a few aphorisms—not prepared by the general staff. The French and the Russians were annoyed at the indiscretion and repudiated the whole story. Naturally such deliberate betrayal of secrets was common enough in diplomacy—during the Boer War, for example, Russia had as a precautionary measure informed London that Germany was proposing intervention. But communications of that sort were generally made in private, not in the course of an interview given by a ruling monarch. The news that the German fleet was being built up against Japan was, the Japanese thought, highly interesting.

But the Germans were more furious than anyone else! Their indignation knew no bounds when they heard that the Kaiser, with the aid of the German general staff, had helped the British slaughter the Boers. And on top of all that Wilhelm had by this one interview irritated four great powers. Every party in Germany, from Social Democrats to Conservatives, was up in arms. *Simplicissimus* published a cartoon showing the Kaiser as a little boy sitting at a desk, his face smeared with ink, while Mother Germania and Father Bülow stand over him shouting: "Haven't we told you never to play 'letter writing'?"

But there was a second surprise forthcoming in connection with this interview. The Kaiser had sent it to the chancellor for checking, before releasing it for publication. Bülow happened to be vacationing at Norderney and sent it unread to the Foreign Office. The foreign secretary was on leave; the assistant secretary did not read it, but passed it on to a privy councillor. The privy councillor thought the basic question of whether it should be published had already been settled and that he was being asked only to check the correctness of certain details; he therefore raised no objections and the document was returned through the same channels. The assistant secretary again passed it on unread; Bülow in Norderney certified that he had looked it over, but did not even glance at it—and so it appeared in the *Daily Telegraph*.

That, at any rate, is Bülow's account of the history of this, the most notorious interview in the world. We can say with a degree of probability that amounts virtually to certainty that this tale is pure invention. There is good reason to believe that Bülow read the text. Why then did he allow the document to pass? Because he did not recognize all the blunders Wilhelm had committed, or because he wanted to make a fool of the Kaiser? Both conjectures are probable; the first is certainly far more probable than Bülow's version.

Bülow submitted his resignation, which the Kaiser refused to accept. The *Bundesrat* considered calling for the Kaiser's abdication. But it did not do so, and Wilhelm quickly regained his composure. When the great debate on the interview was to begin in the *Reichstag*, he went hunting and amused himself royally. "The two days here," he telegraphed to Bülow, "have passed very enjoyably. The hunting went splendidly; I shot sixty-five stags." On this hunting trip he also ,decided important administrative questions; for example, an imperial edict decreed that German sailors, in giving three cheers to His Majesty, must during the second cheer "raise their caps briefly by extending the right arm at an angle of approximately forty-five degrees; as soon as the cheer is finished they are to bend the arm, returning it close to the middle of their chests." Back in the *Reichstag* even the conservative speakers were bitterly castigating the Kaiser. The Kaiser enjoyed himself, meanwhile, at a little cabaret show got up for his benefit at Donaueschingen. The star act was by the chief of the military cabinet, General Count Hülsen-Hüseler, who dressed up as a ballet dancer and displayed his talents. Unfortunately, he had a stroke during the dance and fell down dead. It was a severe loss for the Kaiser; none of his other generals were so good at doing handstands.

Meanwhile Bülow had declared in the *Reichstag* that the strong protests from the German people would teach the Kaiser to exercise greater restraint in the future. "If not, neither I nor any of my successors could continue to bear the responsibility." When Wilhelm returned from his hunting trip, Bülow extracted a public declaration from him that he approved the chancellor's statement to the *Reichstag* and assured him of his confidence.

As so often before, the Eel had slid out of a difficult predicament. But the Kaiser's declaration was both too little and too much. It was too little to put an end to Wilhelm's personal regime; it was too much for Bülow's continuance in office. For now the Kaiser hated the man he had once "worshipped." He quite rightly felt that Bülow had turned against him. He also suspected that Bülow was behind the Eulenburg scandal. Since Cesare Borgia, he said, there had never been so despicable a liar. As a matter of fact, Bülow was far from being in the latter's class. A few months later, still smarting from the public reproof, the Kaiser said to Bülow that Froben would have behaved differently. Froben was the Great Elector's equerry who at the battle of Fehrbellin had reputedly exchanged his horse with that of his master because he knew the Swedes would attempt to shoot down the rider of the noble white charger. Bülow then asked what he should have done. The Kaiser replied that he should have declared in the *Reichstag* that his sovereign had consulted with him before making those statements. Not a soul in the world would have believed him, Bülow replied.

Formally, there was a reconciliation. The Kaiser wired his brother: "I have forgiven Bülow after he begged my pardon, with tears streaming down his face."

In reality Bülow's fate was already sealed. Since he no longer was in the Kaiser's favor, a petty conflict was enough to undo him. During the last several years he had worked with a Conservative-Liberal majority—distributing fruit to the Right and flowers to the Left. But now, when new revenue was needed, he proposed a modest inheritance tax. The Prussian conservatives were not happy about the coalition anyhow, for the Liberals were demanding reform of the three-class Prussian electoral law, upon which the power of the Conservatives in Prussia rested. They therefore gave notice of their dissatisfaction by rejecting the inheritance tax. Bülow decided that this was the point at which to resign. He was aware that the Kaiser no longer had any confidence in him; in choosing a popular issue on which to resign, he hoped to be able to return to office some day. The Kaiser was triumphant.

No doubt the *Daily Telegraph* affair taught the Kaiser to think twice before making speeches. But he remained a troublesome element in the government—he who as monarch should have been the very embodiment of stability. No revolutionary ever did so much harm to the idea of monarchy as did Wilhelm II.

CHAPTER NINE

A Full Circle

*I consider any kind of policy better than a vacil-
lating policy.*

—BISMARCK

I

Bülow had recommended as his successor
the minister of the interior, Theobald von Bethmann-Hollweg. "Bethmann is Bülow's revenge," Ballin, director of the Hamburg-America
Line, said.

When Bülow was going to see the Kaiser for his final audience,
Bethmann accompanied him to the railroad station. In parting he called
after him: "No, you'd better not. Unless . . ." And then he turned his
somewhat stooped six-foot-three figure with crew-cut hair and fur-
rowed face that looked mournfully out into the world, and said to his
driver: "Nevertheless . . ." "Nevertheless" became a common nick-
name for him.

Bethmann was honest and intelligent as a person, but he had none of
the qualities of a chancellor. He stirred sympathy in people, but could
not convince them. However, the Kaiser assured Bülow: "He is loyal
as gold, a good fellow through and through, a tremendous worker, and
full of dash; he'll refurbish the *Reichstag* for Me. Besides, I shot My
first buck at his place in Hohenfinow." When Bülow remarked that
Bethmann knew nothing about foreign policy, Wilhelm replied be-
nignly: "Leave that to Me!"

The new chancellor was a serious-minded person. He assured the
Foreign Office that he considered foreign policy of great importance
and would therefore study up on it so as to be competent to take the
lead. But his first attempts to toddle in the corridors of diplomacy were
very unsteady. When the British ambassador came to see the chancellor
for their first conversation, he found an assistant secretary sitting by
with paper and ink, ready to take down every word—Bethmann's
bureaucratic background was coming to the fore. His first official act
as chancellor was a telegram to the Temperance League. Scion of the
"financial nobility," grandson of a professor, at school nicknamed "the
Governess," he had never in his life gambled, drunk or broken horses.

A melancholic person who always felt the weight of life upon his shoulders, he lacked the sureness to make bold decisions, the sense of being in command of the needs of the day, which had given a man like Bismarck his firmness. He was without passion. Like all weak personalities he was not even consistent in his weakness; instead, he vacillated between anxious hesitation and headlong advances. Foreign Secretary Kiderlen, who had thrice his strength, controlled him without effort. Occasionally the chancellor would take dictation from Kiderlen so that an official note would appear to be the chancellor's own. When Bethmann in his memoirs gets around to the *Panther's* trip to Agadir, he writes clumsily: "The much-discussed mission of the *Panther* was nothing but a promulgation by us, compelled by the obscurantistic conduct of the Paris Cabinet, and one that could no longer be overlooked, of our desire for a thorough discussion, a defensive reply to France's offensive procedures." Men who write such a style are not destined to play a large part on the stage of history.

Bethmann took comfort in the sympathy he enjoyed abroad—not realizing that this was the kind of liking people have for an antagonist's weak advocate. With the naïveté of an unworldly bookworm he once said: "Bismarck was a great man, but nobody trusted him. Prince Bülow was very skillful, but he was not trusted either. I am trusted. Europe trusts me; above all, England trusts me. I can say without conceit that I have become the pillar of European peace." It did not occur to him that a statesman who enjoyed such fine reputation with his country's enemies could hardly be doing a very good job for his own country. He strove to be liked, but nobody can be both liked and successful. An American, commenting on the leading statesmen of Germany and England, declared that if both sat down at the conference table he would be surprised if the Germans emerged from the negotiations still in possession of Berlin. The best verdict on Bethmann was passed by his wife whose first reaction on learning of his appointment as chancellor was to cry out that this was a misfortune. In keeping with his character, after the death of Kiderlen, Bethmann chose as foreign secretary an ambassador named Jagow whose lack of stature, physically and mentally, made him the perfect counterpart for his superior.

Bethmann sincerely desired to smooth over all differences between Germany and other powers by a series of friendly talks. He never overcame this adolescent conception of life. First he approached Russia and had several amicable conversations with Izvolsky's successor, Sazonov. Concurrently Russia was reorganizing her army and increasing the number of her army corps from thirty-one to thirty-seven. Nicky's way of communicating this fact to his dear Willy was to inform him that he had transferred four Russian army corps from the western frontier to the interior. Since Sazonov knew—as he relates in his memoirs—that Germany "was suffering from persecution mania," he made an effort to "soothe this morbid psychological condition." Only because of that he assured Bethmann that Russia's mission with regard to the Christian countries of the Balkans had already come to an end. Sooner than create unnecessary alarm, he did not mention the memorial which the Russian foreign ministry had issued early in 1914, insisting that Russia must dominate the Dardanelles. That aim, the memorial went on to say, could only be achieved "within the framework of a European war"; therefore the foreign ministry must deliberately prepare a favorable political climate "for the occupation of the Straits." The council of ministers approved this memorial.

II

The climate was already prepared. In France the idea of *revanche*, of reconquering Alsace-Lorraine, had slumbered for a time, but had awakened to new life in the twentieth century. The dispute over Morocco had considerably activated it. Kaiser Wilhelm had repeatedly tried to win French favor by polite gestures, but the French were not impressed. When German Ambassador Schön said to French Minister Barthou that the two nations must find some way to live peacefully side by side, he received the reply: "Give us back Alsace-Lorraine and we will be your best friends in the world."

The French-speaking population of Lorraine wanted to return to France; in the German-speaking parts of Lorraine and in Alsace the peasants did not care one way or the other, the petty bourgeoisie wavered, and the upper class was distinctly Francophile. There was a turn toward Germany only after France began carrying out a strong anticlerical policy. Given the desperate isolation of Germany at that time, it would certainly have been worth her while to have exchanged Alsace-Lorraine wholly or partly for French overseas colonies. But any such step would have violated all tradition; only a Bismarck could have risked it.

A curious accident helped precipitate disaster. The French presidential election was imminent and the Left had no strong candidate. Consequently the prospects looked unusually bright for a man of the Right, Raymond Poincaré. Newspapers opposed to Poincaré were bribed with Russian money. The leader of the Radicals, Georges Clemenceau, asked him to withdraw. Poincaré stuck to his candidature, whereupon Clemenceau said: "I have the pleasure of informing you that I no longer know you." During the election Clemenceau predicted: "If Poincaré gets in, there will be war." Poincaré was elected.

The new President came from Lorraine. In his memoirs he relates

that even as a schoolboy he believed his generation's one reason for
being was to win back the lost provinces. As a corporation lawyer he
piled up a fortune of two million francs; he therefore did not need,
unlike most other French politicians, to earn his livelihood by politics.
He had the reputation of being a brilliant legal mind and a man of
rigid character. His friends, however, observed that he was inwardly
uncertain of himself and employed the scaffolding of strict legal
formulae and outward inflexibility to compensate for the strength
which he lacked by nature. He kept a journal, which he wrote every
evening in bed; in it he noted down every cheer he received and every
speech of welcome by every local bigwig in the course of his tours.
Clemenceau, comparing Poincaré and the leader of the Left, Aristide
Briand, said: "Poincaré knows everything and understands nothing;
Briand knows nothing and understands everything." In his inaugural
address to the French parliament Poincaré declared: "A nation can
be peaceable only under one condition—when it is always prepared
for war."

Poincaré was prepared. Izvolsky said he felt reborn. Anxiously the
Belgian ambassador in Paris wrote to Brussels: "I have already had the
honor of informing you that Messrs. Poincaré, Delcassé, Millerand and
their friends are the inventors and proponents of the nationalistic,
militaristic and chauvinistic policy we have observed coming to the
fore again. They represent a danger to Europe."

It seemed as if the devil himself were dealing the cards. In Russia,
too, the belligerent types were taking over. Premier Kokovzev, peaceable and close to financial circles, was dismissed; Goremykin, an ancient
fellow who for years had lived in well-merited retirement, nursing the
afflictions of old age, was exhumed. "This means war," said Russia's
cleverest statesman, Count Witte. Back of Goremykin, who was sheer
camouflage, tough characters were in the saddle. On New Year's Day,
1914, the Russian army newspaper wrote that the Russian people must
grow accustomed to the idea of arming themselves for a war of annihilation against the Germans. But the German ambassador, Count
Pourtalès, reported: "The peaceful intentions of Czar Nicholas cannot
be doubted." "Neither can his absolute unreliability and susceptibility
to all influences," Wilhelm added quite correctly. A bit uncertainly,
the ambassador continued: "Predicting the state of affairs three or four
years hence seems to me very venturesome if one does not possess the
gift of peering into the future. . . ." The Kaiser noted on the margin:
"Such a gift occurs! In sovereigns rather frequently, in statesmen
rarely, in diplomats never. . . . Our good friend Purzel would have
done better not to have written this report. These people who do not
know Russia, and weak, dubious characters among his readers, will
be thrown into total confusion. According to all my information I, as a

military man, have not the slightest doubt that Russia is systematically preparing to wage war upon us. I am directing my policy accordingly."

Wilhelm's concern was well founded. Russia thought she could also count upon England if it came to hostilities. Sazonov, after a visit to London, had reported to the Czar: "Grey told me without hesitation that if the circumstances in question arose, England would go to every length to deliver the severest blow to the German power-position. . . . The King expressed himself in much more emphatic terms."

III

Meanwhile Bethmann was trying to restore amity with England. Under Bülow the naval conferences had broken down. But a few years later two intelligent Jews, the British banker Cassel, and the director of the Hamburg-America Line, Ballin, tried to act as mediators and get new talks going. The man who was then sent to Berlin was Lord Haldane, who had been educated in Germany and was full of good will toward that country. A few years earlier, when Haldane was charged with revamping the British army, the Kaiser had been so supremely kind as to permit him to study the methods of the German general staff.

But Haldane's mission was doomed from the start. Germany already had made up her mind to enlarge her fleet and wanted only to keep the expansion within bounds; the British were genuinely eager to cut down on new shipbuilding for economy reasons. In addition Germany demanded a neutrality pact providing that England would remain a benevolent neutral if Germany were attacked.

When Haldane returned to London with these proposals, Grey rejected them all. If the agreement were going to increase rather than reduce expenditures for the navy, there was no point to England's signing it. But he would not have signed the neutrality pact even if Germany had made big concessions on the naval question. French President Poincaré had bluntly informed him that a British signature to any such pact would mean the immediate end of present Anglo-French relations. For Poincaré the idea of England's remaining neutral during a Franco-German conflict was utterly horrifying. Moreover, he preferred to see Germany spending her money on the navy and not on the army.

The situation was, then, that Germany could be sure of France, Russia, and England as enemies in case of war. Were they the only potential foes?

As far back as the nineties Italy had declared that she could not participate in a war against England on account of her long, unprotected coastline. At the time Hohenlohe had replied that a conflict between the Triple Alliance and England was out of the question. A few years later Italy concluded secret treaties with France in which she agreed to remain neutral if France should declare war on the basis of a German provocation. The war of 1870 was cited as an example of such provocation. Finally, Italy recognized France's claims to Morocco, in return for which France recognized Italy's claims to Tripoli. Discussing this treaty in the *Reichstag*, Bülow, frivolous as always, made the point that in a happy marriage the husband would not take offense if his wife wanted an innocent whirl on the dance floor with another man. But this "innocent whirl" amounted in reality to a dangerous intimacy. With a lawyer's clarity Poincaré declared that what the Italian treaties really came down to was that neither of the two groups of powers could count upon Italy's loyalty; Italy intended to ally herself with the probable victor. For her the Triple Alliance was only a waiting room.

Secure in these friendships, Italy sent a twenty-four-hour ultimatum to the Sublime Porte demanding the right of occupation in the Turkish province of Tripoli since the Italians there "required a peaceful atmosphere in which to live." None of the five great powers of Europe raised objections. Italy had granted timely compensation to England, France, and Russia—Egypt, Morocco, and a free hand in the Straits, respectively. She had no need to buy off Germany and Austria, her two allies. England, who four years before had been indignant over the annexation of Bosnia, and who two years later was to be outraged by Austria's ultimatum to Serbia, had no complaints to make about this Italian demand. On the contrary, Grey assured Italy of his sympathy— after all, he had received Egypt to help him put to rest any awkward moral scruples he may have had. Some Englishmen had more sensitive consciences; in order to placate them, England herself occupied a small part of Tripoli, the Bay of Sollum. She went so far as to refuse Turkey permission to send her troops through Egypt. Nevertheless, the Italians in Tripoli were unable to advance beyond the range of the guns of their warships.

IV

The Italian rape of Tripoli started new balls rolling. The war in Tripoli encouraged the Balkan countries in their designs on Turkey. Hartwig, the Russian ambassador in Belgrade, helped arrange a Serbo-Bulgarian alliance. Greece and Montenegro joined it. Hartwig was a capable, vigorous man, and closely linked with the Russian imperial family inasmuch as his wife was on excellent terms with Grand Duke Nikolai Nikolayevich. The pact provided beforehand for exact division of the Turkish spoils. When Poincaré, on a visit to St. Petersburg, was shown the treaty, he wrote to Paris: "The treaty contains the germ of a

war not only against Turkey, but against Austria. It also establishes
the hegemony of Russia over the two Slav kingdoms, since Russia is to
arbitrate in all matters. . . ." But it never occurred to Poincaré to
propose amendments to the treaty! However, the Czar had eased the
situation to the extent that he postponed the eventual showdown; he
had stringently impressed upon his ambassador in Sofia that Russia
would not be in a position to wage war before 1917; at worst she
might "accept a challenge" by 1915.

But the Balkan states wanted results while Turkey was at war with
Italy. They attacked the Turks, defeated them, and then fought over
the spoils among themselves. Their disputes led Europe to the verge
of a general war. But Russia, being not at all prepared for war, managed to calm things down in Belgrade—very much to the annoyance
of Poincaré who told the Russians that the French were all ready and
were now embarrassed by Russian dillydallying. Benkendorff, the
Russian ambassador to London, wrote: "The situation, as far as I have
been able to observe, appears to be that all the powers are in fact working for peace. But of them all France would accept war with the
greatest equanimity."

Russian Foreign Minister Sazonov had some words of consolation
for the Serbian ambassador. "Serbia should be content with her present
large acquisitions and organize the new Serbia in order, when the time
has come later on, to be in a position to cut out the Austro-Hungarian
tumor, which is at present not so ripe as the Turkish one. Serbia's
Promised Land lies within the domain of Austria-Hungary." When the
Balkan War was over, Pashitch said to the Greek foreign minister: "We
have won the first phase. Now we must prepare the second, against
Austria."

One man nearly wept when peace was preserved. This was the chief
of the Austrian general staff, Baron Conrad von Hötzendorff. Conrad,
in whose personality were united a wholly un-Austrian toughness of
will with a razor-sharp intelligence, had travelled in Russia, Rumania,
Serbia, Bulgaria, and Turkey disguised as a peasant, in order to find
out all he could about these countries and their peoples. He had written
valuable books of instruction, spoke eight languages of the monarchy
fluently. He was clearly aware of the dangers threatening Austria-
Hungary; to his mind the only cure was a preventive war. As soon as
he became chief of staff he put on a series of imperial war games for
the Emperor which were unlike the usual ones in being really rugged.
Franz Joseph was not at all enthusiastic about seeing the troops utterly
exhausted and their uniforms so filthy. Immediately afterward Conrad
requested an audience. When the Emperor asked him what was on his
mind, he received the astonishing answer: "I want to recommend a
war with Italy." Italy was at that time Austria's ally and there appeared

to be no clouds on the political horizon. But Conrad assured Franz Joseph that the Italian artillery was worthless, the Italian fortifications insignificant; it would be a walk to Milan and Venice. He would guarantee success within a few weeks.

Four years later, when Italy was at war with Turkey, he repeated his recommendation. This time the eighty-one-year-old Emperor replied sharply: "My policy is a policy of peace. I recognize that this war may come; it is even probable. But it will not be waged until Italy attacks us." "If only our chances are good then!" Conrad replied. Franz Joseph only repeated: "As long as Italy does not attack us, the war will not be waged!" Conrad was dismissed, but recalled during the Balkan War.

To Conrad, a war with Serbia seemed even more urgent than a war with Italy. During the Balkan War he advised that Austria "settle accounts with Serbia." But again the old Emperor had the last word. "Even in politics one must always be honorable," he said.

Conrad was an unusual man, forthright in character and with a brilliant mind. But old Franz Joseph was not far wrong when he said of him: "Clever, but not wise." Oddly enough, a fine spirit was hidden beneath Conrad's saber-rattling outward manner. A widower, he met at a gathering a woman twenty years younger than himself and after half an hour told her he wanted to marry her. She replied that she had five good reasons for not accepting him: she was happily married and had four children. Conrad declared he would win her; he pressed his suit for seven years, writing her hundreds of the most heartfelt love letters. In the end she obtained a divorce and Conrad extracted from the Emperor permission for the marriage.

V

That was the chief of staff of the Austrian army. And his German opposite number? It is part of what the French call "the delicious irony of Providence" that the German navy, which should have been kept small, was headed by the strongest man in Germany, and the army by one of the weakest.

When Schlieffen reached the age of seventy-three, the Kaiser decided to replace him. He did not ask who was right for the post, since he already had a candidate. There was a friend of his youth whom he called Julius, although the man's name was Helmuth. Julius was an aristocratic goodhearted person, a cultivated army officer who loved books, carried *Faust* with him on maneuvers, and believed deeply in truth and beauty, hypnotizers and quack doctors, and in the theosophist Rudolf Steiner. Soft and meditative by nature, he would assure people that his God was not the God of wrath, but of penitent sinners.

As might have been expected, he was a miserable horseman. His frequent falls while riding suggested weak nerves. He had the excuse that he was not a well man; he suffered from cardiac and liver trouble. Shortly before the war broke out, his doctor had urged him to retire. He had not gone through the regular training of a general staff officer; most of his time had been spent as the Kaiser's aide-de-camp. Under normal circumstances he would have barely qualified for commander of a brigade.

This was the man the Kaiser picked to be head of the German army. He would be charged with preparing for the threatening war, and if war came he would lead an army of millions against the superior forces of the enemy. "His Majesty must be nuts," moaned the chief of the military cabinet in his finest Berlin slang.

The full name of Julius was Helmuth von Moltke; he was a nephew of the famous Moltke. Helmuth promptly told the Kaiser that he had neither the character nor the health to undertake such a job. The Kaiser answered that his abilities were good enough for the peacetime army, and in wartime he, the Kaiser, would take over. This prospect should have prompted Moltke to turn down the post categorically, but he did not. At the time Waldersee wrote in his diary: "The Emperor wishes to be his own chief of staff. May God protect our Fatherland!"

Moltke did his best. But this weak man had a premonition of his fate; of the coming war he said sadly: "Many dogs are the death of the hare." Fourteen days before the outbreak of the war he "was gradually growing skeptical with regard to the political situation." But all he could think to do about it was to have a talk with Rudolf Steiner.

In despair the dismissed Schlieffen wrote: "A commander in chief has been placed at the head of an army. The sovereign who has made the appointment believes his appointee is a strategist. He will be sorely disillusioned. For a strategist is not appointed, he is born and predestined."

CHAPTER TEN

Inside Germany

> *In history nothing matters less than constitutions, although people do not like to recognize this. The character of a state is determined by its administration, its armed forces, its foreign policy; the constitution is a flowing cloak upon which pretty figures can be embroidered. It is possible to rule autocratically with the most liberal constitution, and vice versa.*
>
> —FERRERA

The business of a state is to guarantee its citizens security from external threats, order, liberty and the prerequisites for economic prosperity on the domestic scene.

The Germany of Kaiser Wilhelm II did not fulfill the first of these tasks. A blundering foreign policy steered Germany into isolation. But the government was more successful on the domestic front. The country was definitely prosperous, if its situation is measured not against unrealized ideals, but against the contemporary achievements of other countries. Real income per capita increased by some thirty per cent during the last two decades before World War I.

The state's part in this prosperity, however, came down to its enlightened non-interference with the economic life of the country. It was there to guarantee security and continuity to its citizens. The man who planted a tree could trust that his grandsons would enjoy its shade. Officialdom was kept within bounds. Housing bureaus did not exist; employment bureaus were merely registries. In no country of Europe at that time was there a ministry of the economy; whether there was none because the economy was in good order, or whether the economy was in good order because there was no ministry of the economy, is a moot question. The government was incredibly cheap to run. For incomes of 4,000 marks ($1,000), which in purchasing power corresponded to about 10,000 marks ($2,500) today, the income tax rate was only four and one half per cent; for incomes of 200,000 marks ($50,-000) it rose to eight per cent. The burden of indirect taxes and excises totalled no more than about three per cent. Sales taxes were unknown. A large part of the revenue of the government was derived from the profits which the state-owned railroads produced in spite of low fares and freight rates.

Prosperity was growing in all sections of the population. The disparity of incomes was less in Germany than in England or America. If in 1913 all income above 1,000 marks had been taken from the well-to-do and spread among the rest of the population, there would have remained—after deduction of sums needed for taxes and the formation of capital—just about ten pfennig a day for every employed person. The social gulf, which is expressed most sharply in differences of income, had gradually diminished. Germany owed her favorable social conditions in part to social insurance which Bismarck had introduced —some twenty years before England and France, and fifty years before the United States—and which Wilhelm II had further extended. "Good working conditions" had been one of Wilhelm's early enthusiasms. In regulations on a reasonable work week, light, ventilation, washrooms and shop committees, Germany was in the van of all other nations.

Government institutions and courts were impartial and incorruptible. No one would have dared to try to bribe an official. Even the municipal governments, which in other countries were hotbeds of corruption, were remarkably clean. Liberal-minded mayors were as independent as the courts. To be sure, no government official could hold Social Democratic views. But in those days the Social Democrats were not a reformist party; their demands were similar to those of present-day Communists. The Germany of 1900 was not narrow-minded; the most powerful man in Prussia, Finance Minister Miquel, had been a fiery Communist in his youth. When a political opponent threw this fact up against Miquel, the Kaiser sent his finance minister a telegram congratulating him on his development from revolutionary to statesman, and assuring him of his special confidence.

Germany also had, decades before other European countries, the most liberal election system in the world: equal, secret, and universal. The *Reichstag* could have removed any state secretary—that was the term employed for ministers of the Reich—by persistently refusing to approve his budget; however, it never did so. The ministers were predominantly experts in their various fields. Because of this, Germany lacked those vigorous personalities who came to the fore in other countries as the result of natural selection in the parliamentary struggle for power. On the other hand, these experts could draft legislation with more regard for the real problems and less for the possible political repercussions. It is impossible to say whether partisan ministers would have made better laws. In the field of practical legislation and administration there was little to choose between conservative states like Prussia, and liberal states like Württemberg and Baden.

There was, however, the fundamental fact that democracy in Prussia, in the sense of social mobility, was virtually lacking. The classes were set apart from each other by their views, their associations, and their kinship groupings, far more strictly than in England or France. But the rigidity of this caste system was based more upon tradition and national character than upon the structure of the state.

Where the domestic policy of the Reich failed was in the area where domestic and foreign policy mesh: defense. Germany stood isolated amid hostile neighbors. She therefore had to summon up all the forces of the nation for defense, and introduce universal military training. Such service was provided for in the Constitution, but had long remained on paper. The Kaiser, the chancellor, and the *Reichstag* shared the blame for this. Germany inducted fifty-three per cent, France eighty-two per cent, of all men subject to call. The result was that in 1914 Germany, with a population of seventy million, had only half of her ten million draft-age men trained—no more than France with a population of forty million. If the Germans had put through their universal military service, the field army in 1914 could have been stronger by a million men. The French chief of staff, Buat, wrote ironically after the war that the Germans in peacetime had not made the same sacrifices as the French; otherwise they would have been able to outflank the French armies in 1914 and occupy the Channel ports. "Then the Battle of the Marne would have been impossible."

Buat's comment is to the point. Bismarck had wanted to introduce universal military service, but the Kaiser had opposed it. Such legislation would have taken fighting for and he wanted to be free of any serious fights in order to get rid of Bismarck. Economically the German people could have supported such an increase in the army; it would have required only about one per cent of the steadily rising national income. But the *Reichstag* would have rejected the idea; it had repeatedly refused smaller demands. The people's representatives were unwilling to recognize the danger which arose from Germany's geographical situation and later from the ring of hostile coalitions. They approached the problem solely on the plane of tax rates.

Wilhelmine Germany has been called an "era of false brilliance." It has been represented as a time of perpetual flag-waving, of military bands forever blaring, and feudal-style armies springing up like mushrooms. This picture of Germany's cultural life is not faithful. It was a period when almost twice as many Nobel prizes went to Germans as to any other people. Berlin was considered the foremost theatrical city in Europe. In the drama, the novel, and poetry, Germany gratefully absorbed the creative work of all nations, producing translations that were labors of love. Her own literature received similar appreciation abroad.

Around the turn of the century there was an almost idyllic character about the national life of Germany. But contemporaries were not aware of this. They thought they were living in times of stress. In the course of partisan strife, measures of limited significance were blown up into issues of the first magnitude. When import duties on grain were reduced during the nineties, and raised again ten years later, the opponents of these measures declared in both cases that the existence of the Reich was at stake. A Social Democratic deputy delivered a nine-hour filibuster to avert the impending evil. In sober retrospect it is plain that such tariff laws had only the smallest effect upon the course of German economic development. Other laws were similarly debated with a bitterness which did more harm to the unity and welfare of the people than the disputed legislation could ever do. All those struggles, which agitated the newspapers if not the people more than the loss of a province does today, have rightly been forgotten. All were tempests in teapots. In reality Wilhelmine Germany was a very well governed country with a flourishing economic and cultural life.

What contemporaries did not recognize was the abyss toward which German foreign policy was heading. Blunders in domestic politics imperil only the forms of life, blunders in foreign policy the very existence of a nation. The storm clouds were black on the horizon.

CHAPTER ELEVEN

The Black Hand

*It would not have taken a Bismarck to avoid this
silliest of all wars.*

—BALLIN

I

World War I descended upon mankind
when Europe was being governed by pacifists. None of the statesmen
of those days was by nature a conqueror; almost to a man they were
timid souls who preferred a quiet hour sitting under the willows by a
brook, or a meditative evening reading by the fireplace, to all the fame
of victory. Almost to a man they might have echoed Sir Edward Grey's
exclamation upon the outbreak of the war, when he was congratulated
on the vote in the Commons: "I hate war!"

First of all there were the three Emperors. They would gladly have
sacrificed several years of their lives to have avoided the war, and that
for the simple reason that all three expected defeat and feared they
would lose both their thrones and their lives. In utter despair Wilhelm,
when he saw the war on the point of breaking out, wrote that Germany
would bleed to death in this war and be utterly ruined, but there was
the slight consolation that England ought to come out of it minus India.
Somewhat more temperately Franz Joseph declared that if the monarchy were going to sink, at least it ought to sink decently. The Czar's
advisers managed to obtain his signature to the mobilization order
only by warning him that his life depended on it.

The monarchs were not the only ones whose hands shook when they
opened the fateful portfolios to look at the fateful documents. Their
ministers too had, as Jagow put it, their hearts "not only in their throats,
but in the toes of their shoes." Bethmann-Hollweg, a philosophical man
with a strict sense of duty, who tried touchingly to harmonize the bid-
dings of his conscience with the necessities of politics, wavered between two states of anxiety: fear of war and fear of being too late with
the mobilization order. To his dying day he never understood how so
much bloodstained horror could have sprung from the gentleness of
his spirit.

Russian Foreign Minister Sazonov was a sickly, soft, feminine-Slavic type of person. A religious man, in his youth he wanted to be a monk and would certainly have made a fine Prince of the Church, all the more so since he had the cunning that often goes with weakness. Like all weak men he was thin-skinned. He had been Izvolsky's aide when the foreign minister lost his post because of the diplomatic defeat in the Bosnian affair. Sazonov was determined to show himself a strong man. The continual dinning of the Pan-Slavic press had gradually inculcated in him the belief that Russia had a world mission. He was a man unfitted for the post of foreign minister. His lack of substance, his disinclination for rigorous thinking, his personal touchiness, and his fondness for moral considerations (which in politics, of course, become the sanctions for anything) made him an easy prey for stronger and unscrupulous persons. He was born to be the tool of such men.

British Foreign Minister Sir Edward Grey was also a man of limited horizon. The Liberals, it was said in London, had made Grey foreign minister against his will because they themselves knew nothing about international politics and Grey had a way of looking as though he understood it all. He had a better ear for bird calls; better than the language of men. His memoirs abound in passages like this:

"There are a few days in the first part of May when the beech-trees in young leaf give an aspect of light and tender beauty to English country which is well known but indescribable. The days are very few; the colour of the leaves soon darkens, their texture becomes stiffer; beautiful they are still, but 'the glory and the dream' are gone. Unless Whitsuntide is unusually early, Sundays in the first half of May are the only days on which those who have business in town can be sure of a whole day in the country at leisure. The first Sunday in May was a little too early for the perfection of the beeches round my Hampshire cottage; the second Sunday in May was the perfect day. In my calendar it was known as 'Beech Sunday,' a day set apart and consecrated to enjoyment of the beauty of beech-leaves and to thankfulness for it. It was my habit on that morning each year to bicycle to a beech-wood some nine miles from the cottage. There I lunched once every year on that day at the foot of a certain tree. The wood was entirely of beech; the trees standing far apart; the grey boles grew up straight and clear and smooth for some distance above the ground. High overhead the branches touched and made a canopy; the blue sky just visible here and there; the sunshine coming through the tender, light-green leaves; a breeze stirring them now and then, but very gently. Such was the vision of what I had seen and known year by year, that was present to me in the Foreign Office in the second week of May. I thought of it, looked forward to it, counted upon it."

During the Balkan crisis his beech Sunday was interfered with by the ultimatum to Turkey. "This ultimatum had been necessary, but it was the outcome of a long-drawn-out dispute, and there had been no need to choose even a particular week, still less a Sunday, for its last day. I had now to wait another twelve months to see the great beech-wood as I knew it in its greatest beauty."

The Austrian foreign minister, Count Berchtold, was a fundamentally different type from Bethmann, Sazonov, or Grey, but he too was not a belligerent sort. Everyone knew that he was rich, irresolute, and timid. Berchtold had charm and elegance; in his vestibule were four coats, four pairs of gloves, and four walking-sticks, so that he could change his outfit according to his whim in the course of the day. Insofar as his social and business engagements and his relations with pretty young Viennese shop girls left him any time, he was hard-working. He wrote well, but he was—as Kiderlen once put it when he was irritated —no more than a "cavalier." If Berlin should leave the leadership to Vienna, Kiderlen added prophetically, "that may one day cost us a great deal." In spite of his German name, Berchtold was a Hungarian citizen, although he did not speak Hungarian. Naturally he liked put-ting on an act of being more Hungarian than the Magyars. When he was first appointed foreign minister, everyone thought it a poor joke. He himself declared that only two occasions in the life of a foreign minister held any pleasure: the occasion when, as holder of the office Metternich had once occupied, he received the congratulations of his peers; and the day he would be able to return to his hunting and his racing stable. (Half a year after the outbreak of the war Count Tisza, the Hungarian premier, went to see Franz Joseph to demand that Berchtold be shelved. In the anteroom he met the foreign minister and told him to his face that he was going to urge his dismissal because Berchtold could not cope with his job. Count Berchtold replied with his customary drollery: "By all means, tell him, tell him; I've been say-ing it to him for a long time but he won't believe me." A few minutes later Berchtold was dismissed—but it was six months too late.)

These were the men who held power in the four most important countries in Europe during those fateful days. It may seem astonishing that such peace-loving characters plunged Europe into a world war. But when we have related the events of the evil month, it will become evi-dent that the war broke out not *in spite of* the gentleness and peace-ableness of these men, but *because* their timorousness and insecurity kept them from taking a firm hold and ripping apart the net in which they were struggling like so many fish. Limited intelligence and weak character can bring as much woe to nations as Napoleonic ambition—that is the lesson of those July days of 1914.

II

"The sole purpose of Serbia's existence is to detach Austria-Hungary's South Slav provinces." Such was the credo of Pashitch, the Serbian premier. He had drawn up a memorial on methods for "discrediting the Austro-Hungarian administration in Bosnia and systematically feeding the discontent of the population." Peace and goodneighborly relations could exist between Austria-Hungary and Serbia only if Austria would cease being a great power.

In order to detach those South Slav provinces of Austria-Hungary, the Serbs had created two leagues known as the National Defense League and the "Black Hand." The National Defense League, headed by leading men in the Serbian government, was in charge of cultural propaganda. It arranged lecture tours and literacy courses, distributed incendiary literature, organized an espionage service and trained guerrilla fighters in handling guns, bomb-throwing, and blowing up railroad bridges. The Black Hand was somewhat less innocuous. Its official slogan was "Union or Death." Article 2 of the constitution of this secret society read: "The society prefers terroristic acts to propaganda." Its official seal showed a skull and crossbones, a dagger, a bomb, and a bottle of poison. Anyone entering this society had to "pledge his life." The president was a colonel of the Serbian general staff, Dragutin Dimitriyevitch, alias Apis; his right-hand man was a certain Major Tankositch. Apis was the foremost European specialist in political murder. In 1903 he had done a beautiful job on the assassination of King Alexander. In the following years he had not been quite so successful; plots against Franz Joseph, Nikita of Montenegro, and Ferdinand of Bulgaria came to nothing. He made five attempts to assassinate the governors of Croatia and Bosnia, but only some lower officials were killed; the governors themselves escaped unscathed. On such assignments the Black Hand customarily employed young Bosnians living in Belgrade. The assassins, some of whom committed suicide, some of whom were sentenced to prison terms, were hailed as heroes in Belgrade. In addition, Serbia had established the so-called "frontier officers," whose business was both espionage and the preparation of uprisings in case of war.

The majority of the inhabitants of the South Slav provinces still rebelled against the idea of being ruled by Serbian officials, for the Slovenes and the Croats considered the Serbs poor and uncultured people. But the youth of the poorer classes among the South Slavs, their heads in a whirl of nationalistic, socialistic, and anarchistic ideas, began listening to the siren song of Serbian propaganda. Those in authority in Vienna and Budapest were growing uneasy. Chief of Staff

Conrad recommended burning out that nest of conspirators in Belgrade. There was one man in the Austro-Hungarian monarchy who recognized the folly of such a proposal. That man was the Emperor's nephew, Archduke Franz Ferdinand.

III

After the suicide of Crown Prince Rudolf, Franz Ferdinand had become the heir apparent. He found himself at once surrounded by a group of sycophants. But it developed that he had inherited tuberculosis from his mother; he had to renounce the throne, and his admirers vanished into thin air. Filled with disgust and at the same time with the ardent desire to demonstrate his power to the despicable wretches who had forsaken him, he drew strength from his hatred and, adopting an iron discipline, cured himself. Again he became heir apparent; and again a crowd of flatterers gathered around him. But again he disappointed them. The Emperor wished him to marry a cousin, the Archduchess Marie Christine. He became a regular visitor at her home; the parents were already envisioning the imperial crown upon their daughter's head. But one day, during a tennis game, Franz Ferdinand left his watch lying about. Christine's mother picked it up, snapped open the case, and instead of her daughter's portrait she found in it a picture of one of her ladies in waiting, Countess Sophie Chotek. The presumptuous creature was ordered out of the house that same evening, but this was no solution to the problem, for the heir apparent announced that he intended to marry the Bohemian countess.

Franz Joseph did not know what the world was coming to. Such a *mésalliance* might well lead to disputes over the succession; it might result in the separation of Austria and Hungary, for the two countries held different views about royal and imperial marriages. Was it conceivable that a man would forget his duty for the sake of a mere love affair? But the Archduke refused to yield; he informed the premier that unless he were permitted to marry Sophie he would shoot himself or go mad. The only person who supported him was the Empress Elizabeth. "Marry the woman you love, Franz; otherwise you will have ugly children," she said.

Finally Franz Ferdinand took the plunge; he wedded Sophie in morganatic marriage and the Emperor made the Countess Duchess of Hohenburg. But the situation produced endless humiliations; on all ceremonial occasions Sophie sat below the youngest archduchesses; sometimes she had no male partner to take her to table. Franz Ferdinand feared for the future of his children and became obsessively stingy. He was filled with contempt for humanity, saw the Empire falling to pieces, complained bitterly to his uncle the Emperor: "I have no more influence here than the lowest household servant." "As long as I live no one will interfere with the government," the old Emperor replied. "But I am the one who will have to pay for your mistakes," said the heir apparent.

Franz Ferdinand was a real statesman. He saw the one point at which leverage must be applied; the proper policy was not a foolish preventive war, but peace externally—even at a sacrifice—and reform internally. When a conflict with Serbia was threatening during the Balkan War, he threw his weight into the scales for peace. He wanted "not one sheep, not one plum tree" of Serbia. What the monarchy really needed was internal reconstruction. Austria-Hungary must be transformed into a federal union, he argued, in which each of its ten or twelve nations would have its independent homeland. He ordered plans drawn up, attended lectures on the American Constitution by a professor of international law from Columbia University. "The United States of Greater Austria" was the name his advisers gave to this plan. Within such a framework Franz Ferdinand thought the South Slav question could be solved. If the Croats, Bosnians and Dalmatians had their own state of "Illyria," united with the other parts of the Empire only by a common monarch, a common foreign policy, and a common army, Belgrade would no longer have any attraction for them. On the contrary, with the new South Slav state uniting five million South Slavs, it was conceivable that a poor little country like Serbia would succumb to the attraction of the greater whole.

Of course this plan involved some breakup of Hungary, and the Hungarian nobility were averse to surrendering so much as a square yard of territory. But Franz Ferdinand was the man to force Budapest to accept a new arrangement, if necessary at the point of the sword. It was rumored around among these same pigheaded Hungarian nobles that the Archduke already had written out and laid away in his desk a proclamation to the effect that he would take the oath as King of Hungary only after the Empire had been reconstructed along these lines.

The Archduke was a lonely, bleak figure. The courtiers hated him for his marriage, the middle class for his misanthropy, and the Hungarians for his intentions. But most of all the Serbs in Belgrade hated him, for he and he alone threatened to cancel all their hopes. The cleverest of the Serbian diplomats, Spalajkovitch, declared flatly in 1912 that Serbia must obtain the Austrian South Slav provinces before Franz Ferdinand succeeded to the throne; afterwards it would be too late.

IV

But who was to do this little job? The Czar and Sazonov had, to be sure, repeatedly promised those provinces to the Serbs. But they had expressly added that Russia could not fight before 1917. How likely that Franz Joseph, already eighty-four, would meet his end before that year. Then Franz Ferdinand would reform the Empire and the whole Serbian unification movement would be wrecked. There was only one way out.

Early in 1914, Colonel Dimitriyevitch decided to have the Archduke assassinated; after the outbreak of the war he boasted openly that he had been the "organizer of the murder." Three young Bosnians living in Belgrade, all between eighteen and twenty, undertook to carry out the assassination. Two of them, Princip and Grabec, were attending the *Gymnasium* in Belgrade; the third, Gabrinovic, was a typesetter. All three were puny, undernourished, probably tubercular young men who had broken with their families. The most ambitious of them was Princip—who smarted from the slight of having been sent home as unfit during the war with Turkey. These three youths were provided with arms from Serbian army stores by Tankositch and a Serbian railroad official named Ciganovitch; they were then carefully trained in bomb-throwing and the use of pistols. With excessive solicitude Tankositch gave them cyanide to take immediately after the deed was done; the Black Hand wanted no unnecessary publicity. Then, three weeks before the Archduke was to attend maneuvers at Sarajevo, the capital of Bosnia, these young men were sent through a "tunnel" to Sarajevo. "Tunnels" were the name the conspirators gave to the smugglers' routes over which they carried men, arms, and leaflets into Bosnia. A former Bosnian schoolmaster promised to round up a few additional young men in Sarajevo to lend aid. After the war members of the Black Hand asserted that the Russian military attaché, Artamanov, and Russian Ambassador Hartwig, had been initiated into the plan for the assassination and had given financial support; it was alleged that they had even asked St. Petersburg for instructions. But this story is unconfirmed; Artamanov denied it.

Naturally Premier Pashitch had his liaison men in the Black Hand. As luck would have it, one of these "confidants" was Milan Ciganovitch. Consequently, Pashitch learned of the conspirators' plans by the end of May. The affair troubled him. He had been premier for many years and had, as was customary in the Balkans, become the richest man in Belgrade; French armament firms paid generous commissions. At bottom he was a conciliatory and responsible person; he did not think he had the right to decide by himself on the assassination of the Austrian heir apparent. Therefore he consulted his associates. The cabinet was opposed. The ministers were on bad terms with the Black Hand because ever since the Balkan War the army officers had been attempting to usurp power from the civil authorities. Besides, if there should be hostilities between Austria and Serbia, everything depended upon their obtaining Russia's promised aid, and Czar Nicholas had an understandable prejudice against regicide. The minister of the interior therefore ordered the border guards not to let the would-be assassins cross the frontier. But this gesture was ridiculous. The border guards themselves belonged to the Black Hand. They reported that the gentlemen in question had already crossed. Once again the ministers conferred; they now advised Pashitch to warn the Austrian government. But that, too, was only a gesture. If Pashitch warned the Austrian government of a prospective assassination in general terms, the Austrians would take his action as an attempt at intimidation, and would disregard it. But if he told them frankly that such and such men had left Serbia in order to kill the Austrian heir apparent, he himself would die in his boots within twenty-four hours; the Black Hand did not trifle with traitors. His own head was after all more precious to him than the Archduke's. He issued no warning.

There was, however, something else that Pashitch might have done. He could have sent for the chief of the Black Hand, his own Colonel Dimitriyevitch, and had the minister of war order him to recall the assassins—members of the league were sworn to absolute obedience. It is hard to understand why Pashitch did not choose this solution. To be sure, history sanctioned his action, since the assassination led to war and the war to the unification of the South Slavs. But this was something he could not at the time foresee. Perhaps the forthcoming elections to the Serbian parliament restrained him. Would he not be ruining his chances in that election by calling off the Black Hand? On the other hand, if the assassination succeeded and did not lead to war but only to Austrian threats, he would certainly win the election; under pressure from the hereditary foe the entire population would support the administration. The Austrians had mouthed threats so often before, and had never yet fired a shot.

Humanitarian considerations apparently did not enter Pashitch's mind. After all, he was ready to sacrifice the lives of hundreds of thousands of Serbs; why should he balk at the killing of an Austrian archduke? The fact that Pashitch himself had once been condemned to death and had been saved only by the Austrian ambassador's intercession—that fact carried no weight in view of the needs of the day.

Independently of Pashitch, and on his own initiative, the Serbian ambassador had said to an Austrian minister that during the maneuvers in Bosnia some Bosnian soldier's rifle might well go off unexpectedly.

The minister saw no reason to pass on to his superiors this general remark.

V

On June 26, 1914, two days before his official visit was scheduled to begin, Franz Ferdinand came to Sarajevo for a few hours and wandered about among the shops, dressed in his field marshal's uniform. Since the Bosnian people did not yet know that they wanted to throw off the yoke of the oppressor, they greeted him with cheers. But when he drove into the city at the appointed hour on the following Sunday, June 28, six assassins were waiting along his route. The first bomb rolled off the lowered top of his automobile, severely injuring two army officers in the car following his. The Archduke called a halt instantly and investigated. The wounded men were taken to the hospital. Then Franz Ferdinand continued on his way to the town hall. When his chauffeur started driving fast, he ordered him to slow down so that the people could see him. In the town hall the mayor began his prepared speech: "The people of Sarajevo are delighted to receive Your Imperial and Royal Highness." "With bombs," the Archduke interjected; then he let the flustered official continue and himself read his prepared speech of thanks. The manuscript had been in the pocket of one of the wounded officers and was stained with blood.

When the heir apparent was informed that the terrorists had been arrested, he declared that probably they would now be decorated, that being the usual Austrian practice. The reception over, he was urged to cut the visit short, but he insisted instead on driving to the hospital to see how the wounded men were faring. With an amiable, "I wouldn't be surprised to be on the receiving end of a little buckshot yet," he got into his car. And at this point chance decided the fate of millions. All the assassins except Princip had fled. But at the very spot where Princip was standing, the Archduke's car stopped because the driver had made a wrong turn. The eighteen-year-old student was able to fire two shots at point-blank range; the heir apparent and his wife died in a few minutes. Princip was arrested; he straightway cried out that he was not yet twenty and therefore could not be condemned to death. His accomplices sent a telegram to Belgrade reading: "Excellent sale of both horses."

When the assassination was reported to Franz Joseph, he cried: "Frightful! The Almighty will not be mocked! . . . A higher power has again restored that order which I, unfortunately, was not able to preserve. . . ." His first thoughts concerned the problems of the succession which had arisen from the Archduke's marriage. Franz Ferdinand's enemies were delighted; a man of his rank and manner had few friends. In Budapest Premier Tisza said: "What God bestows upon us we must gratefully accept." The Russians were relieved. In Vienna Berchtold wanted to invite all the princes of Europe to the funeral. He hoped the old Emperor would use the occasion to appeal to the sense of community among the monarchs, who would then see that Austria must receive some sort of redress from Serbia. But Prince Montenuovo, the Lord High Steward, himself the offspring of a mésalliance, hated the late Archduke and his wife; he insisted that a quiet funeral was in order, in consideration of the old Emperor's health. (He had no way of knowing the burdens Franz Joseph's aged frame would have to bear because of this shabby chess-move of his.) Privately he remarked that for Franz Ferdinand and that Chotek woman "a third-class funeral" was good enough.

And so the heir apparent was given a "quiet" funeral. But as the coffins were taken across the Danube on a ferry a sudden cloudburst brought fearful claps of thunder; the horses of the funeral hearse reared up; one wheel of the hearse dangled perilously over the water, and only the courage and firmness of the coachman prevented the coffins from sliding into the Danube. It was all a prelude to the funeral march which would play for four years.

CHAPTER TWELVE

Berchtold's Blunders

It is unwise to place your load upon a dead camel.

—ARAB PROVERB

I

In Serbia the newspapers hailed the murderers as heroes and martyrs, benefactors of mankind for having dispatched a "medieval figure." One newspaper started the story that Princip was in reality a Hungarian count who was punishing Franz Ferdinand for having killed Crown Prince Rudolf years ago.

Meanwhile the assassins were being interrogated. Some of them had "lost," some not taken and some vomited up again the cyanide pills. They betrayed all their accomplices, including Tankositch and Ciganovitch. They could tell no more because they knew no more; as a precaution it had been impressed upon them that the Serbian government frowned upon the conspiratorial group. Consequently, the chief investigator reported to Vienna that no connection with the Belgrade government could be established. Austrian espionage failed completely; if the Austrian intelligence service could have discovered at the time that Pashitch knew about the assassination, the whole world would have approved an Austrian punitive expedition. In fact there was widespread sympathy for Austria at first; the British ambassador to Paris wrote to London that France was scarcely likely to support her ally Russia if Russia should initiate hostilities over so poor a cause. The British ambassador in Vienna noted that the Serbian newspapers were behaving shamefully.

What was Vienna to do? Berchtold came to the conclusion that the moment had come to "settle accounts" with Serbia. The sternest demands must be made, and after they were rejected Austrian troops must invade Serbia. He thought it possible that Russia would support Serbia. But if Russia's sympathies would really extend to the point of the Czar's protecting the assassins of royalty, then it must be assumed that sooner or later Russia would in any case give military support to Serbia's efforts to mutilate Austria-Hungary. Year by year Russia was growing stronger as against Austria. If war were therefore inevitable, it would be better to fight it now while the majority of the South Slavs in the dual monarchy were opposed to separation. Austria-Hungary was faced with the choice of consenting to her own dissolution or "subjugating" Serbia. Berchtold—and in *this* he was in the long run right—was convinced that Austria-Hungary offered her dozen nations a better and safer home than they would have after the breakup of the dual monarchy.

The British historian Dickinson has commented: "One can conceive a world in which Austria would not have wished to hold down a nationality against its will. But that world would not be the world of history, past or present. Never has an empire resigned before the disruptive forces of nationality. Always it has fought. And I do not believe there was a State in existence that would not, under similar circumstances, have determined, as Austria did, to finish the menace, once and for all, by war." Even the papal secretary of state told the Austrian ambassador he considered chastisement of Serbia—though at the risk of a European war—unavoidable if Austria-Hungary were to continue existing. And no state has ever been willing to believe that its day is over.

Berchtold therefore concluded that Austria-Hungary had to fight Serbia. Acting on this conviction, during the days that followed he frustrated all efforts to prevent a war. Moreover, he wanted to win the applause of his noble peers by conducting a vigorous policy; he wanted to be something more than a "cavalier." Only people who have a firm character and firm social standing ought to enter politics.

II

If we judge Berchtold's decision by the ethics of governments, it was not amoral. But it was incredibly foolish.

Berchtold should have asked himself two questions. The first was: what do we do if we actually subjugate Serbia and Russia does not intervene? The Serbs might be made to give up territory to Rumania, Bulgaria, Albania and even Austria-Hungary. But it was probable—and in the course of the crisis became quite certain—that Russia would not hear of any dismemberment of Serbia. Under such circumstances, of what use would be a victory over Serbia? Suppose a few hundred "conspirators" in Serbia were strung up, the country occupied for a year, and *Gott erhalte Franz den Kaiser* played in all the market places —would any of these things solve the South Slav problem?

The second question was far more important: what would happen if Russia intervened? Did Austria have any prospect of coming out of a European war victorious? France would aid the Russians. What about England? What about Italy? Chief of Staff Conrad had suddenly decided that Italy would march alongside Austria. He had come to this belief because Italian Chief of Staff Pollio had recently briefed him on the number of army corps he would send to Germany's aid. Pollio's assurance was worthless; Pollio was only in a position to state what Italy would send *if* the government decided to implement the alliance. But every statesman in Europe knew that Italy was going to do no such thing, especially if England came into the picture. Berchtold even feared Italy would fight Austria. To which Conrad replied laconically: "If we also have Italy to be afraid of, we will not mobilize." But no conclusions were drawn from this vital consideration. In view of the desperate situation, Berchtold's thinking should have centered around a single point: what would England do? If England and Italy were going to come in, the Central Powers were facing superior forces against which they had no chance. In that case the only salvation was to avoid war and choose a different solution to the South Slav question—reform of the Empire. But in none of the papers or memoirs of the Austrian statesmen do we find the slightest hint that they considered these matters. With lordly carelessness Berchtold ignored the crucial issues.

One man was against a war, however, and he happened to be the strongest personality in the monarchy: Hungarian Premier Count Tisza. Tisza was tough. A year ago a deputy in parliament had fired a shot at him. The bullet whistled past his ear. Without even a stammer, Tisza went on with his speech as if nothing had happened. In spite of cataracts in his eyes, he was a renowned horseman at the age of sixty; he had challenged a dozen political enemies to duels. A Calvinist by religion and character, cool and austere, a man of rigid principles, he was feared by friend and foe. When it was known that he was taking the train to Vienna, the imperial ministers trembled; when he reached the capital, they crawled. Tisza's point of view was this: if Berchtold started a war with Serbia, more Serbs would be brought into the monarchy; the holy soil of Hungary would be fouled by even more Slavs, and Hungarian influence would diminish.

He therefore betook himself to Vienna and bluntly told the foreign minister not to press demands that Serbia could not and would not meet. He also insisted upon a positive promise that if Serbia should reject reasonable demands and war should come, not a square yard of Serbian soil would be annexed. If Vienna did not accept this ultimatum of his, he would resign—which would practically mean the separation of Hungary from the Empire.

Berchtold protested that so good a pretext for settling with Serbia would not be likely to come again. Tisza brushed this objection aside. In the present Balkan situation, he remarked, he would not worry about "finding a suitable *casus belli* at any time."

III

The first thing that Berchtold had to know, before taking further steps, was whether Germany was prepared to back his policy. He hoped that the assassination of Franz Ferdinand would have stirred Kaiser Wilhelm personally.

It had. Wilhelm felt that every attempt upon the life of a prince was an attack upon the institution of monarchy. (King Edward VII had reacted similarly to the murder of the wretched King of Serbia; Alexander had, after all, belonged to the same métier as himself, he remarked.) Moreover, Franz Ferdinand had been a friend of Wilhelm's. Nor did the Kaiser think the Czar would help murderers of princes— especially since Russia had not yet completed her military build-up. Therefore it seemed obvious that Austria could punish Serbia without igniting a world war. Only she must act quickly, before the general indignation died down. Reading a report from von Tschirschky, the German ambassador in Vienna, the Kaiser waxed highly indignant. The ambassador wrote that he was calmly but emphatically warning the Austrian government against acting hastily. Wilhelm noted on the margin of the report: "Who empowered him to do that? It is very stupid. It's none of his concern; what Austria chooses to do in this affair is strictly her business. Afterwards, if things turn out badly, it will be said that Germany held back. Tschirschky is to stop such nonsense, if you please! The Serbs have to be settled with, and that *soon!*"

On July 5, one week after the assassination, a letter from Franz Joseph was brought to the Kaiser. The German capital at this time seemed deserted. Bethmann-Hollweg was at his country estate, Foreign Secretary Jagow on a wedding trip, Chief of Staff Moltke was vainly seeking a cure in Karlsbad, his deputy was at the funeral of an aunt in Hanover, Admiral Tirpitz was mountain-climbing in Switzerland, his chief of staff and *his* deputy were also on leave, and the Kaiser was about to sail to Norway next day. The Foreign Office was momentarily being run by Undersecretary Zimmermann, a brash young man who did his best to obliterate his middle-class origins by a dashing military bearing.

Franz Joseph informed the Kaiser that Austria wished to eliminate Serbia as a political factor. Wilhelm replied that he recognized the seriousness of the situation; he did not believe the Czar would aid assassins. In any case, he would stand by Austria-Hungary like a loyal ally. This was his position. Beyond this, it was not for him to advise Austria what to do.

Berchtold could not have wished a handsomer blank check. Bethmann, of whom the British historian Gooch says that he was as peace-

able as he was incompetent for the position he held, was worried at
first, but the Kaiser and Zimmermann soon "put some starch into him."
At the chancellor's request the Kaiser set out on his voyage "in order
not to make the public uneasy."

Berlin's decision was pure folly. Of course Germany had to stand by
Austria. But the least she should have demanded was that she be informed in good time of all Austrian plans, in order to have some control over the game that was being played. Berlin should have realized
that this game required the utmost caution; yet everything was left
up to a "cavalier" whose frivolousness was notorious. Ambassador
Tschirschky, a snob who yearned to be liked by the Viennese upper
nobility, switched his position as soon as he was informed of Wilhelm's
reprimand. He now told the Austrians: "If you put up with this Serbian
insolence, you are not worth being spat upon." If Austria backed down
now, he said, Germany would have to look around for another ally.

IV

That was one risk Berchtold had never intended running. He was
resolved upon war with Serbia. Count Tisza declared he would not be
bound by German opinion. However, even Tisza was growing irate
over the tone of the Serbian press. He finally agreed to a note couched
in the sharpest possible terms, provided Austria informed all the powers
that she sought no territorial aggrandizement. Cession of Serbian territory to other countries would not be ruled out, of course. This declaration, Tisza insisted, must be made when the ultimatum was delivered
to Serbia. Berchtold agreed, but he published the declaration too late.

In Berlin meanwhile Foreign Secretary Jagow had returned from his
honeymoon. He suggested that Austria should, when she presented the
ultimatum, also present Europe with a clear dossier of Serbia's aggressiveness toward the monarchy. Austrian laziness and carelessness
affected the history of the world; this material was not supplied until
many days later, and then only in the German language. By the time
it was translated, the war had already begun.

Jagow also wanted to know what Austria-Hungary really intended
to do about Serbia. To this inquisitiveness Berchtold replied that
Vienna would cross that bridge when it came to it. Jagow, unaccus-
tomed to swimming against the stream, swallowed this arrogant reply.
Still, the little man did not feel very comfortable. On his desk lay a
letter from Prince Lichnowsky, the ambassador to England, warning
him against the blank-check policy. Germany must not follow Austria
blindly, Lichnowsky urged. Helplessly, Jagow wrote back to him that
Germany had only this one ally in all the world.

Meanwhile Count Berchtold was troubled by another concern. Sup-

pose Serbia accepted the ultimatum after all? Tschirschky reported that
the Austrian foreign minister was pondering what additional demands
could be posed in order to render it impossible for Serbia to accept.
Jagow answered with stupid rigidity: "We cannot take any position on
the formulation of the demands, since that is Austria's affair." Kaiser
Wilhelm, however, knew a way out; he noted alongside Tschirschky's
report: "Let them occupy Sanjak Novibazar; then they'll have their
scrap." This was a piece of Serbian territory on the Montenegran
border.

V

In Vienna they were toiling over the wording of the ultimatum. But
it could not yet be sent. Berchtold fully realized that the real decision
lay with St. Petersburg, not Belgrade. And at the moment Poincaré,
the President of France, was visiting St. Petersburg. The Viennese did
not want Russia and France, in the mood of high idealism engendered
by champagne, to promise aid to the Serbs. This was a sensible precaution, but it did not help. Russia's policy for the Balkans was already
established; she wanted the Dardanelles and needed the Balkan countries as allies against Turkey. For this reason she had already promised
aid to Serbia a year ago. Soon after the assassination of Franz Ferdinand, Sazonov told the Austrian ambassador that none of the people
of Bosnia wanted to be ruled by Austria, except perhaps for a few
Catholics and Mohammedans—obviously he did not know that these
two groups constituted a majority in Bosnia. He warned against the
investigations that Austria was proposing to hold in Belgrade. Such
violation of Serbian sovereignty was highly dangerous, he declared.
Did he know that such investigations might prove the complicity of
Pashitch?

The atmosphere in St. Petersburg was therefore already charged
when Poincaré sat down to dinner at a table decorated with the thistles
of Lorraine. At table two Montenegran grand duchesses, the daugh-
ters of King Nikita, told French Ambassador Paléologue that their
father was a hero out of the Iliad. He had written them that the war
would begin this very month and predicted: "Nothing will remain of
Austria; our armies will meet in Berlin; Germany will be annihilated."
Poincaré and Sazonov decided to request Vienna not to make demands
for an investigation which the Serbs could regard as an infringement
of their sovereignty. It was also necessary, they felt, "to smash the
pride of Germany at all costs and stop her once and for all from stepping on her neighbors' toes." Poincaré impressed upon his ambassador
the need for Sazonov's remaining firm; to that end he must receive full
French backing. When Izvolsky and Paléologue parted two days later,

they said to each other: "This time it is war!" (After the war Paléologue became director of the private bank of the Schneider-Creusot armaments firm.)

Meanwhile Berlin was counting upon the Czar's sense of solidarity with the other monarchs of Europe to preserve peace. This expectation was silly. Naturally Nicholas abhorred royal murders, but only when they ran counter to Russian interests.

VI

While Poincaré was still in St. Petersburg, Vienna completed the text of the ultimatum to Serbia. It started out with a number of reasonable demands. An investigation was to be launched against the plotters of the assassination; in particular Tankositch and Ciganovitch were to be arrested. The smuggling of arms into Bosnia was to stop and the participating organizations punished. Pamphlets urging the separation of Austrian territories were to be banned. The National Defense League was to be abolished, its propaganda literature confiscated. All these demands conformed to the customs of international law. Even the demand that the King of Serbia issue a statement disapproving of the efforts to mutilate Austria-Hungary was not intolerable, since Belgrade had in the past come out with such protestations—although not a soul in Serbia had taken them seriously. Serbia was also to dismiss all civil servants and members of the armed forces who were conducting propaganda against Austria-Hungary.

Two of the demands, however, were crucial. Austrian officials were to take part in the investigations—not in the trials—of the accomplices to the plot against Franz Ferdinand; and in the future Austrian agencies were to collaborate in suppressing separatist movements. Objectively, both these demands were justified, since Serbia had repeatedly given assurances that she would stop the propaganda, and had never kept these promises. Nor were the demands "unacceptable" in terms of international law; in Paris there existed a Russian police bureau for the suppression of Russian anarchists, and a similar bureau had formerly functioned in Berlin. Moreover, on the occasion of an attempt in the past to assassinate Prince Michael of Serbia, Austria-Hungary had permitted a Serbian magistrate to take part in the investigations. But for the Serbian government these demands were intolerable because the relations between the assassins and the government might come to light; and if Austrian officials helped suppress the separatist movement, the South Slav areas could never be detached from Austria. Also, if the government started dismissing officials, the Black Hand would strike—and the retribution of the Black Hand was far more to be feared by any minister than war.

Franz Joseph approved the ultimatum, although he commented: "Russia will not accept this; there will be a big war." German Foreign Secretary Jagow was shown the note only twenty-four hours before it was to be delivered. He thought it rather sharp, but Berchtold said to him: "Nothing to be done about it now; it will be delivered first thing tomorrow morning." This was a lie; delivery of the note was scheduled for six o'clock in the evening.

VII

The Austrian ambassador in Belgrade, General Giessl, had given the Serbian government several hours' notice of his intention to present the ultimatum. Pashitch was away campaigning for the elections, he was told. In a kingdom the size of Serbia it ought to be easy to get him back in time, Giessl replied. The truth was that Pashitch had decided to go off incognito to Salonica in Greece for three days, in order to defer decisions. But shortly before his train crossed the border a telegram from the Prince Regent called him back. Serbian Chief of Staff Putnik, the most capable general in Serbia, was also abroad, taking a cure in Austria! On his return trip he was arrested, but immediately released on orders from Franz Joseph. The courteous Emperor then assigned an archduke to accompany him on his homeward journey.

On July 23, at six o'clock in the evening, Baron Giessl handed over the note with a time limit of forty-eight hours for reply. The following morning Pashitch wisely made his decision—that Serbia was incapable of resistance and therefore everything depended upon St. Petersburg. The Prince Regent telegraphed the Czar that Serbia would follow any advice the Russian government chose to give. Pashitch himself doubted that the Russians would help; he informed the leaders of the various parties that without Russian aid Serbia would have to accept the ultimatum.

The momentous decision was now St. Petersburg's. It lay in the feeble hands of Sergei Sazonov. For Austria, which he considered a "monstrous anachronism," Sazonov felt contempt rather than hatred, as he candidly informed the German ambassador. Sooner or later, he believed, a bloody clash between Vienna and St. Petersburg had to come. "No way out of the irreconcilable hostility exists," he declared. At bottom he did not care about the Slavs in the Balkans; before the Balkan War he had offered Turkey an alliance against them, and at the same time he had declared that Serbia's natural destiny was to be hanged by Austria. What really mattered to him was Constantinople. Ever since the Balkan countries had triumphed over Turkey, he had looked upon them as the point of Russia's sword. He sincerely believed that Austria wanted to subjugate Serbia in order to establish her hegemony in the Balkans. In vain the German ambassador, Count Pourtalès, strummed away at his monarchist song and dance; after prolonged consultation the Russian council of ministers decided to support Serbia, if necessary with arms. Russia, however, would not mobilize until Austria attacked Serbia. Simultaneously, preparations for mobilization were begun.

The British ambassador admonished Sazonov to be cautious; he warned that Germany might reply to Russian mobilization by a declaration of war, in order to keep Russia from gaining an advantage. Sazonov responded that Russia could not tolerate Austrian domination of the Balkans, that she was sure of France's aid and would take the risk of a war. Immediately the ambassador telegraphed London that if England did not support Russia now she could expect the end of Russia's friendly cooperation in Asia.

The dice were cast. Austria had resolved to crush Serbia; Russia had resolved not to permit it. Unless one of the two parties changed its decision, war was inevitable. Pourtalès' slight deafness was not a mere physical phenomenon; he was deaf to the overtures of the situation. He telegraphed Berlin that there was no need to fear hasty action. This message was totally misleading. The Bavarian envoy Grimelius (Bavaria had at this time her own diplomatic representative) reported the decision of the Russian council of ministers quite accurately. His telegram was filed away in Munich and never reached the Foreign Office in Berlin.

VIII

Only six hours were left before expiration of the time limit on the ultimatum when the saving word from St. Petersburg reached Belgrade. Immediately the atmosphere changed. The Prince Regent proclaimed mobilization and ordered the seat of government transferred to Nish. The council of ministers drew up a careful reply accepting part of the Austrian demands, but rejecting the most important ones. Above all it would not hear of Austrian officials taking part in the police investigation or Austria's cooperating in the suppression of the separatist movement. Pashitch had to reject these demands not because they offended Serbia's dignity as a sovereign state, but because his government had been privy to the assassination and because separatism was the vital core of Serbian policy. But he was clever enough to propose that all disputed points be submitted to the Hague Tribunal for arbitration. It was improbable that this court, unfamiliar as it was with the methods prevalent in the Balkans, would determine the complicity of the Serbian government.

A superficial reading of the Serbian reply gave the impression that

Serbia was being most cooperative. On closer examination it became apparent that Austria was being given no guarantee that the assassins would be punished and that the separatist movement would be suppressed.

Serbia was cooperative, after her own fashion. For example, Pashitch declared that the government had been unable to locate Austrian citizen Milan Ciganovitch and had therefore issued a warrant for his arrest. In reality none other than the Belgrade chief of police had directed Ciganovitch to clear out of Belgrade and remain under cover for a while. This was all the more necessary precisely because Ciganovitch was an Austrian citizen. By all the rules of international law he should be turned over to the Austrians for inciting to murder; but Ciganovitch was the link between Pashitch and the Black Hand. If he should talk in an Austrian court, the very existence of Serbia was imperilled.

On Friday, July 25, five minutes before six o'clock in the evening, Pashitch handed Giessl the Serbian reply, saying: "We have accepted part of the demands. For the rest, we place our hopes in Austrian chivalry." Before he had returned to his ministry a messenger from Giessl caught up with him and handed him a note prepared in advance; Giessl announced that since the reply had been unsatisfactory, he was leaving Belgrade. "The rupture of diplomatic relations will assume the character of an accomplished fact from the moment your Excellency receives this letter," the note read in choice Austrian bureaucratic jargon. Baron Giessl left Belgrade on the regular train at half past seven, having set a world's record for speed in breaking diplomatic relations.

But there was no such promptitude about the further conduct of the affair. Easygoing Austrian slackness was to do infinite harm. Everything now depended for Austria on her demonstrating to the world that the Serbian reply was only a sham acceptance of the ultimatum. Yet Giessl did not telegraph the Serbian note; he delivered it personally in Vienna on the following day. A commentary on it was sent out on Tuesday and reached the powers on Wednesday, far too late. Meanwhile all the powers had received the impression that Serbia had accepted almost all the demands. Instead of immediately publishing the Serbian reply, Vienna attempted to keep it secret as long as possible. Ambassador Tschirschky did not receive a copy of it, in spite of his repeated urging, until sixty hours after it had been delivered. Since Serbia had mobilized her fifteen divisions by Friday noon, Austria on Saturday evening ordered mobilization of the twenty-two divisions scheduled for deployment against Serbia. But the real mobilization was not to take place until Tuesday: Sunday and Monday "were needed for spreading the alarm."

When Franz Joseph learned of Giessl's departure from Belgrade, he said: "So it's come! Well, breaking diplomatic relations is not necessarily war." Berchtold had assured him that Austria would have to deal with Serbia alone, "and he ought to know," the Emperor commented.

CHAPTER THIRTEEN

Attempts at Mediation

And thus the native hue of resolution
Is sicklied o'er with the pale cast of thought,
And enterprises of great pith and moment
With this regard their currents turn awry,
And lose the name of action.

—HAMLET, ACT III

I

Hardly a statesman in Europe in those days regarded the prospect of war with such great apprehension as British Foreign Minister Sir Edward Grey. It was not the horrors of war which excited his fear—for he thought that England's superior fleet would keep her from harm—nor was it that he had any doubts of victory. The statesmen in London, Paris, and St. Petersburg were confident that the allied armies would meet in Berlin. The tempest in Grey's soul was due to a personal reason. If a war broke out in Europe, the double-dealing he had for years been practicing might come to light. Worse still, his own duplicity might bring on the war he dreaded. "There was often a wakeful time round about four o'clock in the morning—that time when vitality is low and spirits are depressed and the mind is often a prey to doubts and anxieties," Grey wrote. What were the doubts that caused this lover of beech trees to toss in his bed?

England, he constantly reassured himself, had no secret treaty with France. His hands were not tied. In his letter of 1912 arranging joint staff consultations between the British and French armies and navies, he had carefully added the sentence: "It has always been understood that such consultation does not restrict the freedom of either Government to decide at any future time whether or not to assist the other by armed force." In the House of Commons Asquith had publicly declared that England was in no way committed. In private the Cabinet had been profoundly alarmed when he informed them of his discussions with the French. But these other men in the Cabinet were obviously unworldly doctrinaires!

Grey had also negotiated with the Russian navy, a fact which he had flatly denied before the House—but were not such lies matters of plain necessity? The established plan to transfer the British Mediterranean fleet to the North Sea and the French Atlantic fleet to the Mediterranean was essential from a military point of view. Did this plan mean that England had undertaken an obligation to defend the northern coast of France from a German attack? Oh no, not at all—England had no obligations; he had signed nothing; he had concealed nothing from the Cabinet; he had not pledged England's honor. What about Churchill's argument that England was now morally obliged to fight on the side of France? What about Churchill's tart remark that England's brilliant policy had secured her all the duties and none of the advantages of an ally? Would not the House have some grounds for saying that he, Grey, had misled them? But no, after all, he had not put his signature to any treaty; he had given no promises.

But the French did have the impression that England was obligated to help them. They firmly believed this, and the Russians believed it as well. Relying upon this aid, they might let the existing hostilities come to the point of war. What would the members of the Cabinet do then—that prig of a Morley who called himself the conscience of England; and that narrow-minded workingman Burns; and Lloyd George, who was always wooing popular favor; and Asquith, the eternal waverer? Would they declare England neutral, and abandon France to her fate? For they all hated a Continental war like the very devil. And then he, Grey, would be to blame when beautiful, noble France was devastated by the German barbarians. It would be his fault if afterwards England stood dishonored and isolated facing the Teutonic victors alone, with the disillusioned Russians threatening India, and England's position in the world collapsing at all points. . . . It was unthinkable, unthinkable. If things ever came to that pass, Germany would have England at her mercy. There must be no hesitation. There was no question about it. If war came, England must fight on the side of her allies—no, not her allies, her friends. If the Cabinet insisted on neutrality, he would have to resign. Though what good was resignation? Then the evil would take its course. Better yet, he must prevent this war—that is, prevent it so long as it was possible to do so without endangering England's amicable relations with Russia, which constituted the great achievement of recent years.

On the other hand, would it be better to wait and intervene in the war later on? But that might be too late to prevent the defeat of England's allies—no, no, not that word—of England's friends. It was obvious that French Ambassador Paul Cambon would call on him twice a day and ask: Is England going to help us? And if he, Grey, should say no—Cambon would produce the letter of 1912 and announce to the world that France had stripped her northern coast of naval protection for England's sake. Cambon would call in Nicolson and Crowe as witnesses, and Crowe would say that the entire Entente policy had no sense unless it meant that England intended to stand by her friends in a just cause. But if the Cabinet favored peace, how could he tell Cambon England would help? To promise and then not keep his promise, might be the ruin of France. No way out of it—the war must be averted. But how could he avert it? If he told the Germans bluntly, "England will fight against you," they would keep the peace. But this was the one declaration he could not make on his own initiative.

Suppose, on the other hand, he told Cambon: "England will remain neutral." Then the Russians would presumably look around for and find some mode of conciliation with Austria and Germany. But he could not make such a statement either, for Cambon would bring up their talks—and in addition Russo-British amity would be endangered. This was something he did not dare to risk; not when the formidable Russians had fortunately shifted their attentions from Asia toward the West, and were prepared to take up cudgels against that eternal troublemaker and arrogant rival, Germany. Why should a British statesman be interested in preventing a clash between the two? But no, he must preserve peace, must warn both sides—without offending the Russians. . . . But of course both parties would interpret his warnings according to their own wishful thinking; the French would count on his aid and the Germans upon his neutrality. In which case they would both slide into this horrible war and it would be said in the end that England deliberately encouraged both countries to plunge to their destruction. . . .

At this point, perhaps, there lay a possible solution to the problem. The Germans were planning to march through Belgium. For years Field Marshal Wilson had had his room papered with Belgian maps; he had taken bicycle tours all over Belgium to study the terrain, and was certain the Germans would march through that convenient little country. All to the good! If German cannon roared at Liége and Antwerp, if an inoffensive small free nation were assaulted, and if England undertook to defend sacred treaties—then the man on the street could be made to work up some enthusiasm for war.

Suppose now that he told the Germans that to invade Belgium would mean war with England. Perhaps Bethmann would then exert stronger pressure upon Vienna and prevent the war. Possibly. But there could be no certainty about that. And in the final analysis, was it to England's interest to avert a war in which her two chief antagonists would mutually wear each other out? England herself would not suffer very much. All wars were regrettable, of course, but this impending war would not be wholly a misfortune. But no, one must not think in such terms; one must try to stop the war, to do everything possible to avert it without imperilling England's interests. Perhaps it would be possible to keep the peace after all. And if it were not possible, then there was the matter of Belgium, which ought to carry some weight with the hesitant Cabinet. . . . Somewhat calmed by this thought, Grey at last fell asleep.

II

While Sir Edward was tossing and twisting in his bed of irresolution, the most vigorous intellect in his government had long ago come to a firm decision. Sir Eyre Crowe was half German—by temperament as well as by birth and family connections, for he would compose long-winded memoranda at the drop of a hat. His mother was the step-sister of Chief of Staff von Holtzendorff of the Imperial German navy; his wife was the widow of a German army lieutenant; his sister was married to another German admiral. But his mother's brother had belonged to the liberal opposition that had fought Bismarck in Germany, and his own picture of Germany was formed almost entirely by the liberal newspapers. It was not a favorable picture. Germany had no more bitter enemy in the world than Eyre Crowe.

Crowe did not wait to see what Serbia would reply to the Austrian ultimatum, and how Russia would react to the dispute. On Saturday morning—the day the Serbian answer was due—he wrote a memorandum urging unconditional support of France and Russia without regard for the rights and wrongs of the case.

"It is clear," Crowe wrote, "that France and Russia are decided to accept the challenge thrown out to them. Whatever we may think of the merits of the Austrian charges against Serbia, France and Russia consider that these are the pretexts, and that the bigger cause of Triple Alliance versus Triple *Entente* is definitely engaged. I think it would be impolitic, not to say dangerous, for England to attempt to controvert this opinion, or to endeavour to obscure the plain issue, by any representation at St. Petersburg and Paris."

Crowe recommended readying the fleet in order to intimidate Germany. Grey did not act upon this recommendation. There was no need to; by a lucky chance the British fleet was fully ready, having just completed large-scale maneuvers. First Lord of the Admiralty Winston Churchill kept the fleet together on his own initiative, without saying anything about it.

What Grey did do was far more dangerous. All the statesmen of Europe were well aware that the real difficulty involved mobilization. Everyone knew that Germany had a shorter sword than Russia's, but could draw it more swiftly from its sheath. As the general staffs of other countries well knew, German strategy hinged upon this fact. The Germans intended to defeat France before the Russians could complete their mobilization. Given a situation in which both countries would begin to mobilize at the same time, it was fairly obvious that Germany would beat Russia to the game and strike.

Grey's adroit maneuver was based upon this proposition; by it he thought to secure Russian friendship for England and hold Germany in check. On the day Serbia was preparing her reply, a Saturday, Grey informed the Russian ambassador that he was expecting Russian mobilization against Austria if Austria should mobilize against Serbia; he had informed the German ambassador that Germany must not take this step on Russia's part as a pretext for mobilization, but should instead admonish Austria to moderate her demands upon Serbia. The Russian ambassador in London promptly telegraphed these glad tidings to St. Petersburg. Two days later Prince Lichnowsky, the German ambassador, assured Grey that Germany would not consider a Russian partial mobilization against Austria cause for her own mobilization. Grey promptly transmitted this reply to St. Petersburg. In so doing he was countering the policy of his own ambassador in St. Petersburg who was at this time constantly warning the Russians that Germany would interpret mobilization as a deliberate provocation, and who was also telling the Russians that British public opinion would support Russia only if responsibility for the war plainly rested with Germany.

Grey was thus encouraging the Russians to mobilize. His reason for doing so was his desire to deprive the Germans of their most important asset. In his memoirs he recounts how he informed the Russian ambassador of his master stroke. "I was afraid, too, that Germany would reply that mobilization with her was a question of hours, whereas with Russia it was a question of days; and that, as a matter of fact, I had asked that, if Russia mobilized against Austria, Germany, instead of mobilizing against Russia, should suspend mobilization and join with us in intervention with Austria, thereby throwing away the advantage of time, for, if the diplomatic intervention failed, Russia would meanwhile have gained time for her mobilization." Following out this idea with great consistency, he failed to inform St. Petersburg of something he learned two days later which would have greatly reassured and calmed Sazonov: the fact that the Austrian invasion of Serbia could not begin until August 15 at the earliest.

As a result of all this, St. Petersburg counted confidently upon British aid. The British ambassador in Paris reported that Russian Ambassador Izvolsky was whipping up war sentiment. A few months later he reported that when the war did break out Izvolsky had said, "This is my war," but now he was saying: "If I had been responsible for this war in any way, I would never be able to forgive myself."

III

But Grey did not confine himself to encouraging St. Petersburg. Since at the bottom of his heart he would have preferred a peaceful solution, he successively made several offers to mediate. At first he proposed that the four disinterested great powers—Germany, England, France and Italy—mediate between Vienna and St. Petersburg. Paris rejected this suggestion on the grounds that it might weaken the bonds among the members of the Triple Entente. Thereupon Grey suggested that the London ambassadors of these four powers attempt to arbitrate the dispute between Austria and Serbia. Berlin rejected this plan because the tribunal would be composed of four judges hostile to Austria; the British and French ambassadors because of their alliances; the Italian ambassador because Italy had already come more than halfway into the camp of the Triple Entente; and even the German ambassador, inasmuch as Prince Lichnowsky's contempt for Austria was notorious. Lichnowsky was another excellent example of Bismarck's maxim that vanity must be deducted from a man's abilities in order to determine his true worth; the German ambassador's sound judgment was often impaired by childish conceit. At this moment, however, he saw the situation more clearly than his colleagues. On Saturday, July 25, he telegraphed Berlin that a war would not destroy South Slav nationalism, but only intensify it; that it was wishful thinking to imagine that an Austro-Serbian war could be localized; and that Austria must couch her demands in such terms that they would not necessarily lead to war.

On Sunday the Italian prime minister, San Giuliano, made a truly statesmanlike proposal. He proposed that Serbia should accept the remaining demands in the ultimatum "as obligations toward Europe." Thereby Belgrade would be saving face and the tension would be relieved to the extent that all the great powers would be supervising the concord. San Giuliano added that the Serbian ambassador in Rome had indicated that his government would accept such a solution. But London passed this suggestion on in very lukewarm terms. Paris ignored it, St. Petersburg responded evasively, Berlin urgently supported it, and Vienna silently permitted it to be shelved.

In Vienna, Count Berchtold was firmly resolved not to be intimidated. Since he viewed a punitive expedition as Austria's sole salvation, he was even willing to take a European war into the bargain. On Monday Victor Naumann, a German publicist, came to the Austrian Foreign Ministry to express his fears that a European war was impending. Count Forgatsch, Berchtold's right hand, replied with an unbelievable mixture of indifference and arrogance: "Well, then it will have to come." Berchtold even forbade his ambassador in St. Petersburg to mention the fact that Austria would annex no Serbian territory—although he had told Berlin he would attempt to placate Sazonov by such assurances.

In the course of Monday, July 27, therefore, the situation was more and more coming to a head. The news that the British fleet was alerted stiffened the intransigent mood in St. Petersburg and prompted the Kaiser to order the German fleet, then maneuvering off Norway, to return to Kiel. When Bethmann pleaded with him to refrain from this step, which would alarm the world, he responded irritably but accurately that his "civilian chancellor" had not quite grasped the situation.

The truth was that Berlin did not realize at all what was going on. Foreign Secretary Jagow firmly believed that England would remain neutral; after all, he said, "we have not built our navy for nothing." To further strengthen the British inclination toward neutrality, he proposed threatening the occupation of Holland if England should intervene. He was frankly amazed when Tirpitz explained to him that this "bluff" was the surest way to force England to declare war on Germany. On Monday, when he returned home from his honeymoon "ill, weary, but optimistic," he told the British ambassador that Russia was in no position to fight a war. When he heard that the Russian ambassador had said Russia would never tolerate Austria's swallowing up little Serbia, he merely smiled.

IV

From hour to hour the peril of war had been growing. Now a countermovement began. It was sparked by a man whom the world considered a man of violence, although all who knew him knew that at heart he was extremely peaceable: Wilhelm II. The Kaiser had spent his three-weeks vacation in that high-spirited, cheeky mood to which he succumbed so easily whenever he thought matters would not become serious. In the isolation of the Norwegian fjords, surrounded by men who never dreamed of contradicting His Majesty, he had formed his own picture of the dispute. The Serbs were obviously a pack of bandits whom the venerable Emperor Franz Joseph must punish in order to preserve his honor; it was up to the Emperor to decide the nature and extent of the punishment. British attempts to mediate were nothing but impudence; in "vital questions and questions of honor" one could not submit to the judgment of strangers. The Foreign Office's worries about Italy were "sheer rot," as events would soon show. With his mania for knowing it all, he pooh-poohed the very idea of a European war.

But at bottom Wilhelm was intelligent, as he demonstrated by break-ing off his vacation cruise. When he reached Berlin again on Monday, July 27, he found on his desk a telegram from Prince Lichnowsky. The ambassador had wired that in case of war Germany would find Eng-land on the enemy side; London believed that Serbia had been ex-tremely conciliatory.

Serbia conciliatory? By noon on Monday the Kaiser had not yet seen the Serbian reply which Giessl had received at six o'clock on the pre-ceding Saturday. Berchtold had deliberately neglected to pass the Serbian note on to his ally. He blandly rested his case on the formal-ities of international law; since this was a purely Austro-Serbian affair he would pretend to think that the powers had no reason for taking up the British proposals for mediation. Accordingly, it was not until Mon-day afternoon that the Serbian reply to Austria's ultimatum was trans-mitted to the Foreign Office in Berlin—by the Serbian ambassador. That same afternoon Foreign Secretary Jagow informed the French ambassador that he had not yet had time to read the Serbian note. It was nine-thirty in the evening before the text reached the Kaiser. His Majesty, wearied from the voyage, had unfortunately already gone to bed.

So remote from reality was Jagow that it did not occur to him to intervene and prevent Austria's declaration of war upon Serbia, which Tschirschky had announced for Tuesday. There was an air of tragi-comedy about this declaration, as about so many of the events of those days. Germany had long urged the declaration on the theory that a swift blow struck while the assassination of the Archduke was still a current scandal would diminish the danger of a general European war. But the Austrian army would not be ready for war before August 15. Nevertheless Berchtold favored the declaration in order—as Tschirschky candidly admitted—to make it harder for the other powers to mediate. On Monday chance aided his plans; a report came that Serbian soldiers had fired upon a Danube steamer full of Austrian soldiers. Perhaps this report was deliberately fabricated; at any rate, it came in handy for persuading Franz Joseph to sign the declaration of war. The declaration mentioned this "skirmish" as still another provoc-atory action by Serbia, in addition to her unsatisfactory reply. Franz Joseph signed it. On Tuesday it turned out that no skirmish had taken place. At this, Berchtold struck out the reference to it in the declaration of war; he nevertheless sent out the declaration. To the Emperor he wrote: "In the assumption of subsequent approval by Your Majesty, I have taken it upon myself to eliminate this sentence." And then, as if to make sure that this dire decision would not lack all the attributes of light opera, he sent a telegram to the commander on the Serbian front. Small skirmishes against the Serbs were desirable, the commander was

informed; larger engagements which might turn out badly would be
unwelcome.

This accomplished, Vienna now took up the British proposal that the
Serbian reply be used as the basis for negotiations. Chancellor Bethmann had recommended this proposal to his Austrian ally. Berchtold
answered that England's offer of mediation unfortunately had arrived
too late; war was already declared.

V

But the following morning, Tuesday July 28, Wilhelm read the skillfully couched Serbian reply to the ultimatum. The effect upon him
was astonishing. He forgot all about the Serbs being a pack of bandits,
forgot about the advisability of Austria's teaching them a lesson. Completely mollified, the Kaiser noted on the margin: "A brilliant achievement for a mere forty-eight hours. This is more than we had a right
to expect. It is a great moral victory for Vienna; but it also eliminates
all reason for war. Giessl might as well have remained quietly in Belgrade. I would never have ordered mobilization on the basis of this."

Objectively speaking, this pacifistic outburst on the part of Wilhelm
was as mistaken as his earlier bellicose remarks. The Serbian note was
full of loopholes which obviously escaped the Kaiser's notice. But above
all he should not have forgotten that he had granted the "venerable
Emperor" in Vienna full power to eliminate Serbia as a factor in European politics. From this standpoint, Austria was bound to find the
Serbian reply completely inadequate. But Wilhelm did not trouble himself with such considerations. He sniffed powder in the air, and this
was a smell he did not like. He wanted peace; therefore, at ten o'clock
in the morning, he wrote out detailed instructions to Jagow. Austria's
demands had on the whole been met, he said; Serbia's few reservations
could be settled by negotiation; there was no longer any reason for war.

To these comments the Kaiser added a suggestion which today
strikes us as very strange, but which so well accorded with the views
of the times that Sir Edward Grey quite independently arrived at the
same proposal: Austria needed a tangible pledge that Serbia would
keep her promises; the Austrian army also required some satisfaction
for having been mobilized in vain three times in recent years. Therefore Austria should occupy Belgrade until Serbia kept her promises.

This "tangible-pledge" plan was not without its risks. Serbia had
evacuated Belgrade anyhow, so that an uncontested occupation might
just possibly have been arranged. But this occupation would have been
a lasting source of friction. Other pledges—for example, a guarantee by
the great powers—would have been wiser. But in any case, the Kaiser's
plan did offer a peaceable way out.

Bethmann, Jagow and Tschirschky unfortunately watered down the Kaiser's proposal to such an extent that it was rendered wholly ineffectual. Bethmann in particular took the force out of it by telegraphing Tschirschky: "In communicating this proposal you must carefully avoid arousing the impression that we wish to restrain Austria. It is solely a question of finding a method of realizing Austria-Hungary's aim of putting an end to Greater Serbian propaganda without simultaneously unleashing a world war and, if in the end this cannot be avoided, improving to the best of our ability the conditions under which we will have to wage it."

Considering the mealy-mouthedness of this phraseology, it is no wonder that the proud Viennese noblemen made Bethmann wait sixty hours for an answer.

VI

Meanwhile another question had to be clarified: was Russia going to let the drift into war continue? Chief of Staff Moltke, who was daily receiving information on Russian preparations for war, was obsessed by the fear of delaying German mobilization too long. Toward the military authorities of the other German states, however, he presented a pose of self-confidence, in accordance with military tradition. The Bavarian general reported to Munich, for example: "The chief of staff is using all his influence to see to it that the present uniquely favorable moment for striking is exploited. He points out that France is in a position of military embarrassment, that Russia feels far from secure; moreover, the season is favorable—the harvest for the most part in and the year's group of recruits trained."

However, the decisions did not lie in Moltke's hand; Bethmann held the cards. But did he hold any card against Austria? Prince Lichnowsky reported from London that the Austrian embassy there was discussing the award of Serbian territory to Bulgaria and Albania—thereby countering Austria's assurances that she had no designs against Serbian territorial integrity. The Austrian ambassador in Constantinople was even talking about Austrian interests in Greek territory—remarks which were promptly transmitted to London and undoubtedly from there to St. Petersburg. Bethmann telegraphed Ambassador Tschirschky protesting that Vienna was not keeping Germany informed about the Austrian program. But with his customary timidity he added that these remarks were intended only for Tschirschky's personal orientation.

From London Lichnowsky also reported that Serbia was expected ultimately to "swallow" Articles 5 and 6 of the Austrian ultimatum, the collaboration of Austrian officials in the investigations, and that she was awaiting only certain "clarifications." Grey, the report continued, believed that Austria could "chastise" Serbia without war and with Russian consent, and that she could also obtain guarantees for the future. It seemed essential to Grey that Austrian troops should stop at Belgrade and that Austria should then publish her conditions for ending the conflict. This was the very same proposal that Kaiser Wilhelm had made. At the same time Grey declared that if war came between Germany and France England would be "forced to make rapid decisions." (These were the words Lichnowsky reported to Berlin; Grey afterwards claimed he said "England would be drawn in.") In any case, the phrase alarmed Bethmann; on Wednesday he thrice admonished Tschirschky to demand a response to his "tangible-pledge" proposal, which now had the backing of Grey. He pointed out that in case of war Germany and Austria would be fighting four great powers and resolved to "recommend most emphatically" that Austria accept mediation under the proposed honorable conditions. His telegram to Tschirschky concluded with: "Otherwise the responsibility would be extraordinarily grave." Peace and the happiness of generations would have been saved if Bethmann had added just one sentence: "In case these proposals for mediation are rejected, Germany will no longer consider herself bound to act under the terms of her alliance."

CHAPTER FOURTEEN

The Machinery of Mobilizations

If I had not recognized the necessity for this war, it would not have come about.
—SAZONOV

I

Europe was on the brink. The very same Tuesday on which Wilhelm in Berlin sought to swerve away from war, Sazonov in St. Petersburg came to the conclusion that world war was inevitable. He was worried and uncertain, but he felt that he must make sure Russia did not mobilize too late.

What frightened Sazonov above all was Austria's declaration of war upon Serbia. Obviously Austria wanted to strike before mediation proved possible. And since Russia had assured the Serbs that she would come to their aid, her prestige in the Balkans would suffer unless she acted. Sazonov did not know that the Austrians would be unable to march before August 15; had he known this, he might have waited longer. As it was, he envisioned Austrian flags waving over Belgrade within a few days. Therefore Russia had to fight. He was sure of French assistance. As for England, had not Grey himself recommended Russian mobilization? Undersecretary Sir Arthur Nicolson had written to the British ambassador in St. Petersburg that England could not make any definitive promises to the Russians, but there was little doubt that she would do her duty. The British ambassador had also communicated to Sazonov the Italian plan for having the great powers urge Serbia to accept the whole of the Austrian ultimatum. But Sazonov interpreted this as an understandable attempt on London's part to avert hostilities. If war did come, he felt he could count upon England.

It now seemed to Sazonov essential to order partial mobilization against Austria in order to put pressure upon Vienna. On Wednesday morning Chief of Staff Yanushkevich obtained from the Czar permission for this partial mobilization. With the signature in his pocket he sent for the German military attaché and in the most solemn form gave him his word of honor that "not a reservist has been called up and not a horse levied." Mobilization against Austria had been decided upon, but not yet ordered, he said. He did not mention the order in his pocket, nor that for the past three days the "preparedness period" had secretly been in full force. To Paris he sent word that if the French government were thinking of recommending "moderation," he wished it to be known that he would reject such proposals out of hand. To his relief the Paris embassy replied that the French had "not for a moment considered the possibility of exerting a moderating influence upon St. Petersburg."

On Wednesday afternoon the Austrian ambassador called on Sazonov and informed him that Austria could not discuss the text of the ultimatum. But he also gave assurances that Austria would not demand Serbian territory. Sazonov was too polite to mention the contradictory information he was at the moment receiving from London; he averred that the question at issue was not only Serbia's integrity, but also her sovereignty. The Austrian demands were a violation of Serbian sovereignty; if accepted they would alter the balance of power in the Balkans, and this was something Russia could not permit; she would therefore be compelled to mobilize her southern army corps.

Up to this point the conversation had proceeded quietly enough. Then the telephone rang. Sazonov lifted the receiver and learned that the Austrians had "bombarded" Belgrade. Instantly, the Russian became a different man. So the Austrians were trying only to gain time by negotiations, he said; meanwhile they were shelling a defenseless city. Under such circumstances there was no point in making conversation; the interview was over. In reality the news from Belgrade had been enormously exaggerated. Serbian infantry had fired upon an Austrian Danube steamer. Thereupon several Austrian batteries had shelled Serbian fortifications. No houses were damaged and casualties were few. Two days later—typical Austrian procrastination—Conrad issued orders to the Austrian troops to refrain from all shelling of Belgrade, since it was an open city and Austria did not wish to violate international law.

Misfortunes seldom come singly. An hour later the German ambassador, Count Pourtalès, called upon Sazonov. The telegram he had with him was a new product of Bethmann's fears. With his typical compound of timidity and bluff, the chancellor instructed his ambassador to inform Sazonov that "further continuance" of Russian mobilization would compel Germany to mobilize, and that then a European war could scarcely be averted. The fateful flaw in this telegram was its lack of clarity. Only two days before, the German government had informed the British ambassador that Germany would not mobilize if Russia mobilized only on the Austrian border. Bethmann's newest telegram seemed to say that Germany would not tolerate Russian mobilization on the Austrian border either. That was how Ambassador Pourtalès interpreted it. On his own initiative he added that these words were intended not as a threat, but as a friendly admonishment. But such an admonishment was more than Sazonov could stand. Now he knew, he replied, why Austria was taking so unyielding an attitude. This conversation, too, was cut short.

Not half an hour after Pourtalès left, Sazonov held another conference. This time he talked with Chief of Staff Yanushkevich and the minister of war. Both men had been regarding the war as an accomplished fact since Saturday.

This was the decisive conference in the entire crisis. Partial mobilization against Austria seemed to Sazonov inevitable, if Russia were to exert any pressure at all upon Austria. Now he had received the fateful warning that Russian mobilization against Austria would mean that Germany would mobilize. But German mobilization meant war, for everyone in Europe was aware of the German plan: to counter the numerical superiority of her enemies by overwhelming France before the Russians could carry out their deployment. Therefore, if partial mobilization against Austria were going to start the machinery going, it was obviously wiser to lose no time and order general mobilization at once. Sazonov was so excited that he angrily barked at Yanushkevich: "Why isn't the army mobilized yet; it must move at once toward Vienna." Yanushkevich remained calm and urged immediate full mobilization; partial mobilization would be no good from a military point of view since then the corps on the Austrian frontier would draw reserves from those on the German border. If general mobilization were to be carried out in any case a few days later, it would be slowed up by eight or ten days because of the snarls of partial mobilization. Sazonov rightly said that Yanushkevich should have considered this sooner—but this comment did not affect the validity of the argument. Bethmann's message and the technical considerations both suggested the advisability of general mobilization. The Czar was asked for his approval; naturally he was also assured that general mobilization did not necessarily mean war. Nicholas, always inclined to be swayed by the last person to advise him, consented; after the war Yanushkevich admitted that he knew perfectly well that general mobilization meant war. The die was cast. It was Wednesday afternoon, July 29, 1914.

When the Czar and his foreign minister made this decision, they were acting under the influence of three misconceptions which would not have existed if the European diplomats had done their work somewhat more intelligently. They believed that Austria was on the point of invading Serbia; in reality she would not be ready for two weeks, and there was therefore no need to rush decisions. They believed that Germany would answer partial mobilization with German general mobilization; Bethmann had not made himself clear. And they did not know that Kaiser Wilhelm was acting as peacemaker and had sent his "tangible-pledge" plan to Vienna—a plan similar to Grey's and one which Sazonov would have accepted if there were no other way out. Had they been aware of these three facts, they would not have ordered general mobilization.

The bullet had left the barrel, but Fate interposed her hand and held it for a moment. The chief of the Russian mobilization section, General Dobrorolsky, had secured the necessary signatures from the other ministers immediately after the meeting. The minister of the interior prophesied a revolution, crossed himself, and signed. The navy minister predicted a bombardment of St. Petersburg and put a call in to the war minister to ask whether he really ought to sign. At ten-thirty that night Dobrorolsky went to the telegraph office to send out the fatal telegrams. At this point a staff captain who had chased him through the whole city caught up with him. He had a message from the Czar: to order only partial mobilization on the Austrian border. What had happened?

Providence was using the German Kaiser in one last try at turning the course of history. At 6:40 P.M. Willy had telegraphed his dear Nicky that he was continuing his efforts to bring about a *détente;* military measures would only aggravate the situation. This telegram arrived at 9:40 P.M. It contained nothing new, but the Czar asked his adjutant general, a Baltic count named Frederiks, what he should do. The old man said bluntly: "General mobilization means war!" "I cannot take the responsibility for such frightful slaughter," Nicholas cried out in despair. He promptly telephoned his chief of staff and asked about the state of mobilization. Yanushkevich told a quick-witted lie; it was already in progress, he said. The Czar commanded it to be converted into a partial mobilization against Austria. That would produce tremendous confusion, Yanushkevich declared; he could not take the responsibility for such an order. The conversation lasted half an hour, but the Czar stuck to his guns; he himself would assume the responsibility, he said. Consequently, Dobrorolsky had to send out different telegrams at the last moment. The Czar's fear of war had given Europe a breathing spell. The states of Europe had already come within a hair's breadth of reaching an understanding. Would the breathing spell give them enough time for conciliation?

II

When the sun rose over Europe on Thursday, July 30, everything depended upon Vienna. Would Berchtold insist upon smoking out that Serbian nest of conspirators? Or, in the face of the overwhelmingly superior forces encircling the Hapsburg Monarchy, would he accept the tangible-pledge plan and stop his armies in Belgrade?

On that decisive day German Ambassador Tschirschky was having breakfast with Berchtold when Bethmann's telegram was brought to him, the message pointing out the danger of world war with two great powers fighting four. He waited until breakfast was over, then read Bethmann's telegram aloud twice. Count Berchtold listened "pale and silent," so Tschirschky reported to Berlin. In actuality he was waiting to hear whether the phrase "no longer bound under the terms of the alliance" would be employed. It was not.

Berchtold now had to change and go to the palace for an audience with the Emperor. Not on account of this weak-kneed telegram—the Germans were obviously trying to crawl out—but because he already had an appointment.

Conrad was also present at the audience with His Majesty. The tangible-pledge plan was rejected. It would be impossible to occupy Belgrade by a *coup de main* right now, in the midst of mobilization. "If the Serbs should smash us there, everyone would come down on me," said Conrad, who was naturally concerned about his military reputation. In view of Grey's offer to mediate, an uncontested occupation of Belgrade might have been attained, but this settlement was not even considered. Serbia had to be "subjugated." But suppose Serbia should now accept the entire ultimatum without any reservations. If she should be so servile, Berchtold declared, it would still be insufficient; now that events had gone so far, Serbia would at least have to pay all the costs of the Austrian mobilization. Conrad also thought some territorial concessions necessary. Nor was he modest; he wanted Austria to demand Belgrade and the vicinity. Berchtold pointed out that Count Tisza, the Hungarian premier, had expressly declared he would not have any part in the annexation of Serbian territory. The old Emperor, wiser than the other two, at this point called a halt to the bickering. "They will not accept," he said. It was decided to inform Germany in general terms that acceptance of the ultimatum by Serbia would no longer suffice; Austria's conditions would now "naturally have to read differently."

III

Meanwhile the statesmen in Berlin waited in fear and trembling to see whether Vienna would accept the pledge plan. Berlin could sense the trouble brewing in St. Petersburg. The Czar had meanwhile wired the Kaiser that the tone of his telegrams differed greatly from the messages transmitted by Ambassador Pourtalès. The Kaiser, who probably could not recall Bethmann's ambiguous phraseology, wrote on the margin: "What's this?" At the same time the Czar suggested that the dispute be submitted to the Hague Tribunal. According to the views of those days, such a step was unthinkable; the Hague Tribunal had jurisdiction only in legal questions, primarily in questions of interpretation of international law. To the Kaiser the proposal sounded as if the relatives of a murdered man were being asked to submit their quarrel with the murderer to arbitration, instead of having him turned over to the police. Another telegram from the Czar thanked the Kaiser for his intervention—but contained the unfortunate phrase that the military measures for the defense of Serbia had already been taken five days ago. The Czar had meant to say "decided upon," but the Kaiser was scared stiff; he had been afraid all along that Russia would mobilize secretly. He noted on the margin of the telegram: "I cannot engage in any further attempts at mediation since the Czar who requests it has at the same time been mobilizing secretly behind my back. It is only a maneuver to delay us and increase the advantage he has already won. My efforts must cease."

That evening the Kaiser received a report from Ambassador Pourtalès who had had an hour and a half conversation with Sazonov at midnight. Sazonov had stated that Russia's vital interests could not brook any infringements upon Serbian sovereignty; Germany could easily persuade Vienna to withdraw her humiliating demands. Otherwise war would be inevitable.

The Kaiser was overcome by despair. In his agitation his most deeply submerged emotions came to light: his ambiguous feelings toward England, and especially toward his Uncle Edward. He noted on the ambassador's report: "So the notorious 'encirclement' of Germany has at last become a perfect accomplished fact, in spite of all the efforts of our statesmen and diplomats to prevent it. The net has suddenly been drawn over our heads; sneering, England has brought about a brilliant triumph of her *consistently anti-German international policy*, against which we have proved powerless; she has us threshing *isolated* in the net, has twisted our loyalty to Austria into a noose in order to annihilate us politically and economically. An amazing fact which must arouse admiration even in the victim. Edward VII is stronger after his death than I who am still alive. Now all these machinations must be unsparingly exposed, the mask of Christian peacefulness publicly stripped off; the pharisaical hypocrisy in all the talk about peace must be pilloried! And our consuls in Turkey and India, our spies, etc., must rouse the entire Mohammedan world to savage rebellion against this hateful, mendacious, conscienceless nation of shopkeepers. For if we are to bleed to death, let England at least lose India."

But in a telegram to Franz Joseph he once again recommended acceptance of the pledge plan.

Bethmann was equally in despair. He did not have the psychological stamina for such crises. There was no word from Vienna. From St.

Petersburg partial mobilization was reported, and numerous rumors spoke of Russian preparations along the German border. Moltke demanded that Germany proclaim "a state of imminent danger of war," the preparatory period for mobilization. Bethmann insisted that this measure be postponed. But he no longer saw much hope for peace. In a ministerial council he admitted that all the governments—including Russia—had peaceful intentions, but that they had lost their way and started something which could no longer be stopped.

In all the capitals of Europe the nerves of the statesmen were close to the breaking point. Every hour brought fresh telegrams, demanding fresh decisions. Answers had to be approved by all concerned, then ciphered; they were hours being transmitted, were then deciphered, and were meanwhile overtaken by new events; then there would be more endless consultations and constant vacillation between the fear of war and the fear of mobilizing too late. More than one statesman lost hold of his nerves.

When the Austrian military attaché in Berlin met Moltke by chance on Thursday at noon, he found the German chief of staff perturbed by the Russian partial mobilization against Austria and the rumors of mobilization measures on the German border. Moltke was afraid Russia would suddenly invade Austria while Austria had her troops massed on the Serbian border, with Galicia left defenseless—for the monarchy's eastern corps had not yet been mobilized. Two prolonged cures in Karlsbad had not restored Moltke's health sufficiently for this sickly man to bear up under the terrible responsibility. War was inevitable, he thought, and Austria and Germany must not mobilize too late or they would miss their only chance at winning. He therefore told the military attaché that Austria must also mobilize her eastern corps, in view of the Russian mobilization. Then he added: "Any eventual renewed efforts on the part of England toward preserving the peace are to be rejected." The attaché, reporting this conversation in a telegram to Austrian Chief of Staff Conrad, stated: "Germany will unconditionally go along." Those remarks of Moltke's were more than unfortunate, for they counteracted the efforts of his own government to persuade Austria to be conciliatory.

On Thursday evening Bethmann learned that Vienna had refused to negotiate with Russia about the note to Serbia. He telegraphed this information to Ambassador Tschirschky, adding: "Refusal to exchange views with St. Petersburg would be a grave blunder, since it virtually provokes military intervention by Russia, which Austria-Hungary is primarily interested in averting. We are, of course, ready to meet our obligations under the alliance, but we cannot allow Vienna to draw us frivolously and without regard for our advice into a world conflagration. Please take this matter up with Count Berchtold at once, emphatically, and with utmost seriousness." Here Bethmann came close to speaking the necessary words, but still he did not dare to pronounce them; he should have told the Viennese in no uncertain terms that Germany would not back them if they continued to reject the tangible-pledge plan.

IV

When Bethmann at last went to bed at three o'clock on Friday morning he did not suspect that time itself, that juggernaut, had been running down all his efforts. In St. Petersburg the final decision had been taken on Thursday. After Bethmann's misunderstood communication, Sazonov concluded that Germany would answer the Russian partial mobilization with general mobilization of her own. He was determined not to give the Germans this advantage. The Czar must be made to order the total mobilization which he had cancelled at the last minute on Wednesday because of Wilhelm's telegram. Sazonov too thought the war a certainty and naturally wanted to wage it under the most favorable conditions.

Sazonov's fateful decision is difficult to understand. It was obviously to Russia's interest militarily not to hasten the course of events. What was he risking if he waited for German mobilization? He knew—as did all the statesmen of Europe—that the German war plan provided for an attack upon France and only minor defensive measures on the eastern front. The Austrians had mobilized 480,000 men against Serbia; the Russians had already mobilized 1,100,000 men against the Austrians and were therefore more than their match. Consequently there was no danger attached to waiting. On the contrary, it might have been highly profitable; for weeks Austrian Chief of Staff Conrad had been tortured by the dread that the Russians would wait until an Austro-Serbian conflict was in full swing and strike only after half the Austrian army was deep in Serbia's mountainous territory. It would then take weeks for the Austrians to assemble sufficient troops in Galicia. Meanwhile, the Russians might be at the gates of Vienna. This was Conrad's nightmare, and he therefore implored Berchtold to find out definitely, before the invasion of Serbia began, whether Russia intended to remain neutral. It was curious that the Russians did not exploit this opportunity. Was Sazonov too jumpy to see it, or was he averse to waiting for fear a compromise might be reached—a compromise which would limit Serbian sovereignty and therefore weaken Russia's position in the Balkans?

From Paris came the crafty advice that Russia ought to give Germany assurances that mobilization was being stopped; this would not necessarily hinder her from "continuing her preparations in reality, and even accelerating them." It was a further misfortune that Grey—who was honestly seeking a way out—did not act upon Lichnowsky's request to warn St. Petersburg against general mobilization. Grey was as reluctant to offend Sazonov as Bethmann was to offend Berchtold.

At eleven o'clock on Thursday morning Sazonov and Yanushkevich met. The chief of staff telephoned the Czar and asked him to order full mobilization again. The Czar had not slept for several nights and had made up his mind to put an end to the crisis by sending General Tatischev, Kaiser Wilhelm's Russian adjutant general who happened to be staying in St. Petersburg on leave, to the Kaiser with a personal letter in his own hand. Nicholas therefore sharply rejected the chief of staff's request, and cut the conversation short. Yanushkevich just had time to say that Sazonov was with him in the room and would like permission to say a few words. After a brief pause, during which Europe's fate hung in the balance, the Czar consented to speak to Sazonov. Might he see His Majesty today and report to him on the political situation, Sazonov asked. Nicholas replied that he had not a minute free until three o'clock; Sazonov could come then in the company of General Tatischev. Yanushkevich again impressed the foreign minister with the necessity of having the Czar order general mobilization. Just let him receive the order, Yanushkevich said, and he would smash his telephone so that he could not be reached by a counter-order until mobilization was in full swing.

In his report to the Czar Sazonov painted a picture with broad strokes. The situation had deteriorated, he said; Grey's proposals for mediation had been rejected and Germany was secretly mobilizing; the Czar must order general mobilization at once. Nicholas replied: "That means condemning hundreds of thousands of Russians to death." The day before he had received a letter containing only the words: "Fear God. A mother." Sazonov replied that he must order mobilization if he did not want to abandon Russia to "a miserable existence of dependency upon the Central Powers." He added: "It is better, Your Majesty, to invoke war by our preparations, and to carry these out carefully, than to be surprised by war because we are afraid of furnishing any pretext for it. I feel myself brave enough to take the responsibility for a war which will make Russia stronger than she ever was." The Czar was silent. After a while General Tatischev, who had been present throughout, said sympathetically: "Yes, it is hard to decide." The most experienced psychologist could not have chosen a better phrase to change the Czar's mind. Czar Nicholas could not stand being suspected of lack of resolution. "I shall decide," he replied curtly, and ordered the general mobilization. Sazonov immediately telephoned the order to Yanushkevich, adding: "Now you can smash your telephone." It was four o'clock on Thursday, July 30. General Dobrorolsky hurried off to the telegraph office, and this time no one stopped him.

V

On Friday, July 31, final conferences with Tisza on the Anglo-German pledge proposal were being held in Vienna. The day before the Viennese had been worried that the Germans might try to "crawl out" as Conrad put it. But this concern was now removed by the message from Moltke. When Conrad read out Moltke's advice that British mediation should be rejected, Count Berchtold exclaimed: "That's good! Who is in charge of the government, Moltke or Bethmann?" Berchtold pointed out that a simple occupation of Serbia would be a worthless bagatelle, for the Serbian army would remain intact and in two years another attack might be in prospect. As he put it in his inimitable jargon: "The inveterate view in the Kingdom on the Save that the disintegrating seditious activity of shattering the Hapsburg Empire can be carried through with impunity would only receive fresh nourishment." He was not altogether wrong about this; but it should have been worth taking thought whether rejection of the Anglo-German proposal would not lead to just such a shattering of the Empire. It was by now obvious that rejection meant a European war. Would Austria win this war? The Austrian premier, Count Stürgkh, had observed sadly the day before that Austria did not have the financial resources to wage war simultaneously against Russia and Serbia. But, he continued, the thought of a conference was so "odious" to him that he would not consider engaging in one even for appearance's sake.

Following this highly illogical reasoning, Vienna decided to reject the proposed mediation in as polite a way as possible: Austria would not be disinclined to consider a settlement, but only if Russia reversed her partial mobilization against Austria and if the operation against Serbia continued. In truth it had not yet begun. Austria also declared that she was ready to continue the consultations in St. Petersburg. It was further decided to mobilize the corps on the Russian border. But since it was already Friday, the first day of mobilization was set for the following Tuesday, August 4. Franz Joseph sent a telegram to Wilhelm informing him of this decision and adding: "I am conscious of the import of my decision and have taken it with trust in God's justice."

VI

During the early hours of Friday morning, before dawn, a spy from the Russian town of Kolo came in to see the sergeant of a border garrison in East Prussia and reported that red mobilization posters had been put up in Kolo. The sergeant sent the man back across the border at once with instructions to tear down one poster and bring it to him. When he had the poster on his desk, he telephoned the nearest general headquarters and read the text. Word of the Russian mobilization was thence telephoned to Berlin. Moltke declared that he wished to wait until the red poster reached the general headquarters at Allenstein; decisions of such magnitude could not be made without completely clear documentary evidence. At eleven o'clock Pourtalès confirmed the Russian general mobilization. From that moment on the German generals hourly expected Russian cavalry divisions to come galloping across the border; only swift action could fend off the superior Russian forces, they believed. Bethmann therefore decided to give Russia a twelve-hour ultimatum calling upon her to rescind her mobilization order against Germany and against Austria. Simultaneously the "preparation period" was imposed; it bore the unfortunate label: "State of imminent danger of war."

Since the German war plan envisioned smashing France before the Russian deployment was completed, nine-tenths of the German troops were to be sent into action on the western front. According to the German schedule, they would finish off France by the fortieth day after mobilization, after which the troops would flow back to the east. But suppose France, knowing of this plan, remained neutral for a while in order to give the Russians time to engage the German army? France's intentions had to be ascertained. Consequently, the German ambassador in Paris, von Schön, was ordered to inquire whether France would remain neutral in case of a German-Russian war. There was, however, still the possibility that France would say yes, only to declare war two or three weeks later. The German armies could not stand fully armed on the French frontier while the Russians completed their mobilization. A further condition was therefore made; Schön was instructed to demand as a pledge—if France declared her neutrality—temporary occupation of the forts of Toul and Verdun.

The German general-staff plan also provided for an advance through neutral Belgium because it was believed—probably with good reason— that the belt of fortifications on the French border would give trouble. Therefore an ultimatum had to be sent to Belgium demanding the right of passage.

The German strategic plan was no good at all. The elder General Moltke had always intended, in case of a two-front war, to remain on the defensive against France and to invade Russia. His successor, Schlieffen, took the view that an attack to the east would be fruitless because of the vastness of the Russian spaces—which was also a valid argument. At bottom there was no military solution to the problem.

Germany and feeble Austria were in the long run in no position to cope with a Russo-Franco-British alliance—probably strengthened by the Balkan powers and Italy. The plan of swift deployment and defeating each enemy singly would no longer work; the enemy had seen to that long ago. The French fortifications would slow up an attack in the west, and in the east Russia had prepared for a temporary retreat from Poland. And as would soon be shown, Russian mobilization went forward more rapidly than had been expected.

To repeat: there was no military solution. The problem could be solved only by political means. Germany should never have allowed the entente among her enemies to arise, and once it had been established she should have broken it up even at the cost of great sacrifices.

To make matters worse, the ineffectual strategic plan was also carried out badly. From the moment Russian general mobilization began, the men in Berlin were bent on putting their machinery of mobilization into action. The war itself was considered inevitable. And at this moment nothing was so dangerous as a belief in irrevocable disaster. Even if the German strategic plan were adhered to—and no alternative could be whipped up at this late date—there still remained a few days for negotiation. Germany engaged in her first act of war—the invasion of Belgium—on the morning of August 4. There had been at least three days' leeway. Instead of losing time with a hopeless ultimatum to Russia, the German mobilization should have been announced at once, but at the same time an offer of mediation should have been made—which would almost certainly have been accepted. Neither St. Petersburg nor Paris had rejected the tangible-pledge plan. The day before, Grey had repeated this suggestion, adding that if Austria accepted he hoped he could persuade Russia to cease military preparations. "I would sound out Petrograd whether it would be possible for the four disinterested Powers to offer to Austria that they would undertake to see that she obtained full satisfaction of her demands on Serbia, provided that they did not impair Serbian sovereignty and the integrity of Serbian territory, which she had already declared her willingness to respect. . . . All Powers would, of course, suspend further military operations or preparations." Austria had rejected the plan, but Bethmann could have forced her to accept it if he declared that Germany would have no part in the war which would otherwise ensue. Along with this proposal, Germany should have demanded that all powers immediately call off their mobilizations. The pledge plan would almost certainly have been accepted, which would have been incomparably better for all concerned than the war which all fully realized was now imminent.

Bethmann had all the more reason to take this course because he learned at last, on this Friday morning, that England, too, was ranged against Germany. At ten o'clock in the morning British Ambassador Goschen called upon him to bring him Grey's reply to a "neutrality proposal" which had been submitted to London two days earlier. The chancellor had asked whether England would remain neutral if Germany pledged herself to annex none of France's European territory and to restore the integrity of Belgium after the war. This offer was prompted by a remark King George of England had made a few days before to Prince Heinrich, the Kaiser's brother, to the effect that England would attempt to remain neutral in any European war. Grey rejected the proposal in terms hardly customary in diplomatic intercourse before a declaration of war. Not for a moment, he said, could this suggestion be considered; such an agreement would be an eternal blot against England's good name. In more conciliatory language he added that if this crisis were passed, he would try to bring about an agreement guaranteeing Germany against hostile policies on the part of the Entente Powers. Bethmann, his nerves still shattered by the news of the Russian general mobilization, listened apathetically to Goschen's statement, and asked to have it in writing.

VII

Grey vacillated; Churchill, Nicolson and Crowe did not vacillate at all. Churchill did not absolutely want war—almost with tears in his eyes he had implored Ballin at the end of July: "My dear friend, don't let us go to war." But *if* war came, he accepted British participation as a matter of course. On July 30, five days before the British declaration of war, he ordered his Mediterranean cruisers to fire upon German warships if these attempted to interfere with the transportation of French African troops to the mother country. This was taking the law into his own hands as no admiral in militaristic Germany would have dared to do. He felt that England was morally obligated to come to the aid of France. The fact that the majority of the Cabinet favored neutrality did not disturb this thirty-nine-year-old fire-eater. He knew that the pro-war group—Grey, Haldane and himself—was far stronger than a dozen friends of peace.

At first, however, the Cabinet rejected his recommendation that England begin mobilizing. Lloyd George declared that all business circles were horrified by the thought of war; the money market was in such a panic that the discount rate had to be raised from 4% to 8%. The Cabinet was firmly resolved upon neutrality. But Sir Eyre Crowe once more took up his pen: "The theory that England cannot engage in a big war means her abdication as an independent State. . . . A balance of power cannot be maintained by a State that is incapable of fighting and consequently carries no weight. . . . I venture to think that the contention that England cannot in any circumstances go to war is not true, and that any endorsement of it would be an act of political suicide." These remarks were elementary and could at most surprise the dreamers in the Cabinet. But Crowe added practical conclusions: "The whole policy of the *Entente* can have no meaning if it does not signify that in a just quarrel England would stand by her friends. This honourable expectation has been raised. We cannot repudiate it without exposing our good name to grave criticisms. . . . I feel confident that our duty and our interest will be seen to lie in standing by France in her hour of need."

On Friday afternoon Russian general mobilization—the Russians had kept back the news—and the German ultimatum to Russia were reported simultaneously. Crowe knew what he had to do. Boldly falsifying, he informed Grey that Germany had given Russia a time limit of twelve hours for demobilization, and that Russia had responded with general mobilization. Sir Arthur Nicolson declared that Russia's precautions were eminently prudent and in no sense provocative—an astonishing verdict upon a measure which both Russians and French knew would necessarily start a world war. Grey continued to answer Cambon equivocally; the Belgian question would be crucial, he said. Cambon understood, however, and wired Paris that Grey favored immediate intervention. The Russian ambassador also recognized clearly that Grey was for participation in the war while England as a whole was still against it; he let St. Petersburg know by telegram that British public opinion still had to be prepared for war. Three years before he had reported to St. Petersburg that the German plan for marching through Belgium had, according to Grey, one great advantage for the Entente: it would stir the indignation of the entire British public, whom otherwise it would be difficult to arouse to favor war.

VIII

In Paris, Cambon's wire gave great satisfaction. Poincaré had meanwhile returned home and was inspiring everyone with vigor and confidence. France and Russia alone could easily trounce Germany, he had told Izvolsky some weeks before. He had already telegraphed to St. Petersburg: "The pending negotiations still allow room for hope that peace can be preserved. In my opinion it would therefore be worthwhile if Russia, in pursuing the measures of preparedness and defense which she believes are required, were to take no direct step which would provide Germany with a pretext for whole or partial mobilization of her forces." (In his *Memoirs* Poincaré contrived to omit the words "which would provide Germany with a pretext"; thus the passage indicated that France had advised Russia against partial or total mobilization. Certainly this was one of the boldest expurgations in the entire literature of the war.) Simultaneously, the Russian military attaché in Paris reported to St. Petersburg that Paris was manifesting "unconcealed joy at the opportunity to exploit the favorable strategic situation." The French generals had the same ideas as German Chief of Staff Moltke.

On Friday, July 31, Ambassador Schön transmitted the German demand that France state within twenty-four hours what attitude she would take in case of a war between Germany and Russia. The French at once wired to St. Petersburg that their reply would be that they intended to consult their interests. The Russian military attaché sent the following bulletin: "The French war minister informed me in a vivacious, cordial tone that the government was firmly resolved upon war and asked me to confirm the hope of the French general staff that all our efforts would be directed against Germany and that Austria would be treated as a *quantité negligeable*." This message was sent out on August 1 at one o'clock in the morning—sixteen hours before the German declaration of war upon Russia and two and a half days before the German declaration of war upon France.

The French government saw one great obstacle in its path: the Socialist leader Jean Jaurès. Jaurès was an idealist; in daily life he was incapable of taking the right tram, but on the platform he was an inspired orator. He had spoken openly against the war, averring that the French nation recognized only one kind of treaty: the pact with humanitarianism. A few days earlier, when Izvolsky came from a consultation with the French ministers, Jaurès had shouted: "There goes the warmonger." The Russian ambassador had pretended not to hear, but his monocle had slipped from his eye. Jaurès had threatened to publish his material on the part Izvolsky had played in Poincaré's election campaign. "We shall tell the people the truth even if we are shot down on the next street-corner!" he announced. Two hours later he was actually shot down by an irresponsible acting on someone else's order—perhaps Izvolsky's. The trial was deferred until after the end of the war, and the murderer was then pronounced not guilty.

CHAPTER FIFTEEN

The Lamps Go Out

> *In the European card game we must keep the deal and not allow ourselves to be forced, by impatience, complaisance, vanity or the provocation of our friends, from the phase of waiting into the phase of premature action.*
>
> —BISMARCK

I

Late Friday evening Lichnowsky received a report from Chancellor Bethmann on Russia's mobilization and Germany's ultimatum to Russia. Lichnowsky sent this telegram to Prime Minister Asquith, since Grey could not be located. Asquith promptly drafted a telegram for King George to send to the Czar. He did not know that Grey had advised the Russians to mobilize five days earlier. King George had already gone to sleep, but he got up and received the prime minister in his night clothes at two o'clock in the morning. The telegram was sent off. It read: "I cannot help thinking that some misunderstanding has produced this deadlock. . . . I therefore make a personal appeal to you to remove the misapprehension . . . and to leave still open grounds for negotiation and possible peace." Next morning Grey was hardly pleased by this interference with his particular province. Meanwhile the French were reporting attacks by German troops—the fictitious atrocity stories which always spring up in such circumstances.

When Grey arrived at his office on Saturday morning, he found awaiting him replies from Germany and France to an inquiry he had addressed to them regarding Belgian neutrality. France promised to respect it; Germany answered evasively. Count Berchtold wired that Austria was ready to accept British mediation in regard to Serbia. But this was couched in so indefinite a form that it was worthless; in reality Austria intended not to yield a single point of her demands. Grey disregarded the message from Berchtold; he was busy with a new project, the origin of which is uncertain. Perhaps it had been conceived during the nocturnal conversation between the King and Asquith. The plan was alarmingly simple: France was to remain permanently neutral while Russia and Germany fought it out. Then England would have no cause to intervene and could sit by and watch her two principal rivals draw each other's fangs. It was a game England had been proficient at for centuries. German Ambassador Lichnowsky assured Grey that in such a case Germany would certainly not attack France. On a purely formal basis, the idea was possible. According to the terms of the Franco-Russian alliance, France was obligated to help Russia only in case of German aggression. Since Russia had mobilized first, the question of who was the aggressor was at least debatable. But in reality the formal aspect of the situation was meaningless, for it would have meant that France was abandoning all her previous policy and surrendering all hope for Alsace-Lorraine. Such a shift in French policy was inconceivable. Nevertheless, Lichnowsky enthusiastically wired Berlin of this new turn of affairs.

At noon there was another Cabinet meeting in London. John Morley pointed out that a victory of Russia would endanger England's interests in Asia, and that the British people were scarcely prepared to accept the Czar's cossacks as comrades in a struggle for freedom and justice. The Cabinet again rejected Churchill's recommendation of immediate mobilization and decided to caution Germany about Belgium, but for the present to make no decision. After the meeting Morley clapped the First Lord of the Admiralty on the shoulder, saying: "Winston, we have beaten you after all." Churchill merely smiled—prophetically. For the rest, he sent instructions to the navy which were tantamount to mobilization orders.

Grey had the ungrateful task of informing French Ambassador Cambon of the Cabinet's indecision. Cambon refused to transmit this reply to his government. Bitterly, he remarked that because of the Anglo-French naval agreement the French coasts were undefended. Grey, who throughout this talk had to deny his own convictions, said he "would ask the Cabinet to consider this point about the French coasts." By way of consolation he added that this question and the question of Belgian neutrality might alter public feeling in England. The conversation was a shock to Cambon; distraught, he stumbled into Sir Arthur Nicolson's room. Sir Arthur took his friend's hand and led him to a seat. Cambon could only repeat again and again: *"Ils vont nous lâcher"* (They are going to abandon us). After Cambon had recovered somewhat, Nicolson went to see Grey. Sir Edward was pacing back and forth in the room, despair written all over his face. His undersecretary of state asked him whether England had really refused to aid France in her dire need. Grey was unable to speak; he merely made a gesture of desperation. "You will render us . . . a by-word among nations!" Nicolson cried in horror. He left his superior and returned to Cambon. The ambassador had meanwhile regained his composure somewhat. To the foreign editor of the *Times* who had happened into the room and asked what he was doing here, he replied: "I am waiting to find out whether the word 'honor' has been struck out of the English dictionary." To Nicolson he remarked that he would now produce "his little paper"; he meant the letter of 1912. Nicolson advised him against doing so officially, for he knew that this "little paper" was Grey's sorest spot.

Grey was in truth in a desperate predicament. He had to prevail on the Cabinet and Parliament to keep a promise whose existence he must simultaneously deny. Was England obligated to help France legally, morally, or merely as a consequence of existing agreements? That was the core of the problem which Grey did not dare to touch because he had a guilty conscience. He hoped to tack around it by arguing that England's burning immediate interests, not ancient agreements, demanded that she take France's side. Upon the question of Belgium he was pinning his hopes of securing England's intervention.

The conversations with Cambon and Nicolson had been a fearful trial for Grey. Now came another. No sooner was Sir Arthur out of the room than German Ambassador Lichnowsky appeared. Grey read to him the Cabinet's warning: that Germany must not violate Belgian neutrality. Lichnowsky responded with an adroit question—whether, if Germany gave a promise not to violate Belgian neutrality, England would engage to remain neutral. As a matter of fact, only a person as ignorant of the general situation as Lichnowsky would have dared to pose such a question. If Sir Edward answered yes, Germany would have been in a fix, for the German General Staff would not have discarded its sole war plan even at the price of British neutrality. But Grey, inwardly resolved to persuade the Cabinet to agree to England's participation in the war, answered that England would make no promises. Lichnowsky promptly went a step further; he pressed Grey to formulate conditions under which England would remain neutral. Sir Edward replied that England must keep her hands free. Lichnowsky made a great mistake in not communicating this conversation to the British press at once; had he done so, public opinion would have been rallied to his side. On the margin of the report of this conversation the Kaiser noted: "So they are deceitful scoundrels!"

II

In Berlin, meanwhile, it had been learned that Ambassador Pourtalès had delivered the twelve-hour ultimatum to Sazonov at midnight; the time limit would therefore be up at noon on Saturday, August 1. Chancellor Bethmann had become obsessed with the strange notion that he must transmit the declaration of war to St. Petersburg on that same day. War Minister Falkenhayn, Chief of Staff Moltke and Admiral

Tirpitz—all the chief military men, that is—were opposed to the declaration of war. They pointed out that for the present no military operations against Russia could be undertaken and that there was therefore no point in Germany's incurring the grave stigma of having declared war first. But Bethmann saw the whole matter in purely legalistic terms; if he did not have a war with Russia, he could not declare war on France, and without a declaration of war against France he could not deliver the ultimatum to Belgium—which was slated for the following day. These arguments were ridiculous. The demands made on Belgium were aggression under international law, whether based upon an existing or only a threatening war with France. A fine point like this could not justify the Belgium ultimatum and by no means outweighed the tremendous disadvantage of Germany's sending out two declarations of war.

Notwithstanding his agitation, it is hard to believe that Bethmann overlooked this point. Probably he was most strongly influenced by another fear, for when Ballin asked him brashly why he was in such a damned hurry about the declaration of war against Russia, he replied that without a war against the Czar he could not win the support of the Social Democrats. This was a wretched argument indeed. Throughout this period Bethmann was apparently fretting over his forthcoming *Reichstag* speech justifying the war.

In any case, the protests from the military men came too late. At noon the Kaiser and Bethmann, without consulting anyone else, had sent instructions to Ambassador Pourtalès to transmit the declaration of war unless Russia agreed to demobilization. On the other hand, Bethmann temporized for five hours before applying to the Kaiser for the German mobilization order. Such wavering was typical of him. To him, the prime urgency was to clarify the legal situation rather than to do what was necessary in the real world. The mobilization order was not sent out until five o'clock in the afternoon.

A few minutes later came Lichnowsky's telegram detailing Grey's proposal of the morning that France should remain neutral. Kaiser Wilhelm was delighted. This happy outcome was obviously the result of his firm attitude. If France were really to remain neutral, the German army need not deploy in the west; it could confine its operations to the east. Moltke shuddered. Since 1911 deployment in the east had not been discussed or planned for by the general staff. Could this omission be rectified by improvisation now? It seemed hardly likely. The chief of staff declared that Grey's proposal was only a feint. Change the deployment plans, he said, and the Kaiser would possess not an army ready to strike, but a loose horde of armed men without supplies. Angrily but accurately the Kaiser exclaimed: "Your uncle would have given me a different answer."

Admiral Tirpitz alone kept his head; he was in fact the only strong man in this group of weak personalities. With calm and statesmanlike authority he declared that whether or not Grey's suggestion was a bluff, it could not be rejected out of hand, for if it were then published, Germany would be placed in the wrong. It was therefore decided to accede to the British proposal if England could guarantee France's neutrality. The declaration of war against France and the ultimatum to Belgium were temporarily shelved. If French neutrality were secured, the army would deploy as planned in the west and would then be shifted to the east. Chief of Staff Moltke went home and suffered a nervous collapse.

Only a few hours later this gleam of hope vanished. Grey had meanwhile got in touch with his ambassador in Paris; the ambassador declared that French neutrality was inconceivable. In response to a telegram from the Kaiser King George replied that there must be some misunderstanding. That night the Kaiser sent for Moltke and told him irritably that he could carry out the deployment as he pleased.

In the meanwhile Bethmann was waiting for news from St. Petersburg. Was Germany at war with Russia or not? The Kaiser once more telegraphed the Czar asking him to accept the German ultimatum and warning him against violations of the German frontier. The warning was somewhat out of order, for by this time the German ambassador, according to the Kaiser's own instructions, should already have delivered the declaration of war.

III

In St. Petersburg Pourtalès waited restlessly in his embassy for the Russian reply to the ultimatum. It should have arrived by noon on Saturday. It did not come. Instead, at six o'clock on Saturday there came instructions from Berlin for him to deliver the declaration of war at five o'clock. The declaration contained two alternate passages —one for the eventuality that Russia rejected the ultimatum, the other if she had not replied to it. At seven o'clock Pourtalès handed the note to Sazonov—in his stress he had failed to delete the alternate passage. Unable to speak, he went to the window and burst into tears. Sazonov embraced and kissed him, and assured him: "Believe me, we will see each other again." Pourtalès asked for his passports; Sazonov was so confused that he did not grasp the meaning of this request. Pourtalès had already made arrangements for his departure; with unsteady footsteps, he left the room. He telegraphed to Berlin his transmission of the declaration of war, but the telegram never arrived. Five hours later the Czar received the Kaiser's telegram warning him against crossing the frontier. Sazonov telephoned Pourtalès to ask what this meant, in view of the existing state of war. Pourtalès said he did not know; he would ask Berlin and request that the reply be transmitted through the Italian embassy. Then he left Russia.

The other appeal to the Czar, from King George, had also been in vain; the King need not have risen from bed at two in the morning. Nicholas replied that he had been compelled to order general mobilization by Austria's mobilization, her bombardment of Belgrade, her concentration of troops in Galicia, and by Germany's secret military preparations. None of these four "causes" had existed before the Russian mobilization. The Czar had been fed with lies by his own ministers.

In Paris, meanwhile, Poincaré had made up his mind that "France will not let war be declared upon her"; he insisted that France herself must declare war. His ministers were wiser than he and firmly vetoed this idea. The foremost concern of the French government was whether England would support France. In order to give London the impression of peaceable intentions, the French troops were instructed to halt ten kilometers before the frontiers, so that clashes would be avoided. Since most of the fortifications were ten kilometers from the borders and since in some cases the order was not obeyed or armed customs officials were sent ahead of the lines as scouts, this was an adroit move—impressive and without significance. On August 2, when the French gathered that they could count on England's assistance, the ban was lifted—twenty-four hours before the declaration of war. Paris, moreover, reported to London that 20,000 Germans had crossed the border near Nancy without previous declaration of war. This was a fabrication which made a great impression upon the British war party. But then, in Paris, too, everyone was in a state of nerves. The naval minister forgot to carry out Poincaré's order to patrol the Channel against torpedo boats. The war minister went into a rage and gripped him by the throat, at which the naval minister challenged his colleague to a duel. Poincaré had to separate the disputants and the scene ended in tears, embraces and the resignation of the naval minister.

IV

On Sunday evening the German ambassador in Brussels had received Germany's twelve-hour ultimatum to Belgium. It demanded the right of passage for German troops on the ground that, according to reliable reports, French troops intended to march into Belgium. If Belgium would adopt an attitude of benevolent neutrality, Germany would withdraw immediately after the war and pay the country compensation. In point of fact the French plan did not now envision an invasion through Belgium. Belgium was determined to defend her neutrality from attacks on all sides. She therefore flatly rejected the ultimatum. Many Belgians doubted that the Germans really intended to invade, since such an invasion would probably bring in its train a British declaration of war. Perhaps the ultimatum was only a feint intended to draw French troops to the north. Or perhaps the Germans hoped to induce the French to invade Belgium in order to engender a conflict between France and Belgium.

On the morning of August 4, however, Germany settled these doubts. She informed Belgium that she now unfortunately found it necessary to carry out her previously announced security measures. Only then did Belgium ask England for aid and take up contact with the French army. France was not surprised; the possibility of a German march through Belgium had been considered in French war games ever since 1878, whereas Germany had not adopted the plan until the turn of the century. The British general staff had rehearsed a possible German invasion of Belgium in 1905. The Schlieffen plan had been betrayed ten years earlier by a German army officer who called himself *Le Vengeur*—not that his idealism stopped him from accepting money. French mobilization, which General Joffre had been vehemently urging for days, was finally approved at four o'clock on August 1, one hour before the German mobilization.

On August 3, Berlin decided upon a declaration of war against France. By then reports had come in that French patrols had crossed the border and French aviators flown over with bombs destined for railroad lines near Nuremburg and Karlsruhe. These reports, too, were for the most part fabricated. The general staff foolishly cited these as grounds for the declaration of war which was of course being made because of the Russo-French alliance.

The telegram to Ambassador Schön containing the text of the declaration of war arrived in completely garbled form on the afternoon of August 3. With great difficulty Schön managed to draw up a passable text, and with deep emotion handed it to French Premier Viviani. The premier icily denied the charges of French violations of German territory; sick though he was from jaundice, he politely saw Schön to his car. The only person who was really pleased was Russian Ambassador Izvolsky, who exclaimed gaily: "Congratulate me; now my little war is beginning. It took me only four years at my post to attain my goal." Izvolsky died soon after the end of the war, completely impoverished; he had been living in Southern France on a small French pension.

V

On Sunday morning London still seemed peaceful. Asquith received Lichnowsky and said to him with tears in his eyes: "A war between our countries is wholly unthinkable." Reporting this statement to Berlin, the ambassador added that at present there was not the slightest intention upon England's part to declare war on Germany. In actual fact the war party gathered around Nicolson, Crowe and Churchill had already launched their counter-offensive against the neutralists. Their fieriest member was Field Marshal Wilson, whose role in Britain was similar to that of Yanushkevich, Moltke and Conrad in the other capitals of Europe. Wilson prompted the Conservative Opposition to send a message to Asquith declaring that they were in favor of supporting France whether or not Belgian neutrality were violated. Wilson also relayed the hint to Cambon that he ought to threaten Grey with a rupture of relations—a suggestion highly embarrassing to Grey, since such an act would have shown the House that France believed she had reason to count on British aid. When Grey learned of the German declaration of war upon Russia, he decided to inform Cambon that England would not permit the German fleet to enter the Channel. Such was the state of tension that for the first time in British history the Cabinet met on Sunday. It approved, subject to the consent of the House of Commons, Grey's assurance that the French northern coast would be protected. But uncertainty still prevailed; Churchill told Balfour, the leader of the Conservative Party, that he was under the impression that half the Cabinet would resign if war against Germany were declared. In that case, Balfour replied, the Conservatives would form a coalition government with the remaining Liberals.

At the same time, public opinion was gradually turning against Germany. News of the German declaration of war upon Russia, of the alleged invasion of France by 20,000 men, and of the threatened violation of Belgian neutrality, was beginning to have its effect. The French and British press did not indicate that German mobilization had taken place only after the Russian mobilization.

On Monday morning, Morley, Burns, and two other ministers tearfully announced their resignations on the grounds that the Cabinet was headed toward war. Had Lloyd George joined them, it would have meant a Cabinet crisis, with a majority of the ministers opposed to entry into the war. The Cabinet then decided to do nothing until the House met in the afternoon. Even at this late date one of the most respected newspapers in England, the *Manchester Guardian,* was warning against support for Serbia, a country of the blackest reputation. It was difficult to tell which way public opinion was swinging.

The decision in the House now depended upon Grey's speech. And this speech was a masterpiece. Grey still maintained that England's hand was free; he knew the House would not receive kindly any news of obligations undertaken behind its back. He wisely concealed the fact that the exposure of the French northern coast rested upon an agreement between the French and British Admiralties. He read out his letter to Cambon of 1912, but suppressed the last sentence which mentioned the discussions to be held between the general staffs. He then reported the Belgian King's appeal to England, and stressed the fact that Belgium's independence, as well as Holland's, would be lost if the Germans were victorious. If France were "on her knees," he said, Europe would be subject to a single power. To remain neutral, in view of the letter he had just read, England would forfeit her good name and her prestige throughout the world—in saying this Grey was tacitly admitting the existing obligations. On the other hand, she would suffer no more by participation in the war than she would by standing aside.

The entire House, with the exception of the Socialist Ramsay Mac-donald, responded with tumultuous applause.

Still the Cabinet postponed the declaration of war and the commitment of an expeditionary force—dilatoriness that brought on an outburst of tears from Field Marshal Wilson. Instead, on Tuesday, August 4, Grey sent an ultimatum to Germany demanding assurance by midnight that Germany would respect Belgian neutrality. Grey was suffering fearfully from the weight of his responsibility; he told Walter Page, the American ambassador, that he felt like a man who had wasted his life.

All through the week the British ambassador in Berlin, Sir Edward Goschen, had been emphasizing to Grey Chancellor Bethmann's peacefulness. As late as August 1, after the German declaration of war against Russia, he still did not believe there would be war between England and Germany. He had even sent a letter to England deploring the fact that German mobilization was stripping his entire household of servants; he would probably have to get along with only his British valet and his Swiss second cook. Now he was confronted with a somewhat larger tragedy. Bethmann was dreadfully wrought up when Goschen brought him the ultimatum, which amounted to the declaration of war. When Goschen continued to insist that the violation of Belgian neutrality was the reason for the war, Bethmann lost his patience. Was Great Britain to "make war on a kindred nation who desired nothing better than to be friends with her," just for a scrap of paper? His entire policy had "tumbled down like a house of cards," he said. Goschen argued with him, but he, too, was in such a state that he asked permission to remain in the anteroom for a short while; he could not show himself to the staff of the chancellery in his present condition, he said. In the *Reichstag* on the following day, however, even Bethmann referred to the invasion of Belgium as an "injustice" and could only vindicate it by saying that this was a case of necessity knowing no law. Such admissions are hardly common in political life; only a legalistic, bureaucratic personality would have given his enemies such an opening.

Bethmann offered to resign, but the Kaiser told him: "You have got me into this mess; now you'll have to stew in it." A strange decision, for if Bethmann's indecision had helped to bring about the war—as it had—there was every reason to replace him by a more forceful and capable chancellor. Bethmann himself was well aware of his guilt. A few months after the outbreak of the war he said: "We have our share of the responsibility for this war. To say that this thought depresses me would be to fall short of the truth. The idea obsesses me; I live with it all the time." Grey felt much the same way. He was convinced that he had dragged England into the war when the public and the other ministers of his government could not come to any decision. In his memoirs, which contain more deliberate untruths than those of the other statesmen, it is easy to see how painfully Grey was struggling with his conscience. The rest of his life was sad; during the war he resigned, and lost his sight.

CHAPTER SIXTEEN

Whose Was the Guilt?

The nations slithered over the brink into the boiling cauldron of war. Amongst the rulers and statesmen who alone could give the final word which caused great armies to spring from the ground and march to and across frontiers, one can see now clearly that not one of them wanted war. Had there been a Bismarck in Germany, a Palmerston or a Disraeli in Britain, a Roosevelt in America, or a Clemenceau in authority in Paris, the catastrophe might, and I believe would, have been averted; but there was no one of that quality visible on the bridge in any great State.

—LLOYD GEORGE

Whose was the guilt for the First World War? The question is far more complex than the quick verdicts of politicians would indicate. No government wanted the war! Yet every one of the participating states was resolved upon a world war sooner than surrender certain aims. These aims were:

For Serbia: wresting the South Slavic areas from the Austro-Hungarian Monarchy.

For Austria: subjugating Serbia in order to prevent such dismemberment.

For Russia: preventing any lessening of Russian influence in the Balkans.

For France: standing by her Russian ally, since all hope for the recovery of Alsace-Lorraine rested upon the alliance with Russia.

For England: standing by her allies France and Russia, who were the only powers on the Continent capable of checking Germany.

For Germany: standing by her ally Austria-Hungary, who was her sole support in the world.

In order to place the "war guilt" we must therefore decide whether these aims were "morally" justified. In regard to the Austro-Serbian dispute it may be said that the Serbs were within their rights in wishing to unite all South Slavs under the scepter of Black George's dynasty. To which the reply is possible: the welfare of the South Slavs who belonged to the Austro-Hungarian monarchy was far more secure within that prosperous and cultivated state than out of it; the majority of those South Slavs wanted no part of Serbia.

If we wish to examine these problems rationally, we must free ourselves of the notion that any country began the war for "idealistic" aims. Idealistic aims have never mattered a farthing to any state; it is, moreover, improbable that any people would empower their government to fight for anything but their own interests. Serbia was not fighting for the "liberation" of her brother Slavs, but for Serbian territorial aggrandizement. Russia was not concerned with the "small Slavic countries," but with her power position in the Balkans. England was not defending "international law" which had been infringed by the violation of Belgian neutrality; she was fighting for the maintenance of her own power in Europe.

As the result of such considerations many persons will conclude that no "aims" justify a war, that the only just war is a purely defensive one. But in that case it can be said that Austria-Hungary desired only the preservation of the Hapsburg monarchy, while Russia and Serbia sought its destruction and were therefore the aggressors. Also, the destruction of Austria-Hungary would give Russia the chance for further expansion; she would be free to take Constantinople. Only two countries in Europe had designs for conquest: Russia and her ally France. From this point of view, the scales fall in favor of the Central Powers. British and American historians have admitted that Austria was fighting for her self-preservation and Russia for her prestige. Harry Elmer Barnes comments in his *The Genesis of the World War:*

"American readers can perhaps get some of the Austrian feeling by imagining the attitude of the United States if Theodore Roosevelt and his wife had been assassinated at El Paso, Texas, on July 4, 1901, while watching a review of the Rough Riders, their assassins having been members of a notorious Mexican secret society which had plotted for years against the United States, with the Mexican papers acclaiming the assassination as a noble and heroic act. There is little probability that under these circumstances the United States would have delayed even long enough to send an ultimatum to Mexico. In all probability American military forces would have been rushed into Mexico without any formal diplomatic exchanges whatever."

From the moral point of view the conduct of every one of the participating countries must be condemned. They all allowed themselves to be guided exclusively by what they supposed to be self-interest; they were out to achieve their aims no matter whether it meant war. This attitude is not surprising; it is inevitable as long as the disputes among nations are not decided by some international authority which has at its beck and call sufficient physical power to enforce its decisions. What is astonishing is that none of the governments concerned clearly realized that they were all drifting into a world war. Each of the five great powers might have avoided war if it had behaved a bit more prudently. World war broke out in 1914 not because the heads of state were especially belligerent, but because they were extraordinarily unskillful.

Russia was the most expansionist of the great powers. She was willing to make war for Constantinople; she had promised Serbia Austrian territory and regarded the dismantling of the Hapsburg monarchy as essential. But she was militarily unprepared; she hoped to be able to play for time. In two years she expected to be able to enforce sweeping changes in her favor. For this reason she would have preferred peace in 1914. But Sazonov's nerve failed. Against Russia's true military interests he first ordered partial mobilization and then, from sheer panic and fully knowing it meant war, he went ahead with a general mobilization. Yet war was necessarily far more perilous to the Czarist government than the Anglo-German compromise proposal could have been.

Austria-Hungary had formed the natural but misguided plan of putting an end to the Serbian nuisance by waging war upon that country. War was hardly the best way to go about achieving such a purpose, but Austria insisted on carrying through her plan, even when it became certain that a world war would result, and even though many Austrian statesmen thought world war might very easily mean the end of the Austrian Empire.

France assured the Russians unconditional aid, thereby encouraging them to commit follies. France was desperately afraid of losing her Russian ally if she recommended moderation, and hoped, moreover, that war would enable her to regain Alsace-Lorraine.

Germany was far from wanting the war, or even preparing for it. Her military collaboration with Austria had been conducted on so tenuous a basis that, for example, as late as July 22 Conrad refused to inform the Germans which army corps he intended to mobilize against Serbia—whereas England and France had worked out joint deployment plans. In 1919, when the Socialist Kautsky was sent into the German Foreign Office in order to obtain proof of the imperial government's war guilt, he reported dispiritedly: "I was very surprised after looking into the documents. My original view proved to be untenable. Germany did not deliberately work to bring about the World War. At the end she tried to avert it."

For decades Germany had not made use of favorable opportunities for a preventive war. She had sought no spoils, whereas her opponents had hanging from their belts the scalps of Transvaal, Egypt, Morocco, Tripolitania and Korea. Germany had looked on while the world was

being divided up. She had been loud-mouthed, but timid and conciliatory in action. Finally, Germany did not even believe that she
would win, and certainly could not have wanted a war whose outcome
both the Kaiser and the chancellor thought highly dubious. Even in
the summer of 1914 Berlin's policy was that of a sheep in wolf's clothing. The Kaiser gave to Vienna the same blank check that Poincaré
had given St. Petersburg. The Germans left to the Austrians the terms
of their ultimatum, and although at the last minute Germany made a
sensible attempt to arbitrate, she never clearly said that she would
withdraw her support if arbitration were not accepted. When the
Russians mobilized, the Germans lost their heads. In short, they took
precisely the course calculated to brand them in the eyes of the world
as solely responsible for the war. They misjudged the whole situation,
misunderstood the true state of Russia's and France's preparedness for
war, and pinned their hopes on the frail fantasy that the newly
founded Anglo-German friendship would prove stronger than England's traditional interests. Finally, overwhelmed by harsh reality, the
Germans sank into a morass of resignation. Their whole foreign policy
had been one of blunder; they staggered into war not out of belliger-
ency, but out of folly.

And *England?* Grey might have averted war if immediately after
the Serbian reply he had told the German ambassador: "If there should
be a war between Germany and France, I shall come out in favor of
supporting our allies, and I have reason to believe that a section of my
own party and all the Conservatives will be of my opinion. If you
should trample on Belgian neutrality—and it has been rumored for the
past eight years that you intend to—this probability will become a
virtual certainty. As you know, I cannot make any binding commitments without Parliament, but I shall resign if England does not stand
by her friends." Had this happened, Bethmann would certainly have
played his lone trump and forced Vienna, by threatening to abandon
her, to accept the Anglo-German compromise. The crisis would then
have passed peacefully and without having exposed the Central Powers to any danger.

The situation demanded of Grey only one thing: forthright language.
He did not speak forthrightly. On the one hand he proposed a compromise that went a long way toward meeting Austria's demands. On
the other hand he encouraged Russia to mobilize. It has been supposed
that he intended from the first to have Bethmann rush headlong into
the trap. But this supposition is wrong. Grey's policy was equivocal
because he was the prisoner of promises he had made to the French
behind the back of Parliament, and in part also behind the back of his
own Cabinet. He was bound to France by obligations of honor, but he
had to deny the existence of these obligations while at the same time

persuading Parliament and a reluctant Cabinet to meet them. To him it seemed natural that England must not forsake her allies—neither Russia, for the sake of England's Asiatic interests, nor France, for the sake of the European balance of power. Of all the statesmen of Europe Grey had, as he stumbled into the war, the interests of his own country best in view. But he was concerned entirely with England's political power; that commercial rivalry with Germany played a part in England's decision is sheer legend. In general, economic questions had nothing to do with the outbreak of the war.

All the countries of Europe were responsible by their folly for the outbreak of the war. To assign each its share of guilt is difficult. Perhaps the most accurate formulation is the famous comment of the French historian Fabre-Luce: "By their actions Germany and Austria made the war possible; the Triple Entente by their actions made it inevitable."

The tragedy of 1914 shows how difficult it is to grasp historical events in legalistic and moral terms. Luther wrote: "Law is a lovely bride when she remains in her bed. But when she climbs into another bed and would rule theology, then she is a great harlot." What is true of theology is true of history. The problem of 1914 is not one of law or morality; it is a problem of incompetent statesmanship.

Statesmen and historians both have pointed out that this war would never have occurred if some of the posts in European governments had been held by other men. Lloyd George, in the passage quoted at the beginning of this chapter, has listed men who were famous not for their peacefulness, but for their energy. Certainly not every century can be expected to produce a Bismarck. But other men would have sufficed, men who had only lately been at the helm, or were at the moment in other than the crucial posts. Kokovtsev in Petersburg, Caillaux in Paris, Morley in London, Tisza in Vienna—had these four been foreign ministers, the war would never have started.

But in that case would the war not have come a few years later? Colonel House, Wilson's friend and adviser, writing in May 1914—before the assassination of Archduke Franz Ferdinand—had declared that Europe was full of envy and hatred; he believed that as soon as England gave her consent, France and Russia would fall upon Germany and Austria. Would it not seem that the three great problems underlying the war—the Straits, the Austro-Hungarian nationalities question, and Alsace-Lorraine—must inevitably have led to war?

This question can be answered with an unequivocal "No." The problem of the nationalities in Austria-Hungary could have been settled peacefully by the transformation of that state into a federal union. A strong German government would have been able to force such a change upon Austria—perhaps in such a manner as to restore Germany's friendship with Russia—since the Russians could have been given that indigestible morsel known as Galicia. Russian statesmen often hinted at such a solution; even Bismarck sometimes thought of abandoning Austria-Hungary to the mercies of Russia. Without Russian aid France could have done nothing about Alsace-Lorraine. On the Straits question the Central Powers needed only to act upon Bismarck's prescription, in which case the matter would have remained up in the air because of the antagonism between England and Russia. All in all, it is quite possible that peace in Europe might have been preserved for decades, had not the ship of Europe, fatally steered by weak and timid hands, run afoul of the Serbian reef.

CHAPTER SEVENTEEN

The *Blitzkrieg* Fails

In war men are nothing; one man is everything.
—NAPOLEON

I

During the first days after the outbreak of the war the Kaiser's face was that of a man going through hell. Chancellor Bethmann's ordinarily stooped figure seemed to shrivel. Chief of Staff Moltke suffered a nervous breakdown. Secretary of State for Foreign Affairs Jagow kept up a steady mutter to the effect that Germany must try to extricate herself as soon as possible from this frightful war.

There was good reason for this mood. Opposed to 120 million Germans and Austrians were 280 million of the enemy; on the side of the enemy were also 420 million colored colonial peoples. The enemy could immediately mobilize 10 million men, twice as many as the Central Powers. What chance had Germany if every German company had to fight two of the enemy, if every German battery were engaged with two of the enemy's?

If the situation was bad on land, it was worse on the seas. The enemy could cut Germany off from world trade. How could a nation sustain blockade when it drew a fourth of its food and raw materials from abroad? Could Germany win the war against such superior forces?

Since the dismissal of Bismarck there had been only one man who had studied this vital problem with the knowledge and thoroughness it merited. And this man believed he had found a solution. As early as 1905, Chief of Staff Schlieffen, inspired by the spirit of prophecy, had horrified his associates by working out war games in which Russia, France, England, Belgium and Serbia were united against Germany and Austria. He had endeavored to show that even such a war could be won. One thing was clear: any such war must be short, for with time the enemy superiority in resources would be sure to tell. The only hope was to defeat the enemies swiftly and one after the other. There was no point to attacking Russia first off, since at the beginning of the war the Russian army would not have completed mobilization and would therefore retreat into the endless spaces where in the past so many European armies had been swallowed up. Therefore France must be defeated in eight weeks, before the Siberian corps would reach Poland to swell the Russian forces. Yet the French fortifications running through Verdun-Toul-Epinal-Belfort could not be breached by a sudden onslaught. Since Germany had no time for siege operations, she must strike through Belgium.

Schlieffen's plan was certainly the boldest ever conceived by any strategist. To oppose three or four million Russians he wanted to post in the east, for the time being, only 200,000 men; in other words, the defense was virtually being entrusted to 1.3 million Austro-Hungarians. Some 1.8 million Germans would be deployed in the west. Of these, only 200,000 men were to remain in Alsace-Lorraine to protect South Germany. The other 1.6 million would invade France through Belgium and Luxemburg. With Metz as pivot they would complete a gigantic loop. The right wing of this offensive army was to be powerful and backed by heavy reserves. The invasion was to begin on the fourteenth day after mobilization; by the thirty-eighth day Schlieffen proposed to encircle Paris from the rear, cross the Seine at Rouen, take the enemy in his rear and, advancing eastward, drive the enemy up against the Swiss border and the Moselle fortifications (see map, page 167).

The plan called for a monster "Cannae," as Schlieffen customarily called encirclement battles—a Cannae in which the encircling troops would cover more than three hundred miles. Again and again Schlieffen urged that a frontal victory in which two armies clashed directly was a "vulgar victory" which would not save Germany. The enemy must be annihilated by a gigantic encirclement. It was probable, of course, that the French would meanwhile penetrate into Alsace-Lorraine; they might even invade South Germany. But that would be all the better; every division that was involved on the Rhine would be one less for France on the crucial front. If the French did not attack in Lorraine, another 80,000 men must be shipped from Lorraine to join the attacking army. Only in this way could the Germans win the war. In a prolonged struggle Germany would probably bleed to death. "Make my right wing strong," were Schlieffen's last words on his deathbed.

II

To his successor von Moltke, the plan was too bold. But he was not the man to find a substitute plan. Instead, he merely watered it down. Temporarily abandoning Alsace-Lorraine seemed to him too dangerous; in actuality occupation of the country by French soldiers would have increased sympathy for Germany among the population. Therefore, instead of Schlieffen's 200,000 men, he deployed a good 450,000 in Alsace. He also planned to use on this front the 200,000 Italians who had been promised him by the Italian chief of staff; he innocently believed these forces to be forthcoming, whereas Schlieffen had always considered Italian aid illusory. But in strengthening the Lorraine defensive front, Moltke necessarily weakened the offensive army. Schlieffen had called for a proportion of 8:1 between the offensive and the defensive wings. Moltke's proportion was 3:1.

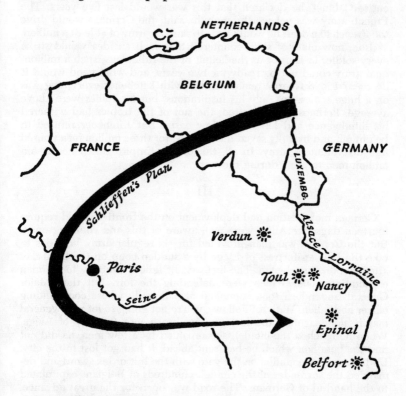

In France Commander in Chief Joffre deployed part of his army on the Franco-Belgian frontier, for he knew of the German plan to invade through Belgium. The united army of the French, Belgians and British was some 200,000 men stronger than the German army in the west. Years ago British Chief of Operations Wilson had asked French General Foch how large the British auxiliary army would have to be.

"A single British soldier would suffice, and we will see to it that he is killed soon," Foch had replied grimly. England did a great deal more; she transported 130,000 men across the Channel without losing a single soldier.

Lord Kitchener of Khartoum, the British Empire's most vigorous soldier, became secretary of state for war. He had suppressed the Indian rebellion, had killed the Mahdi and converted his head into an inkwell; he had defeated the Boers, and now, to the dismay of the entire Cabinet, he declared that this war would last five years. The French army was not worth much, he said; the Germans would drive the French like deer; he would have to raise an army of at least a million. Wilson, now chief of staff, countered that such an idea would strike every soldier in Europe as the height of the ridiculous; such a million-man army could not be ready for two years, and what good would it do then? Lloyd George remarked that with Kitchener everything was on a huge scale—not only his inspirations, but his follies were above average. Perhaps, he suggested, the sun of the tropics had withered his intelligence and left only a few oases. But Kitchener refused to be put off, and his folly saved the country, for three million men poured into his volunteer army. In all, the British Empire called nearly ten million men to arms during the war.

III

German mobilization and deployment on the frontier would require fourteen days; the Allies were well aware of this and counting on it. But the German war plan provided for six regular army brigades to take the Belgian fortress of Liége by a sudden coup on the third day after mobilization began. The first assault failed; contrary to German expectations, 30,000 men were defending the fort. But then Major General Ludendorff took command of a brigade whose commanding officer had fallen. With a, "Fellows, you're not going to let your general march alone against the fortress," he broke into the city of Liége. When he reached the citadel, accompanied by a few men, he did not find the batallion which he had sent ahead; it had got lost in the city. Undeterred, he pounded on the gate with the hilt of his sword and demanded the surrender of the citadel. Hundreds of Belgians capitulated to the handful of Germans. The road was open for the great advance.

In one furious offensive the army of the west marched through Belgium into France. The armies on the right wing, the First commanded by Kluck, the Second by Bülow, had for the time being considerable numerical superiority over the enemy. In fourteen days they fought their way forward some two hundred and fifty miles, an unprecedented achievement for troops marching on foot. By the end of August, however, the cavalry divisions could no longer operate cross-country; the horses were too worn. The French government was already declaring Paris an open city—a declaration rescinded on the following day. Joffre was on the point of retiring his armies behind the Seine, was even considering retreating to a line running through Dijon and Besançon. French, the commander of the British Expeditionary Corps, wired to Kitchener that his confidence in the French leaders was waning rapidly and that his troops could no longer withstand the assault of a single German army corps. The British commander was already proposing that the army be transported back to England. But at this critical point, Moltke's incompetence suddenly became plain. Moltke's famous uncle had once remarked that mistakes in deployment could not be remedied; the nephew was now to learn how true this was. The unfortunate man committed three strategic deadly sins in succession; any one of them would have been sufficient to deprive Germany of the laurels of victory.

It would be wrong to say that Moltke led the army of the west badly, for he did not lead it at all. Instead of moving with his headquarters in the train of the offensive, he remained first in Coblenz and then in Luxemburg; consequently his "orders" often took twenty-four hours to reach the right wing. Nor did he keep sending liaison officers up front; this would have implied distrust of the army commanders, he felt.

Everything depended upon the superior German offensive wing's doing more than just pushing the enemy back; it had to encircle and annihilate the enemy armies. The offensive failed to do this because the Germans had no overall leadership. They had, as Joffre remarked later, entrusted an express locomotive to the driver of a hackney cab. As a result, Joffre succeeded in getting his army behind the Marne in tolerable order.

Meanwhile the French had attacked in Lorraine. Now the very strength of the Lorraine army proved fatal. Its commander, Bavarian Crown Prince Rupprecht, declared that a Bavarian soldier could not be asked to retreat before an enemy toward whom he felt distinctly superior. Moltke was not the man to decry such heroics; he emphasized that he wished to give only "suggestions," not orders to his generals. The enemy, about equal in strength to the defenders, was defeated. If only Moltke had at this point shifted 250,000 men to the right wing! The railroad cars were standing ready in accordance with the Schlieffen plan. But instead he now ordered a breakthrough between Toul and Epinal, in the center of the French line of fortifications. If Schlieffen had considered this operation easy, he would never have proposed the march through Belgium. The attempt failed.

Moltke misinterpreted the situation. He believed that the French were fleeing in a wild rout to the south before the German attack

on the right wing. The trophies of a rout—prisoners and artillery—
were missing, but that did not trouble him. "In six weeks it will all
be over with," said the chief of his Operations Section. Basing his
plans on this faulty judgment, Moltke committed his third mistake:
he decided to send six army corps to East Prussia, for bad news was
coming from that front. Fortunately the staff chief in the east declared
that he did not need these corps. Moltke reduced the number to two
—some 80,000 men—but he took these two from his offensive right
wing which was in any case too weak to carry out the encirclement.
The army commanders of the right wing did not dare to protest, let
alone to sabotage the order. Not content with this, Moltke further
weakened the right wing by three more corps which he needed to
besiege several fortresses. Here, too, the forces he threw in were too
large; timid as he was, he dared not take any risks and therefore lost
everything. Instead of the offensive wing's having Schlieffen's 8:1
relationship to the defensive army in Alsace-Lorraine, the proportion
was now 2:1. Consequently the Germans could no longer encircle Paris
from the west; they had to pass to the east of that huge bastion.

Meanwhile the enemy was gathering his forces. Joffre was no strategic genius. But he was a buoy against which the tempests surged
in vain. He had nerves of steel; events could not shake him. The fate
of France might be in balance on the point of his sword, but he lost
no sleep over it. Because of his monumental phlegma, he emanated
complete calm and communicated this assurance to his subordinates.
His army commanders obeyed his orders *sans discuter*. He dismissed
thirty-three generals, including two army commanders, reinforced the
army with reserve troops, brought divisions from Lorraine to Paris,
and to the north of the capital he built up a new army of 100,000
men under General Manoury. This army was to strike at Kluck's right
flank. Kitchener came to Paris and saw to it that the British remained
in France. When Kluck realized that an attempt would be made to
encircle him on the right, he decided instantly to solve the problem
by attacking. Retreating to the right, he threw his entire army against
Manoury. In vain the commandant of Paris commandeered 1500 taxi-
cabs to send the last man in the capital to Manoury's aid. Kluck encircled him with tremendously superior forces and threatened to cut
him off from Paris. Manoury rapidly retreated. By September 9, Kluck's
troops could see the Eiffel tower on the horizon.

Kluck's shift to the right had left a gap between him and Bülow's
Second Army. It was guarded only by weak forces, mainly cavalry. But
the enemy—in this area consisting mostly of the British Expeditionary
Corps—moved into this gap with great hesitation. Thrown back con-
stantly for three weeks, they distrusted their own strength. The Second
Army had to draw back its right wing only very slightly. Moreover,

further to the left, in the area of the Third Army, the Germans had completely overcome the enemy and were approaching the Seine. To be sure, Foch, the army commander there, had sent to Joffre his famous message: "My right wing is hard pressed, my center is yielding; it is impossible for me to move; the situation is splendid—I am attacking." But there was more bravado than truth in this courageous report.

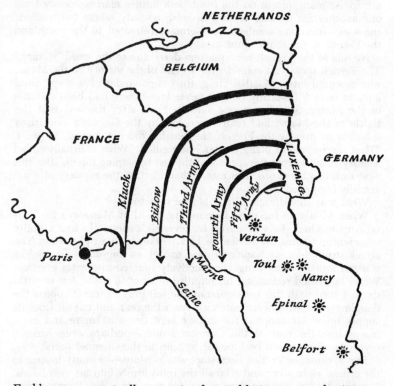

Foch's army was actually retreating fast and losing guns and prisoners. The German victories by the First and Third Armies were creating a dangerous situation for the enemy groups who were slowly filtering into the gap between the First and Second Armies. If after the victory over Manoury Kluck should turn the greater part of his army against these troops, and if the Third Army should swing to the right, the British forces might be cut off.

Suddenly the entire German front from Paris to Verdun received the order to retreat. The soldiers at the front, who for three weeks had driven the enemy before them and who were still pushing southward, flushed with the prospect of victory, did not understand the order. The troop commanders raised objections. The enemy was even more perplexed. Anxiously he had waited for fresh attacks on the morning of September 10; suddenly his advance scouts reported that the Germans were withdrawing. The French did not believe their eyes; they scented a trap. At many places on the front both armies marched away from one another for a time; as in a Spanish comedy where two ruffians run away from one another, the Germans retreated to the north and the French to the south simultaneously.

No one in the French headquarters dared to use the word "victory." The French spoke of a miracle; the legend of the victory on the Marne was invented later. Marshal Haig, then commander of a corps, used later to remark ironically that he never knew there had been a Battle of the Marne. When someone said to Foch after the war that the Battle of the Marne had really been lost by the Germans more than it had been won by the French, the marshal did not contest the point. "That can be said of many battles," he replied. "What is usually called 'victory' is most often the success of the last remaining forces." But this neat turn of phrase obscures rather than clarifies the mystery of what actually happened.

What was the Miracle of the Marne in actuality?

When Moltke in far-away Luxemburg heard of Manoury's flank attack upon Kluck, he was seized by feverish anxiety. He had a guilty conscience; against all advice he had weakened the right wing. The attack struck him, as Napoleon used to say, *en flagrant délit*. Moltke was not a man whom danger instinctively spurred to greater exertion. When he sensed resistance, his impulse was not to strike, but to withdraw. Faced with this new situation, he fell prey to fear. Suppose the dangling right wing were encircled from the rear and cut off from its supply lines? Or suppose the enemy kept throwing more and more troops into the rear of the German armies—perhaps even Russian divisions which could be brought by ship to the Channel ports?

For a commander the next step was obvious—he must hasten to the crucial right wing and take all the reins firmly into his own hands. But this Moltke did not dare to do. He was not a field commander; he was the nephew of a great man. Had not a spiritualistic medium predicted to his wife that the war would end badly? In his despair he hit upon a curious notion. Instead of sending his deputy, say the chief of his Operations Section, to the right wing, he dispatched a young officer, his chief of Intelligence, Lieutenant Colonel Hentsch. A certain sympathy of kindred natures must have influenced this choice; Hentsch had many of the qualities of the chief of staff: he was uncertain, pessimistic, sickly. Moltke could be sure that Hentsch would act just as timidly as he himself would. He ordered Hentsch to urge the armies to hold out and, if a retreat were necessary, to coordinate their movements. But in his morbid fear of issuing clear, direct commands, he did not set these instructions down in writing. Hentsch's interpretation of them was that he had full powers to order a retreat if necessary.

When Hentsch reached the headquarters of the Second Army on September 8, he found Colonel General von Bülow gravely worried. Bülow had resented Kluck's swing to the right and feared that the French and British would penetrate deeply into the gap between the First and Second Armies. Then they could cut Kluck's army off from the rest of the army in the west. To make matters worse, Bülow's staff chief, Lauenstein, was also ill and irresolute. To balance the staff weakness, at the beginning of the war the most energetic general in the army, the same Ludendorff who had stormed Liége, had been assigned to the Second Army. But meanwhile it had been necessary to recall Ludendorff and send him to the east. The situation called for only one sensible procedure; to get in touch with Kluck at once and find out how his battle against Manoury was going and when he would be able to detach troops to close the gap. But neither Bülow nor Hentsch thought of this. Instead, they mutually coddled one another's pessimism. Together they decided that the Second Army must retreat.

Next morning Hentsch went to see Kluck. He found Kluck's chief of staff, General von Kuhl, one of the finest officers in the army, standing in a village street in a triumphant mood. Manoury was defeated, he announced. Here was good news that Hentsch had not expected. Instead of wiring Bülow at once that yesterday's decision to retreat had been taken on false premises and must be rescinded, he declared that the Second Army had shot its bolt and was retreating. Kluck would have to retreat also in order not to lose contact. Kuhl protested; Hentsch referred to his authorization and to Bülow's retreat, which he said was already in progress. Finally Kluck and Kuhl yielded and issued the orders for withdrawal.

After the war General Gröner, later to be Reichswehr minister, avowed that Kluck should simply have arrested Hentsch and, in his name, telegraphed to the army commanders:

"Glorious victory on the right wing. All armies attack, keep enemy engaged; Second Army especially not another step back; yours is the responsibility for still greater success in battle. Forward to fame and victory for Kaiser and Reich.

> The Commander of the First Army and the
> Envoy of the High Command."

This suggestion has a certain picaresque appeal. But no general in imperial Germany could have done anything of the sort.

Two days earlier, when he was out of touch with the right wing,

Moltke had excitedly recommended a retreat to the Kaiser. The Kaiser, once again wiser than his counselors, had quietly refused. Now, when the news of the retreat of the First and Second Armies reached head-quarters, Moltke disregarded the advice of his staff and in his over-anxiety ordered the other armies also to retreat. He suffered a complete psychological breakdown and reported to the Kaiser: "Your Majesty, we have lost the war!" As the French general Malleterre has said, Moltke was the perfect model of an incompetent commander in chief.

After the war the question was raised: what would probably have happened if a real man instead of Hentsch had gone to inspect the right wing and had ordered the battle continued. In that case the German armies would probably have defeated the enemy on that right wing. But their forces would hardly have sufficed to carry out Schlief-fen's plan and roll up the entire French army against the frontier in Lorraine. Moltke had prepared the offensive too inadequately from the start, and conducted it too slackly. Nevertheless, the bridgeheads for the succeeding battles would have been much stronger.

IV

The Kaiser relieved Moltke of his position and appointed Minister of War Erich von Falkenhayn as chief of staff. It was not a happy choice. Falkenhayn was one of the handsomest officers in the army; six feet tall and a veritable war god in appearance, he never lost his composure for a moment, even in the gravest crises. His exterior charm was a thin veneer over an utterly cold, sarcastic personality. Toward his Austrian allies he dispensed with his diplomat's courtesy and as-sumed the intolerable arrogance of a Prussian junker. He kept his own counsel and was generally thought a double-dealer. Early in his career, when he was still only a colonel in Metz, his colleagues would say: "That man is done for; Falkenhayn shook hands with him." Madly ambitious, he seemed to have an inexhaustible capacity for work; he bore the heavy burdens of his office with casual ease. From the first day his appointment aroused discontent; he was younger than all the army commanders and commanding generals. As a minister or parlia-mentarian, Falkenhayn would have been destined for success; supreme leadership in war was less his dish. Daring was not in his character; great operations struck him as too risky. Consequently, he hit on the strange theory that Germany must win the war by husbanding her forces; she must limit herself to the defensive and to occasional limited attacks. Unfortunately, time was working for the enemy—thanks to the blockade, to Kitchener's rapidly growing army, and to the wavering of Italy and Rumania.

When Falkenhayn took over, 1.7 million Germans were facing 2.3

million of the enemy on the western front. The German right wing and
the French left wing facing it were hanging in the air. The Germans
and the French therefore attempted to strike one another on the flanks,
and both were thereby forced to extend their fronts to the sea. Falkenhayn wanted to break through to the Channel ports. Ruthlessly,
he threw in the new corps which consisted of young volunteers. They
lacked artillery and officers; the volunteers were inadequately trained
and were inclined, because of their enthusiasm, to advance without
cover. They sang *Deutschland, Deutschland über alles* as they stormed
headlong into the enemy fire. The British communiqués spoke admir-
ingly of boys of seventeen who marched fearlessly forward and died
by the thousands. "The fruit of a century of national discipline," the
British called this behavior.

The stony-hearted Falkenhayn was uselessly sacrificing Germany's
future; the leaders of the years to come, who should have been given
preliminary training on quieter fronts, died gloriously and in vain with
the national anthem on their lips.

V

At the outset the Russians had deployed two armies against East
Prussia. Rennenkampf's army was to attack from the east, Samsonov's
from the south. Each of these armies was about 200,000 men strong;
a smaller reserve army waited near Warsaw. The German army in
East Prussia was able to place about 180,000 men in the field against
the enemy (see map page 176).

In command of the East Prussian Army was Colonel General von
Prittwitz whom the enlisted men called "the fat soldier." He was a fine
raconteur and a gourmet, inconsiderate and rude toward subordinates
—but well liked by the Kaiser. So far as anyone knew, he had never
distinguished himself as a strategist. The general's instructions were to
pin the enemy's superior forces down, but not to risk his army. If necessary he was to retire across the Vistula, sacrificing East Prussia.

Schlieffen had recommended waiting for the Russian offensive with
a defense in depth. Instead, Prittwitz attacked Rennenkampf's army,
but while the battle was still in progress he received word that Samsonov had crossed the southern frontier of East Prussia in the German
rear and was threatening to cut his army off from the Vistula. The
operations officer of the East Prussian Army, Major Hoffmann, was a
tough Berliner, six feet three inches tall, a man who lived hard and
had been accustomed for years to washing away his hangovers with
a couple of bottles of wine before breakfast. Calmly, he remarked: "The
chief's nerves won't bear up under this news; we ought to keep it from
him until Rennenkampf is beaten." But Prittwitz himself had already

received the report and against his staff's advice ordered the battle against Rennenkampf broken off and a retreat behind the Vistula. When Moltke, who was still chief of staff at this time, asked him over the telephone whether he would at least be able to hold the Vistula line, he answered irritably: "With the few men I have how can I defend a river that can be waded across?" Moltke then did nothing at all. But a few younger members of the headquarters staff telephoned the corps commanders and learned that these men also considered Prittwitz's decision a mistake. Prittwitz himself had meanwhile decided to attack Samsonov on the eastern side of the Vistula. Before he could inform Moltke of this decision, he was relieved of his command.

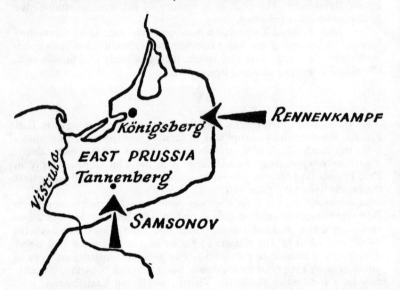

At Supreme Headquarters there was no doubt about who should be sent to East Prussia. The most energetic officer in the army was now considered to be that general who on his own initiative had assumed command at Liége and taken the city by storm: Ludendorff. "I know of no other man," Moltke wrote to him. "Perhaps you can save the situation in the east." But Ludendorff was young and only a major general; it was out of the question for him to be commander in chief in the east. He was therefore appointed staff chief; the supreme commander had still to be found. Since Ludendorff had a reputation for intransigeance, his commander would have to be someone who would give him a free hand. After some hesitation the retired General von

Hindenburg was selected; his imperturbable calm virtually guaranteed that he could get along with anyone. Hindenburg entered Ludendorff's special train at Hanover, and during the trip they agreed to throw their entire weight against Rennenkampf. From the train Ludendorff issued orders for deployment. These for the most part accorded with the preparations Major Hoffmann had already made.

The plan was splendid in its boldness. If Ludendorff left only a thin curtain of cavalry to hold Rennenkampf, he could assemble 150,000 men on the battlefield. With this force he decided to encircle Samsonov's 200,000 men while Rennenkampf's army remained only a day's march away. Hindenburg was well aware of the perils; when he reported his plans to Moltke he added: "Morale high, although possibility of disaster not excluded." Fortunately the Germans possessed the key to the Russian wireless code; consequently they knew their enemy's plans.

Everything depended upon whether Rennenkampf would march. At one time during the six-day Battle of Tannenberg it appeared that he intended to come to Samsonov's aid; his cavalry advance guard was only ten miles away from the German front. Ludendorff considered breaking contact with the enemy. But at that moment Hindenburg's imperturbability proved its worth; he decided to take the risk. Rennenkampf did not make a move to come to the aid of Samsonov. Perhaps personal enmity between himself and Samsonov played some part in this decision; during the Russo-Japanese war the two men had come to blows on the railroad station in Mukden, and only a direct order from the Czar had prevented a duel. In the battle Samsonov lost 92,000 prisoners and 50,000 dead, and committed suicide. The Germans had only 5000 casualties.

During the last day of the battle Moltke telephoned Ludendorff and informed him that he wanted to send several army corps from the west to the east. Ludendorff was game enough to tell him he did not absolutely need this assistance; if the troops were necessary in the west, they had better remain there. Nevertheless Moltke sent two corps which arrived too late in the east and were sorely needed on the Marne.

A few days after the Battle of Tannenberg Ludendorff also defeated Rennenkampf. Warned by Samsonov's fate, the Russians escaped the encirclement by withdrawing swiftly across the border, but they lost 40,000 prisoners. Within two weeks Ludendorff had not only defeated, but virtually annihilated armies more than twice the size of his own.

VI

On the southern sector of the front, which was held by the Austro-Hungarian armies, it was quite a different story.

Austrian Chief of Staff Conrad also had a bold plan; fate would have it that his ideas were abundant and good, but that he did not possess an army capable of executing them, whereas the German chief of staff had the best military instrument in the world but was so inhibited that he did not dare to commit it.

Franz Joseph had rightly said of Conrad: "What we need is a chief of staff who is somewhat less of a genius, a man who would know how to cook with water." But Conrad did not intend to cook with water; his plans always had a Napoleonic sweep. Instead of waiting for the superior Russian forces to attack and wear him down in a frontal battle, he wanted to advance into Russia, conduct a war of movement in which the superior training of the Austro-Hungarian army could be turned to advantage. But Galicia was enveloped by the enemy on two sides, and nothing is more difficult than to operate from a central position against surrounding forces superior in numbers. Conrad assumed that until the twenty-eighth day after mobilization the Russians would hardly be able to commit more than one to one and a quarter million men against him. This assumption was correct. To this force he could oppose about one million men, if he left a quarter of a million to operate against Serbia.

In concocting his plan Conrad was also relying upon two promises from Moltke. The German chief of staff had assured him before the war that the Germans would launch an attack from East Prussia toward Warsaw, and that by the fortieth day after mobilization the first corps would be transferred from the west to the east. Both promises were frivolous. Since Moltke had only 200,000 men in East Prussia against twice that number of Russians, he could not hope to take the offensive toward Warsaw. And on the fortieth day after mobilization, even if the Schlieffen plan were carried out perfectly, the great battle of encirclement in France was just scheduled to begin. Moltke had, moreover, neglected to come to an agreement with Conrad on details. When the war started, he began immediately backing down on his promises, but by then it was too late for Conrad to call off his offensive.

Everything turned out differently from what the ingenious Austrian commander had foreseen. First of all the deployment failed. Austria had mobilized first against Serbia. Although it became clear by the second day of mobilization that at least a partial Russian mobilization was impending, Conrad continued with foolish and self-complacent optimism to count upon Russia's standing by while Serbia was "chastised." Consequently, he began transporting the army to the Serbian border. When after two days he learned of the Russian partial mobilization, he did not dare revise the first deployment order. Consequently the Second Army, which in case of war with Russia had been assigned the defense of southern Galicia, was sent to the Danube. Conrad then compounded the blunder by allowing the commander of the Second Army to throw his forces into the battles against the Serbs so that this army would not stand idle while the railroads to Galicia were being cleared. Naturally these useless engagements further delayed the transportation of the Second Army to Galicia.

When Conrad ordered the offensive in Russia, a good fourth of his million soldiers were missing; some of them arrived by driblets during the battle. In addition, the Austrian plan was known to the Russians; it had been betrayed to them years ago by an Austrian colonel who as a result of his homosexual tendencies had fallen into the hands of a Russian espionage organization.

"Just see to it that the Germans don't leave us in the soup too long," were Conrad's parting words to a liaison officer whom he sent to Moltke. But when the officer presented Conrad's requests in Berlin, Moltke merely remarked: "You have a great army; you'll beat the Russians by yourselves."

Conrad's first inroad into Poland succeeded; the proud regiments of the ancient monarchy carried the black and yellow flags deep into the enemy country. But after a week the mistakes in deployment took their toll; the Russians were far superior in men and artillery, and the Austrian divisions were rolled back. They paid for Conrad's audacity with 200,000 dead and 100,000 prisoners—a third of the army. The Austrian army never recovered from this defeat; its best officers remained on the field of battle.

The officer corps had been the vital element of the army. Those officers of the monarchy had received a marvellous military training because they did not despise intellectual work, as their colleagues in the north frequently did; moreover the boredom of Austrian garrison life gave them plenty of time for study. As for the common soldiers, Germans, Hungarians and Croats fought with their traditional bravery, but the Czech, Polish and Italian troops could be held together only by the corps of active officers; under the direction of reserve officers, who in their hearts often hoped the enemy would win, these troops began deserting in a body. Thus the loss of the first battles decided for good the fate of an ancient and famous fighting force. As it happened, however, the Russian army suffered the same fate. In the bloody battles of 1914 it lost its old leadership, mostly Balts who were faithful to the Czar and who alone could have prevented the victory of the Revolution.

It was only human nature for Conrad to blame his defeat on the failure of the Germans to carry out their promised offensive. When his liaison officer returned from the German headquarters, Conrad received him with the quip: "Well, what are our secret enemies, the Germans, doing? And how about that comedian, the German Kaiser?" Relationships between the two armies were tense. Falkenhayn's arrogance was hard for the Austrians to bear. Austrian officers, with their happier dispositions and their ancient culture, could afford to be on an easier social basis with one another; they had the security of aristocrats. To the Prussians, however, this ease and sociability seemed like a lack of fiber. The insolent Berlin phrase that Conrad only held up the Russians "until the military arrived" caused a great deal of bad blood. The Austrians themselves felt that the Prussians were "more efficient," but they did not care to hear this repeated every day.

When the Austrians had retreated back to the San River, Falkenhayn decided to send the East Prussian Army down into Silesia so that it could march shoulder to shoulder with the Austrian allies into southern Poland. The Germans led the advance as far as the fortifications on the Vistula defending Warsaw and Ivangorod. But meanwhile Grand Duke Nikolai Nikolayevich, the supreme commander of the Russian forces—an uncle of the Czar and a tough, gifted strategist—had amassed such vastly superior forces that the Germans had to retreat to the Silesian frontier. The Russian steamroller, upon which the French were pinning their hopes, had begun to move. In Silesia preparations were made to dismantle the great armament works, and in Prague the Czech women sewed flags and baked cakes with which to greet their Slavic liberators.

At this juncture Ludendorff produced one of his most brilliant inspirations. He was loath to face the Grand Duke in a frontal battle in which the superior forces would certainly win. Employing the close-meshed network of railroads, he secretly shifted his entire army toward Thorn on the Vistula, in order to attack the advancing Russians on their right flank. He left only Austrian forces to guard the Silesian border; Conrad, always enthusiastic about bold plans and a genuine nobleman in his readiness to support others, had instantly placed his troops at Ludendorff's disposal. Hindenburg and Ludendorff implored Falkenhayn to send them a few more divisions in order for them to be able to cut off the Russians, who had ventured deeper than ever before into the Polish cul-de-sac. But Falkenhayn wanted to harvest a victory in Flanders; he did not begin sending reinforcements, a few at a time, until December, by which time the battle was over.

Ludendorff's surprise worked. The steamroller was not constituted to fend off flanking attacks. The Grand Duke, defeated at Lodz, retreated to the Vistula. If Falkenhayn had sent the thirteen divisions which he allowed to bleed uselessly to death in Flanders, the battle would have been a second and even bigger Tannenberg. But without those divisions the disproportion in forces was too great. The Germans had to retreat slowly again. A German army group of some 40,000 men was dispersed and encircled near Brzeziny. The Russians had already set aside sixty railroad trains for the transportation of prisoners when the group broke out of the envelopment without losing a gun, and even took 16,000 prisoners with it. By the time the first snows fell, the danger from the Russian steamroller had been averted. Conrad, too, had thrown the enemy back southeast of Cracow; it was his one victory in the entire war.

In east and west now the fronts were frozen. In the west it was possible to walk through a system of continuous trenches from the North Sea to the Swiss border; the efforts of both sides to diminish the hazards ended up in the new concept of positional warfare. The German part of the eastern front was under the command of Hindenburg, who now bore the title of Supreme Commander in the East. Two attempts by the Austrians to invade Serbia had failed ingloriously, at great cost in blood.

VII

Meanwhile two other powers had entered the war. On August 15, 1914, Japan presented Germany with an ultimatum demanding cession of the protectorate of Kiaochow. As has been mentioned earlier, the Japanese employed the very language the Germans had used fifteen years before when they expelled Japan from the Asiatic mainland after the Sino-Japanese War. Bethmann wanted to accept the ultimatum; Tirpitz insisted on its being rejected. Quite rightly he argued that an alliance with Japan, necessary as it was for Germany, could be attained sooner by stalwart resistance than by surrendering Kiaochow without a fight. After a struggle lasting two months, the Germans ran out of food and ammunition and had to lay down their arms.

The second new participant in the war was Turkey. The Sick Man on the Bosporus was well aware that Russia and England would, if they won, usher him in short order to death's door. Consequently the Turks signed an alliance with Germany on August 2. This alliance did not hinder Turkish Minister of War Enver Pasha from offering an alliance to Russia also at the end of the same month. But Russia refused the offer; the Russians and French were so sure of victory that they decided to let Turkey stay in the enemy camp, so as to be able to divide up the country after the war. England had to promise Russia that she would be awarded Constantinople in the coming peace—a violation of a centuries-old tradition for the British. In October Turkey declared war upon the Entente Powers—against the will of the Sultan, who feared for his throne.

Turkey proved to be a dubious asset. The country had thirty-six million inhabitants, but half of these were Arabs who wanted to shake off the Turkish yoke. Aside from the incomplete Bagdad railroad, there were few rail lines. The roads were wretched and the bridges mostly useless. To transport a heavy shell from Ankara, the terminus of the railroad, to the Russo-Turkish front in the Caucasus, took at best thirty-five days by camel. German Secretary of the Treasury Helfferich, who had been one of the directors of the Bagdad railroad, proposed completion of the line within the year. But Falkenhayn rejected the idea; he hoped to be able to end the war sooner than that.

Nevertheless, in spite of her weakness Turkey pinned down sizable British forces during the following years.

CHAPTER EIGHTEEN

The Breakout to the East Fails

The most important element in strategy is clarity about one's intentions.
——VERDY DU VERNOIS

I

When the German Kaiser considered the military situation soberly during those Christmas days of 1914, the picture he saw was grim. Germany had only half the manpower of her enemies. As a result of the blockade, time was on the enemy side. It was impossible to win victories by simultaneous offensives in all directions; yet it would seem that only such feats would convince all Germany's foes that further war was useless. Obviously Germany's only chance was to split away at least one enemy. But which one? The British could not be persuaded toward peace; they sat unassailable in their island building up an army of millions from which they expected victory. The French were placing their hopes in Kitchener's army and the Russian steamroller; until these two resources had been tried and found wanting, they would not conclude peace. Russia was the only possibility. The year 1914 had shown that the Germans could defeat Russian troops even when the odds were two to one. The eastern front ran in a gigantic arc; if a pincers attack were launched from East Prussia and East Galicia, it might be possible to nip off this great arc (see map page 184). Two armies advancing from north and south would be able to cut the Russian supply line. If this super-Cannae were successful, Russia would scarcely be able to raise an entire new army of equal strength, in spite of her human reserves; an army required not only men, but also equipment and training officers. The Russians were already short of arms and ammunition; their armaments industry was inadequate and they were almost cut off from foreign supplies. If they suffered a disastrous defeat, revolutionary uprisings could be expected—that is what had happened during the Russo-Japanese War. If Germany then offered the Czar a peace on the basis of prewar boundaries, and if she broke faith with her Turkish ally and threw in Constantinople as well, a separate peace with Russia would be a virtual certainty. Then the whole world situation would

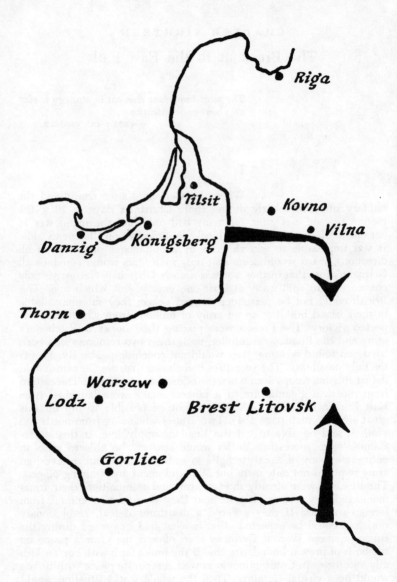

look very different. In addition, a decisive victory in Russia might well be the best method for keeping two neutrals, Italy and Rumania, out of the war; it was also the only way to strengthen Germany's wavering Austrian ally. The two generals who had already magnificently proved their competence, Hindenburg and Ludendorff, therefore proposed assembling all available forces in the east and cutting off the Russian frontal arc by a gigantic pincers movement.

It seems unlikely that Kaiser Wilhelm considered the matter in such fundamental terms. At the time he did not even ask Falkenhayn for a written briefing on the situation, that is, a clear analysis of relative forces, possibilities and plans.

Falkenhayn was opposed to Hindenburg's and Ludendorff's plans. For the great pincers offensive the eastern front would need at least 200,000 men from the west; to take these men away was impossible, Falkenhayn thought. He was wrong. Naturally there was a risk in withdrawing troops from the western front. But unless such gambles are taken, a war against overwhelmingly superior forces cannot be won. On the western front at that time 1.9 million German effectives were facing 2.8 million of the enemy; the proportion was therefore five to eight. The following years showed that even when the odds were still more favorable to the Allies, they could not succeed in breaking through. Falkenhayn should not have hesitated even to take up rear positions, which could have been prepared by ruthlessly drafting the home labor forces. Another possibility was to apply an old idea of Schlieffen's—transferring the home replacement troops into occupied territory as reserves.

But Falkenhayn was of the opinion that a pincers offensive extending over nearly four hundred miles would not succeed. Probably he was wrong. We know now from Russian documents that the Russians were exceedingly ill supplied with arms and munitions. Troops in training frequently had only one rifle for ten men. Replacements were often sent to the front without weapons and had to wait patiently under German shell fire until they could take over the rifle of a fallen comrade. As early as the end of 1914 the Russian chief of staff reported that many soldiers wanted to go home because they had no boots, because the Russian artillery did not fire and the foot soldiers were being "popped off like so many partridges." Ivanov, the commander of the southern front, reported in June 1915 that 150,000 of his men had no firearms. During the summer the Russian batteries were in many places limited to four shots per gun per day. Chief of Staff Yanushkevich wrote to the war minister that if need be shells should be delivered without fuses. Even if they did not explode, they would at least create the impression of artillery fire. "A drowning man clutches at a straw," he added. It seems hardly likely that an army in such straits would have been able to fend off the pincers movement. Of course Falkenhayn was not aware of these details, but it had been reported to him that the Russians were short of ammunition.

Falkenhayn's arguments against the offensive were insubstantial. When a man has only frivolous arguments to offer, he is usually concealing other conscious or unconscious reasons. That was the case here. Hindenburg's popularity offended the ambitious chief of staff. For a big pincers offensive it would have been necessary to give Hindenburg command of the entire eastern front. And if he then succeeded in winning a tremendous victory, he would certainly soon be taking Falkenhayn's place as chief of staff. Every man possesses the capacity to convince himself that such shifts are bad for the nation. Falkenhayn soon transferred Ludendorff to the Carpathians in order to separate the two popular generals—a move which seems further to prove that he was acting out of personal motives. Hindenburg had to protest to the Kaiser in order to force Falkenhayn to rescind this order. By rejecting the plan for a grand assault in the east, Falkenhayn threw away Germany's next to the last chance to end the war on tolerably reasonable terms. Ludendorff told Chancellor Bethmann that if Falkenhayn remained chief of staff, the war would be lost. Bethmann vainly urged the Kaiser to drop Falkenhayn.

II

Chief of Staff Falkenhayn was not without plans himself. He bolstered the eastern front with fresh troops; he wanted the Russians expelled from East Prussia, which they had once more invaded. In a battle during the winter another 90,000 prisoners were taken. But Falkenhayn stuck to his opinion that no decision must be sought in the east; Germany must content herself with "paralyzing the Russian offensive strength by partial blows."

The Austrian section of the eastern front was wavering. In the Carpathians, in spite of German "corset stays" here and there, it was threatening to collapse. In that event, the road to Budapest would be open to the Russians. Falkenhayn had no choice but to help immediately. He decided upon an offensive at the outermost point of the eastern front, near Gorlice. The attacking army was to be commanded not by Hindenburg, but by General Mackensen, a cavalry officer. This dapper, youthful-looking colonel general was ideally suited for collaboration with allies; he had a way of saying "no" more courteously than other people when they said yes. But he was not a strategist; consequently Colonel von Seeckt, the future creator of the Reichswehr, was assigned to him as his staff chief. Seeckt was a cool-headed, strong-willed officer who by keeping his mouth shut had gained a reputation for superhuman cleverness. In his dry way he commented that such breakthrough operations had been *verboten* before the war. By the tenets of peacetime military science breakthroughs were always dangerous because the army breaking through might be cut off.

Seeckt's breakthrough succeeded, but no sooner did it do so than Falkenhayn called a halt. Since his idea was to "paralyze" the Russian army by "partial blows," a great advance would be violating basic principles. Above all Germany had to "husband" her forces. This was just another way of expressing the principle of wasting strength piece-meal until Germany was ruined. Seeckt and Conrad had to plead persistently in order to obtain permission to continue their attacks; the same farce was repeated for every phase of the advance. According to Falkenhayn, the goal of the operation was "a decision adequate for the purposes of the High Command"—a thoroughly mysterious oracular formula. Lvov, the capital of Galicia, was taken. Mackensen was promoted to field marshal and Falkenhayn ordered the operation against Russia concluded and the troops shifted to the west. Hindenburg, Mackensen, Seeckt and Conrad objected and once again proposed the great pincers movement. When Ludendorff argued that the Russians were weak on the northern front near Vilna, Falkenhayn's chief of operations, Tappen, said: "They're always wanting to attack where there is no enemy"—a criticism revealing incredible depths of folly. Again Falkenhayn rejected the pincers idea. He ordered Hindenburg to advance alone from East Prussia toward the south. Hindenburg appealed to the Kaiser, who confirmed Falkenhayn's order. When Hindenburg nevertheless prepared for an envelopment movement toward Vilna with the forces at his disposal, Falkenhayn withdrew part of the troops hitherto under his command and formed a new army group subordinate directly to the chief of staff in person. In vain Hindenburg protested; he demanded that his title of "Supreme Commander in the East" be changed on the grounds that it was now sheer irony. Major Hoffmann henceforth referred to Falkenhayn only as "that scoundrel."

The campaign in the east thereafter followed Falkenhayn's plans: the Russians were pressed back in frontal attacks. When the chief of staff at last let loose the offensive against Vilna in September 1915, it was already too late to cut off the Russians, who by now were retreating. Moreover, Falkenhayn soon afterwards began withdrawing troops from the east for the western front.

The campaign over, Ludendorff made contemptuous reference in a letter to "the sort of warfare which was favored during the summer." Falkenhayn replied sarcastically: "Whether your Excellency agrees with the views of the High Command is no longer of consequence, since a decision by His All-highest Majesty has been handed down." He averred that the campaign had succeeded in "damaging Russia in a fashion completely sufficient for our purposes"; he was convinced that the war would be won if Germany went on being careful not to overstrain her inner and outer resources and did not go chasing after military laurels of dubious lasting value.

Falkenhayn was profoundly mistaken. Russia had not been sufficiently damaged. She reinforced her army and the following year was able to smash the Austrian front and draw a new ally, Rumania, into the war. The Czar's empire had called up thirteen million men, and an equal number of men were waiting at the gates of the barracks. When a British liaison officer in St. Petersburg expressed his regret over the heavy casualties, the war minister answered: "Don't worry about that; men are all we do have a surplus of."

III

The success of the Germans and Austrians in throwing back the Russians during 1915 was due to two factors: the superiority of German generalship and the inferiority of Russian equipment. The Russians would not have been so poor in arms if England had followed the advice of a man who alone among the statesmen and generals of the First World War bore the distinct stamp of genius: Winston Churchill.

The young First Lord of the Admiralty argued that everything depended upon providing the Russian multitudes with sufficient arms. There was only one way to obtain a swift and safe route to Russia, and that way had the additional advantage that its capture would completely eliminate one enemy, dispose of all cares about the Orient, and probably secure for England a million additional allies. Churchill urged that England conquer Constantinople. Then arms and ammunition could be shipped to Russia through the Black Sea, Turkey would conclude a separate peace, and Rumania, Bulgaria and Greece would range themselves on Serbia's side and march against Austria. The war, he maintained, could be decided by such an attack upon the "soft underbelly" of the Central Powers.

Part of the British Cabinet was opposed to this "fantastic adventure." But the vigorous personalities—Field Marshal Kitchener and Sea Lord Fisher—were for it. Reluctantly, the government consented to the plan. But half-hearted decisions are generally not carried out in the most effective or intelligent manner. Committees were set up. Fisher wrote to Churchill that never in world history had a committee won a victory; one man was needed.

The operation was not a simple one. Constantinople was separated from the Mediterranean by the strait of the Dardanelles, 37 miles long and 2½ miles wide. On the southern shore lay Asia Minor, where ancient Troy had looked up to the oak groves of Mount Ida. The northern shore of the Dardanelles formed the narrow peninsula of Gallipoli (see map below). A number of age-old forts barred the passage. But until February 1915 the peninsula was feebly defended; two or three divisions could undoubtedly have landed and taken it. The British, however, began the battle for Gallipoli—one of the crucial battles of the war—by committing every imaginable blunder.

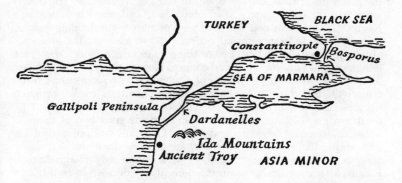

First of all they gave a warning signal: several warships bombarded the forts. The Turks promptly threw 60,000 men into the peninsula. German General Liman von Sanders took command and a German admiral was entrusted with the naval defense; they had at their disposal five hundred German soldiers who had come through Rumania in civilian dress. It was a full month before sixteen British and French battleships attempted to force the entrance. The guns of the *Agamemnon* churned up the mound of rubble that was the site of Troy. The ships had a superiority in guns over the forts—58 to 18—but the forts remained strong enough to prevent the clearing of mines. Three battleships were sunk, three others severely damaged. The admiral retreated with his squadron. He did not suspect that the Turkish guns had only eight shots apiece left, that aside from the mines already laid there were no others available, and that the Turks would have no chance to obtain more ammunition or mines in the near future. The retreat of the British fleet from Gallipoli was one of the strangest examples of the role of chance in world history.

The Turks realized that the British would now attempt to land troops. Liman von Sanders exclaimed: "If only they give me a week's time." The British Cabinet waited a full month. As a result of the naval losses, the British had lost their taste for the offensive. Resistance to the bold enterprise grew. The Dardanelles suddenly acquired a new defensive wall: an immovable mountain of bureaucratic opposition to thorough,

vigorous measures. The army and the navy tossed the ball back and
forth between them. The evil day when decisions would have to be
made was postponed again and again.

Gradually 80,000 men were assembled on the Greek islands before
the Dardanelles—in violation of Greek neutrality. After a long bombardment by the guns of the warships, 50,000 men were landed upon
the peninsula of Gallipoli and upon the coast of Asia Minor. The troops
were British, Australians, New Zealanders, and French Senegalese
Negroes. But Liman was by now well prepared; the landing parties
met stubborn resistance on all quarters. Nowhere were the attackers
able to penetrate more than two or three miles inland. There was great
indignation in London. They had come so close to the goal; was the last
leap to fail? After all, the whole of Gallipoli was no more than three
miles wide and thirty miles long. But the committees could not make
up their minds to commit more ships of the line to the support of
the troops; a U-boat had appeared and already sunk two of them.

A Cabinet crisis delayed the decision. Churchill was relieved of his
post and made Duke of Lancaster, an office without duties usually
assigned only to Cabinet members with advanced arteriosclerosis.
Finally, after many anxious consultations, it was decided to land troops
once more. Their commander, General Stopford, was fetched out of
retirement. The landing took place uncontested this time, but Stopford
took no advantage of the surprise. He had his men bathe and wait;
he himself did not go on land for many hours. In the meanwhile there
remained between him and Constantinople, for a full thirty-six hours,
no more than a thousand Turks without a single machine gun. It was
a strange battle indeed. Facing one another in the valley of the Sca-
mander and on the opposite shore, where once Achilles had chased
Hector around the walls of Troy, sturdy Anatolian peasants who put
their trust in Allah fought with the sons of far-off New Zealand and
Negroes from Senegal. The issue at stake was whether the British
would be able to supply arms against the Germans to the soldiers of
the great Russian Empire—a cause that moved the hearts of the men
on both sides far less than the fate of beautiful Helen had stirred the
men of Hellas and Ilium. If Zeus had still sat enthroned upon the
cloudy heights of Mount Ida, he would hardly have known which army
he should back.

Both armies were suffering. When Liman, who had his headquarters
only three miles back of the trenches, sent sandbags up front, the
impoverished Turks used the precious cloth of the bags to far better
purpose to patch their miserable uniforms. Ammunition was scarce;
the Germans were smuggling 30.5 cm. shells across Rumania in beer
barrels. The Turkish batteries often fired the blanks used on maneuvers
in order at least to give their infantry the feeling of having artillery

support. If one out of twenty of the real shells exploded, they were doing well. But the attackers, by now 120,000 men strong, also lay in wretched trenches. Churchill wrote irritably: "Had the Germans held the positions we have been holding for all these months, a system of subterranean habitations, lighted by electric light, lined with concrete, and properly warmed and drained, would have been in existence." Considering the ease of supplying the troops—ships could anchor within a stone's throw of the trenches—there was good reason for such indignation.

The previous commander, General Stopford, was replaced by General Munro. "General Munro was an officer of swift decision. He came, he saw, he capitulated. Without going beyond the Beaches, he familiarized himself in the space of six hours with the conditions prevailing on the 15-mile front of Anzac, Suvla and Helles, and spoke a few discouraging words to the principal officers at each point" (Churchill). Munro argued for evacuation; Kitchener, who had meanwhile come to Gallipoli, agreed with him. For by now the Germans, through the Serbian campaign which we shall shortly discuss, had established land communications with Constantinople. They had won the race. Any day now gray steel helmets might appear among the red fezzes of the Turks. To be sure, evacuation seemed a highly perilous procedure. Experts foresaw the loss of half the troops. But the generals were mistaken up to the last. Excellently prepared and favored by luck and fog, the evacuation cost the British not a single man, although they did lose a great deal of equipment.

For eight months, rainless months in a murderous climate, the bitter, bloody battle had gone on. Some 66,000 Turks and nearly 80,000 Britons had lost their lives, and 120,000 had been hospitalized. Nothing whatsoever had been achieved. No one perceived that the plan had been good, and had come to grief only through faulty execution. Winston Churchill was generally considered a visionary and adventurer. He received no further assignments in the conduct of the war. Perhaps the worst consequence of the Battle of the Dardanelles consisted precisely in this, that the most vigorous and brilliant mind in the British Empire was henceforth excluded from the councils of war.

IV

By the Triple Alliance Italy was obligated to give aid if Germany and Austria were attacked. She therefore had the formal right to remain neutral, since Germany had been first to declare war. The Triple Alliance treaty also provided that if Austria occupied Balkan territory even temporarily, she must come to an agreement with Italy on compensation. Berchtold had frivolously ignored this clause in the treaty. But these matters were, after all, only petty formalities. From the first Italy had resolved to wait and see which way the wind blew. As early as the beginning of July she had assured France of her neutrality. The most Bismarck had ever expected of his ally was that Italy would post "a bugler" in the western Alps and make the French a little nervous. But not even this modest hope was fulfilled.

On August 2, 1914, Italy declared her "benevolent neutrality"—this much she was obligated to do under the Triple Alliance. But her benevolence was of a peculiar sort. Immediately after the Battle of the Marne the Left press demanded that Italy join the presumable victors—join them early enough, while the rewards for doing so were still high. One snobbish group in this unmilitary people, a group headed by futurist painters, announced with the cheap enthusiasm of the un-armed militia man that the principal thing was for Italy to fight at all, no matter on what side.

Italy informed Vienna that she had "compensation demands" to present. She hesitated, however, to formulate these demands—not out of embarrassment, but because she wanted to drag out the negotiations. When the demands were at last presented, they proved to be consider-able; Italy was asking for all of southern Tyrol as far as the Brenner Pass, for the right bank of the Isonzo, for several Dalmatian islands and a free hand in Albania. Trieste was to be made a free city. All these concessions of territory were to be made immediately, for Italy reasonably suspected that a victorious Austria-Hungary would no longer meet obligations under such an agreement.

Vienna would have been wiser to meet these demands—except for the German part of southern Tyrol, which Italy would not have pressed for. After such concessions, Italy could hardly have mobilized her army. The other side was not offering very much more. Russia, in-toxicated with confidence in victory, even asked whether Italy ought to be "admitted into the war." None of the territory Italy was asking for was indispensable to Austria-Hungary. She was in a bad spot and could not afford any additional enemies.

But Vienna had learned nothing from the mistakes of the past few months. The Austrians despised the "rabbits," as they called the Italians because of their numerous progeny. For a century they had bested the Italians in every encounter; were they now to surrender without a fight parts of the country which had suddenly become "the most precious jewels in their treasury"? In vain Germany thrust that adroit diplomat Prince Bülow into the negotiations. In vain the Vatican, which strongly favored the Central Powers, tried to prevent Italy's entrance into the war. When Pfiffl, the Cardinal of Vienna, timidly conveyed to Franz Joseph the Holy Father's request that Austria mollify Italy, the eighty-four-year-old Emperor rose red-faced and pushed the cardinal to the door without hearing him out.

The Austrian foreign minister at this time was Count Stephan von Burian, a Hungarian. He belonged to that character type who are least suited to political life, for he was a doctrinaire bureaucrat. King Ferdinand of Bulgaria remarked of him: "Herr Burian is a professor and thinks all Europe is his classroom. But Europe does not listen to him." Burian conducted the negotiations as badly as possible. He started out by refusing to consider any of the demands so that Italy was forced into the arms of the enemy. Then, at the very last, he virtually consented to everything; by that time, unfortunately, the Italians had signed a treaty in London two weeks since.

The victory of Gorlice came a week too late. Italy, obligated to "benevolent neutrality," handed Austria-Hungary a declaration of war. After the war the Germanophile statesman Giovanni Giolitti asserted that Italy had at the time acted justly and with moderation. One wonders what she would have done had she decided to be unprincipled! Wilson, too, assured the Italians after the Armistice that they had entered the war to fight for the principles of right and justice.

The Austrians had only 30,000 men, mostly militia, on the Italian border. The situation was fraught with opportunity for the Italians. But they disappointed the new allies as they had their old ones. They did nothing. The Central Powers at first practically disregarded the new enemy, a nation of forty millions. Count Luigi Cadorna, the Italian commander, did not attempt until July 1915 to break through the Austrian front on the Isonzo. During this battle and the subsequent ten battles on the Isonzo the Austrian army was able to beat off the Italian attacks with the odds in men one to two, sometimes one to three, against them.

V

During the Dardanelles struggle Falkenhayn had cast frequent and uneasy glances toward Turkey. He knew that the British were only a hairsbreadth from success. The Bosporus would be safe only if the Central Powers crushed Serbia, thereby opening a land route to Constantinople. And only then would it be possible to supply Turkey with sufficient matériel for her to attack the Suez Canal. But Falkenhayn did not care to undertake to smash Serbia unless the Bulgarians assisted, and the Bulgarians did not want to come in until the campaign in the east was decided in Germany's favor.

King Ferdinand of Bulgaria had hoped, during the Balkan War, to take Constantinople and crown himself as the successor to the Byzantine emperors; he had the robes of one of these emperors, rented from a theatrical costumer, laid away in a trunk for that occasion. But Serbia, Rumania and Russia had put spokes in his wheel. Ever since he had been pondering revenge.

During the last year before the war Bulgaria had moved closer to the Central Powers, although only after—as the Bulgarian prime minister put it in his memoirs—"the powerful and convincing tongues of the various banks had spoken." Germany granted a loan to Bulgaria, and the Bulgarian finance minister then succeeded in forcing a treaty through Parliament—although a small insurrection broke out among the deputies and it took a drawn revolver to quell it and get a majority vote.

Before the alliance with Germany was signed, King Ferdinand surprised the Kaiser by making the assertion—which was hard to check —that he had a personal fortune of several millions stashed away in London. If he declared war on the Entente, this fortune would be lost. He could therefore take up the sword only if, in case the war turned out badly, which God forbid, Germany guaranteed to compensate for this loss. Germany underwrote this, and in 1930 the Bruening Government was still paying installments on the account. It must be conceded that this represented a real refinement in the gentle art of bribery, even by the high standards of the Balkans.

On October 7, 1915, Mackensen crossed the Danube—more than half a mile wide at this point—and two days later took Belgrade. The Serbs fought with the courage of desperation. They lost their country, 80,000 dead and 150,000 prisoners; but 100,000 men escaped to Albania. For a while Serbia considered a separate peace. Pashitch circumspectly laid the groundwork. First of all he had Chief of Staff Dimitryevitch, who had organized the assassination of Archduke Franz Ferdinand, court-martialed and shot. This gesture was intended both to placate the Austrians and to get rid of an accomplice who knew too much. Naturally, Pashitch had a good pretext; he asserted that Dimitryevitch had been planning the assassination of the Serbian prince regent, Alexander. The fabricated evidence for the court martial was supplied by a creature named Danilovitch. Very few persons knew that the man hiding behind this alias was none other than the Ciganovitch who in 1914 had trained the assassins of Franz Ferdinand in bomb-throwing. Dimitryevitch died with savoir-faire. A few minutes before the execution the presiding officer of the court offered him a drink of brandy from his own glass; before he drank Dimitryevitch asked the officer whether he was sure he had no venereal disease. Ciganovitch, who had so willingly served the Serbian state, died in bitter poverty after the war. A state loves betrayal, but not the betrayer.

VI

The relationship of Greece to the Entente wavered wildly. When the war broke out there was only one man in the entire Balkans who had clear vision. Venizelos, the Greek prime minister, said Churchill, was the only man who recognized the moral reasons for the war; he alone had a measure of the relative strength of the two sides; he alone appreciated the inexhaustible resources of the British Empire. One of the purveyors of those resources which so impressed the Greek prime minister was the British armaments manufacturer Zaharoff, originally a fellow-countryman of Venizelos who had worked himself up from a no-account fireman, jailbird and tourist guide to one of the richest men in the world. As Sir Basil Zaharoff he became a Knight of the Order of Bath and of the Grand Cross of the Legion of Honor, and received an honorary doctorate from Oxford. Zaharoff took so kindly an interest in the personal finances of Venizelos that the prime minister decided to offer England an alliance. At the time, Grey refused it. An alliance with Greece meant an immediate declaration of war from Turkey and Bulgaria; it would also have offended the Russians, who considered Greece a rival for Constantinople. Thereafter, two parties fought it out in Athens. King Constantine, the brother-in-law of Kaiser Wilhelm, favored neutrality; Venizelos was for war. When during the Serbian campaign the Allies proposed to make a landing in Greek Salonika, the King dismissed Venizelos and proclaimed his country's neutrality —in accord with the wishes of the people, who had no heart for war. But the Allies respected Greek neutrality no more than the Germans had respected that of Belgium; to protect the Serbs they landed 50,000 men in Salonika and advanced toward Serbia. They were however too late with their aid and retreated back to Salonika.

Falkenhayn could not bring himself to attack the intruders. By holding his hand he hoped to keep Athens neutral. But he had not reckoned with the bludgeoning methods of the British. England was not content with Greek neutrality; she demanded active aid. Following the advice of Field Marshal Wilson to take Constantine by the throat, England blockaded the importation of food and sent an ultimatum threatening to bombard Athens and demanding the surrender of German ships in Greek ports, the deposing of the King and the recall of Venizelos. Athens yielded. A reign of terror eliminated the last recalcitrant elements, and Greece declared war on Germany.

VII

The hardest battles of the year 1915, however, were fought not on the Vistula, the Isonzo or the Danube, but in northern France. Joffre thought he could shatter the German front by mass attacks after heavy artillery preparation. But the British and the French were repeatedly beaten back. Operations on the western front petered out into "bloody meaninglessness," in Lloyd George's phrase.

Joffre and the British supreme commander, Haig, were convinced that all that mattered was "to kill off Germans." Lloyd George and Churchill disagreed. During those attempts at a breakthrough in 1915, England and France lost half a million dead and 1.3 million wounded. The German losses were not half so great. This method of waging war merely by "extinguishing human lives" seemed to Lloyd George the cruellest kind of blundering; the men who fell in those ghastly offensives could have been used to conquer Gallipoli or save the Serbs by a massive attack from Salonika. A third of the ten million shells which were fired in futile attacks in the west could have prevented the Russian retreat. A manpower superiority of 3:2 was obviously insufficient for penetrating well-fortified positions. If that were so, German breakthroughs could also be discounted; consequently, a good part of the western front army could be transferred to areas where easier successes were possible and where old allies could be saved or new ones won. England must make use of her command of the seas.

Such were Lloyd George's arguments, but he did not succeed in convincing the generals. In the spring of 1915, Joffre had promised that he would be crossing the Rhine by October; he seemed not a bit abashed when by the end of the year he had reconquered only eight of the twenty thousand square miles of occupied territory. In vain Churchill proved that the casualties in France were proportionately far higher than those at the Dardanelles; Churchill was still considered the adventurer and Haig the sober expert.

The year 1915 had been one of disappointment for the Entente. In France, on the Isonzo, at the Dardanelles, the Central Powers had held their ground; and in Russia and Serbia they had thrust the ring of besiegers far back. But nowhere had they made large gains. England and France therefore did not doubt that they would win ultimately; in the long run their superior resources must tell. Russia's vast manpower was still far from exhausted; Kitchener's army was still being built up. By the middle of 1916 all four great powers were to be ready to begin a new offensive simultaneously.

CHAPTER NINETEEN

The Mounting Assault

> *The definition and limitation of war aims remains a political task during a war, and the way of solving it necessarily influences the conduct of the war.*
>
> —BISMARCK

I

At Christmas 1915 Falkenhayn sketched out an analysis of the situation. The Russian offensive power had been broken, the Serbian army annihilated, the Italians had learned that they could not attain their "predatory ends," he wrote. Each one of these assertions was wrong. Falkenhayn then went on to calculate that Germany had some twenty-six extra divisions over which she could dispose freely. These would not suffice for a breakthrough in the west. Therefore what should be done?

At this point the German chief of staff put forward the strangest proposal in military history: he advocated a frontal attack against the strongest antagonist at his strongest point. In other words, he wanted to attack the French at the fortress of Verdun. Falkenhayn did not propose taking Verdun. All he hoped to achieve by his offensive was a "bleeding to death of France's strength." France was now "weakened to the limit of endurance," he argued. Whether or not the fortress could be captured was not significant. What was sure was that France would have to throw in her last resources to defend a key point like Verdun.

Every step in Falkenhayn's line of reasoning was wrong. If a battle of attrition were to be fought, there was no need to launch it against the strongest French position; anywhere else the French would have put up bitter resistance. Attacking Verdun could cost the Germans approximately as many casualties as the French. And the idea of attrition was senseless, since the enemy's manpower potential was double that of Germany. If Falkenhayn had asked Ludendorff, for example, he would have heard that the Supreme Command in the East considered the offensive against Verdun a criminal act. But Falkenhayn was not in the habit of discussing his plans with anyone. The Kaiser assented to his proposal.

All historians agree that the Verdun offensive was a mistake. But what else should Falkenhayn have done in order to use the half year at his disposal before the Russian army recovered its striking power and Kitchener's army was ready?

On his desk lay a proposal from Conrad to cut off the Italian front by launching an attack from Tyrol (see map below). The prospects were similar to those afforded the year before by the prospective pincers movement against Russia. On a 125-mile front Cadorna had only five divisions; his other thirty-three were posted on the 100 miles of Venetian front. Conrad wanted to break through in Tyrol with some 300,000 men; he asked for German aid to the tune of 150,000 men. With this force he would "tie the whole sack on the Isonzo."

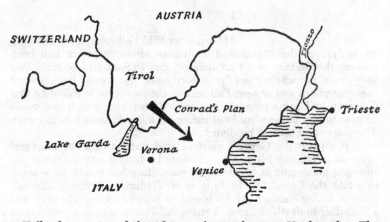

Falkenhayn rejected this plan, preferring his own Verdun idea. The argument he presented was that victory on the Isonzo would not decide the war. That was a pointless objection; the capture of Verdun would not have decided the war either. But if the offensive from South Tyrol had been successful—and to judge by later experience it would have been—then the Italians would have lost the core of their army. Even if they did not conclude a separate peace, that profoundly unmilitary people would not again have been able to muster the strength for an attack; the Austrians could have held the new front line running from Lake Garda to Venice with weak forces.

There were other possibilities. There was an attack upon Rumania, for which Falkenhayn had made all the preparations. There was a further assault upon Russia. After the war both Lloyd George and Churchill declared that if Falkenhayn had conquered the Ukraine, instead of senselessly throwing men against Verdun, Russia would have collapsed and England and France would have been forced to sign a disadvantageous peace. The Black Sea and even the Caspian Sea would have been the proper goals of the Germans, these English statesmen argued. "Literally a few thousand Germans could have dominated Northern Persia, and eastward beyond Persia lay Afghanistan and the threat to India," writes Churchill. General Hoffmann of the Supreme Command in the East also recommended a fresh offensive against Russia. Had it succeeded, the siege of Germany would have been broken and the danger of starvation eliminated. But a march toward Kiev involved the gravest dangers. It would have meant extending the eastern front by some 700 miles when the enemy had almost a two to one superiority in the west. Perhaps such a tremendous enterprise might have succeeded if the classes of 1897 to 1900 were called up prematurely, if all reserve and rear-area troops were ruthlessly combed out for the one great exertion, and if Turkish and Bulgarian troops were also employed. But it is impossible to say for certain that such a venture would have come off.

II

Crown Prince Wilhelm was in command at Verdun. His staff understood Falkenhayn's Verdun plan as any soldier would understand it— that Verdun was to be taken. The offensive almost succeeded in the very first days, and that for a curious reason. Joffre's aviators had informed him that an offensive was impending; deserters had brought similar reports. But the general could not imagine that Falkenhayn would run headlong up against his strongest position; he therefore thought the Verdun attack was a feint. For this reason he at first sent in reinforcements hesitantly. The Germans gained ground. But Falkenhayn had no reserves at hand to exploit this early success. He was convinced that the British would undertake a relief offensive and was holding troops in readiness against this. "If you want to defend everything, you defend nothing," Schlieffen used to say. The general who attempts to secure himself against all dangers cannot force a decision anywhere. By the time Falkenhayn's reserves arrived, the French reinforcements had also been brought up. Within ten days the number of defenders rose from 150,000 to 800,000. French generals threatened their infantrymen that they would have them mowed down by their own artillery if they retreated.

Now the battle of attrition began. Within an area of a few square miles one and a half million men lay in mud and blood facing one another. The inferno of Verdun lasted almost half a year. The losses on both sides were about equally high. Meanwhile the Anglo-French army on the western front, which Falkenhayn was going to "bleed to death,"

increased in numbers by 400,000 men. Time and again Crown Prince
Wilhelm asked permission to stop the battle, but his ambitious staff
chief was an adherent of Falkenhayn's attrition idea. After six months
the German forces had moved a few thousand yards closer to the city
of Verdun; half a year later the French, by a surprise offensive, took the
entire area back. Falkenhayn, as certain persons on the staff of the
Supreme Command in the East remarked, had "bloodily squandered"
a whole year.

III

Conrad had meanwhile decided to wage his offensive against the
Italians alone. For this purpose he removed five of his best divisions
from the eastern front. From his desk at the war ministry, April seemed
like a good time for such a venture. Unfortunately April in the Alps
meant snow still six feet deep; the army had to wait, and Cadorna
doubled the number of his troops at the point of attack. Nevertheless,
the breakthrough was successful. The Tyrolese and Styrians, the Hungarians and Bosnians who had advanced in torn shoes and with bleeding feet over precipitous cliffs and through deep ravines, over smooth
alpine grass and loose scree, now saw the Venetian plain spreading
before them. Cadorna was already preparing to evacuate the entire
Isonzo front—when his reinforcements unexpectedly held the line. Conrad considered trying again to break through. But at this moment he
received a surprise blow.

The Russians had prepared an offensive on the eastern front. When
Cadorna appealed for help, Marshal Brusilov, commanding in the south,
decided to attack the southern half of the eastern front, which was held
by Austrians. He did so without preparation, without assembling troops
for the offensive. His operation resembled a large-scale reconnaissance,
a knocking on a wall that had shown signs of crumbling. On this sector
the Russians scarcely outnumbered the Austrians.

Now Conrad paid the price for having stripped the front of five crack
divisions of German-speaking Austrians and of numerous batteries. The
defense was conducted by the armies under the command of the Archduke Joseph Ferdinand, of Count Bothmer, and of Pflanzer-Baltin.
Joseph Ferdinand was a man who loved life. He loved it twice as
much when it was embellished by a good table, gay music, Viennese
chansonettes, and hunting. The Archduke was a goodhearted fellow;
he kept the troops happy by sending brass bands up to the foremost
trenches. But military discipline suffered under his easygoing command.
The generals forgot how to issue precise orders; the troops forgot how
to obey. Conrad, too, exercised only loose control of his armies. He
was a strategist, but not a field commander, respected but not feared.

To interfere vigorously and tighten discipline at the front was not his dish. When the Russians marched, the Austro-Hungarian troops ran away. Whole battalions surrendered to a handful of mounted Cossacks. In three days Brusilov took 200,000 prisoners. Without an encirclement, without superior forces, without strategic art, he had won a victory twice the size of Tannenberg. The armies of the Archduke and of Pflanzer-Baltin dissolved; the retreat became a rout. The Emperor Franz Joseph, whose last months of life were saddened by this terrible defeat, said: "If only we had German leadership." This cry of despair was understandable. For the army of the Bavarian general Count Bothmer stood like a rock in a raging sea. Of its five divisions, only one was from Germany proper. But the will of this one man seemed to extend to the entire hundred thousand soldiers under his command, for his Austro-Hungarian divisions held also. This defense was a brilliant demonstration of the importance of leadership. Bothmer did not retreat until the two armies on his left and right had been thrown far back and he had to withdraw or lose contact with them.

As soon as the offensive began, Conrad asked Falkenhayn for aid. Falkenhayn hesitated. By the time he made up his mind the gap in the front had been enlarged and he had to throw in 400,000 men. After five weeks they stabilized the lines, but meanwhile the Austrians had lost 750,000 men, of whom 380,000 had been taken prisoner. It was the greatest coup of the war. The collapse of the Austrian front seriously strained relations between Germany and Austria. At the Supreme Command in the East, whose area of command had now been extended to the south, General Hoffmann noted: "My fondness for the Austrians has increased remarkably in the past two weeks. They are impossible! They run away, they lie, they send false reports, and at the same time they are utterly insolent and make difficulties wherever they can. I wouldn't mind fighting a war against that bunch some time!"

IV

While Falkenhayn was throwing division upon division into the gap left by the Austrian rout, the guns on both sides of the Somme began to thunder with a fury unequalled before or afterwards. On a six-mile front an area of less than forty square miles was churned up again and again by thirty million shells and mines. The battle lasted for four months. The entire area became a field of shell-holes. In these holes, in which rain water collected, lay the soldiers. Night after night the mess crews would not get through, and when they did the soldiers could scarcely swallow their food, so poisoned was the air by the smell of decaying corpses. Daily, hourly, fresh hailstorms of shellfire poured down upon the devastated fields. But when the red flares rose and the word "attack" was passed from shell-hole to shell-hole, the starving, louse-ridden soldiers manned their machine guns again; hand grenades flew at the oncoming enemy, barrages roared from the overheated muzzles of the batteries, and in the evening the army communiqué would report dryly that strong enemy assaults had been beaten off. The courage of the German soldiers made up for the numerical and technical superiority of the enemy and for the mistakes of the German command. Falkenhayn was stubborn enough to continue the offensive against Verdun even after the start of the Battle of the Somme. He did not call off his own attack until the Somme had been aflame for two weeks.

V

Falkenhayn had led the German army for some two years, and in this period his hair had turned white. He had held the fronts, even pushed the enemy back, but he had failed to recognize the key problem of the war: that merely holding firm was not enough, since time was working against Germany. His strategy of attrition meant no more than patching holes. Finally his whole policy came down on his head when a disaster took place which he had not counted on, and which he had neglected to insure against while there was still time: Rumania declared war on Austria. Suddenly 750,000 fresh enemy troops were hurled against the besieged Central Powers. When the war broke out, Rumania had had a mutual aid treaty with the Triple Alliance. King Charles of Rumania was a Hohenzollern; but his entire country was opposed to war on the side of the Central Powers; the Rumanians had a deadly hatred of the Hungarians, who ruled despotically some three million Rumanians. King Charles did not long survive the outbreak of the war. His son Ferdinand, influenced by his pretty and vivacious wife, leaned toward the Allies. But haggling was so much a part of Rumanian politics that even after Brusilov's victorious offensive Rumania negotiated for two months. Finally the Russians handed an ultimatum to Bucharest, and the Rumanians marched.

The Kaiser was playing cards when he received the news. His first reaction was that the war was lost; Germany must ask for peace. Then he decided to dismiss Falkenhayn. Hindenburg and Ludendorff were the only possible successors. Sharing the responsibility, they took over the leadership of the German army under the titles of Chief of Staff and Deputy Chief of Staff. They also tacitly assumed the conduct of German foreign affairs.

The change was not one of persons, but of philosophies. A torrent of energy poured through the German military organization. Armaments production was stepped up, auxiliary military duty for all male Germans proclaimed; the replacement army was combed for eligible men, basic training improved, the defense placed on a more flexible basis. As always when reforms are undertaken, much was done to excess. Steel furnaces were built which were never fired up. But the mistakes in detail did not detract from the overall achievement.

Paul von Hindenburg came from a family of impoverished Prussian nobility. His mother had been the daughter of a middle-class army doctor. His strong points were his unshakable calm, pedantic exactitude —he would put in every missing comma in a document—and the tenacity he inherited from generations of landed proprietors. Even during crises he would go to bed at ten o'clock—"and really sleep," one of his subordinates remarked with envious admiration. He was warm-hearted and had a sense of humor; when a victory was won on a Saturday, he would wait until Sunday to report it, so that the school-children would have a holiday on Monday. When a sculptor admired his "sculptural" head, he remarked smilingly that before the Battle of' Tannenberg nobody had ever noticed it. When he was honored at solemn ceremonies, he complained that he felt like the elephant at the zoo on Sunday. A year after the victory at Tannenberg he happened to arrive at the city of Insterburg, which he had liberated during that battle. An anniversary celebration was in progress at the moment. Hindenburg was not recognized and was ordered to drive around the city in order not to interfere with the parade. Hindenburg smiled and ordered his chauffeur not to enter the town. In later days when he was asked who had really won the Battle of Tannenberg, he usually replied that he did not know, but that if the battle had been lost, he would have lost it. Almost seventy at the time of his appointment, he found that his mind wearied under the strain of decisions, so that in the latter stages of the war he left everything to Ludendorff. When Ludendorff made a suggestion in matters of great importance, he would answer: "I cannot think of anything better either; God help us." Toward the end his staff scarcely bothered to tell him where the divisions were located.

The man who was thus entrusted with the fate of Germany, Erich Ludendorff, was of different caliber. His father, who had Swedish blood, came from a family of Pomeranian merchants, had gone bankrupt as a tenant farmer running a large estate and thereafter became an agent selling hail insurance. His mother was of the ancient German military nobility. There seemed to be no limit to Ludendorff's energy. He was a first-rate organizer, ready to assume any and all responsibility. Even as a lowly young staff officer, he had been at sword's-point with everyone around him. There were, however, a good many persons who believed that his toughness was more assumed than natural. Toward women he showed a peculiar weakness; he was fond of erotic adventures and rather liked hearing himself referred to as an "old sinner."

Urgent as the situation was on all sides, Ludendorff decided to deal with Rumania immediately, even at the cost of stripping other fronts. He needed Rumanian oil and he wanted to make an example of this new enemy. While Rumanian hordes were flowing like lava down into the valleys of undefended Transylvania, Ludendorff threw together two feeble armies consisting of German, Austrian, Bulgarian and Turkish troops—a good part of them militia. One army was placed in Transylvania, the other in Bulgaria. Falkenhayn was given command of the northern army. He had turned down the post of ambassador to Constantinople and had asked for a front-line command irrespective of his rank. This man who had failed as chief of staff proved to be a brilliant field commander. He led his 60,000 men across the 6000-foot Szerduk Pass in the Transylvanian Alps, a narrow corridor twenty-five miles long and six miles wide, and won battle after battle against the Rumanians, who outnumbered his forces by three to one. But in spite of all attempts to encircle the enemy, he did not succeed in annihilating the Rumanian army. After three months, however, most of Rumania was occupied, even though Falkenhayn had been "hindered by innumerable needless instructions from Ludendorff," as he put it.

VI

Even before the collapse of Rumania, 1916 had produced two bitter disappointments for the British: on the Euphrates and on the North Sea.

At the outbreak of the war the German Military Cabinet had not thought fit to assign an army to Field Marshal Colmar, Baron von der Goltz. Goltz had written books and was considered too learned; he was also seventy-one. Actually he was energetic and robust. If he had commanded an army group during the 1914 advance, the Battle of the Marne might well have taken a different course. The Kaiser appointed him governor general of Poland, but he was eager for a front-line assignment. He was therefore assigned "to the person of the Ottoman Emperor." His job was, as he said bitterly, "to sit cross-legged on a divan in the Sultan's anteroom, smoke a lot of cigarettes, drink coffee incessantly, and wait for orders that would not come." But Goltz did not stay in Constantinople. He wanted to strike at England and therefore took command in Mesopotamia. When he left he said: "Now we shall see whether I am a genuine field marshal."

Mesopotamia, the Biblical Eden, was as Lloyd George later said "the paradise of the steel helmet." On the British side the generals ran things by themselves, without interference from the war minister in London, since the India Office was in charge of this area. They ran things very badly indeed. The supply of guns, ammunition, vehicles and medical equipment was miserable. From Basra General Townsend marched against Bagdad with an army of some 15,000 men, of whom only 3000 were Englishmen, the rest mostly Indians. The Turks under von der Goltz defeated him at Ktesiphon and encircled him at Kut-el-Amara. A relief army of 20,000 men was sent up; its equipment was so inadequate that the carts in which the wounded were to be carried out were upholstered with corpses so that the soldiers would not have to lie on hard boards.

Von der Goltz himself had only about 20,000 men. Nevertheless he insisted on continuing the siege, even in the face of the British relief army. He even dispatched a few of his companies to Persia in order to protect that country, where anarchy reigned, from the Russians. His emissaries reached the Emir of Afghanistan. At home people made fun of these missions; Goltz was said to be trying to play Alexander the Great. The field marshal himself never exaggerated his chances; he knew the supply situation too well to imagine that he could do anything sensational.

The besieged Townsend tried in vain to bribe the Turks to withdraw by offering them two million pounds. After one hundred and fifty days he capitulated. The Mesopotamian mess, as Lloyd George called it, had cost the British 40,000 men—twice the actual strength of the opposing Turkish army. But Goltz did not live to see the capitulation; ten days before he had died of typhus.

A year after his death the British conquered Bagdad. Joint German and Turkish offensives against the Suez Canal failed. But Turkey kept some half a million British troops tied up. Lloyd George's proposal to make a landing in the rear of the Turkish army in Palestine struck the generals as too bold.

VII

England's control of the sea also suffered a blow that year. The greatest naval battle in world history took place, and the British did not win it.

Admiral Jellicoe considered the primary duty of his fleet the maintenance of the blockade, and in this he was undoubtedly right. The fleet was also to guard against a German attempt to invade England, and to protect English seaborne traffic. These tasks did not call for actual battle. Jellicoe therefore intended to use his squadrons only if victory were a certain thing. If there were a naval battle, he expected the Germans to try to lure him to destruction by retreating through mine fields or U-boat zones. This was a danger he was not going to risk. Jellicoe was, as Churchill remarked, the only man on either side who could lose the war in an afternoon.

Tirpitz had not foreseen any such caution on the part of the British when he built up the German navy. The German admirals each had a set of very different plans, and for the first two years the naval war was fought chiefly among themselves. The Kaiser and the Naval Cabinet were against a large-scale attack; they pointed out that the British North Sea fleet was nearly twice as strong as the German navy in battleships and torpedo boats, three times as strong in cruisers. Given such superiority, a naval battle would almost certainly result in the annihilation of most of the German fleet. Then the British would be able to sail into the Baltic, which had hitherto been an uncontested German inland sea, and would supply Russia with arms. What was more, they would be able to stop submarine warfare as well, for only the active German fleet prevented the British from sealing in the U-boats by mine fields. And even if the German fleet won a naval battle, the English would still be strong enough to maintain the blockade—a consideration to which even the aggressive Admiral Scheer had to bow. Consequently, a naval battle must be avoided.

Those who favored the German fleet's coming out and fighting pointed out that in naval battles chance tended to play a greater part than in land battles. They admitted that the German ships were inferior to the English in guns, but they had better armor and high accuracy. Therefore it would be perfectly possible to win a naval battle. The creator of the fleet, Grand Admiral von Tirpitz, argued that after the war the fleet would never receive a pfennig from the *Reichstag* unless it committed itself and the blood of its seamen "gloriously and rationally." Not that his policy was consistent; sometimes it seemed as if he advocated bold measures precisely when he expected the Naval Cabinet to be adamant against them. But as time passed and the fleet continued gathering rust in the ports, the aggressiveness of the admirals mounted.

In June 1916 the long-awaited battle took place at the Skagerrak. Scheer had come out with the entire navy to challenge the British. Jellicoe, who held the key to the German wireless code, knew of the project and at once sailed to meet him. In both fleets the battle cruisers led the way: ten British and five German ships. At five o'clock in the afternoon the cruisers began firing at a distance of ten miles, and after half an hour the Germans had sent two British cruisers with their entire crews to the bottom; the Germans themselves had suffered no losses. At this point the German main fleet appeared on the scene. Immediately, the British cruisers withdrew to team up with their fleet.

It was 7:30 P.M. when the main fleets clashed. After only an hour's fighting, Scheer broke off the engagement. The British had a superiority of almost two to one; moreover the visibility was bad and he had, in his hasty pursuit of the cruisers, come upon the British main fleet with his ships in an awkward formation. In the dark of night the Germans escaped back to Wilhelmshaven.

The outcome of the battle was amazing. The Germans had sunk 115,000 tons and lost only 61,000 tons. Sixty-one hundred British sailors had met their end, as against only twenty-six hundred Germans. On the other hand, the majority of the British battleships had scarcely got into the action. A battle from which the Germans had retreated could scarcely be called a German victory. But for the British, accustomed to triumphs at sea, the engagement was a setback.

VIII

England made up for the two reverses at the Euphrates and the Skagerrak by a single stroke: she placed at the head of the affairs a man who for all his demagoguery grew with the tasks confronting him, who united the strength of the lion with the cunning of the fox and steered the British Empire successfully through the storms.

David Lloyd George had originally been a pacifist liberal; during the Boer War he had often come near taking actual beatings because of his pro-Boer attitude. But once he assumed office, he saw matters in a different light. He learned how to growl for all the world like the British Lion. As Chancellor of the Exchequer he had imposed high taxes on the rich and introduced social insurance on the German model. When Kitchener went down with a British cruiser on the way to Russia, Lloyd George became minister for war. Up to then England had maintained her army on volunteers. Lloyd George introduced conscription.

But being war minister did not satisfy him. He was convinced that Great Britain could not win the war so long as Asquith was prime minister. His own passionate ambition was inclined to reinforce this idea. Asquith shared with Chancellor Bethmann-Hollweg of Germany a characteristic irresolution. He had spent his life in the parliamentary whirl and at bottom conceived of his job not as winning the war at any cost, but as keeping his discontented Cabinet together. For decades he had demonstrated his skill at mediation and waiting for things to ripen. But as Churchill wrote: "In War everything is different. There is no place for compromise in War. That invaluable process only means that soldiers are shot because their leaders in Council and camp are unable to resolve. In War the clouds never blow over, they gather unceasingly and fall in thunderbolts."

Lloyd George was the precise contrary to Asquith. Defeats and disillusionments, previous views and adversaries' arguments—all such things did not trouble him. Every morning he began a new life. He threw into his work all the temperament of a Welshman and all the tenacity of an Englishman. He examined problems thoroughly and listened to advice, but he made decisions more by intuition than by logic. In peacetime such an approach is not always successful. In wartime it was ideally suited to bring to bear all the power of the British Empire. Skilled parliamentary intriguer that he was, it was a small matter for Lloyd George to overthrow the Asquith Cabinet and put himself into the saddle. Without any bias, he chose the best minds in England for his colleagues. When he wanted to take Churchill back, however, he ran into difficulties. "For days I discussed with one or other of my colleagues Churchill, his gifts, his shortcomings, his mistakes, especially the latter. Some of them were more excited about his appointment than about the War. It was a serious crisis. It was interesting to observe in a concentrated form every phase of the distrust and trepidation with which mediocrity views genius at close quarters." It took all his cleverness to obtain at least the post of minister for armaments for Churchill. The new minister immediately put through a tremendous increase in war production.

IX

When the Russian offensive ground bloodily to a stop, people in St. Petersburg began talking about a separate peace. Prime Minister Stürmer was considered Germanophile; the Entente unjustly accused him of having been bought by the Germans. Count Witte, the cleverest statesman in Russia, had told everyone who would listen—including the French ambassador—that by staying in the war Russia was only pulling England's chestnuts out of the fire. Russia's holy mission in the Orient was merely a romantic delusion, he argued, and the self-important Balkan peoples were nothing but carelessly baptized Turks. But unfortunately for Europe Count Witte died in 1915.

Germany had made many overtures to Russia through court and banking circles. But here, too, Chancellor Bethmann always hesitated to commit himself. He could not bring himself to the point of offering Russia the prewar *status quo* and Constantinople into the bargain, thereby sacrificing Germany's Turkish ally. Consequently, Russia had not even replied to his overtures. During those months the Czar was no doubt considering which was the greater peril: to have the war go on forever and be executed by revolutionaries, or to make a tolerable separate peace and be assassinated by the Pan-Slavists. If, however, he were given Constantinople as a present for the Pan-Slavists, he would be safe. But while he was considering, the Germans slammed shut the door to a separate peace. They founded the new state of Poland.

The governor general of Poland was a General Beseler of the engineering corps, by nature more a theoretician than a soldier. One day, under the promptings of a number of Polish candidates for ministerial posts, he came out with the statement that if a Kingdom of Poland were set up, the Poles would supply the Central Powers with an army of at least 200,000 men—or if conscription were introduced, of one million men. It can scarcely be said that many Poles encouraged Beseler in this hope; one Polish politician told him, when asked whether Poland would supply 100,000 volunteers, that there were not that many potential suicides in Poland. Austrian Chief of Staff Conrad also warned against the idea. But Beseler's project had some support. It had occurred to Chancellor Bethmann-Hollweg that the creation of a Polish state might correct the bad impression which had been made by Germany's violation of Belgian neutrality. In his memoirs he writes with naive helplessness: "Everywhere in the country we encountered the idea of the restoration of an independent Poland; in the long run we could not go on ignoring this aspiration." Moreover, Austrian Foreign Minister Burian hoped to be able to establish an Austrian archduke as King of Poland. In that case, the House of Hapsburg would surrender Galicia to the new Poland and would incorporate the new Polish kingdom into the dual monarchy. Burian had the effrontery to term this "Austro-Polish solution" a sacrifice on the part of Austria. Ludendorff felt nothing but contempt for the proposal; he hoped to kill it by demanding cession of a "buffer strip" to Germany. The buffer strip extended almost to Warsaw and would have brought seven million Poles into the German Reich.

The whole project of setting up a Polish state was a blunder. Such a state was bound to lay claim to Prussia's Polish provinces. But Bethmann was an innocent, Ludendorff clung to the straw of a Polish army fighting on Germany's side, Burian thought of his archduke, and the Kingdom of Poland was proclaimed to exist—although for the present it had no king. No Poles turned up at the recruiting offices. A small Polish legion composed mainly of Austrian Galicians had to be disarmed again because it attempted to desert to the Russians. The Czar outbid the Germans by proclaiming a Poland which would include the Polish areas of Germany, Austria and Russia; Stürmer was overthrown; and Germany and Austria began an endless bickering over the candidate for the Polish throne.

X

Perhaps the establishment of Poland shed a faint glow over the last hours of a man whose sorrow-filled life came to an end shortly afterwards. Eighty-six-year-old Franz Joseph came down with a case of grippe. He felt the chill of death upon him, asked for the sacraments, and after he had received them sat down at his desk once more to work as he had done all his life. Toward evening he lay down on his iron army cot after impressing upon his valet that he wished to be waked as usual on the following morning, because he had a great deal of work to do. Dutifully he inquired of his doctor: "Am I lying properly?" Then he fell asleep for good. Following the Spanish court ceremonial, two days later Chief Marshal of the Court Prince Montenuovo tapped with a golden staff upon the gate of the Church of the Capuchins in the Neuer Markt: Franz Joseph of Hapsburg was asking admission after a pilgrimage of eighty-six years. The gate opened and bearded mendicant friars admitted the mortal remains of Franz Joseph. Twilight had fallen upon the Austro-Hungarian Empire.

For almost seventy years Franz Joseph had governed the Empire. He had seen come and go Napoleon III and Bismarck, Czar Nicholas I and Cavour, Lincoln and Gladstone. Fate had heaped upon his head misfortune upon misfortune. He was spared the last and worst: the collapse of his Empire.

His grand-nephew Karl succeeded to the throne. Karl's enemies maintained that he was thirty, looked like twenty, and spoke like ten. But this was unjust. Willingly, though with effort, he had absorbed what education the first five classes of the *gymnasium* had to offer. He had been a hard-working but not a passionate soldier and had married a devout, plain princess of the impoverished and proud House of Parma. Like Joseph II he was full of natural kindliness and had little worldly experience; but he was without the diligence, the ambitious drive, and the cleverness of this great ancestor. When he heard of the coal shortage in Vienna, he personally examined the stores at the railroad terminals and sent horses from the court stables to help transport the coal. He tried to introduce improvements in all things, but when he changed personnel he usually replaced a stronger man by a weaker one. The principle that a monarch has to do what is proper rather than what is kind, was beyond him. During the Tyrol offensive he had been in command of a corps; when he saw men lying on the ground from sheer exhaustion, he halted the advance. Premier Körber—his predecessor, Stürgkh, had been shot by the Socialist deputy Adler—remarked thoughtfully: "The old Emperor endeavored for fifty years to destroy the monarchy, and did not succeed." He paused, and continued: "But this young man will take care of it in two years."

Chief of Staff Conrad was appointed army commander in Tyrol. His successor, Arz von Straussenberg, had to conduct his business while moving around, for the Emperor kept travelling about and insisted on the chief of staff's accompanying him.

XI

The Allies had lost over 600,000 men on the Somme, of which 250,-000 were killed; the German losses were half that number. Lloyd George felt that this bloodletting could not go on. "One-third of the Somme guns and ammunition transferred to the banks of another river, the Dnieper," he wrote, "would have won a great victory for Russia and deferred the Revolution until after the War." To be a general in positional warfare was a stupid occupation, he declared; all the strategist had to do was to sit at his desk and distribute several million shells among the various sectors of the front, then send his men running up against the enemy barbed wire here and there. Every battalion commander faced more difficult tasks than the commander in chief. But the prime minister could not hope to put across his views against the opposition of his generals. They had their plans all ready: in March 1917 they were going to launch a new offensive on the western front. Joffre was replaced by young General Nivelle whose surprise attack had snatched back the meager German conquests at Verdun. Nivelle promised the government he would drive the Germans back across the Rhine. The Entente was optimistic; the governments reasoned that at the beginning of the war the Germans had been better equipped than the British or the Russians; that accounted for their initial successes in the first two years. In the long run superior resources must win.

The French, the Russians, and the British therefore believed they would be able to achieve their war aims. The French were demanding at least Alsace-Lorraine; in addition they had obtained a treaty from Russia assuring them a free hand on the left bank of the Rhine. The Russians wanted above all to break up "anachronistic" Austria-Hungary. Sazonov was in favor of incorporating the Polish-populated Prussian provinces into a new Poland ruled by the Czar; he would also set up a separate state of Hanover, give German territory to Belgium, and divide up all the German colonies. On the other hand he considered Italy's claim to Dalmatia gross impudence—all the more so since Saint Isaac of Dalmatia was one of the foremost saints in the Orthodox calendar. England was modest; aside from taking over the German colonies, her two war aims were the weakening of Germany and of Russia. By the end of 1916, however, she did not feel that either of these aims had been sufficiently realized. Italy wanted new provinces —as she always did after lost battles. This time she was claiming territory on the Brenner Pass and on the Isonzo. As for Turkey, the Arab areas were to be made independent under British patronage and the rest of Turkey divided among Russia, England, France and Italy. All these details had been carefully fixed in treaties.

After French blood had flowed in torrents in the Battle of the Somme, the Socialist Brizon concluded a speech in the Chamber of Deputies by asking whether France had not suffered enough, whether the time had not come for a negotiated peace. Premier Briand—a man of the peaceful Left—answered: "What is this, Monsieur Brizon? Ten provinces of your native land are occupied by the enemy and you come forward saying, 'Let us negotiate, let us ask for peace.' How little you know France if you imagine that a saving of billions of francs, or even a saving of blood, would be acceptable under such humiliating circumstances. What kind of peace would France receive? It would be a warlike peace indeed. If you wish the light of peace to shine above the world, Monsieur Brizon, if you wish the ideas of liberty and justice to reign, you must call for victory and not the kind of peace we could obtain today." By a vote of four hundred and twenty-one to ninety-six the Chamber decided to post this speech on placards all over France. French patriotism, drawing upon memories of French greatness in the past, was still strong and fervent.

With the Allies in such a mood, it occurred to Austrian Foreign Minister Burian at the end of 1916 to make a peace offer—or more precisely, to broach the idea of peace negotiations without indicating any definite conditions. He overlooked the fact that it takes only one to start a war, but two to conclude a peace, and that there was a gap wide as the mouth of hell between the two groups' conception of reasonable conditions for peace. The Germans had their eyes fixed upon the "war map"; that is, they were obsessed with the vast territories they already occupied. But this war map did not show the trump cards in the hands of the Entente: the British domination of the seas, the blockade which was slowly starving the Central Powers, and the human reserves on the Allied side.

German Chancellor Bethmann was hardly so foolish as to believe the offer would be accepted. But he wanted the German people and the neutral countries of the world to see that Germany was not to blame for the continuance of the war. Accordingly, thirteen days before Christmas a proposal to discuss the possibilities of peace was dispatched. The tone of the note was one of confidence in victory; one neutral diplomat commented that the Central Powers were threatening peace or else. . . . As a basis for discussion the Central Powers had also cooked up quite a menu among themselves, one which would please the most jaded appetite. They planned to ask for cession of the iron-ore region of Briey, the fortress of Liége and part of the Congo Territory, loose annexation of Poland, Lithuania and Courland, reduction in size of Serbia and Rumania. But Germany and Austria were not subjected to the embarrassment of having to lay this program on the table: within four days the leading statesmen of the Allies refused to consider "a proposal which is empty and insincere." In Berlin the leader of the Pan-Germans declared: "We can thank God on our knees that our peace offer was not accepted."

The shadow offer was a folly—a double folly because it interfered with a step toward peace which did have some prospect of success. The President of the United States, Woodrow Wilson, had long been considering asking both sides to state their conditions for peace. He had warned Germany against offering peace on the grounds that such a proposal would only be interpreted as weakness. Wilson's sympathies were with the Allies, but he wanted to be a peacemaker. Bethmann reacted to Wilson's attempts at mediation with mixed feelings; he feared the President's known partisanship and the German public's dislike for Wilson. For these reasons he had disregarded Wilson's advice and gone ahead. Nevertheless, the American peace proposal came a few days later.

The Central Powers replied to Wilson in a conciliatory tone, but evasively. They specified no conditions. Bethmann did not dare mention the *status quo ante* as a condition, for he feared the Pan-Germans. But he also did not dare to ask for more for fear of shutting the door against agreement. Washington advised the naming of hard conditions, on the basis of which bargaining could take place, but Bethmann's rigid sense of justice kept him from giving this serious consideration. The Allies, on the other hand, protested against being treated on the same level as the Central Powers. King George of England wept at being put on a par with the wicked enemy. The Allies gave as their war aims the dissolution of Austria-Hungary and Turkey, the restoration to France of Alsace-Lorraine, and fair reparations. Wilson told the German ambassador these demands were nothing but a bluff. In a speech to the Senate (January 22, 1917) he demanded a peace without victors or vanquished. He also warned the banks against extending foreign loans—a first attempt to exert pressure upon the Allies. But the Allied reply was such as to strengthen Germany's determination to carry out a fateful decision which she had taken at the beginning of the year 1917.

CHAPTER TWENTY

The Crucial Error

*The worst German blunder in the War was the
quarrel with America. It was at best a reckless
miscalculation; at its worst it was an inconceivable folly.*

—LLOYD GEORGE

*It seems to me a horde of madmen are govern-
ing us.*

—MAX WEBER, *March 1916, on
the U-boat question.*

I

At the end of the year 1916 Ludendorff
considered the military situation. He was deeply convinced that Germany could not content herself with holding out; she had to win the
war. To sign a peace without acquiring territory in the east and west,
would have meant that she had lost the war. But how could he possibly
force a victorious peace upon Germany's foes? The forces against the
Germans in the west were two to one. If the enemy with those odds
had not succeeded in breaking through the static positions, how could
Germany do it with half the enemy's manpower? There were no troops
she could withdraw from other fronts. In the east the Russians had
a twofold or threefold superiority, and the Austrians had little fight left.
In Italy and at Salonika also the enemy's strength was double Germany's. Obviously there was only one way to win: to introduce some
new method of warfare. And such a method was on hand: unrestricted
submarine warfare. The German Admiralty declared unequivocally
that use of this weapon would force England to her knees within six
months.

The entire question of submarines was curious. Tirpitz had not
thought much of them. At the outbreak of the war Germany had 27,
England 55, and France 77 submarines. Moreover, only about half the
Germans' submarines were seaworthy. Since two years were required
to build a U-boat, the deficiency could hardly be made up. And the
skeptical Tirpitz ordered few built. By the beginning of 1915 Germany
had twenty U-boats which could be used against the enemy. Of these,

a third were in drydock and another third sailing to or from an assignment; only seven submarines were in actual striking positions. With these seven Germany in February 1915 declared "unrestricted submarine warfare." The waters around Great Britain and Ireland were specified as a war zone; every enemy merchant ship would be sunk without warning, and neutral merchant ships ran the risk of being sunk since the British were abusing the flags of neutrals. Germany maintained that she had been forced to take this step because of the blockade which England, contrary to international law, had imposed upon Germany.

As always, international law was not very clear about the matter. Maritime problems were governed by the London Declaration of 1909, under which only certain war goods were "contraband" and only the importation of contraband could be stopped by blockade. Food was definitely not contraband. The Declaration of London had been drawn up at the instigation of England; it began by stating that the signatory powers recognized unanimously that the Declaration was "in accord with the generally accepted principles of International Law." But the House of Lords had not ratified this agreement, whereupon Germany had also refused to ratify it. Legally, therefore, no government was bound. England now declared all vital goods contraband—especially all foodstuffs. To the extent of her powers she prevented contraband goods from reaching Germany through neutral countries. Her intention was to starve Germany. Such aggression against non-combatants violated what was at that time conceived to be international law. The neutrals, the United States in particular, protested in vain.

When Germany now sent out submarines to attack merchant vessels, a real problem in international law arose. It was customary for warships to stop merchant ships, examine them, and if contraband were found, either take them as prizes or rescue the crew before sinking the vessel. A U-boat could not do this. Since the British were secretly arming merchant ships and flying neutral flags above them, a submarine that ventured such courtesies would have been sunk very swiftly.

Germany therefore announced that henceforth she would sink merchant shipping in the war zones without warning. Neutrals would be endangered only if they insisted on entering such zones. Unrestricted submarine warfare, Germany declared, was a reprisal against the English blockade; she would cease U-boat warfare if England lifted the hunger blockade. During the Second World War both England and America tacitly accepted the German view of international law by employing unrestricted submarine warfare against Japan.

But if the U-boat campaign of 1915 was no crime, it was—in Talleyrand's phrase—something worse: a blunder. Those seven U-boats could not seriously imperil England's maritime commerce, but they could and did do something else: they apprised England of the possibilities of the new mode of warfare and prompted the then First Lord of the Admiralty, Winston Churchill, to take immediate defensive measures. All merchant vessels were armed, supplies were laid in, and domestic agricultural production stepped up. After the war Churchill commented that if Tirpitz had waited until he had 200 U-boats, the consequences would have been incalculable.

But the warfare of those seven U-boats was far more injurious to Germany in another respect. One of them sank the British passenger liner *Lusitania,* one of the biggest ships in the world. In addition to a large cargo of ammunition the ship was carrying more than 1000 passengers, including several hundred Americans. Most of them were drowned. The American press promptly blared that this sinking was an act that Attila the Hun would have blushed to commit. No one mentioned that these Americans had had no need to sail aboard the *Lusitania* into a war zone. The German government was keeping a shipping lane open for American vessels. The German ambassador in New York had even published a newspaper advertisement warning prospective passengers; by a fateful oversight, however, the notice did not appear until the day the ship sailed. For all of this, the United States Senate tabled a motion to prohibit Americans from travelling on armed British vessels. In taking this stand America was defending the cause neither of international law nor humanitarianism; she was demonstrating only her firm resolve not to recognize any blockade against her British friends. For the pro-British in America the drowning of two hundred Americans was a gift from heaven, a propaganda point for swinging public opinion all over the United States to their side. The United States demanded that Germany cease unrestricted submarine warfare.

What was the German government to do? Was it to risk a declaration of war by the United States in order to sink 170,000 tons of shipping monthly—an amount England could replace forthwith by new construction? Germany called off unrestricted submarine warfare. But at the beginning of the following year, 1916, the folly was reënacted. Although the number of seaworthy U-boats had risen to a bare fifty, of which some were needed in the Mediterranean, so that at any given time there were never more than fifteen submarines roving the sea lanes, Germany once more declared unrestricted submarine warfare. The attempt failed as it had the previous year; the sinkings amounted to only 200,000 tons monthly—against a total English merchant fleet of twenty million tons. Again a liner with American passengers aboard was sunk. This time the United States instantly threatened to break diplomatic relations, and once more Germany yielded. One of the victims of this second campaign was Admiral Tirpitz; he resigned because his advice had been disregarded.

II

Now something astonishing happened. Public opinion in Germany, fed by the reports given out by the Admiralty and Tirpitz, rebelled against laying down "Germany's sharpest weapon." It never occurred to the submarine fanatics to examine objectively whether the prospects offered by unrestricted U-boat warfare outweighed the dangers of an American declaration of war. They turned the problem upside down; the story was that Chancellor Bethmann was too soft-hearted, and afraid to take the one drastic action which would decide the war. Clubs were formed "for the rapid crushing of England." The members of these clubs were not, as one might assume, determined to sail in submarines or fly in planes against England; they considered their patriotic duty done when they sent fierce telegrams to the chancellor and the *Reichstag*. The *Reichstag* soon declared itself by an overwhelming majority in favor of resuming unrestricted submarine warfare. Thus the enemy was given due notice of what was to be expected, and the hopes of the people became fixed more firmly than ever on this particular mode of warfare. Maximilian Harden came out strongest for it. He proposed Admiral Tirpitz for chancellor and wrote in his absurd, stilted language: "The diving boat is as decent an implement of war as any other. There's a loophole in the wall of legalisms; German seamanship will slip agilely through and hire away the island plutocrat's best cook."

All this enthusiasm was based upon a few memoranda handed out by the German Admiralty in which the effect of unrestricted submarine warfare was calculated down to the last nut and bolt. England, the argument ran, possessed a merchant fleet of twenty million tons. But of these, twelve million tons were required for military transports, coastal shipping, or were undergoing repairs; consequently only between seven and eight million tons were available to supply the civilian population. This shipping was supplemented by some four million tons from other countries. The U-boats could sink at least 600,000 tons monthly; moreover, two-fifths of the neutral shipping would be frightened off by submarine warfare and would refuse to continue sailing to England. All in all, submarine warfare would cut England's seaborne commerce within five months by 39%—the estimates were that precise. Such a pinch England could not endure. Admiralty Chief von Holtzendorff therefore concluded "that British resistance will be broken within half a year at most." U-boat warfare was, he argued, "the proper means for ending the war victoriously." Tirpitz wrote a tract in which he "guaranteed" that England would have to sue for peace within six months. All these men were well aware that proclamation of unrestricted submarine warfare would draw America into the war; the German ambassador in Washington, Count Bernstorff, and his military attaché, the future Chancellor von Papen, had made this amply clear. But Holtzendorff assured the nation on his word as a naval officer that not an American would set foot on the Continent. Tirpitz' successor, Capelle, declared in the *Reichstag* that the military significance of American intervention would be "zero, zero, zero!" If the Americans really attempted to send troops, the transports would be the most welcome quarry for the U-boats. Warship convoys for merchant ships would serve as fine targets for torpedoes. "The Americans cannot swim and cannot fly; they will not come," Minister of Finance Hergt added. "America's help is a phantom," Tirpitz was still announcing at the beginning of 1918.

In actuality the navy's calculations were so amateurish that any non-specialist could easily point out the fallacies. The argument was based on British tonnage, which was absurd. It should have been based upon world tonnage and should have undertaken to estimate what portion of that world tonnage England could draw upon. For it was obvious that before surrendering, England would secure shipping from other countries—by heavy payment and by blunt threats. First of all she could appropriate the 2.5 million tons of German shipping now interned in American and other neutral ports; these alone would make up for the sinkings of four months. Secondly, England would surely resort to the centuries-old device of convoying her merchant vessels. Furthermore, the British could significantly reduce the length of the dangerous sea voyage by having goods sent to French, Spanish, Portuguese or Italian ports and shipping them the rest of the way by railroad to the Channel ports. It would be cheaper to build new railroads than to capitulate. For example, England needed only some 15,000 tons of grain daily; four freighters could easily bring that amount across the English Channel, for nets and warships had made the Channel virtually submarine-proof. With the Channel safe from hostile shipping, England had ceased to be an island. Then there was the possibility of large stockpiles; the neutrals estimated that England had enough provisions to last her population a year. Finally, England could begin importing goods which took less shipping space: flour instead of grain, canned meats instead of livestock.

All these considerations were by no means the product of hindsight. In March 1916, the economist Max Weber sent all responsible persons a paper branding submarine warfare as "the policy of adventurers." But nobody went to the trouble of studying his conclusions. The possibility that the American nation, with twenty-three million men of military age, might join Germany's enemies, was blandly ignored by the ardent jingos. In vain Vice Chancellor Helfferich protested: "Once we have played our card of ruthless U-boat warfare and it proves to have been no trump, we will be lost, lost for centuries to come." Hindenburg and Ludendorff were convinced that there was no other way to win the war. If this were so, it was mandatory for Germany to seek a conciliatory peace instead of taking a course which would certainly make for an even more thorough defeat.

With the Supreme Command and the Admiralty, the *Reichstag* and public opinion, all demanding that this "last weapon" be put to use, the Kaiser, chancellor and vice chancellor shifted their ground. On February 1, 1917, unrestricted submarine warfare began. That day marked the death of Imperial Germany.

With bated breath Germany waited for victory. At first everything seemed to be going according to prediction; during the first six months the U-boats reported an average of 900,000 tons of shipping sunk monthly. We know today that the published statistics were about one and a half times as great as the real losses, chiefly because the Admiralty clapped on a certain number of tons for presumed losses from mines. Actual sinkings came to about the promised 600,000 tons.

Were the British forced to their knees? Did famine break out in England? Were the American troop transports stopped?

There was, of course, not the slightest trace of famine in England. The British did not even find it necessary to introduce food rationing. Race horses continued to receive high-quality oats. Not until February 1918, when the submarine danger had long since been eliminated, was rationing introduced for quite other reasons. Even then the rations were more than ample. As for the Americans: by the end of the war they had sent two million soldiers to France without losing a single man at sea. In sum, submarine warfare had made no inroads on Allied strength; everything had turned out just as the few warning voices had foretold. The British met the emergency by obtaining neutral ships, setting up convoys and increasing new construction; by the second quarter of 1918 current shipbuilding exceeded sinkings.

Lloyd George had succeeded in forcing through the convoy system against "the blind obstinacy of the Admiralty." His saving inspiration was almost defeated because of a bookkeeping error. The admirals declared that convoys were impracticable because two thousand five hundred ships a week entered British ports. Lloyd George pointed out that this figure took in every single loading of coastal steamers; of ocean-going vessels, there were only one hundred and twenty per week which needed protection.

But the German navy was also the prisoner of tradition. Submarine construction was not intensified. Admiral Capelle told a *Reichstag* committee to consider the chaos which would ensue in the regular promotion and organization of the navy if battleships were replaced by U-boats and airplanes. In peacetime, he pointed out, the maintenance costs resulting from excessive construction of submarines would be intolerable. It was not until the middle of 1918, shortly before the collapse, that he contracted for the building of three hundred and forty submarines.

III

The proponents of submarine warfare later pointed out that at the beginning of the U-boat campaign Admiral Jellicoe described the situation to American Admiral Sims in the gravest terms. That was clever of Jellicoe, since his prime purpose was to obtain as many American vessels as possible; it was policy to portray matters as desperate. Before the elections in 1918, Lloyd George and Churchill also solemnly declared that the decision had hung by a hair; they meant their fellow-citizens to appreciate what great work they had done in overcoming a fearful peril.

Later Churchill examined the entire submarine question more objectively, and in his *World Crisis* he concluded: "Whether the vehicle will break down the bridge does not depend on chance. It depends on the weight of the vehicle and the strength of the bridge. When both these are unknown beforehand, anxiety is natural. But once it is known that the bridge will bear at least ten tons and the vehicle at the most weighs no more than eight, all misgivings are proved to have been unfounded. To say that the vehicle 'nearly' broke down the bridge is untrue. There was never any chance of it. Whereas any one of a score of alternative accidents would have given the German Army Paris in 1914, the seafaring resources of Great Britain were in fact and in the circumstances always superior to the U-boat attack."

It has occasionally been argued that the U-boat war would have been successful had it been started in 1916, at which time the British defensive measures were not yet so strong. This argument is foolish. The British could have introduced the convoy system and could have increased new construction just as well in 1916 as in 1917. Since in 1916 Germany had only half as many U-boats as in 1917, the toll she could have taken then would have been only half as large.

The question has also been raised whether the United States might not have entered the war even without unrestricted submarine warfare. President Wilson's sympathies lay with the Allies. Had there been reason to fear a "German" peace, he would certainly have tried to bring America into the war. His representative, Colonel House, had agreed with Sir Edward Grey in 1915 that Wilson would propose a peace conference and support the Allies' minimum demands—presumably the prewar *status quo* and cession of Alsace-Lorraine to France. If Germany rejected this formula, House warranted that the United States would enter the war. But at the end of this document Wilson added the word "probably," and this reservation was enough to make Grey drop the plan. As Lloyd George emphasized, Wilson always kept one eye cocked toward the German and Irish voters in the United States. He also intensely wished to be hailed as a peacemaker; given the sentimentality of the American character, such a title would have assured his reëlection. Consequently, Wilson would not have brought America into the war if Germany had offered peace on the basis of the prewar *status quo*. Possibly Germany would have been able to propose a plebiscite in Alsace-Lorraine on condition that England held a plebiscite in Ireland—a demand that would have aroused great enthusiasm in the United States. Thus Germany might well have been able to keep America out of the war if she had given up the useless submarine warfare, and if she had made a reasonable peace offer.

After the war the United States Senate rejected Wilson's plan for a League of Nations on the grounds that it would involve America in needless wars. Wilson replied that even without a League of Nations the United States would have to intervene in unjust wars of aggression. One senator promptly drove him into a corner by asking whether the United States would have entered the war if Germany had not committed certain aggressive acts. Wilson answered that he hoped and trusted that America would have entered the war for the sake of justice. But this was an answer he had to give in order not to contradict what he had just said. There is no proof that Wilson would have managed to win the consent of Congress to a declaration of war if Germany had offered peace on terms of the prewar boundaries.

Mistakes are seldom committed singly. In January 1917 Germany offered Mexico several American states in return for aid as an ally. Mexico was neither sufficiently strong nor sufficiently trustworthy to be made the recipient of such proposals. News of the offer immediately reached Washington, since the British had the key to the German wireless code. The "Zimmermann note" made it easier for Wilson to obtain from Congress a declaration of war.

The United States went into the war with great vigor. She immediately instituted conscription, and within two years trained four million soldiers. And she lost no time applying against Germany all those blockade measures which she had vainly objected to England's employing.

CHAPTER TWENTY-ONE

Domestic Conflicts

> *We in Germany have not yet had sufficiently
> long experience of party strife to weaken its ef-
> fects and permit national leaders to put the
> Fatherland above their parties.*
>
> —BISMARCK

I

All the nations of Europe entered the First
World War with enthusiasm. The Germans, the French, the Russians
and the British were all convinced that they were taking up arms only
for the defense of their threatened native soil.

But when the black-white-red flags of Germany waved over Brussels
and St. Quentin, over Warsaw and Libau, the wind blew from another
quarter. "Where a drop of German blood has been spilled, there we will
stay!" cried the nationalist-liberal leader Bassermann, insulting a great
nation's mourning by a meaningless claim. Redrawing the map of Europe became an armchair occupation of innumerable philistines who
possessed neither the judgment to recognize what was attainable nor
the courage to stake their own lives for their aspirations. The Pan-
German League demanded not only Belgium, but France as far as the
Somme; Lille and Calais, Amiens and Sedan, and the mining region
of Briey were to become German. Then, they argued, Germany would
be close enough to Paris to prevent a fresh assault by the French.
France was to turn over this land to Germany "clear of human beings."
Poland, the Baltic provinces, and the Ukraine were to be detached from
Russia and annexed in some form to Germany and Austria-Hungary,
so that the Germans would have land in which to settle. The new frontier was seen as running from Lake Peipus to the mouth of the Dnieper.
The British colonies were divided up, Ireland was granted independence, Siberia was assigned to Japan.

When these proposals were submitted to the government, Chancellor
Bethmann's comment was that the war had obviously "not removed, but
intensified to the point of absurdity" the lack of political understanding
among the members of the Pan-German League. The Pan-Germans
promptly accused him of being a lackey at heart. Erzberger, the leader
of the Center, who at that time was closely allied to heavy industry,

wanted to annex not only Briey and Northern France, but also the British Channel Islands. Nationalism sprouted its wildest growths. A professor of philosophy named Lasson at the University of Berlin actually rushed into print with the following statements: "We are morally and spiritually superior to all other human beings; there is not our like in all the world. Our organization and our institutions cannot be surpassed. Germany is the most perfect political structure known to history, and Chancellor von Bethmann-Hollweg is the foremost of living men."

While the Allies carefully cloaked their selfish ambitions in the guise of "liberation of the oppressed nationalities," such pen-pushers as Maximilian Harden did their best to strike a superman stance. No meek morality for them: "We want to win, we must win, not prove to the berobed and bespectacled that we are honest people of peaceful complexion. Cecil Rhodes, who was a grand fellow, a giant in patent-leather shoes and afflicted with tuberculosis, shouted into the cheese-colored mug of a carping critic: 'This war is just because it is useful to my people and increases my country's power!' Hammer that sentence into all hearts. It is worth a hundred white books. Paste it up on all the walls. Post it on blood-red paper on all official buildings, on every street corner in the towns and villages. Write underneath: 'The gang want our lives. A bastard brood is puffed up with the crazy notion that they can annihilate the grandsons of those who defeated the Roman cohorts. Bare the sword! The footstep of the impudent foe disgraces our soil. Kill them! In the Last Judgment you will not be asked for your reasons!' . . . Have we been deceived, cheated, betrayed? We will not believe that. No time for leisurely examination to see whether the proof is strong or weak, solid or crumbling. . . . The ancient, primeval condition of eternal Nature returns whenever Mars dons his golden armor and commands his twin sons, Horror and Terror, to hitch the steeds to the chariot of war." In a vehement, vainglorious, Wagnerian diatribe he pointed the way to the wild ocean's waves: "Now we know what we are fighting for. For that narrow gate, that churning Channel, that opens and closes the way to the seas. There we must raise the banner of the Reich. . . . What Germany wants is plain to the spirit that can picture a Belgium, France, Italy, Austria, Russia, Spain, Walachia and the South Slav lands animated by German discipline, German will, German diligence, knowledge and ability." As far as he was concerned, the war to attain these ends might last for fifty years. "We will fight this cause through till the youth artlessly smiling today, caps and coats decked with flowers, will hasten from the next to that remotest of all battlefields, their hair grayed."

All these wild dreams are hard to understand. To wrest anything like such vast territories, Germany would have had utterly to subjugate all the allied great powers. It hardly seemed likely that the two Central Powers could crush all of Europe under their heel. The idea of the Pan-Germans was to secure Germany "against all future aggression"; they overlooked the fact that a country so secured would dominate all of Europe—and the world was not going to stand for any such domination. Napoleonic war aims only impeded what was for Germany the one way out of her predicament—splitting her enemies. But even if by a miracle the Germans had been presented with one of these coveted territories as a gift, they soon would have discovered it to be a doubtful blessing. If Belgium were annexed to Germany in any manner, the black cloud of a British desire for *revanche* would threaten Germany far more grimly than the French *revanche* had done. Shifting territory back and forth without regard for the preference of the inhabitants had been possible in the age of dynastic wars (and was to become so again in the era of totalitarian states), but during that brief, happy episode of liberalism it would have made for constant trouble. Germany's war aim could only be to break up the alliances of her enemies and return to that condition within her old borders which had made her powerful, fortunate, and prosperous during the era of Bismarck. One of the few persons who felt this was Chancellor Bethmann. But he was unfortunately not the man to lend force to such an idea.

II

In 1914 all the nations had entered the war confidently. The Russians and the French had trusted in their military might, the British in the fact that they were British, and the Germans in the nobility of their cause and the great tradition of their army. On many railroad cars transporting soldiers to the front the men had scribbled: "Additional declarations of war against us may be deposited here."

That mood had fled long ago. When the snow melted after the third winter of the war, the German people no longer wanted the crown of Poland or the ore of Briey; they wanted nothing but peace. Hunger lurked behind these feelings. In peacetime the Germans had raised three-fourths of their food on their own soil. But in wartime, agriculture could not be maintained at the peacetime level. Nor could the controlled economy distribute the smaller supplies equally. Before the war the Germans had consumed daily $\frac{1}{3}$ lb. of meat and two ounces of fats; by this third winter they were down to less than one ounce of meat and $\frac{1}{3}$ ounce of fats. Sometimes the rationing system allowed half a herring per person; persons living alone had to seek some companion in misery with whom to go and claim their herring. The food value of the rations had dropped to 1100 calories, about a third of the amount needed. To supplement official rations, of course, there was the food which could be obtained by subterfuges. But most city-dwellers had no such private sources. With hunger hitting different sections of the population with such varying force, the unity of the people was shattered. Labor efficiency dropped to a third of normal. Even the army in the field was reduced to 2500 calories per man per day. In Austria the situation was still worse: front-line troops received only one ounce of meat daily, against nine ounces for the men in the German army. Austrian soldiers received five ounces of barely edible corn and a little dried vegetable. The Austrian quartermasters corps announced that the worms found in the rations might be unpalatable, but were by no means bad for health. While the Austrian city folk were starving, Hungary was enjoying surpluses.

Joffre and Foch once declared irritably that the English fleet was not worth one bayonet. In reality the blockade did much to win the war for the Allies.

III

The Allied statesmen, however, were not depending upon hunger alone to wear down the resistance of the Central Powers. They also organized a tremendous propaganda campaign. The underlying theme of their propaganda was that this war was a struggle of Good against Evil, of humane, peaceable, democratic governments against the military despotism of Germany. British liberals, who were basically pacifistic, needed such slogans to appease their consciences. They had to believe that England was fighting for the cause of justice and freedom. President Wilson had inherited from his ancestors, Scotch Puritans, the self-righteous tendency to damn his adversaries; in his proclamations he called the American people "the light of the world, the only idealistic nation." He really believed the war was a crusade for tolerance and democracy; Czarist Russia as an ally was conveniently overlooked. Territorial ambitions were veiled; fortunately for the Allies, some of the regions they wanted to detach from the Central Powers were actually seeking independence.

Allied propagandists were not finicky about their methods. They alleged, for example, that the bodies of German soldiers were ground up to be used as fertilizer; as evidence they published fake photographs and a fabricated diary of a German soldier who described his job in a "corpse factory"; the diary had been planted in the pocket of a fallen German soldier. After the war the British intelligence service frankly admitted these falsifications.

The propaganda of the Allies had three purposes. First, it aimed to win over the neutrals. It was remarkably successful in doing so; in the course of time almost all the countries in the world declared war on Germany.

Second, the propaganda was intended to strengthen the fighting morale of their own peoples, and to convince the Americans that the war was a crusade for democracy. The British did not need such urging; they believed heart and soul in the justice of their cause. The French bent backwards to preach furious sermons of hate: "People of France! You do not hate enough. . . . You are dealing with a nation that has sold its soul to the devil. With a nation following in the train of the most satanic, most infamous, most repulsive and cruellest pack of criminals the world has ever seen. Cease to think of Germans as they are today as human beings."

The third task of Allied propaganda was to influence Germany. Sixty-six million leaflets were dropped down upon Germans in the army and at home. A large part of them were written by German deserters. As British Propaganda Minister Northcliffe admitted, little was accomplished until the summer of 1918. But when the military defeat became apparent to the Germans, the propaganda took effect.

The Allied propaganda campaign received tremendous impetus from the demonstrations and proclamations of the Pan-Germans themselves. A French secret report of 1917 declared that these were "as good as hard cash" because they "welded together the moral alliance of the nations against Germany." If the efforts of the Kaiser and the chancellor to give German policy a liberal coloration had been successful, the "crusade against Prussianism" would not have seemed so necessary.

By the time the roses began to bloom in the fourth year of the war, all German hopes of victory were withered. Submarine warfare had failed. England showed no signs of starvation. America had declared war. Within another year her millions could be in Europe to decide the issue. But in the east there was a faint gleam of hope: the Russian Revolution. Revolutionary Russia could hardly be expected to go on pouring her full strength into the war.

IV

Here was Germany's chance. The United States was three thousand miles away; how soon her help would arrive and how great it would be was still uncertain. Russia was beginning to weaken. For Germany everything therefore depended on how to make use of the brief respite when the Russian collapse became evident and American aid was not yet tangible. She should have had plans all ready. In the summer of 1917 the deputies to the German *Reichstag* should have been asking themselves: how can we use this interval?

In order to obtain peace in the west, Belgium had to be evacuated and compensated. Giving up Belgium would not be a loss, but a gain; and paying compensation would be far preferable to protracting the war into the perilous year 1918. But it was clear that evacuation of Belgium would not be enough. Heartened by the prospect of American aid, France would no longer make peace unless she was given Alsace-Lorraine. Perhaps the position of the Central Powers in the east could be strengthened in some way. In that case, Alsace-Lorraine might be traded off for some French colonies. Such a solution was certainly better than continuing the war until the American troops arrived in force on the Continent.

Germany therefore had to wait until her hands were free in the east and—perhaps—until she could lay hold of a few spoils of war. Until then, the government should be engaged in paving the way for a compromise peace. Given the temperament of Chancellor Bethmann-Hollweg, such a solution did not appear to be out of the question. His lack of hardness made him a poor wartime chancellor, but with the reputation for sincerity he enjoyed among foreign statesmen he was the right person to negotiate for peace. The logical thing to do, therefore, was to support Bethmann. Above all, for the time being the word peace must not be spoken aloud. Germany had proposed negotiations only six months before; a repetition of the offer would be interpreted as weakness. If any peace proposals were to be made, Germany must use neutrals as a screen for them; fortunately for her, the Pope was already sending out peace feelers. A satisfactory settlement was hopeless as long as the Western Powers were counting on Russia; the gulf between the views and claims of both sides was still too wide.

All this should have been clear and cogent enough. Nevertheless, in June 1917, a deputy who occupied a key position in German politics came to precisely opposite conclusions. He was the most energetic personality in the Center Party: Mathias Erzberger. An intelligent grade school teacher, he had won by application and behind-the-scenes intrigues the reputation for being an expert in economics and a man of dubious integrity. He had no experience of the world and was devoid of political instinct, but these lacks did not diminish his self-assurance, since he was not aware of them. He was as hard-working as an ant and as thick-skinned as an elephant, was certain that he had at his fingertips all earthly and numerous heavenly affairs. For all his burning ambition and furious diligence, he had a taste for good living; the result was a grotesque physical appearance.

The U-boat campaign had failed. The next step, as Erzberger saw it, was to have the *Reichstag* propose peace and overthrow Chancellor Bethmann-Hollweg who had fought the idea of submarine warfare and who of all the German leaders was most inclined toward a compromise settlement. To this end Erzberger formed an alliance with Ludendorff, who had put across unrestricted submarine warfare and who was determined to have no peace without victory. The power of the *Reichstag* was growing in Germany, and Erzberger wanted to try it by the overthrow of a chancellor. To be the henchman of Ludendorff he was glad to topple his former patron, Bethmann. It was a masterstroke on Ludendorff's part to maneuver the pro-peace majority of the *Reichstag* into ousting the one chancellor who shared their desire for peace, and replacing him by a man who advocated Ludendorff's strong stand.

Erzberger, speaking before a *Reichstag* committee, described the miscarriage of the U-boat campaign and the starvation in Austria; Austrian Foreign Minister Count Czernin was in close touch with him and had encouraged him in his plans. He asked for a formal resolution by the *Reichstag* favoring a peace without annexations or reparations, in other words, a peace on the basis of the prewar *status quo*. The government must pay no attention to the frantic protests of the Pan-Germans; it would be cheaper to lock up 25,000 Pan-Germans in hydropathic institutes than to continue the war. Erzberger overlooked what was most important: that the enemy governments would have no part of a *status-quo* peace. His stand was an expression of that attitude so common to Germans: "I have done what is right; if that does no good, at least I have satisfied my conscience." He lacked intelligence to see that this peace resolution would defer peace rather than bring it nearer.

Ludendorff, however, saw his opportunities clearly. Erzberger met with two of Ludendorff's faithful adherents, the National-Liberal deputy Stresemann and a Colonel Bauer. Three days later Stresemann declared publicly that the leadership of the Reich was feeble, was floundering from one failure to the next. Colonel Bauer invited the Crown Prince to Berlin and introduced him to six carefully selected party leaders; the Crown Prince asked these men whether they favored Bethmann's dismissal. None of the deputies returned the obvious question: Who will be his successor? Naturally the wisdom or folly of dismissing Bethmann depended upon who the next chancellor would be— but this most vital aspect of the whole matter was not discussed at all. Five of the six spoke against Bethmann; the Center Party drew up a resolution stating that Bethmann had declared war and therefore was not the man to conclude peace. From Erzberger's point of view, Bethmann was too belligerent, from Ludendorff's too pacifistic. Both men collaborated to overthrow him without knowing who would succeed him.

Bethmann was too misanthropic a personality to have many friends. He lacked the gift for handling men and the cheerful energy for handling affairs. The Kaiser, however, liked his conscientiousness; a few days before the parliamentary struggle came out in the open he had listened to a lengthy report from his chancellor and had remarked: "Am I to dismiss this man who towers head and shoulders above all the others?" But the opposition was too strong. The Crown Prince informed his father of the views of the party leaders; simultaneously the Kaiser received a telegram stating that Hindenburg and Ludendorff would resign if Bethmann stayed. Had Bethmann been a statesman, he would not have yielded. He would have described the situation clearly to the three majority parties—the Center, the Progressives and the Social Democrats—and shown them that he alone could properly represent their peace policy. He would then have persuaded the Kaiser to reprove the rebellious generals and order them to confine themselves to military affairs and stay out of politics. But it was child's play to intimidate Bethmann. He lacked fight, and therefore creative powers, for creation is struggle.

V

Now, however, the vital question arose: who was to take over the rudder of the Reich? Bethmann himself had recommended Count Hertling, the prime minister of Bavaria, who was a Catholic professor of philosophy and a *Reichstag* deputy of the Center Party. But the frail old gentleman rightly declined the office. Bülow was proposed; he had the experience and the skill, though whether he had the necessary toughness was uncertain. Ludendorff favored him, but the Kaiser would not have him; he had not forgotten Bülow's "betrayal." The majority parties had agreed that if the question was put to them they would propose a lawyer from Baden named Fehrenbach who for thirty-three years had led the Freiburg Glee Club with great success. However, they were not asked.

Finally one of the Kaiser's military aides suggested a man named Michel or something of the sort whose work had something to do with the bread supply; his distinction was that he had recently made a terrific speech declaring that he would run his sword through the body of anyone who stood in his path. The man turned out to be Michaelis, who was under-secretary of state and food commissioner of Prussia and who had recently stated that he intended to carry his plans through against all opposition. The Kaiser did not know the man but thought he sounded all right; Michaelis was sent for. It turned out that in his military career he had risen no farther than deputy sergeant in the militia. The Kaiser said to him: "I hereby promote you to major; you need no more than that and God's help to make a great chancellor."

This account of the affair is from Bülow's venomous pen, and is undoubtedly fictional. But it gets to the heart of the matter: a hardworking Prussian administrative official was appointed chancellor at a crucial time in the history of the Reich solely because he happened to have used a vigorous turn of phrase in a speech.

Michaelis was a man with a strong sense of duty, and of a religious though not entirely straightforward turn of mind. He was in the habit of saying that a man must often give himself the order, "Forward, march!" and "take as a guide him who is the Saviour of us all." When the chancellorship was offered to him, he opened the book of mottos of the Moravian Brethren and found under that particular day Joshua 1, Verse 9: "Be not afraid, neither be thou dismayed: for the Lord thy God is with thee whithersoever thou goest." Accordingly, he accepted, although he fully realized that he would have to promise the *Reichstag* to further and the Supreme Command to oppose the peace resolution. To the Socialist deputy Scheidemann he remarked that hitherto he had never been more than a fifth wheel on the wagon of high policy. Deputy Payer described the impression he made upon the party leaders in these words: "We parted so depressed that Bethmann's friends could not even gloat over the poor choice of successor, as would have been only natural." When the new chancellor telephoned the news of his appointment to his wife, she cried out in alarm: "Oh come, why, you're crazy."

During the period preceding the appointment of the new chancellor (July 1917) the Kaiser for the first time in his life had a talk with the representatives of all the political parties in Germany. In his most adroit manner he made conversation by remarking that his son Fritz was off in Galicia knocking the democratic stuffing out of the enemy. "Where the Guard steps forward, there is no democracy." At the end of this war, he said, Germany would arrive at an understanding with France and then the entire Continent, under the leadership of the German Emperor, would begin a "second Punic War" against England. To Erzberger he said: "My officers inform me that they can scarcely find an enemy vessel upon the high seas." Erzberger replied that in that case he could not understand how the Admiralty managed to report monthly sinkings of 600,000 tons. The peace resolution was voted by the *Reichstag*. The new chancellor declared that he was in agreement with it "as I understand it," he added. The deputies missed this at first and applauded; only some time afterwards did they ask the chancellor to explain himself.

The *Reichstag* had overthrown Bethmann, but it had omitted to find a successor whose policy had anything to commend it. On the contrary, the *Reichstag* accepted a policy on the part of Michaelis which made peace even more remote than ever. Erzberger contented himself with a declaration that if only he could speak with Lloyd George, he would be able to come to an agreement on a basis for peace within a few hours. At the same time Lloyd George was saying that the only way to deal with bandits and murderers was to knock them down.

The peace resolution of the German *Reichstag* aroused little response abroad. The newspapers gave it short shrift, saying that it was a sign either of weakness or dishonesty; in any case the German *Reichstag* made no real decisions, they maintained. A few days after Erzberger's masterstroke the House of Commons overwhelmingly rejected a peace resolution offered by Ramsay Macdonald; only nineteen voted for it. In Paris Premier Ribot demanded not only Alsace-Lorraine, but a buffer state on the left bank of the Rhine. The Chamber of Deputies was modest; it declared that it would be satisfied with Alsace-Lorraine and war reparations.

Within Germany the effect of the peace resolution was peculiar. Grand Admiral Tirpitz founded a Fatherland Party whose million members were firmly resolved to win at their café tables a peace with territorial expansion for Germany.

VI

With Europe ready to go at the war with redoubled energy, a small plea for truce was heard. The Pope offered to help mediate a peace, thereby saving both sides the unpleasant necessity of making the first gesture.

The offer was received sourly by all sides. When Italy entered the war, France, England and Russia had promised her to keep the Pope out of all peace negotiations. France now bluntly informed London that she had no intention of being drawn into any deal of this kind. England was wiser. She suggested to the Pope that he first ascertain whether Germany was ready to evacuate Belgium. This issue should not have been pressed. Germany had the war map on her side, England the time factor. If the belligerents sat down at a conference table now, and if the negotiations then came to nothing, it would probably be difficult to persuade the soldiers to continue the war. In that case Germany would be holding the occupied areas as trump cards. Consequently, Asquith, who was now leader of the Opposition, had recently directed to Chancellor Michaelis the public question: would Germany evacuate Belgium if peace were concluded? Michaelis had not replied. What was he to answer now to the flat question asked by the papal nuncio?

A Crown Council was called. The Kaiser decided that Belgium was to be given her freedom. But the new secretary of state for foreign affairs, Kühlmann, had an unfortunate inspiration. He decided that Belgium was a "pledge" which should not yet be surrendered, but should be saved for the negotiations. Once you had made a concession, after all, you got nothing for it. He also decided to disregard the Pope's mediation and rather make overtures to London via Spain.

Both ideas were mistakes. Kühlmann might have made the evacuation of Belgium conditional upon restoration of the *status quo* everywhere. And he overlooked the fact that a peace feeler via Madrid—the third within the year—would be interpreted as weakness.

Michaelis resented the Pope's mediation even more than Kühlmann. He kept one eye cocked for Hindenburg's and Ludendorff's reaction. At the Crown Council they had had to bow to the Kaiser's decision. But they were by no means converted. On the contrary, two weeks later they sent a telegram to Michaelis protesting the rumors that the Crown Council had given up all of Belgium. Not a bit, they maintained; the decision had referred only to the coast of Flanders. Liége had to be German territory. Ludendorff argued in a memorandum that Belgium must be divided up into Flanders and Wallonia. The mines of Briey had to be annexed. Belgium must be attached to the Reich in some form; then Holland would follow suit and thus let Germany fall heir to her rich colonial possessions in Indonesia—not to speak of a great colonial empire in Africa and the needed strategic terrain in Poland, Courland and Lithuania. As far as the generals were concerned, the decisions of the Kaiser and the *Reichstag* resolution were of no import. And Michaelis realized that it was wiser not to oppose the two powerful generals; Bethmann's fate had been instructive.

The *Reichstag*, be it remembered, had a strong majority favoring peace. A committee of seven demanded that Germany make it clear to the Pope that she would restore Belgium to full sovereignty and integrity if peace were concluded. But Michaelis and Kühlmann had no difficulty steering things their way. They did not dare tell the blunt truth to the committee; had they done so, the *Reichstag* might have refused to vote any more war credits. Kühlmann therefore gave the members of the committee (made up of the best brains in the various political parties) a little lesson in diplomacy. It was wiser, he said, in replying to the Pope to refer only to the *Reichstag*'s peace resolution and to say nothing definite about Belgium. The deputies failed to see the deadly difference between giving a straight answer to a straight question and citing a document which was subject to various interpretations. They agreed that Kühlmann's way was best. The nuncio, acquainted beforehand with what the reply was to be, declared that it was completely unsatisfactory. But the God-fearing Michaelis concealed his comment from the committee. To make sure the Pope fully understood that the answer was negative, Michaelis wrote a letter to the nuncio behind the committee's back. The time, he stated, was not yet ripe for a declaration on Belgium. To the Spanish mediator England made answer that she was ready to receive any communication; with that the negotiations died a natural death. To seal their end completely, the peaceable Czernin announced that Austria would cede not a foot of soil to Italy. The nuncio replied that if this were the case, the Pope could go no further in mediation.

We know today that in the fall of 1917 the Allies would not have signed a peace on the basis of the prewar *status quo*. Nevertheless it was a mistake for Michaelis and Kühlmann—in defiance of the clearly expressed desires of the Kaiser and the *Reichstag*—to have repulsed papal intervention by refusing to agree to the evacuation of Belgium. A German declaration that Belgium would be set free if the prewar *status quo* were restored would have acted like a bombshell upon public opinion in England. It would then have been unequivocally clear that the peoples of Europe were continuing to fight only for Alsace-Lorraine. The offer might well have been accepted once Russia was definitively out of the picture.

The *Reichstag* had not met the test. It could have won; it had only to threaten to refuse war credits. Moreover, this time it had the Kaiser on its side. But it failed through weakness of will. Since the chancellor was also a nonentity, a vacuum was created. Into this vacuum Ludendorff moved. In a negative sense, at least, he became despotic ruler of the Reich; no major questions could be decided contrary to his views. The *Reichstag* submissively served as his footstool. The rule of the Kaiser was replaced by a veiled military dictatorship.

VII

At this point the leading spirit in the *Reichstag*, Deputy Erzberger, committed a blunder of extraordinary import. Austrian Foreign Minister Czernin wanted peace even if it meant sacrificing Germany. He was one of the first statesmen in the Central Powers to realize that peace could not be had unless Alsace-Lorraine were ceded to France. He also knew that Germany was dead set against abandoning this territory. He therefore suggested to the Germans that Germany annex Poland. Austria would even throw in Galicia. In return, Germany must leave Alsace-Lorraine to France. Czernin was not being entirely altruistic; he conceived of Austria's taking over the greater part of Rumania by way of compensation.

Czernin was bright enough to realize that this offer was scarcely alluring to the Germans. There was a saying in Vienna: "The one who loses the war will get Galicia." He therefore applied a certain amount of pressure. He drew up a memorandum for Germany's edification stating that Austria was no longer able to continue the struggle and would have to make peace this year. Germany, too, was at the end of her resources, his memorandum argued; if peace did not come soon, a revolution would sweep everything away.

The Germans were too well aware of the purpose of this memoran-

dum to let it alarm them. They refused the Galician morsel. But at this
point two political dilettantes made history. The Empress Zita of Austria gave the memorandum to Erzberger. The leader of the Center
Party realized what was up. Czernin's dark picture terrified him; he
rushed through his peace resolution, overthrew Bethmann, and when
he was shortly afterwards reproached for his precipitous policies, he
drew the confidential memorandum from his pocket and read it aloud
to a gathering of over one hundred persons. Then he went to Switzerland and presumably showed it to a number of people there. Two weeks
after the peace resolution a copy of the document lay on Lloyd George's
desk. It put the finis to any inclinations toward peace that England
might have had at the time.

VIII

Meanwhile Michaelis went on governing the Reich, his incompetence uncontested. Only a month after his appointment the *Reichstag*
had decided to vote him out of office. Then a parliamentary *Bierabend*
took place at the Chancellery, and the following day Glee Club Leader
Fehrenbach put off the attack upon Michaelis, arguing: "He was so
nice to all of us last night." Consequently, the unfortunate man hung
on for a hundred days. Not until after the war did he mournfully realize
that his situation at the time "was not based upon clarity and truthful-
ness." He had accepted the peace resolution without believing in it,
and he had waited for military triumphs that did not come.

Once more Fate offered Germany a chance. Everything now depended upon the choice of a new chancellor. Who among the Germans
was strong enough to stand up in the face of the entire world and save
the storm-wracked ship of state from a perilous but not desperate situation? A nation of seventy millions had to number in its midst at least
one man who was both lion and fox, who was tough and energetic
enough to halt the downward trend, intelligent enough to understand
what was attainable, and clever enough to win the support of the people. Was there not one man between the Meuse and the Memel who
was the equal of Lloyd George and Clemenceau?

The *Reichstag* proposed Count Hertling for chancellor.

Georg von Hertling was a professor of medieval philosophy. Grown
gray in the service of the Center Party, he had risen in the wild scram-
ble of Bavarian parliamentary politics to the office of prime minister
and had been awarded the title of count. He could deliver fascinating
lectures on Dante and Thomas Aquinas; he himself noticed that on
such subjects he spoke with greater animation than on political matters. Unfortunately his health was not good, and he was seventy-four
years old. His eyes were failing so that reading was difficult for him;

the general weakness of age forced him to go to bed at eight o'clock; and travelling was too much for him. Before his appointment the journalist Viktor Naumann told Hertling that he had pressed for his appointment. "But I also said: 'Count Hertling has one fault. He has no energy.' At that Hertling pushed his glasses up on his forehead, looked hard at me and then said: 'That was a cheeky thing to say, but you are right.'" Hertling was a resigned, contemplative person. Feeble as he was, his best hours for work were the two first of the morning, and these he employed, even as chancellor, to write his memoirs in a prolix and commonplace manner. Twenty years before, Chancellor Hohenlohe had said of him that Hertling was a man who never in his life had drunk a glass of good wine, kissed a pretty woman or owned a pair of well-fitting trousers. In regard to peace, he went along with the views of the Supreme Command. He had more confidence in Ludendorff than Ludendorff himself. A *grand seigneur* of the old school, he hated the parliamentary system.

Hertling's chancellorship proceeded just as everyone who knew the old man had foreseen: nothing happened. The chancellor worked on his memoirs, the Kaiser resigned himself to inaction, the *Reichstag* marked time, and the one energetic personality in the country, Erich Ludendorff, held the reins. He worked behind the popular figurehead that old Hindenburg had become and filled as best he could the political vacuum which had appeared as a result of the Kaiser's uncertainty, the *Reichstag*'s cowardice, and the chancellor's feebleness. Uninhibited by doubts, untroubled by political knowledge or instinct, Ludendorff held to his course. Two dozen traditional phrases constituted his intellectual equipment. He did not quite know what he was heading toward, but it was certain that he would keep his foot down on the accelerator.

CHAPTER TWENTY-TWO

The Year 1917

It is men who make history.
—TREITSCHKE

I

Throughout the war the domestic situation in Russia had steadily deteriorated. In a country where eighty per cent of the population could not read and write, a modern war presented a tremendous problem in organization. The government was too infirm and too corrupt to solve this problem. The harvests shrunk, the communications system broke down, famines struck the cities, the army was disheartened by defeats, lack of munitions, and a miserably poor medical corps. Vodka had been forbidden since August 1914. Morale sagged. What were the Russians actually fighting for? The censorship let through an article asserting that England was determined to fight to the last Russian soldier. Men on the Right began entertaining thoughts of a separate peace, for if the toll of the war went on mounting, the Left might succeed in making a revolution, or at least in forcing through reforms. The Allied ambassadors started a strong whispering campaign to the effect that Russia's defeats were due to treason. The Czarina, who was of German origin, and above all her adviser Rasputin, were suspected of evil-doing.

Rasputin was an uneducated monk of uncanny vitality about whose unwashed figure the odor of sanctity had collected. He blew his nose between his fingers, scratched his head, and had the ladies of the court enchanted. He possessed hypnotic powers which he utilized to heal the Crown Prince, who had inherited haemophilia from his mother. According to Rasputin's teachings, man could not win salvation without penitence; in order to be penitent, however, it was necessary to sin. The sin of lust was a convenient one for the purpose. Seducing women meant "purifying" them. Politically, he favored peace; perhaps Russia would not have forced the issue in 1914 if Rasputin had not been temporarily off the scene, convalescing from a stab in the abdomen inflicted on him by a woman at the time of the Serbian crisis. Rasputin would have counselled moderation. With peasant instinct the monk sensed that war was bad for the Czar. Now, three years afterwards, he was for calling a halt to the hostilities. Some guards officers who were hot for continuing the war invited him to a dinner and served him poisoned cheese and wine; Rasputin swallowed the cyanide without harm and the officers had to resort to their pistols to put an end to him. The story circulated among the people that Tatyana, the Czar's daughter, had been present at the murder disguised as a cavalry officer; because the monk had once tried to rape her, it was said, the dying Rasputin had been emasculated in her presence.

The Czar made overtures to Vienna. Sir George Buchanan, the British ambassador, thought the situation so dangerous that he negotiated with the Duma deputies of the Left parties on the establishment of a republic. He also considered assassination of the Czar, but could not make up his mind.

Before Buchanan's men could put through any kind of action, the kettle boiled over. The St. Petersburg armament workers, protesting against the shortage of bread, went on an "Italian" strike: they came to work but did not lift a finger. The factory management locked out 30,000 men. Street riots immediately broke out, and when army units were sent to quell them, the soldiers went over to the workers. Nicholas sent word from army headquarters that the rebellion must be crushed, but the St. Petersburg troops revolted, and from all parts of the front the generals wired that their troops would not march on St. Petersburg. Only two generals, one a Balt and the other a Tartar, were willing to fight the uprising. Nicholas abdicated. A ministry composed of representatives of the bourgeois Left and the Socialist Right took control. But with incomprehensible blindness the new government neglected to take the one step which was essential if it were to hold power: making peace. Whether Ambassador Buchanan's advice to the current leaders was backed by hard cash, no one can say. If at that time Germany had offered Russia peace on the basis of the prewar *status quo,* the Russian army would in all likelihood have simply gone home.

But Germany wanted to wait and see; consequently, eighty of her divisions were nailed down in the east. Meanwhile the Supreme Command took a step fraught with graver consequences than any other event of the First World War: it allowed two Russian professional revolutionaries who had been living in Switzerland to travel in sealed cars through Germany to Sweden, whence they reached St. Petersburg. The Supreme Command did not suspect that one of them, Lenin, would give a new direction to world history. Kerensky, the head of the transitional government, exhausted his eloquence in persuading Russian divisions to try one more offensive which failed as soon as it ran into German troops. Lenin, who at the time of his arrival could scarcely have had 50,000 adherents, easily outtrumped the muddled theoreticians with a clear watchword: peace, bread, and land! In a nation where only one fifth of the people could read he was able to capture only a minority, but for a man of his will power this small minority sufficed to overthrow Kerensky.

The Russian Revolution broke out exactly five weeks after the declaration of unrestricted submarine warfare. Had the Germans waited those additional five weeks, or the St. Petersburg workers lost their patience five weeks sooner, Germany would never have embarked on that ill-fated experiment. France would then have had to go through 1917 unsustained by the prospect of America's aid. According to Churchill, she would not have been able to hold out. "The war would have ended in a Peace by negotiation or, in other words, a German victory."

II

In 1917, a new man became head of the French army. His name was Nivelle; he was just sixty and it was he who had reconquered the lost territory at Verdun. He promised to end the war by a mighty pincers offensive which would cut off the protruding salient in the German front. The British were wild with enthusiasm about Nivelle. He was the first French general whom they could understand, not only because he spoke a clear and forthright language, but because he also spoke English. His mother had been English.

But Nivelle's grand project went up in smoke. In February, on the advice of Crown Prince Rupprecht of Bavaria Ludendorff evacuated the salient and retreated to the strongly fortified "Siegfried Position." In the evacuated territory, villages, roads, railroads and wells were destroyed—a procedure which the lower officers considered somewhat extreme. The retreat was prepared with the utmost care and was carried out with clockwork precision, without the slightest interference from the enemy. When French army commanders noted signs of retreat and recommended reconnaissances in force, Nivelle declared that a German withdrawal was impossible. Like many men of action, he refused to believe what did not fit in with his plans. What should be done now? Pétain, the savior of Verdun, urged waiting until the Americans arrived. But that did not suit Nivelle's whole style. With Haig he settled on a new offensive. The British would attack at Arras, the French at the Chemin des Dames, a ridge along the Aisne. The commander in chief was sure of victory. After tremendous artillery preparation he expected to break through without losses and advance twenty miles in three days. Then it might be necessary to take a breathing spell, but it would be hard to hold back the troops once they were loosed.

After ten days of artillery preparation Nivelle issued the order of the day: "The hour has come! Confidence! Courage! Long live France!"

The French infantry climbed out of the trenches to march across the German positions, which the artillery had presumably taken care of. But out of shell-holes and water-holes machine-guns chattered in their faces; the Germans were still there, and their hand grenades proved that they were ready to fight. Within a few days the French offensive had collapsed. In vain two cavalry divisions waited for the command to charge into action. Over thirty thousand French dead lay among the tangle of trenches and shell-holes; over 100,000 wounded were sent to the military hospitals. In the folly of overconfidence Nivelle had provided for only 10,000 beds; only one out of ten wounded men received a cot. For days they lay in heaps in pestilential cellars, without attendance, oozing blood and pus, the dead bodies of their fellows among them. In many cases the severely wounded were laid on tent canvas along the sides of the roads. Members of the Chamber of Deputies, who had been invited to watch the grand advance, were witnesses of the massacre. Nivelle wanted to put the blame on his army commander Michelet, but General Michelet stormed into headquarters, wrenched open the windows in the commander in chief's office, and shouted at Nivelle so that everyone could hear: He, Michelet, had warned against this offensive; it was cowardice and infamy for Nivelle to charge him now with the mistakes he himself had committed. The whole army demanded the head of the "bloodsucker" Nivelle. The government sent him to Algiers, but that was not enough. Mutiny ran like wildfire through the French army. Leaflets were circulated: "You must bleed so that England can destroy a trade rival!" A remark of a general overheard on the telephone, "You can use the corpses as sandbags," sped through the armies. Forty-five divisions were in a state of unrest; the troops refused to fight. Between Soissons and Paris there remained only two reliable divisions. But it was not a revolution; it was only a strike by disillusioned soldiers. There were no attacks upon the officers. Indignation seethed back of the lines also. A million workers laid down their tools. A cry arose that Poincaré and all his ministers should be loaded into a boat and set adrift at sea. A number of ministers in Paris and London declared privately that if Russia dropped out of the war now, peace would have to be made.

The new commander in chief, Pétain, acted with great sagacity. He had neither Joffre's forced joviality, nor Nivelle's contempt for human life, nor Foch's mathematical mind, but he had a heart; twenty-three years later that was to be his doom. He called off all attacks, declaring that he would wait for tanks and for the Americans. He went from regiment to regiment and addressed the troops, praising their bravery, handing out decorations to hundreds, investigating complaints about food and furloughs; he set up commissions on provisioning and miti-

gated the incessant drilling. Simultaneously, the court-martials were
grinding out one hundred and fifty death sentences—of which only
twenty-three were carried out. Some two thousand men were sent to
the penal colonies. Extreme harshness was employed toward a Russian
brigade which had beèn sent to France; here the mutiny was liquidated
by artillery. When the unions threatened a general strike in order, as
Clemenceau said, to "taste the sweetness of civil war," the government
commuted the sentences of some of the men condemned to death—
against the advice of all the generals. Not a word of these troubles
crossed the borders. The policy of iron fist in a velvet glove was completely successful. A few months later the very divisions that had muti-
nied fought magnificently.

The skies had clouded indeed for the Allies during this period when
the Russians were making a revolution, the French were mutinying,
and the Americans were still three thousand miles away. But while the
German government was composing peace resolutions, the British government and people held firm. To maintain the western front had now
become the task of the English. Haig knew only one way to do it: by
smashing head on into the German positions in Flanders. He launched
frontal attacks for four months, losing nearly half a million men—twice
as many as the Germans. Haig's critics cried that this was not strategy
but madness. At the end the fronts were unchanged. When one of the
British generals saw the mud-holes of Paschendaele for the first time,
he exclaimed in a voice breaking with sobs: "Have we really sent men
out to fight here?" For the first time British soldiers taken prisoner
affirmed that they would gladly shoot down their officers.

III

In that same fateful year of 1917, the armed forces of the dual monarchy were also in a desperate plight. The field army comprised 3.5
million men, the home army half a million. But only 780,000 men of the
field army were actually engaged in combat; the rest were in reserve
or serving as supply troops. The eastern front was quiet, but on the Italian front the Austro-Hungarian army was fighting against odds of two
to one. For two and a half years they had resisted; now they were flagging. Conrad asked for twelve German divisions for an offensive. He
wanted to attack simultaneously in Tyrol and on the northern part of
the Isonzo front, near Tolmein, in order to cut off the entire Italian
front. Ludendorff responded that he could spare no more than seven
divisions, and these only for a short time. The attack could therefore
be carried out only at Tolmein; the north-south advance from Triente
to Venice had to be cancelled.

This was one of the great blunders of the war. Ludendorff surely could have released another five divisions. For instance, he might well have sent the six western divisions which he used for a cheap victory at Riga. But Ludendorff had other plans, as we shall soon see.

The Tolmein offensive was a bold undertaking. The attackers had odds of three to two against them and were operating in mountainous terrain. But the Italians were terrified before the offensive began, and after a brief skirmish abandoned their artillery and supply train and fled westward. King Victor Emanuel, who was at the headquarters in Udine, escaped from Austrian forces with only a few hours to spare. If the Austrians had not complicated things by stubbornly insisting on keeping ahead of the Germans, the advance would have forged on even faster.

The Italian army suffered only 10,000 dead and 30,000 wounded— but lost heavily in other ways, there being 300,000 prisoners and 400,000 "dispersed" troops. The latter discarded their uniforms and formed themselves into gangs of bandits who for weeks terrorized the populace. Sicilians deserted by the division. As in France, relief troops were looked upon as "strikebreakers." If the British and French had not sent a few divisions to the Italians' aid, the front would scarcely have been stabilized again. Had an additional offensive been launched against the Italian rear from Tyrol, a million prisoners would surely have been bagged. But General Foch forced Cadorna to hold on the Piave. By December 1917, 1.3 million Allied troops were facing a 900,000 man German-Austrian army, and the front froze hard once more.

IV

The Hapsburg army had drunk a last full draught from the cup of victory before the feast was over. Emperor Karl and Foreign Minister Czernin had long felt that it was twilight over Austria. A few months before the *Reichstag*'s peace resolution, they had attempted to end the war by highly unconventional methods. A brother-in-law of the Emperor, Prince Sixtus of Bourbon, was a Belgian artillery officer; as a member of the former French royal family, he was not allowed to hold a position in France's army. Desirous nevertheless to serve France, he acted several times as an intermediary between the Emperor Karl and Poincaré. Now the Emperor wrote to Sixtus, asking him to transmit a letter to the French President. In this communication Karl promised to "apply all his personal influence to support France's just claims to Alsace-Lorraine." Poincaré replied that France insisted on the frontier of 1814—that is, an area taking in the Saar. She also required reparations and guarantees on the left bank of the Rhine. Within a year, he pointed out, a million well-equipped American soldiers would be added to the Allied forces. The Allies would not negotiate with Germany until she had been thoroughly defeated, but they were willing to conclude a separate peace with Austria. Austria could be awarded Bavaria and Silesia, but would have to give South Tyrol and Dalmatia to Italy.

Karl might be generous with Germany's Alsace-Lorraine, but he hated the thought of sacrificing territory of the dual monarchy. A separate peace struck him as going too far. Discussions ceased.

In August 1917, Karl again broached the question, this time via two diplomats who met in Switzerland. Once again the French played the part of a tempter who from the high mountain showed the Hapsburgs all the treasures of this world. If Austria-Hungary would pull out of the war and cede Triente and Trieste, the Kingdom of Bavaria, and Poland as she had existed before the first partition, would be enrolled in the Hapsburg federal union. Silesia would become Austrian once more; even Saxony and Rumania were dangled before Austria-Hungary. The Hapsburg state would then extend from the Baltic to the Adriatic; the black and yellow double eagle would wave over Danzig, Posen, Breslau, and Munich. The French envoys reported trenchantly to Paris: "Poland lures them, Bavaria attracts them, Silesia frightens them." The Emperor Karl could not fail to see that such a settlement would only mean exchanging his present war for a war with Germany, which would certainly not be popular in his country. He therefore asked for conditions for a joint peace involving both countries. Paris replied: cession of Alsace-Lorraine, of the Saar, and of the former Polish territories. Knowing that there was no use even transmitting such terms to Berlin, Vienna fell silent.

The Austrian peace overtures came to a dramatic finale. In the spring of 1918, Count Czernin mentioned in a speech that French Premier Clemenceau had wanted to start peace negotiations some time ago, but that the preliminary discussions had broken down over the question of Alsace-Lorraine. Clemenceau promptly replied that the Emperor Karl himself had admitted the justice of France's claims to Alsace-Lorraine. Czernin was alarmed. He knew nothing about the monarch's letter. He therefore asked the Emperor to give him his word of honor that he had not made any such admission. If he did not receive this assurance, Czernin said, there would be nothing for him to do but commit suicide. Karl gave his word of honor and authorized Czernin to denounce Clemenceau's story as a lie. Clemenceau promptly published the text of the letter. Karl now cried it was a fraud. But no one believed him. Czernin then made the wild proposal that the Emperor take a leave of absence on grounds of health and appoint one of the archdukes as regent. The Emperor refused, and Czernin resigned.

V

Czernin would hardly have been so foolhardy as to cross swords with Georges Clemenceau if he had known the sort of man he was dealing with. Clemenceau had been through a great deal in the seventy-six years of his life. He had been a doctor, had taught French and riding in a girls' school in the United States, had been imprisoned for slander, and had written innumerable newspaper articles—enough to fill some hundred 350-page volumes. He started his political career as a Jacobin, favoring a militia in place of the army, calling for the separation of Church and State and the elimination of the presidency and the Senate. More than once he was ruined personally and politically; at one time he was involved in the Panama Scandal; another time he was accused of taking bribes from England. Accordingly his speeches were shouted down with the English phrase "Oh yes!" and people spat at him. His newspaper went into bankruptcy. In the nineties it was said that·he must have a head of iron to stand up to all the brickbats that had been hurled at him. "It is courage that makes a man's greatness," he declared. When he entered the government as a minister, he broke with his friends on the Left, ordered striking workers shot down, and answered his savage critics by explaining that now he was on the other side of the barricades. When the Socialist leader Jaurès took him to task for defection, he said irritably: "You are not God." "And you are not the devil," Jaurès replied. "How do you know that?" Clemenceau retorted.

Clemenceau's political opponents were chary of attacking him, for his pistol was feared as much as his tongue. As an old man he fell in love with an English sculptress, a pupil and model of Rodin's, who for her part was in love with a Bavarian army officer. Clemenceau gave her up, but only after an emotional crisis which broke his last ties with ordinary life. He became a nihilist who found an outlet in activity. Once he reproached his secretary for not being a man of action. The secretary asked what he meant by "action." The old man answered: "Anyone who asks that question does not act. One must act as one breathes. Acting means being thrown out of equilibrium. In order to act, one must be mad. A relatively reasonable person contents himself with thinking." He was fond of telling the story of the Oriental Emperor Baber who had the heads of his political enemies delivered to him every morning, and when the heap grew smaller said crossly: "They are relaxing." As premier he went on a hunting party with his ministers. A novelist in the party confessed that he shot wretchedly and was always afraid he would hit one of his fellow hunters. With a lordly gesture toward his Cabinet, Clemenceau said: "Please take your choice." His humor was of the acid variety. At the time he was first appointed minister, he came to his office at ten o'clock in the morning and went through all the rooms, accompanied by his bureau chief. No one had come to work as yet except for one official who sat sleeping at his desk. The bureau chief wanted to wake him, but Clemenceau interposed: "Don't do that, or he will go away too." When a ministerial councillor met him with: "Have I the pleasure . . . ?" he replied, "It is no pleasure to meet me. I am Clemenceau!" He was fond of calling himself a cross between conservative and anarchist.

This diabetic old man now took the rudder of France into hands which were always clothed in gray cotton gloves; he suffered from eczema. Poincaré had selected him reluctantly as a last trump, knowing that Clemenceau thought him "as lyrical as a dictionary," and had remarked that it was dangerous to entrust the fate of a country to a man whose breast contained a filing case instead of a heart.

Clemenceau promptly introduced the closest censorship of the press. Yielding must no longer even be considered. "Justice must take its course; the country must see that it will be defended," he thundered. He ordered a number of traitors and defeatists—some guilty, some innocent—executed or arrested, and appointed the strongest available man to every government position.

CHAPTER TWENTY-THREE

Peace in the East

It is not hard for the German Empire to respect the rights of other nations, since through no merit of our own we require no enlargement of our territory, nor could we achieve such expansion without intensifying the centrifugal forces in the realm.

—BISMARCK

I

Lenin was a genuine statesman. As soon as he came to power and had dissolved the Russian National Assembly at the point of the bayonet, he did the thing which could best fortify his position: he offered peace to the whole world.

Ludendorff telephoned to Hoffmann, who by now had risen to the rank of major general: "Is it possible to sit down at a table with such people?" "It is possible, your Excellency. Your Excellency needs the troops from the east and for that we have to have peace." Hoffmann concluded an armistice, and just before Christmas, 1917, peace negotiations began in the hall of the theater at Brest-Litovsk.

The Russian front dissolved. The Russian peasant soldiers did not want to arrive too late at home when the estates of the big landowners were divided up. The Germans therefore had no reason to fear any further resistance. For the present they could make their own conditions. But was it wisdom to throw only the sword of the victor into the scales? It should have been Germany's primary aim to free her hands in the east and scare the British with the prospect of German-Russian amity. Only by playing on this fear could Germany secure a general peace before the Americans arrived in Europe.

On the other hand it seemed evident that the "border states"— Poland, Lithuania and Courland—could not be turned over to the Bolsheviks, so that they could set up their dictatorship in areas so close to Germany. Could revolutionary Russia be allowed to approach so closely to Berlin while the entire German army was fighting near Paris? Clearly, the Russians would have to relinquish the border states, and since one of their slogans was the "self-determination of nations," this price could well be asked of them. But what was to be done with the three countries? Were they really to be allowed to determine their own destiny some day, or should they be annexed to Germany under some formula or other? Ludendorff was bent on retaining them; moreover, he wanted Poland to cede large areas to Germany. The civilian heads of the German government, Hertling and Kühlmann, did not have the power to oppose Ludendorff, and at bottom found the plan appealing. After all, Germany could do much for these new nations in the sphere of culture and government; above all she could spare them the chaos of the new order. But was it really a blessing for Germany to take in thirty million discontented "protégé citizens"? Threatened as she was in the west, was she strong enough to force upon these buffer states in the east a *pax germanica?* Liberated peoples are not grateful but demanding, Bismarck used to say. Would it not be wiser to continue to occupy those Baltic and Polish lands for the time being, but to promise on the Kaiser's word of honor that after the conclusion of peace the Germans would immediately withdraw as soon as a new government was firmly established by popular election? Or the occupation of the Baltic area by Swedish troops might be proposed; the Swedes would hardly want to do this, but the gesture would rob anti-Germans of their arguments. Hertling, however, was blind to the principal task: to render public opinion in England favorable to peace. Kühlmann and Czernin went to Brest-Litovsk without having any clear purpose in mind.

Richard von Kühlmann was an esthete. As Hertling dwelt by preference among the scholastic philosophers, Kühlmann loved to linger in antique shops. He was a connoisseur of painting and terra cotta, as well as of women and good food. His father, of a recently ennobled Bavarian family, had been director of the Turkish railroads in Constantinople; he himself had married very rich. There really was nothing compelling him to bicker at Brest with these unkempt peoples' commissars and at the same time quarrel with this mulish Prussian, Ludendorff, who from his headquarters in Kreuznach kept throwing spokes into the wheels and rejecting all suggestions simply because they came from the Foreign Office. But after all, when he became sick of it he could throw the whole thing up. . . . During that crucial year Germany had an emperor who had lost courage, a chancellor who was worn out and feeble, and a foreign minister who cleverly twisted his way through the problems of the day with an amused and supercilious smile.

The Russians did not handle the negotiations badly. They put on European airs and daily dined at the table of Prince Leopold; it was as though they had checked their bombs in the cloakroom. Since they considered it their task to convert national wars into civil wars, they sent out a rain of leaflets and wireless messages encouraging all the peoples of Europe to revolution. When Kühlmann protested against this propaganda, the leader of the Russian delegation, Joffe, looked at him with astonishment in his gentle eyes and declared in a mild, almost pleading tone: "But I hope, you know, that we will succeed in unleashing revolution in your country also." The Russians proclaimed as the basic principle of peace: "No annexations and no reparations," and invited all the governments to participate in the negotiations. The Germans readily accepted this principle on condition that the Western Powers would accept it also; they were certain this condition would not be met. The conference adjourned for a short time to give the other governments time to reply; when no answers came, Hertling was very pleased. The Kaiser, the Crown Prince, and Ludendorff now urged the chancellor to retract publicly his adherence to the *Reichstag*'s peace resolution. Hertling, who had never thought the resolution meant anything, was not quite so foolish as to say so.

The Russians expected to receive their old borders and then to be able to settle with Poland and Lithuania as they pleased; after all, a Polish National Assembly could be dissolved by bayonets as easily as the Russian one. But one day Hoffmann casually mentioned to Joffe at breakfast that by a peace without annexations Germany understood Russian relinquishment of the border states—an area half as large as Germany proper. To their dismay the Russians discovered that the Germans knew how to exploit the elasticity of idealistic doctrines just as well as they themselves.

II

Leo Trotsky now took over the leadership of the Russian delegation. He was a strong personality with a versatile mind and the oratorical gifts of a shyster lawyer. Though he was playing the game without a single good card in his hand, he played brilliantly. From the theater at Brest he delivered revolutionary speeches, enjoined the German soldiers to kill their officers, and deliberately protracted the negotiations. One day Hoffmann informed him that after all the Germans, not the Russians, had won the war, and that the border states would have to be ceded. Trotsky turned down this view of the matter as too narrowly military. Then Hoffmann tried another tack. In Kiev a Ukrainian government had been formed; it had sent a couple of students to the conference as representatives. With these people the Central Powers abruptly concluded a peace treaty—the so-called "bread peace," for its purpose was to obtain Ukrainian grain for Germany. As bad luck would have it, a few days before the Bolsheviks had conquered Kiev and expelled the local government. The only territory this government controlled, Trotsky sneered, was the two rooms the Germans had placed at the disposal of its peace delegates. He thereupon produced two Ukrainians of his own whom he introduced as the new Ukrainian government.

But Trotsky had prepared an even more dramatic play. He bluntly declared that Russia was herewith ending the war and sending her armies home without concluding a peace treaty.

The Congress was flabbergasted. Could this sort of thing be allowed? Kühlmann said it could. But Hoffmann said no, and Ludendorff agreed with him. Germany therefore declared that she regarded Trotsky's statement merely as the announcement of an armistice. Without opposition the German troops occupied Latvia, Estonia and the Ukraine. They penetrated by railroad as far as Georgia. The Russian army had indeed gone home.

Was it sensible for Germany, on the eve of the decisive struggle in the west, to occupy an area as large as Germany herself? A million men were thereby immobilized in the east, although only men over thirty-five were kept in the eastern army. The Western Powers were also being given a splendid chance to pillory Germany's aggressive policy. Did the taking of these territories offer such advantages as to outweigh these disadvantages? The Supreme Command declared that the Baltic countries had to be liberated from Bolshevist rule for the sake of the Germans living in them; but only eight per cent of the population—big landowners and the urban middle-class—were of German origin. As for the Ukraine, it was taken over to secure the supply of grain. The German Food Board declared that this was "urgently desirable, but not absolutely necessary." In spite of the occupation of the country, the extra grain obtained was of little account—only about one pound of grain per head for Germany. Well-paid smugglers would probably have provided that much grain without the trouble of military occupation.

After the Germans had marched for several days, Lenin concluded peace. Russia relinquished the border states. The Russian envoys signed without even bothering to study the document; they were yielding only to force.

And the German *Reichstag?* Did it recall the peace resolution it had passed only six months before? The majority parties apparently found that the resolution applied only in bad weather. The *Reichstag* approved the Treaty of Brest-Litovsk; the Socialists abstained from voting. Once again the Left majority in the *Reichstag* had played Ludendorff's game.

Under the shadow of the sword Germany began setting up new governments in Poland, Lithuania and Latvia. Meanwhile, Russia was threatening to fall apart. British troops landed in Archangelsk and Murmansk. Former Czarist generals raised armies which, supported

by the Allies, expelled the Bolshevist government from large areas
of Russia. The German ambassador and the German commander in
chief in the Ukraine were murdered. The Russian government readily
supplied a list of more than one hundred people who had been shot for
participation in the murder of the ambassador. But the names of the
assassins, which were widely known, were not among them—a foolish
piece of recalcitrance, since it would have been easy to report that
they, too, had been shot. Germany exploited the chaos in Russia to
extract an additional treaty from the unhappy country, in which Russia
also surrendered Latvia, Esthonia and Georgia and promised payment
of six billion marks in gold and goods to make up for certain unfulfilled
obligations undertaken in the Treaty of Brest-Litovsk. In return
Germany promised to withdraw her support from the White Russian
counter-revolutionaries and to keep her Turkish ally from invading
Baku. Turkey promptly threatened to repudiate the Turko-German alliance. The Bolshevists went so far as to ask the Germans for help in
suppressing revolts in Great Russian territory.

General Hoffmann was entertaining different plans. He proposed
breaking the treaty, marching to Moscow and installing a new government. Even the weak divisions of the eastern army could carry out this
action, he maintained. The German military attaché in Moscow had
stated he could restore order there if he were given two battalions.
The new Russian government would then be assured that after a general peace the old borders of Russia would be restored—including
Poland. And Germany should then form an alliance with the new
Russia. The German government would have no part of such daring
plans; it contented itself with the supplementary treaty. When that
treaty was at last signed in the fall of 1918, Germany was on the verge
of collapse. A Dutch newspaper wrote: "The Germans go on grabbing
even on their deathbed." The treaty was only a scrap of paper. In
the following years Lenin united and consolidated Russia.

Peace with Russia was followed by peace with Rumania. Originally
the Germans had wanted to depose King Ferdinand—who came from
the Catholic branch of the Hohenzollern family. But Austrian Foreign
Minister Czernin objected that kings were a dime a dozen already and
would become utterly worthless if more of them were thrown on the
market. Moreover, Hungary was demanding a broad border strip and
Bulgaria all of Dobruja, Rumania's province bordering the Black Sea.
Turkey, which had helped in the conquest of Rumania, promptly demanded several areas she had formerly ceded to Bulgaria. As if that
were not enough, the Supreme Command wanted the port of Con-
stanza for Germany—thus establishing a second Kiaochow in the heart
of enemy country. This plan had the effect of infuriating both Bulgaria and Turkey, but Ludendorff declared that the Bulgarian alliance

involved heavy burdens; it would be no great loss if Bulgaria dropped out of the war. The upshot of it was that Dobruja was to be ceded to the four countries jointly; thus the problem was only postponed and both Turkey and Bulgaria irritated. The Hungarians received their border strip and the Germans all prospecting rights in Rumania—which meant oil—as well as the Rumanian railroad network and the promise of grain deliveries over a long span of years. The Kaiser was opposed to the excessive demands of the Supreme Command. But he was unable to put across his wishes against the opposition of the general staff.

CHAPTER TWENTY-FOUR

The Last Offensive

> Suppose Germany saying: "You are weary of
> war; so are we. We are prepared to surrender
> Alsace and Lorraine. We will evacuate Bel-
> gium. We'll cry quits; without indemnities on
> either side."
> Such a proposition—though improbable—was
> not impossible, and it is conceivable that our
> Allies might have been willing to accept some
> such terms, forcing us to an inconclusive peace
> unless we could carry on alone. In that case,
> Germany would have been left dominant in
> Austria, the Balkans, Turkey and Syria; with an
> open road from the North Sea to the Persian
> Gulf. She would have won all she fought for;
> supremacy in Europe and easy access to the
> East.
>
> —LLOYD GEORGE

I

At the end of 1917 and the beginning of
1918 the Quadruple Alliance, taking in all fronts, was approximately
equal in strength to the Allies. Only a quarter of its troops were held
in the east. On the western front both antagonists were about equal.
But from the spring on the influx of Americans steadily shifted the
balance from month to month. Erich Ludendorff was facing the hardest
decision of the war: should he attack in the west before the Americans
were ready to fight? He considered the situation.

For the first time since the beginning of the war Germany had
numerically equal forces in the field. This moment must be exploited.
The Allies, he knew, were not planning an offensive; they were waiting
for the Americans. The British military commentator Colonel Reping-
ton had, Ludendorff reflected, publicized the fact that Lloyd George,
deducing from his own cowardice that his people were also craven,
intended to avoid the conflict on the key front in France and instead
win cheaper victories in the Orient. Ludendorff would therefore have
the initiative. To be sure, a German offensive would cost him 100,000
men; moreover, his best soldiers would fall, for in the attack Death

chose the bravest. Still, if you wanted to break the enemy front you had to accept casualties. But would he succeed in taking the Channel ports? Of this there was no guarantee; in war you had to risk something. Finally, if the Germans did win a battle, would the Western Powers then agree to a peace repaying the sacrifices? Ludendorff's chief of operations held that Germany was not strong enough to crush the enemy completely; France would continue the struggle while waiting for the United States to send her millions. Would it not be better, therefore, to offer peace now, while fear of the coming offensive filled the hearts of the enemies? But at best what kind of peace could be obtained under such conditions? It would be a peace of renunciation; Germany would not acquire a square yard of additional territory in the west, would be required to grant Alsace-Lorraine autonomy; and might even have to cede some territory. The German people certainly did not want that kind of peace, Ludendorff assured himself. Despite the fact that regimental commanders reported that the soldiers had no wish for annexations, wished only peace—it was not true. Moreover, aspirations for territory grew with distance from the front. No, he did not want the onus of having needlessly given up Germany's rightful claims; moreover, the dynasty could not survive a compromise peace. The Supreme Command, which had for so long preached a peace with victory, could not now confess that it had been wrong. If the civilian government concluded such a peace, all very well—that was its affair. He could then declare that his views had been overridden. But he himself must think as a general. He must play the grand card that Fate had placed in his hand. There could be only victory or defeat! It was the commander in chief's business to take risks.

II

In some of his reasoning Ludendorff was not altogether wrong. Since the collapse of Russia the Western Powers had been waiting in fear for the German offensive in the west. Lloyd George did not look forward to the prospect of being beaten by the Germans in France and then rescued a year later by the Americans. Early in the new year Lloyd George asked the generals whether England would be in a better military situation within the next twelve months; if not, it would be better to discuss the conditions for peace. His Chancellor of the Exchequer and his President of the Board of Trade were defeatists, he said. Bonar Law remarked that Germany might be willing to return Alsace-Lorraine if she were given a free hand in the east. Former Foreign Minister Lord Lansdowne published a letter arguing for peace by negotiation. The unions enthusiastically backed him. The Socialist Ramsay Macdonald called for armistice negotiations; however, he added, he himself would don the khaki if the Germans wanted to keep Belgium in their clutches. Lord Robert Cecil affirmed that England must not insist unconditionally upon the return of Alsace-Lorraine. Prime Minister Smuts of South Africa, who at that time exerted great influence in London, persistently declared at meetings of the Cabinet that the Germans could not be beaten. Lloyd George was finally compelled to address the trade unions. He made it plain that England did not intend to contest Germany's position in the world as a great power, nor to impose a different form of government upon her, nor to dismember Austria-Hungary. He demanded only restoration and indemnities for Belgium, reconsideration of the "great wrong of 1871," autonomy for Austria's nations within the framework of the monarchy, and freedom for the Italian and Rumanian inhabitants of Austria to rejoin their homelands. As for Russia, let her settle with the Germans as she thought proper. However, he favored an "independent Poland comprising all those genuinely Polish elements who desire to form part of it." An international conference should deal with the question of the German colonies; the interests of the natives would have to be given primary consideration. He concluded with the words: "On these conditions the British Empire would welcome peace; to secure these conditions its peoples are prepared to make even greater sacrifices than those they have yet endured."

This was a distinct change in tone from that of the Allied reply of a year ago. Nor did Lloyd George mean these offers to be his last word; other concessions could have been won by negotiation. Churchill declared after the war that simply out of hatred for the Bolshevists England would have granted the Germans a free hand in the east provided Belgium were restored and France granted considerable concessions in Alsace-Lorraine. Lloyd George's view of the possibilities is quoted at the head of this chapter. After the war the strongly Germanophobe Conservative M.P. Leo Maxse asserted that the prime minister had been so pessimistic at the beginning of 1918 he would have accepted any tolerable offer of peace. England owed her salvation to her enemies, Maxse added; had it not been for the German Supreme Command and the Fatherland Party, Berlin would undoubtedly have made an offer which would have induced England to drop all of her war aims.

On January 8, 1918, a few days after Lloyd George's speech, President Wilson announced his Fourteen Points. He, too, demanded the evacuation and restoration of Belgium and self-government for the peoples of Austria-Hungary. He further called for righting of the "wrong done to France by Prussia in 1871 in the matter of Alsace-Lorraine," and the establishment of "an independent Polish state which should include the territories inhabited by indisputably Polish populations." These two points were put so generally that they could have been given any interpretation that accorded with the military realities.

Shortly before the great offensive, when Ludendorff had one of his men, a Colonel von Häften, sound out an envoy of Field Marshal Wilson's, the conditions transmitted were even more favorable to Germany than those which Lloyd George had laid down in his public speech. They were evacuation and compensation of Belgium, autonomy for Alsace-Lorraine, abrogation of the Treaty of Brest-Litovsk, and settlement of these questions at a general peace conference. Ludendorff not only rejected these conditions, but concealed them from the government of the Reich. But at the same time he retained Häften, who favored a peace by negotiation, as a liaison officer to the government; he even handed to the chancellor, with his approval, a memorandum by Häften in which the colonel said flatly that the efforts of the army alone would not be sufficient to obtain peace.

This contradictory behavior on Ludendorff's part bespeaks the terrible conflict in his own soul at the time. Outwardly, he was still the steel-hard advocate of victory; by his own show of confidence he stirred up the proudest hopes, thereby building up German public opinion into a dangerous obstacle to a peace by negotiation. But in the depths of his heart he was ready for such a peace, so long as he himself did not have to accept the responsibility for it; he wanted to blame an unpopular peace on the pen-pushing diplomats. His tactics toward the civilian heads of the government lacked candor and his decisions were colored by his personal ambitions; he undertook the great offensive not because there was no other way to achieve peace, but because the offensive offered the single possible way to win the victorious peace to which he was committed.

Ludendorff did not understand that a portending offensive is a stronger political weapon than one which has been carried out. Uncertainty produces more fear than an accomplished blow. If Germany at that time had publicly stated her designs: restoration and indemnifying of Belgium; autonomy for Alsace-Lorraine; exchange of a few French-speaking border areas for French colonies (France was considering the cession of Madagascar, the Congo, or Indo-China); a reasonable settlement in the east corresponding to the desires of the nations—the Western Powers would probably have had to agree. They would no longer have been able to ignore their pro-peace politicians and to go on driving their soldiers into the mouths of German cannon. The deputies from Alsace and Lorraine were ready to declare that they would consider their problem solved if their country were set up as an independent federal state with a democratic constitution. Such a compromise peace would have left Germany the victor; with Russia so weakened, her own position would be stronger than in 1914, and she would have proved that she could stand against the whole world. Ludendorff's war cry that there could be only victory or defeat was a stupid slogan. There were, as there usually are in this world, any number of intermediate possibilities.

Germany would not hear of compromise. Disregarding the starvation at home, Ludendorff risked Germany's destiny on the dubious chance of a great offensive in the west—and lost his gamble. Neither Kaiser nor chancellor nor *Reichstag* raised objections to this offensive which was as much a political as a military blunder. It was virtually out of the question that the offensive could force a peace with victory. And if it failed, the Americans would be landing in Europe and Germany would be lost.

III

It was as if the divided emotions in Ludendorff's heart carried over into the operation he now planned. He decided not to try to break through the enemy front in a single surprise assault, but to hit the line several different blows. When he outlined this plan to Major General Hoffmann, the commander of the eastern front said: "Your Excellency, any cadet who tried to solve the problem in such a way would flunk his examination." But Ludendorff nevertheless could not bring himself to concentrate all his disposable forces on any one point. He left a million men in the east; in the course of the year it turned out that he was able to withdraw half that number from the eastern front. These were, to be sure, men over thirty-five, but they would have been good to have for quiet sectors of the front and for building up rear-echelon positions. He also left 270,000 horses in the east, although he had only enough horses to render 51 of his 192 western divisions "mobile." Curiously overestimating his own situation, he did not request Austrian divisions, although the German general in charge of liaison with the Austrians believed some would be forthcoming if he asked. Instead, he encouraged the Austrians to launch an offensive of their own. Without German "corset stays," it failed completely, and Austrian Chief of Staff Conrad was subsequently pensioned off.

All in all, Ludendorff dispersed his forces in a fashion that is hard to understand. He also lacked tanks. Some time before the war the Prussian minister for war had been shown early models of tanks; he had not been impressed. Even after the Allies had been so incautious as to bring out their first tank models during the Battle of the Somme in 1916, the German Supreme Command did not profit by the live exhibit; it disregarded the advice of its chief of ordnance and did not order tanks built.

As always in war, mistakes on one side were counterbalanced by mistakes on the other. Ludendorff wanted to strike his main blow against the seam between the British and the French fronts. The Allies had for weeks anticipated that this would be the point of attack; nevertheless they did not reinforce the weak British divisions because the French were convinced that what was being prepared at this point was only a feint. Even when the offensive surged forward with the Germans having odds of two to one, the French were disinclined to come to the aid of the British. Dissension between the allied generals reached a danger point. The British considered retreating to the Channel ports, the French to Paris. "The more I hear of this war," remarked a witty Frenchman at the time, "the less I think of Napoleon's generalship. After all, Napoleon had an easy time of it—all he had to do was fight *against* coalitions." Thus the Germans succeeded in punching a salient forty-five miles wide and fifty-five miles deep into the enemy front. They took 90,000 prisoners. Pétain, Haig said, was terrified that the Germans would smash first the British and then the French in pitched battles. But after a week the offensive came to a halt just outside of Amiens. Ludendorff had not held a reserve army in readiness —although afterwards he proved to have sufficient forces to make three more attempts at a breakthrough. England sent across reinforcements of 300,000 men. The Americans increased their monthly shipments of troops to more than 200,000. When the American divisions, composed almost entirely of stalwart young men in their twenties, rattled through the streets in their trucks, roaring out their songs, the French took heart again. It was like a tremendous blood-transfusion from across the ocean; the tormented body of France, bleeding from hundreds of wounds, felt the influx of new life. Of equal importance was the Allied appointment of a joint commander in chief on the western front. Clemenceau would have preferred taking supreme command himself, with Foch as his chief of staff, but Haig pushed through the nomination of Foch. There was a certain malice underlying this proposal; most Allied generals were expecting further defeats and wanted Foch to bear the blame for them.

The grand offensive had broken down and the deep salient now constituted a weak point in the German front. It was virtually certain that fresh offensives launched with weaker forces against a reinforced enemy would also fail to bring victory. At this point Ludendorff should have informed the chancellor that this was the last chance for starting peace negotiations. But he could not humble himself to do this.

Two additional attempts to break through bogged down after a few days. The pro-German Swiss military commentator Stegemann wrote to a friend: "Germany's military position is brilliant and hopeless." In the three months of attacks the Germans had lost 190,000 men in dead and prisoners, the Allies 340,000. But at the same time the Allied front had been strengthened by 600,000 Americans. Millions more were in training. These American troops enabled the statesmen of the Allies to talk in strong language once again. It was against the background of American soldiers that Clemenceau answered a query on his foreign and domestic policy: "My foreign and my domestic policies are one and the same. Domestic policy: I am waging war. Foreign policy: I am waging war. I am always waging war. Russia fails us: I shall go on waging war. Unhappy Rumania is forced to capitulate: I wage war. And I shall continue to wage war to the last quarter of an hour, for that quarter-hour will be ours."

It was certainly time for the German chancellor to recognize that the midnight hour was nigh. But those in power in Germany remained blind. Crown Prince Rupprecht of Bavaria wrote to Chancellor Hertling that a compromise peace must be concluded; Ludendorff, too, he said, was staking everything on a *deus ex machina* which would not descend. Every week was precious. Hertling replied arrogantly that he still believed in victory. At a new war aims conference Ludendorff demanded the splitting of Belgium into Flanders and Wallonia, and a long occupation of these two new countries. He also wanted Austria to abandon her claims to the crown of Poland; the new Poland was to cede a broad border strip to Germany.

In the *Reichstag* Foreign Secretary Kühlmann ventured the self-evident truth that without the work of diplomats the sword could not restore peace. Ludendorff countered by forcing the dismissal of the hated foreign minister. Kühlmann's successor, Admiral Hintze, was one of the Ludendorff coterie; he quickly came through with the statement that he felt sure the next offensive would decisively defeat the enemy. This offensive was to be started to either side of Reims, tying up the French reserves and preparing the ground for further assaults against Calais, against Paris, and in Alsace.

But Kühlmann had barely been removed when the Reims offensive failed on the first day. This time the defenders were equal in numbers to the German attackers, and the surprise did not come off. Germany was at last forced on the defensive. The only man in Europe who did not believe this was Ludendorff. He promptly assembled divisions for still another offensive in Flanders.

CHAPTER TWENTY-FIVE

The Collapse Begins

*We now need no longer fear any possible sur-
prises by Foch, since we have drawn the fangs
of General Foch's operational army. We have
nullified the enemy's plans for the year 1918
and the enemy no longer has any chance to
seize the initiative.*

—STATEMENT BY THE GERMAN
MILITARY PRESS OFFICE,
JUNE 8, 1918

I

Foch had not even needed to draw on his
reserves for the shattering of the Reims offensive. Now the French
marshal tried a new tactic. A few days after the German assault had
broken down, the French infantry advanced without previous artillery
preparation, but protected by hundreds of tanks. They overwhelmed
the thin German lines and, marching ahead several kilometers, came
across German troops employed in taking in the abundant harvest.
The German soldiers threw away their scythes and fought where they
stood. By sundown the French had taken twelve thousand prisoners.
From that day on the Allies marched steadily forward, and the Germans
steadily back.

That evening Ludendorff made the admission to his staff that the
war could no longer be won. What mattered now was not to lose it;
Germany must play for a draw. For years Ludendorff had been saying
again and again that there could be only victory or defeat. In the
past he had been wrong; there had been numerous chances for a draw.
Now he was wrong again; a draw was impossible and the only point
in continuing the fight was to render the defeat less bitter.

The plan for the Flanders offensive was shelved. Ludendorff's advisers also recommended a withdrawal from the salient won in March
and a repetition of the "Siegfried position" retreat of the previous year.
This meant for Ludendorff owning up that his great offensives had
been useless—and he was incapable of recognizing his own errors.
When asked whether the Kaiser should be prepared to expect rectifi-

cations of the line to ease the problems of defense, Ludendorff thrust out his chin: "Defense? I hope we will be able to continue the attack upon Amiens as soon as the troops have been somewhat rested." If the general himself believed this, he was blind. If he were deliberately deceiving the Kaiser, he was guilty of violating his oath of allegiance.

If deception it was, he could not maintain it long. Five days after Ludendorff made this statement, Haig attacked the salient which had been conquered in March. The British soldiers advanced in the morning mist behind five hundred tanks. Several German divisions, weakened by influenza and the shortage of potatoes, caved in. Some 24,000 prisoners and four hundred guns were lost within forty-eight hours. After the failure of the grand offensive the morale of the troops had deteriorated. The soldiers were fagged out. Withdrawn from the front in a state of exhaustion one day, they would be taken back to it in trucks the next and thrown into a new witches' cauldron. The cry of "war boosters, strikebreakers" which had been heard in the French and Italian army now rang out among the Germans as they jeered at attacking relief divisions. British cavalry had opportunities to charge now, and the British losses were slight.

The Kaiser immediately came to headquarters. Ludendorff burst into reproaches against the soldiers. Wilhelm succumbed to discouragement as quickly as he had, six months earlier, to the intoxication of victory. As always, he was unable to strike a middle course. A balance-sheet must be drawn up and the war ended, he said. And he ordered a Crown Council.

A great deal depended upon this Crown Council. The Reich might still be saved from complete collapse. Would Ludendorff give an honest description of the direness of the military situation? Would Foreign Secretary Hintze be given powers to conclude a compromise peace before Germany had to accept a peace by capitulation? Would the Kaiser realize that he would have to sacrifice his coat in order to save his shirt?

Before the discussions began, Ludendorff took Hintze aside. "Three weeks ago I told you I felt certain I could force the enemy to make peace," he said. "Today I no longer feel that this is so."

"What form, then, will the war take?" Hintze asked.

"We will gradually paralyze the enemy's will to fight by our defensive strategy."

Ludendorff and Hintze sat down at the conference table with Hindenburg and Hertling; the Kaiser was temporarily left out of the discussions. At once the generals put on a bolder mien: The army was established on enemy territory and it would stay there! When Hintze pointed out that Austria-Hungary was on the verge of collapse and Bulgaria ready to drop out of the alliance, Ludendorff thrust aside such pessimism. Nevertheless Hintze insisted that it was necessary to take steps toward peace; what about Belgium and Poland? Ludendorff became the man of iron again; the program for Belgium must remain: division into Flanders and Wallonia and an extended occupation, as had already been decided. In Poland he must insist on the Bug-Narev Line, a frontier strip around Posen, a military convention, and an economic alliance. Ludendorff had learned nothing whatsoever in the past few months.

Foreign Secretary Hintze, son of a businessman and posturing as a globe trotter, was a virtuoso affecting the demonic type. He prized wit above all; when he called upon Soviet Ambassador Joffe he discarded his orders and put a red carnation in his buttonhole. He resembled somewhat the sophisticated, disillusioned man of the world in an Oscar Wilde comedy. But he was not so cynical as to make light of the gulf between Ludendorff's situation and Ludendorff's demands. The Crown Council was due to take place next morning. Hintze went to see Hertling beforehand and declared flatly that he would resign unless the Crown Council authorized him to seek peace. Instead of assuring him of support, the chancellor said: "In that case you must let an old man like me go first."

When the Crown Council opened, Ludendorff took the floor at once. But he said not a word about the situation at the front, only complained about the slackness back at home. It was left to Hintze to describe the military situation. The foreign secretary repeated what Ludendorff had told him the day before; he also stated his blunt opinion of Germany's allies. The Kaiser remarked that they must look for a suitable moment to start negotiations with the enemy. That moment would come after the next success on the western front, Hertling said. Hindenburg agreed that it would be best to wait until the situation improved before undertaking negotiations. The minutes of the session recorded: "Field Marshal Hindenburg hopes that the army will continue to remain in enemy territory." Ludendorff crossed out the word "hopes" and replaced it by "points out."

The "balance-sheet" the Kaiser wanted drawn up had turned out to be a neat bit of bookkeeping sleight-of-hand. The demands of the hour were a change of program and a change in leadership. Everything depended on sending a peace feeler through some neutral without delay, while at the same time demonstrating to the enemy by vigorous measures in home politics that the hoped-for collapse would not take place. Someone who was considered a "strong man" should be given the reins of government. He would have to gain the support of the parties of the Center and Left—the Right was needed for an Opposition. He would have to raise the privates' pay—the enlisted man received 15.90 marks per month as against 210 marks for the lowest rank of commissioned officers—as well as increase the pensions for widows and orphans. He would have to introduce electoral reforms, ostentatiously take action against profiteers and luxurious living, comb the home army and the draft-deferred men for more effectives—after which it was possible that a tolerable compromise peace could be achieved by relinquishing Alsace-Lorraine. For this program to make sense, Ludendorff should have been replaced by one of the prominent army group commanders.

But nothing of the sort happened. "Deeply moved," Ludendorff recounts, he shook hands in parting with Foreign Secretary Hintze. Like all men of action Ludendorff had the happy gift of losing sight of his own duplicity. Two weeks later he described the situation so blackly to his associate, Colonel von Mertz, that Mertz asked whether he should not pass on this picture to the representative of the Foreign Office. "Out of the question," Ludendorff replied. "The Foreign Office is so scared now (he used a much more graphic term) that if it finds out the real situation, there will be a catastrophe."

II

Thus disaster took its course. His hands a-tremble, Hertling went on trying to smooth over the contention of the political parties in the *Reichstag*. Hintze waited for some triumph on the western front and meanwhile confidentially informed the Belgian government that Germany wanted "only" guarantees from Belgium after the war, not dependency status. Ludendorff rejected all proposals by the army group commanders to withdraw the troops to shortened lines in order to save reserves, gain time, and give the soldiers a chance to rest. Political reasons were against it, he said. Vice Chancellor Payer believed that permission to declare publicly Germany's intention to restore Belgium's freedom had to be given not by the Kaiser but by Ludendorff. The result was a lamentable scene at headquarters in which the general laid down to the vice chancellor his "conditions" for the declaration—when in reality Germany's intentions toward Belgium no longer mattered in the least. The struggle was continuing only to determine whether Strassburg and Posen would remain German, and whether Wilhelm would keep his crown.

Gradually, however, even Chancellor Hertling was growing frightened. Three weeks after the Crown Council he requested a written report on Germany's military prospects. For a month Ludendorff did not condescend to answer him.

In Vienna, meanwhile, Count Burian had again become foreign minister. Since the western front had begun wavering and the imminent collapse of the Central Powers was becoming evident to all, the nations of the dual monarchy had begun raising the cry: Separation from Austria. The Emperor Karl recognized that peace alone could save his crown, but he could not find the right way to achieve it. Count Burian wanted simply to propose to all the belligerents that they meet in The Hague for peace negotiations. Given the predicament of the Central Powers, this naive gesture was hopeless and no more than a pitiable sign of weakness.

Rather than let the Austrian offer go through, Ludendorff gave his authorization to a peace feeler via Holland. But it was too late. Like many Hungarian statesmen, Burian saw no farther than his nose, and he was mulishly stubborn to boot. He sent out his cry of distress. It went unheard. American Secretary of State Lansing was said to have spent only half an hour composing a note of rejection. Clemenceau replied with a speech to the Senate which concluded: "On to stainless victory!" Simultaneously, the Fatherland Party in Germany issued a statement calling for an independent Flanders and a free hand for Germany in the east.

Meanwhile the military situation in the west was steadily going from bad to worse. At the beginning of the year Ludendorff had had 3.5 million men in the west. Since then he had—too late—brought in another half million from the east. But the grand offensives had cost the army 1.5 million more men than could be replaced, and every month the army was shrinking by another 80,000 men while 300,000 Americans were being added monthly to the enemy forces. By the end of September only 750,000 infantry troops were opposing the enemy. Fortified rear positions did not exist. Foch was capturing an average of 3000 German prisoners a day. At the end of August Foch said: "The Germans may still escape if they make up their minds to abandon their baggage." But Ludendorff could not bring himself to give up this "baggage"— the vast supplies of war materials and equipment the army had accumulated. Still less did he want to lose prestige. The British, too, had to disband divisions for which they could no longer find replacements—but "General Tank" and the Americans quickly filled the gaps in the lines.

The Allies now felt that victory was certain, but they did not expect the decisive campaign to come until 1919. Smuts even thought the fighting in the west would continue through 1919, and that the Germans might advance once more in the east. It would take until 1920 to finish them, he believed—and wondered whether by then the victory would be worth winning. British Chief of Staff Wilson was counting on a German-Turkish offensive from Baku across Afghanistan into India and was speculating on the possibility of sending Allied troops through Siberia to defend India. With weird military logic he argued that even if the Germans were expelled from France and Belgium, they could still conquer Asia. "Theoretical rot," Haig commented.

The point is that the Allies still feared the fighting spirit of the German soldier. An intelligent German government could have played on this fear to obtain a fairly tolerable peace. The British government wanted, if possible, to avoid further great sacrifices of lives. It was hardly inclined to spill more English blood in order to build up French hegemony on the Continent. As late as October 2, when Ludendorff had already drafted his plea for an armistice, Lord Robert Cecil said that peace would be much nearer if a German statesman would only do one thing: declare Germany's willingness to evacuate Belgium completely and to settle all other questions without annexations or reparations.

III

Neither Hertling nor Ludendorff took a comprehensive view of the situation. Ludendorff did not realize that the fate of the western front was being decided not only on the Aisne, but also on the Piave, at Salonika, and on the Jordan. At Salonika about 160,000 Bulgarians were facing a somewhat stronger army of Greeks, Serbs, Frenchmen, Englishmen, and Italians. The Bulgarians no longer had any heart for fighting. In the spring of 1918 Ludendorff's gluttony for more land and the selfishness of the Turks had denied Bulgaria the entire Dobruja. As a result of this disappointment, the pro-German Cabinet had been ousted. The ministers of the new government preferred good English guineas to German marks.

Ever since the Balkan War, that is, for seven years, Bulgarian peasant women had been toiling behind the plow while their men, barefoot, in ragged uniforms, on wretched rations, without blankets or firewood, had endured the bitter winters of the high mountains. What their distress began, bribery finished, for the Bulgarian generals were as fond of hard currency and horses as their statesmen. The few German divisions in the Bulgarian army had been shifted to the west in the summer of 1918; only three German infantry battalions and thirty-two batteries were left. In vain King Ferdinand complained: "My Bulgarians want to see spiked helmets." In vain the German commander on the Bulgarian front begged for at least one full division for a mobile reserve. Ludendorff allowed six divisions under Mackensen to remain idle in Rumania, a country which had bowed out of the war. But he sent not a single man to reinforce the Salonika front, even when an offensive was threatening there. In the middle of September the Allies attacked; at the point of assault they had a superiority of two to one.

The Bulgarian army was routed, and the entire army group began retreating toward the north. The Bulgarian government asked for an armistice. It took effect on September 29, opening the way for the Allies to Constantinople, Belgrade and Rumania. King Ferdinand abdicated in favor of his son—thereby becoming the sole monarch of the Quadruple Alliance to save the throne for his family. In a telegram to the Kaiser he recommended that Wilhelm follow his example. Wilhelm replied: "I consider your action altogether senseless, or at least premature."

IV

A few days after the Salonika army had smashed the Bulgarians, the British attacked the Turks in Palestine. The Turkish army in those parts was under the command of Liman von Sanders, who had won the Battle of Gallipoli. The supply officers of the Turkish army reckoned that they had to feed about 100,000 men. But the actual number of soldiers varied according to whether a battle or a pay call was impending. For fighting, about 20,000 men could be counted on; in addition there were 3000 Germans. The enemy was five times as strong.

Conditions in the Turkish army were even worse than in the Bulgarian army. Even the officers wrapped skins around their feet; during the past winter half of the army in Mesopotamia had died of starvation. In the Caucasus, ready to die for Enver Pasha's dreams of a Pan-Turkish Empire, were 40,000 fine fighting troops, but their German allies had promised Moscow to stop them from marching upon Baku. (Nevertheless, the German Supreme Command reinforced this Turkish front with German armored trains.) Strong Turkish divisions were also tied down by rebellious Arabs under the brilliant leadership of the young British colonel T. E. Lawrence. Of the two million men the Turks had enlisted during the war, some 500,000 had fallen in battle or died of disease, and 750,000 men had deserted. In the interior of the country these deserters were busily making careers out of banditry.

Equipped with five planes and two cannon, the ruins of the Turkish army in Palestine awaited the new offensive. In vain Liman requested reinforcements; Ludendorff had only recently withdrawn from this front a rifle battalion which never had a chance to meet the enemy again before the war ended. When the British at last attacked, with tenfold superiority, a two-hour barrage did the trick; the Turkish troops fled and vanished without a trace. Liman von Sanders was almost captured in his headquarters at Nazareth by British cavalry patrols; the army staff had to fight its way to safety in hand-to-hand combat.

The remnants of the Turkish army retreated far to the north; the British took 75,000 prisoners. Of the German components of the army

Colonel Lawrence wrote: "Exceptions were the German detachments; and here, for the first time, I grew proud of the enemy who had killed my brothers. They were two thousand miles from home, without hope and without guides in conditions bad enough to break the bravest nerves. Yet their sections held together in firm rank, sheering through the wrack of Turk and Arab like armoured ships, high-faced and silent. When attacked they halted, took position, fired to order. There was no haste, no crying, no hesitation. They were glorious."

About this same time the British conquered Mesopotamia. Like two gigantic serpents the two British armies coiled northward, each seizing a leg of the Turkish army and swallowing it whole. The front in the Orient collapsed.

CHAPTER TWENTY-SIX

Ludendorff Asks for an Armistice

*The profession of soldier often saps even the
strongest personalities with surprising swiftness. A vigorous intellect and driving will may
within the span of a year be reduced to a sterile
mind and faint heart. Such has often been the
tragic course of great military men.*

—HINDENBURG

I

For more than a year General Ludendorff
had been bearing a tremendous burden. He had to defend the German
Reich against a whole world of enemies, and in addition he had assumed the task of governing the country. He had gone on hoping that
he would be able to dictate to Europe a peace that would carry Germany's power and his own fame to dizzy heights. Now this hope had
been swept away, and his nerves gave out. He ate little, lay night after
night without sleeping, involved his army commanders in telephone
conversations that went on for hours, fussed over trivial details, issued
contradictory orders, refused to listen to objections, and hunted everywhere for scapegoats. His subordinate commanders and the officers of
his staff complained that he was intolerably nervous, indecisive, and at
times absolutely passive. The best mind left in the Supreme Command,
Colonel Bauer, recommended dismissing him at once. Ludendorff's
prestige had fled. All the important army commanders agreed that he
was no longer the man he had been; one of them said that Ludendorff
risked the final resources for his personal prestige, on a gambler's
operation. Finally the army's chief psychiatrist, Dr. Hochheimer, was
consulted. He found the general suffering from overwork and in the
grip of extreme tension. For three weeks the doctor attempted, by mas-
sage, breathing exercises, and friendly admonition, to induce the general
to relax. A staff officer wrote home: "In Ludendorff's garden the roses
are blooming, and on his doctor's orders His Excellency must enjoy
them daily." Hochheimer was satisfied with the success of his treatment
—as psychiatrists usually are. But it soon became apparent that Ludendorff's problem could not be solved by smelling roses.

The situation was growing more and more fearsome; retreat, prisoners, insufficient replacements, superior tank forces, more and more American divisions; there were by now 1.5 million Americans in action. In the southeast two fronts had just collapsed; suppose the western front also caved in? Almost every night Ludendorff said to his chief aide: "Heye, now they've broken through." When word came that influenza had broken out in Marseilles, Ludendorff—as he himself said —grasped at this news like a drowning man at a straw. "A glance at General Ludendorff's clouded face, at his eyes now roving restlessly, now staring blankly, revealed spiritual agitation of extraordinary intensity, as the puffed-up look of his features told of sleepless nights," reported Major Niemann, the liaison officer to the Kaiser. Finally several generals told Baron von Lersner, the Foreign Office representative at headquarters, that if the enemy should attack with all the forces at his disposal, there would be a large-scale breakthrough; all that was needed was determination on the enemy's part, and the German army would be routed. Lersner asked Ludendorff to report this to Berlin. Ludendorff growled: "Don't press me. I created Hindenburg's fame, and the field marshal knows nothing officially as yet."

Finally Heye, without consulting Ludendorff, requested Foreign Secretary Hintze to come to headquarters. From Lersner's reports Hintze had already concluded that at the proper moment President Wilson must be asked to mediate a peace. But first, in order to prepare the people for what would be a terrible shock to their hopes, a "revolution from above" had to be made and a new government formed. He decided to go to headquarters on September 28, 1918. When on the eve of his departure he informed Chancellor Hertling of his views, the old man called him a pessimist. Habitué of the world of parliamentary intrigues, Hertling imagined that the purpose of the whole action was only to pry him out of the chancellorship. To confirm his suspicion, the Supreme Command had just informed him directly that it had changed its mind about a Cabinet shuffle and thought a new government with more popular representatives was necessary. He decided to follow Hintze to Spa, where general headquarters was located. To close associates he remarked that he was sure of the Center, and that in any case he already had a furnished apartment in Munich. The chancellor's mind was going the way of his flesh.

II

Late in the afternoon of that same September 28, Erich Ludendorff heavy-heartedly descended the stairs to the office occupied by Field Marshal Hindenburg. He had at last brought himself to a decision, he told Hindenburg. A breakthrough was threatening; the armies had to have a rest; they must propose an immediate armistice. With great

calm and decency Hindenburg replied that he had come to the same
conclusion of his own accord. He wanted to spare Ludendorff part of
the responsibility for the hardest decision of the war.

The plea for an armistice—for an offer in such a situation is inevitably a plea—was an incomprehensible idea. Would Ludendorff, in
the days of triumphant German offensives against the Russians, Serbs,
Rumanians or Italians, have granted the enemy an armistice so that
their armies could recover? It was certain that the Allies would agree
to an armistice only under conditions that would preserve their present
superiority. In fact, they would obviously seize upon this sign of weakness to make demands that would improve their position. Certainly
they would protract the negotiations; they had no reason not to. An
army in full retreat that asks for an immediate armistice is raising the
white flag.

And how would the German people take such a development? Only a
few weeks earlier the generals had been promising them Belgium,
Poland, and the Baltic countries; now they suddenly saw themselves
confronted with the greatest defeat in their history. The masses are
given to crude reactions; it was obvious that they would be overcome
by despair at this apparently sudden change of weather. Since the
armistice negotiations would obviously drag out for a long time, would
not every German soldier have the feeling that it was not worth dying
for a lost cause at the last minute? The young Americans were still
hot for battle; such a thought would be far less likely to occur to them.
A request for an armistice was a confession of the hopelessness of the
struggle. How, if the armistice talks came to nothing, would it be
possible to persuade the German people to go back into the struggle?
Everyone knew that Germany was fighting against time, that every
month brought more Americans to France. Count von der Schulenburg,
chief of the Crown Prince Army Group, said later of this decision: "The
worst thing that could happen to us was this confession to the world
that our military collapse was impending. This forced request for an
immediate armistice meant just that. Spring the word 'armistice' upon
an army straining to the utmost, as was ours, and it will no longer
be capable of stubborn resistance. After all, no one likes the idea of
being shot up at the eleventh hour. That is all the more true of soldiers
who are at the end of their rope. And in making the offer we revealed
the extent of our weakness to the enemy. Ludendorff alone is responsible for this decision. A general who holds in his hand the destiny of
a nation of seventy millions must have strong nerves. If he loses his
nerve, he must go; to keep him on is unthinkable. . . . An army like
ours had no need of raising the white flag on September 29."

When Foreign Secretary Hintze arrived at headquarters, Ludendorff
told him: "The condition of the army requires an armistice to avert a

catastrophe." Hintze was stunned; he had no idea that the situation was so dire. Bitterly he replied that this sudden change from the fanfares of victory to the dirges of defeat would have a woeful effect upon the army, the people, and the monarchy. The armistice request must at least be accompanied by an invitation to peace negotiations, he said, and Wilson's Fourteen Points should be taken as the basis for these. It was also necessary for a new government to be formed. Responsibility had to be placed upon a broader basis. Hindenburg suggested without a trace of irony that at least the annexation of the Briey ore basin should be made one of the conditions of peace. Ludendorff cut him off: "Now is no longer the time for that."

Following the conference, the generals and the foreign secretary reported to the Kaiser. Wilhelm remained composed; he was, he said, agreeable to the request for an armistice. But Hertling, who arrived that afternoon, broke down completely and handed in his resignation.

A new chancellor had to be chosen in this, Germany's gravest hour. Under the rules of parliamentary system, by which the government of Germany had now decided to abide, it was the *Reichstag's* business to pick the chancellor. But the *Reichstag* had not a single member on the Right or Left to whom it could entrust the helm at this time. At a moment when power was passing from the monarch to the representatives of the people, the *Reichstag* could think of no one to propose except the heir apparent of one of the South German states, Prince Max of Baden. The Prince, who was also a general in the Prussian army, had worked skillfully and energetically during the war on prisoner welfare and the exchange of prisoners among the belligerents. Several times in the course of the war he had delivered sensible and conciliatory speeches recommending negotiation to all parties. It was he who had coined the phrase "conscience of the world." For a long time the moderates on the Left had wanted him as chancellor. But he had evaded such proposals with embarrassment; power did not lure him, and by this very fact he demonstrated that he was not by nature a political man. After Bethmann's fall the administrative head of the Cabinet had proposed him, but the Kaiser had replied with his weird logic that he would accept advice from an older statesman, but not from a younger member of a royal family. Now Prince Max was the only candidate.

Something happened that astonished the generals. Prince Max was prepared to risk his life, his name, and his possible succession to the throne and accept the ungrateful task of heading the government in this crisis. But this soft-hearted, emotional advocate of a peace by negotiation flatly refused to issue the request for an armistice. In this moment of peril, he declared, a new chancellor must appeal to all the forces of the nation for a last-ditch effort; there must be no talk of peace while the army was retreating. Briefed on the military situation, he announced that in his first *Reichstag* address on October 5 he would proclaim peace aims which would go far toward meeting the desires of the enemy; this done, he maintained, the Allied soldiers would lose a good deal of their martial fervor. He would state Germany's willingness to evacuate Belgium, surrender Alsace-Lorraine if need be, and negotiate on a new peace in the east. Then, he argued, Germany must wait for the reaction. If the situation were as grave as the Supreme Command described it, he said, nothing would be saved by a request for an armistice; capitulation would be inevitable. Bravely he declared his willingness to take responsibility for the postponement; the danger of delay was less than that of a premature request for an armistice. Out of unfounded pessimism the fatal submarine campaign had been started early in 1917; this mistake should not be repeated.

These arguments were wise, but the generals gave them no support; the only backing Prince Max received was from two clever Jewish businessmen. Walter Rathenau declared a request for an armistice premature and called for an all-out national defense effort. The banker Warburg told Colonel Häften, the representative of the Supreme Command: "It seems strange to me that I as a civilian must today appeal to the military men: Continue the struggle. I know that my only son, who is now being trained, will be in the trenches in a month's time, and yet I implore you not to call a halt now." But Ludendorff was deaf to appeals. On September 20 he stormed unannounced into a room where the Kaiser and Hertling were discussing the problem of a new chancellor and asked in a tone of extreme agitation: "Hasn't the new government been formed yet?" The Kaiser replied harshly: "I am not a magician." Whereupon Ludendorff said: "The government must be formed at once because the request for peace must be sent today." The Kaiser said: "You should have told me that two weeks ago."

On October 1 the vice chancellor asked whether the sending of the offer could not be postponed for a while. Ludendorff replied that if by eight o'clock that same night it were certain that Prince Max of Baden would form a government, the offer could wait until next day; otherwise it had best be sent at once. In the course of the afternoon Ludendorff sent two more telegrams to Berlin urging that the armistice request be sent immediately. Today, he said, the troops were still holding and the offer could be made with dignity; at any moment the enemy might break through, and then no less favorable time could be imagined for suggesting peace. He felt like a gambler, he added; a division might collapse at some point along the front from one hour to the next. That night he had Lersner send another telegram urging that the offer be transmitted to Washington via Berne, Switzerland, as speedily as possible because the army could not wait another forty-eight hours. In vain Prince Max again summed up the arguments against a plea for an armistice; General Ludendorff dismissed it all with the words: "I want to save my army." His special envoy in Berlin declared that it was not a matter of days, but of hours.

Prince Max asked Ludendorff whether he fully realized that acceptance of Wilson's Fourteen Points meant giving up Alsace-Lorraine and perhaps Posen and West Prussia as well. Ludendorff shirked the question by replying that concessions in Alsace-Lorraine must be considered, but none on the Polish frontier. The general simply ignored the fact that in the armistice request he so desperately wanted these concessions were already made. Without a trace of irony Heye wrote later: "Ludendorff would tolerate no half-measures. Realizing now that the government would not, without his urging, find its way to an 'honorable peace,' he himself intervened with his usual energy." In other words, with the greatest of energy he raised the white flag.

On October 3 Prince Max accepted the post of chancellor. A conference was held, the Kaiser acting as chairman, to draft the text of the armistice request. The new chancellor opened the meeting by stating: "I am against the request." The Kaiser interrupted him: "The Supreme Command thinks it necessary, and you have not come here to make difficulties for the Supreme Command."

Prince Max replied: "I am prepared to agree to immediate dispatch of the note only on one condition: that the Supreme Command gives me a written statement—one which I will be able to transmit to the Cabinet today, and later publish—that the military situation on the western front renders impossible a postponement until my *Reichstag* speech the day after tomorrow." Hindenburg, who had come to Berlin, was harried with questions from all sides, but answered calmly and levelly. "His calmness," reports Vice Chancellor Payer, "was in pleasant contrast to the overwrought tone of the Supreme Command which has so distressed us in the past several days. But his position differed in no whit from theirs and he demanded with equal firmness, though in somewhat milder a manner, the immediate dispatch of the note." The Supreme Command came forth with the written statement Prince Max had asked for. Thereupon the members of the government, including Payer, agreed that it was not for mere civilians to contest the decision of the military in this matter. Prince Max alone and his foreign secretary, Solf, continued to protest. The Prince proposed sending an offer of peace without the request for an armistice. That, he said, would be an announcement of liquidation but not of bankruptcy. But Ludendorff, consulted on this point by telephone, vetoed the idea. On the night of October 3, Prince Max, against his better judgment, dispatched the note.

Even before Prince Max of Baden's appointment had been confirmed, Vice Chancellor Payer had thought it proper to inform the leaders of the various party fractions in the *Reichstag* of the military situation. For this purpose Ludendorff sent Major von dem Bussche to Berlin to explain matters to the deputies. With a carelessness amounting to treason Payer allowed the presence at the conference of two self-declared enemies of Germany: the Pole Seyda and the Independent Socialist Haase, both of whom were in contact with foreign countries. Bussche spoke calmly, weighing his words. The decisive factors were the lack of replacements and the enemy tanks, he said. The war could no longer be won, but it might be possible, by various shifts, to hold out for months. The request for armistice and peace negotiations were necessary before the enemy recognized Germany's weakness. If the enemy offered only a humiliating peace, the fighting would have to be resumed.

The deputies heard all this in utter consternation. They wilted in their seats. Ebert, the leader of the Socialists, was deathly pale and unable to speak. Stresemann looked as if he were about to have a stroke. Von Heydebrandt ranted that his Conservative Party was being ruined by the lies of the Supreme Command. As the deputies filed out of the room, Seyda was noticeably beaming and Haase called triumphantly to a fellow-member of his own fraction: "Now we have them." The briefing had been in strict confidence, but within a matter of hours the story was all over Berlin. Payer later declared apologetically that since the life and death of the whole nation was at stake he had therefore—therefore!—considered that he had no right to exclude the leaders of any of the parties, thereby impugning their discretion. The vice chancellor, too, was one of those politicians whom God in his wrath had appointed to rule Germany.

With the new government being formed, the leader of the Social Democrats, Philip Scheidemann, ruled that his Socialists must stay out of it. "Why should we enter a bankrupt enterprise at this moment of utmost despair?" he asked. While he was speaking, Ebert entered the Chamber, walking like a broken man; he had just heard Major Bussche's briefing. He spoke up, saying that it was not a question of party, but of the Fatherland; the party must do its duty, at whatever cost to its own future. If the Socialists did not go along with the bourgeois parties now, he said, there would be a revolution, and anyone who had seen how things had turned out in Russia could not wish for another such upheaval, not even in the interests of the proletariat.

III

The next few days proved that Prince Max's military judgment had been better than Ludendorff's. The front held. Ludendorff had exaggerated his predicament; Prince Max's plan might well have been followed. Military history is wont to pass harsh verdicts upon generals who raise the white flag when it is not absolutely necessary. In misfortune Ludendorff had displayed the same immoderateness as in good fortune. For years the pro-Ludendorff press had hammered away at the slogan of victory or defeat and scorned the very possibility of negotiation. Now when it was vital to be steadfast, Ludendorff gave a despairing cry for help—thereby letting Germany's enemies know that the victory they had not dared believe in was practically theirs. After the war Ludendorff maintained that the request for an armistice had been necessary in order to determine as quickly as possible whether the enemy was prepared to make peace. Actually, the confession of imminent collapse only stiffened the enemy's resolution to continue the war.

If instead Prince Max had announced new German war aims, and if at the same time a new war minister had been chosen to personify the will to continue fighting, France and England would in all probability not have pushed the contest to the finish. At the end of October Ludendorff himself admitted privately that the armistice request had been the worst mistake in his life.

In his inaugural address to the *Reichstag*, Prince Max had wanted to discuss Wilson's Fourteen Points in detail, that the world might know how Germany regarded them. But the War Cabinet, of which Payer, Scheidemann and Erzberger were members, demurred. They were not aware, as Prince Max remarked, that master races like the Anglo-Saxons respond to servility with harshness. The attitude of the War Cabinet was reflected in Erzberger's miserable outburst: "When I am down on the ground and someone is kicking me in the stomach, I do not say things that will annoy him."

The Constitution was amended to provide for straight parliamentary government. The administration rested on the confidence of the *Reichstag*, Cabinet ministers could be recruited from the ranks of deputies, and the war minister had to approve the appointment of army officers.

On October 8 Häften admitted that the armistice request had been unnecessary. The following day Wilson's reply came in. The President demanded an explicit acceptance of the Fourteen Points; also a pledge that all occupied territory would be evacuated in the event of an armistice. He wanted to know in whose name the chancellor was speaking.

The government, with consent of the Supreme Command, submitted to the first two conditions; in answer to Wilson's third point it referred to the constitutional amendments which had meanwhile been made. Foreign Secretary Solf asked Ludendorff whether he could hold the front another three months. Ludendorff replied: "No." Asked further whether Germany would be able to take up the struggle again if efforts to obtain peace failed, he said: "If there is a pause in the fighting in the west." That, of course, could not be without an armistice.

A few days later came Wilson's second note. It laid down three principal conditions for an armistice: the existent Allied superiority must be maintained; submarine warfare must be stopped; the German nation must no longer be controlled by an arbitrary power. The first point was a matter of course. The second was unimportant, since U-boat damage was lagging far behind new construction and there was not, since the loss of Rumania, sufficient fuel for submarines. As for the third point, the government could again point to the recent constitutional changes.

Now, at the end of October, Ludendorff sprang another surprise. He had realized that his armistice request had been a blunder for which the nation and history would never forgive him. Therefore he resumed his role of strong man and would not hear of calling off the submarines. When the chancellor asked him whether he thought the war could be ended next year under better conditions, he replied: "Yes." Foreign Secretary Solf snapped that if this were so he had been very wrong in his analysis of September 29, for meanwhile the situation in the Balkans and in Turkey had greatly deteriorated.

By the end of October the battle strength of the German divisions had shrunk to about twelve hundred rifles apiece. The Allies on the western front had two hundred and twenty as against one hundred and ninety German divisions; the French division numbered twice as many men as the German, the British three times and the American twelve times. If battle strength were reckoned in manpower, the Allies had a three- or fourfold superiority. Moreover, the German army was shrinking by 80,000 men per month; the enemy's forces were increasing by about 200,000 men monthly. The war minister offered to scrape up 600,000 men. But for "immediate delivery" he had only 75,000. To be sure, these "scrapings" and the undernourished eighteen-year-old boys had little heart for fighting; many field commanders would as soon do without such replacements.

The situation was equally bad in the other theaters of war. In Russia there were some twenty divisions, in Rumania six, in the Caucasus one, in Turkey special formations comprising about 30,000 men, in Finland a cavalry brigade, and in Hungary one division. These troops could not be released for the western front, Ludendorff insisted; they were needed to stop the advancing Allied army in the Balkans, for the Austro-Hungarian army was in such a state that it could not hold its own borders.

The government sent a quiet and dignified reply to President Wilson, agreeing to the cessation of U-boat warfare but emphasizing that it was confident the President would not champion dishonorable demands.

Wilson now dispatched a third note. The Allies, he said, would require extraordinary safeguards. If the United States, he added, "must deal with the military masters and the monarchical autocrats of Germany now or later, it must demand not peace negotiations but surrender." The purpose of this was obvious: to drive a wedge between the German people and their government.

Ludendorff straightway issued a message to the army telling the soldiers that the Wilson note was unacceptable. The message was couched in language scarcely suitable for a general who only very recently had said the game was up. Had Ludendorff been right on September 29, any further defense at this point was useless. Had he been wrong then, his guilt was enormous, for he had forfeited Germany's last chance for a decent peace. In either case, the general was thoroughly discredited. By threatening to resign, the chancellor procured Ludendorff's dismissal. At the express wish of the Kaiser and the chancellor, Hindenburg remained chief of staff. Prince Max wanted to reply to Wilson's latest note with some asperity, but his underlings again declared that proud language did not become a country in such a fix as Germany was. Prince Max then decided to postpone calling for a last-ditch national defense until really unacceptable demands had been made. He never guessed that when the moment came the revolution would have snatched every weapon from his hands.

CHAPTER TWENTY-SEVEN

The Downfall of Austria-Hungary

*What is there to fill the place of the Austrian
state in Europe? Any new political structures in
this area would be permanently revolutionary
in character.*

—BISMARCK

I

The Emperor Karl of Austria was a man of
noble views and meager ability. Soon after he ascended the throne he
issued an amnesty for the traitors among his loyal peoples. "I am choosing this day on which My most dearly beloved eldest son, whom God
in His mercy has given to Me, celebrates the day consecrated to the
saint whose name he bears," Karl's proclamation read. "Thus the hand
of a child who some day will direct the destiny of My peoples is leading misguided prodigal sons back to their father's house." The prodigal
sons did not return penitently to the paternal tent, but, with the worst
intentions, went abroad. When the Emperor, on a visit to the front
soon afterwards, heard of fresh desertions, he exclaimed petulantly, "I
should like to know what the men are thinking of?" "That they will be
amnestied," Chief of Staff Conrad replied.

As long as the Central Powers had reason to hope for a favorable
termination of the war, the Slavic nations in the Hapsburg Empire adhered to the monarchy. The same leaders of the Czechs and South
Slavs who a year later were to trample the Austrian flag underfoot had
in 1915 declined the Allies' offer to liberate them from the yoke of the
Hapsburgs. The utmost they demanded was national autonomy within
a Hapsburg federal union. The South Slavs of Austria-Hungary would
far rather rule themselves than be governed by "Belgrade illiterates."
As late as the end of 1917, President Wilson maintained that he did not
wish to weaken the Austro-Hungarian Empire, and General Smuts assured Count Mensdorff. the Austrian ambassador in London, that the
Allied note demanding the dissolution of the Hapsburg Monarchy had
been a mere bluff.

But when Germany's glory and power were splintered into a thousand
fragments on the western front, all the rats deserted the sinking ship

of the Hapsburgs. Now, in the fall of 1918, Karl decided to make all the concessions which, if made a year before, might possibly have saved his throne. But his reforms required the consent of Hungary. He therefore asked Count Stefan Tisza for once to pay a personal visit to the South Slav areas to see for himself what the temper of the people was. Tisza complied, but his mind was sealed. In Bosnia he assured a delegation that Serbia would emerge from this war so small that Bulgaria would be able to swallow her for breakfast. When someone replied that Bulgaria was defenseless at the feet of the Allied Salonika army, he said grudgingly: "Perhaps we will go under. But before we do we will crush you!"

II

The Emperor Karl now decided to act—far too late. His peoples were to be given autonomy. The Hungarian prime minister reminded him of his coronation oath and declared coolly that Hungary must not be tampered with, or else he would block Austria's supply of food. Consequently the Emperor's manifesto had to say that all these liberties did not apply to Hungary. Thus most of the South Slav regions remained separated from the projected "Kingdom of Illyria," and the new Kingdom of Czechia did not include the Slovaks because they too belonged to Hungary. Taken all in all, the manifesto made only the vaguest concessions to the "loyal peoples."

The Emperor's manifesto was Austria-Hungary's obituary. As Count Andrassy, the last foreign minister of the monarchy, remarked: "In order to prevent anyone from murdering us, we are committing suicide." When the Austrian prime minister invited the nation's leading citizens to a conference so that he could explain the manifesto to them, they did not trouble to come. The South Slav National Council rejected this and "all other proposals of whatever complexion." Four years before, the Czechs had been all eagerness to crown the Emperor of Austria as King of Bohemia!

The Hungarians now obtained an agreement that henceforth the connection between Austria and Hungary was to be no more than a pure personal union. This new arrangement threw Budapest into a delirium of joy. The Hungarians were now confident that their country would emerge from the war with all its territory intact. Unthinkable that the Fourteen Points might also be applied to Hungary. An attempt was made to assassinate Count Tisza, but the bullet missed, and with his customary calm the count said to the arrested terrorist: "Look here, young man, why did you do this? Now you have only made trouble for yourself."

When Austria appealed for a peace conference, Wilson waited two weeks before replying that the idea of a federal union was no longer good enough. These words sounded the tocsin of liberation for all the nations within the monarchy. Each was resolved to go his own way. The living body of Austria-Hungary was torn asunder. The chaos caused the greatest suffering in the army. Troops in combat lines were still receiving 200 grams of meat per week, and hundreds of men deserted rear-echelon positions for the front lines in order to obtain a share of this abundance. Horse meat was considered a delicacy. Men feverish with malaria had to stand naked and shivering in the open air while their one shirt, which had just been washed, was drying. During the last battle a staff officer found a detachment immediately behind the front lines clad only in underwear; they were supporting troops and there were enough uniforms only for the men in the foremost trenches.

At the end of October the Italian army, strengthened by English, French, Czech and American troops, launched an assault upon this pitiful horde which had a total strength of about 1.5 million, of whom 350,000 men were combat troops. Yet once more Germans and Magyars, Croats and Serbs, Slovenes and Galicians, and even a few Czech regiments, displayed an amazing comradeship in arms. For four days this army without a country fought for every rock; several hills changed hands three times.

Republics were proclaimed in Prague and Zagreb. At the same time Hungary recalled her troops; they were needed to save the sacred soil of the Fatherland from the advancing Salonika army. The Hungarians simply withdrew from the battle line. Soldiers of the other nations refused to leap into the breach. The army dissolved. When General Arz von Straussenberg reported the situation to the government, Finance Minister Spitzmüller took out his watch and said: "It is now half past twelve. That gives us a little time for lunch. After that we must ask for peace immediately."

An Austro-Hungarian commission headed by General Weber crossed the front lines to the Italians. The Italian conditions were: immediate demobilization of Austria and free passage through her territory for the Allied troops. These conditions were transmitted to Vienna. At this point there took place a grotesque farce in which dying Austria managed to sum up, in one phantasmagoric symbol, all her weaknesses.

The Emperor and the government decided to accept the conditions and wired their decision to General Weber. General Arz went to the telephone and ordered the Chief of Operations to cease all hostilities immediately. Finance Minister Spitzmüller objected: the armistice agreement must first be signed by both sides, he said. But Foreign Minister Andrassy wearily waved aside this objection: "Let him be! Is the slaughter to go on forever?" It was then about three o'clock in the

morning of November 3. But a few hours later Karl, on the advice of
the Empress Zita, withdrew his consent to the armistice conditions; he
felt he ought to consult with the Council of State. The telegram to
General Weber was rescinded. The order to cease hostilities had already gone out.

Meanwhile General Weber sat in Padua awaiting Vienna's decision.
In the interval he discussed the procedure for putting the armistice
into effect. Among other matters it was agreed that hostilities would
cease twenty-four hours after signature; that would give time for word
to reach the entire front. Finally a coded radiotelegram arrived for
Weber, but he could not read it since he had not taken with him, on
this visit to the enemy, any code keys. The Italians, however, reported
that the Austrian troops had stopped fighting everywhere and were
under the impression that an armistice had been concluded. Weber
replied that he had been granted no authority to sign the armistice.
Lieutenant General Badoglio, the head of the Italian armistice commission, was inclined to suspect some infamous trick in this strange
business. Finally several Austrian officers, whom Weber had sent back
across the front lines, reached Padua again. They reported that they
had received a secret order to accede to the conditions, but that the
order had subsequently been rescinded. Badoglio grew increasingly
suspicious. Either Weber must sign the armistice agreement by midnight November 3 or he would refuse to negotiate any further. Weber
resolved to sign on his own responsibility. But then another difficulty
arose. The Austrian officers who had just come from the front objected
to the interpretation that "immediate" cessation of hostilities meant a
time-limit of twenty-four hours. The Austrians, they pointed out, had
already stopped fighting. They muttered "bad faith." Badoglio's fist
crashed down upon the table: "The negotiations have failed; the war
goes on!" he thundered. This terrified the Austrians and they promptly
gave their signature; it was 5 P.M. on November 3. Badoglio generously
declared his willingness to consider the armistice in force after twenty-
two instead of twenty-four hours. In other words, it would begin at 3
P.M. next day—thirty-six hours after the Austrians had already laid
down their arms. Simultaneously Badoglio ordered flying columns to
cut through the retreating Austrian troops. Ignoring the dismayed protests of the Austrians, the Italians made prisoners of war of all the enemy soldiers they overtook.

Thus the Italians captured 427,000 prisoners, winning their first great
victory in centuries. Vienna's consent arrived a few hours after the
signing of the armistice.

In Budapest a republic was proclaimed, after Karl, speaking in a
trembling voice over the telephone, had forbidden the use of force
against the revolutionaries. The new Hungarian minister of war, Bela

Linder, stated: "Playing soldiers will stop. I want to see no more soldiers." The Emperor Karl had assured his "faithful friend" Kaiser Wilhelm that if the Allies attempted to march across Austria, he would place himself at the head of his German Austrians and die fighting. But even had he wanted to do this, he would not have had the opportunity. Salzburg and Tyrol objected when Bavarian troops occupied the Brenner Pass; a nasty situation arose which was cleared up a few days later, however, when the Bavarians stuck red cockades on their hats and went home. On November 10, 1918, the Schönbrunn Palace band played *Gott erhalte*, the hymn of the monarchy, for the last time. Karl stood at attention, gray-haired and haggard. Haydn's melody had become the funeral dirge of the seven-hundred-year-old Empire.

CHAPTER TWENTY-EIGHT

The Fleet Mutinies

*The Coriolani are not rare in Germany, but
they lack Volscians. . . . What does such a
man care about the smoking ruins of his fatherland, so long as he stands upon them.*

—BISMARCK

I

In his fourth note President Wilson had an-
nounced that the conditions of the armistice would preclude a resump-
tion of the fighting. One group in Germany was struck to the heart by
this news: the officers of the navy. For they knew they would have to
surrender the German fleet.

In the course of two decades they had built this fleet into the second
strongest in the world. In the Battle of Jutland it had compelled the
admiration of the enemy. And yet it had always been denied the laurels
of victory. On the high seas ship after ship had been sent to the bottom
by the stronger enemy forces. Even at Jutland it had had to retreat.
The U-boat campaign, bravely and tenaciously as it had been fought,
had ultimately failed. Were these officers now to compound disgrace
by turning their warships over to the enemy? Certainly the fleet had
been able to keep the Baltic Sea closed, thus blockading Russia and
assuring Germany her supplies of Swedish iron ore. But how pallid
such a practical accomplishment seemed to be when compared with
the glorious victories of the land army. No, the fleet must never become
an object of barter in a shameful peace; rather let all the ships go to
the bottom of the ocean with banners flying. Better to die in honor
than to live on in humiliation. Admiral Scheer issued orders for the
entire fleet to sail toward the mouth of the Thames, thereby challeng-
ing the British fleet to battle.

It was a stirring idea, worthy of the proud tradition of the German
soldier. No country can survive unless it contains some men who are
willing to make such gestures. But at this particular moment Scheer's
plan was fatal. Clausewitz once commented that in any prolonged
struggle the commander must take into account the subversive factor
of war weariness in the army and among the people. Scheer was blind

to one prime fact: since the request for an armistice the sailors considered the naval war over and done with. They were not professional
soldiers, but peaceable citizens who hoped to be able to celebrate
Christmas at home with their wives and children. For the fleet to go
to sea now represented, in their eyes, crazy bravado. Let the officers
in the mess raise their glasses to toast a glorious defeat; the sailors
only shook their heads. Had not one commander stated that the new
government of the Reich consisted of idiots and criminals who ought
to be shot? Was the purpose of this naval action to frustrate the armistice negotiations? The sailors wondered whether the new government knew of this planned voyage to the death.

In fact it had not heard of it! Scheer had concealed his project, and
later denied that he had even planned it. A man of Scheer's stature
was certainly aware that such an operation had its political aspects
and therefore needed the government's endorsement. It has been remarked, with a certain bitter twist, that the mutiny in the fleet had
started out by being a mutiny of the admirals against the government.

II

Scheer's project set off a train of far-reaching troubles. When the fleet
at Schilling Rheede received orders to put to sea, the sailors on several of the ships put out the fires and smashed the anchor winches.
The *Thüringen* and the *Helgoland* were put out of commission. The
mutineers announced that they would defend the coast if the British
came, and that they would also sail out to clear mines; but they would
not participate in a senseless suicide attack. Some let it be known that
they would carry out the thrust against the British navy, but only if
ordered to do so by the government.

Admiral Scheer had to drop his plan, but he made up his mind to
crush the mutiny by force. A torpedo boat and a U-boat were sent up
to the *Thüringen;* the crews of these vessels, which had been constantly engaged with the enemy, were reliable. The mutineers barri-
caded themselves on the forecastle. When the torpedo boat aimed a
10.5 cm. cannon at them, sympathizers on the *Thüringen's* sister ship,
the *Helgoland,* threatened to fire upon the torpedo boat. The U-boat
promptly made ready its torpedoes and warned that it would sink the
Helgoland with all men on board. Simultaneously, a 30.5 cm. gun on
the *Thüringen,* which happened to be manned by a loyal gun-crew, was
trained on the *Helgoland.* At this point the mutineers decided to surrender; they were taken off the ship and brought to Kiel.

The situation might still have been saved. But at this point the naval
chief committed an act of fateful folly: he sent a squadron into Kiel.
At once the sailors united with the dockworkers and attempted to lib-

erate the prisoners. They gathered in a mob; the guards fired; men were killed on both sides.

Up to this point the mutiny had had no political character. But now the sailors fell under the influence of extreme Leftist agitators. These persuaded the sailors that if they seized power and raised the red flag, an immediate peace without cession of territory or reparations would be possible. The sailors boasted that if the British fleet entered Kiel, it would sail out again flying the red flag. Admiral Souchon, commanding at Kiel, could not make up his mind. Twice he appealed to the army for help, twice retracted his appeal. A number of detachments of troops under firm leadership broke through to Kiel. But Souchon began negotiating. The sailors' representative at first made only modest demands: less "sirring" of officers, less saluting, easier duties, longer furloughs. Then came the principal demand: release of the prisoners. The admiral nodded consent. But when the sailors went on to ask for the Kaiser's abdication, he sharply refused to consider the matter.

Meanwhile soviets of soldiers and workers had formed everywhere. Noske, the Social Democratic deputy, arrived in Kiel as representative of the government. He learned that there were no longer any troops willing to fire upon mutineers. Next morning red flags were flying on all the ships. On only one vessel had the officers resisted; two of them were shot, a third severely wounded. Noske offered the rebels freedom from punishment if they would return to their duties. But they hit upon the idea of sailing to other cities—Lübeck, Hamburg, and Bremen—and bringing revolution to the reserve troops.

III

The sailors' mutiny had not arisen out of any desire to proclaim a republic, but out of the simple urge on the part of the men to come home alive and spend Christmas with their families. The conversion of this mutiny into a revolution was due to the disgraceful blindness of the ringleaders, who did not suspect that their vanity would plunge a whole nation to ruin. At this critical moment the folly of a few poor specimens of humanity had the power to sway destiny. It was the traditional German lack of political sense which brought on the catastrophe; in these days of extreme peril another nation would instinctively have closed ranks and not overthrown, a few days before the armistice, the very government which could and was determined to restore peace. The sailors did not sense that at this moment revolution was neither necessary nor possible. Their leaders were wretched rabble, at bottom unconcerned with political questions, interested only in stores of provisions and government treasuries. They did not spread the revolt out of conviction, but out of vanity and cowardice; a general revolution would be the surest way to escape the consequences of their misconduct. The revolutionaries of 1789 had marched against external foes; those of 1918 sold their uniforms. One looks in vain for anything like the grand gesture of the Oath of the Tennis Court during those shameful November days of 1918.

But the pettiness of the rebels had its counterpart in the irresolution of the garrison generals. When the coastal cities were hit by the red epidemic, the army wanted to start a counterattack from Hanover. But the reserve troops, composed exclusively of slackers and the unfit, could not win any battles. Two hundred sailors disarmed the Hanover garrison before the counteraction could begin. If a few well-armed battalions had been formed out of officers and resolute volunteers, they could have dispersed the rebel hordes, who had neither arms nor leaders. But at the key points there were lacking the few hundred real men who might have put up such resistance in good time.

CHAPTER TWENTY-NINE

Revolution

How can a king be swept away
Like so much dust before a broom?
If in the soul their royalty lay
Such would never be their doom.

—GOETHE

I

All revolutions may be seen in two aspects
—there is the soil which is ready for the sowing, and there is the seed
which is dropped into that soil.

The soil of the revolution was hunger, disillusionment, and the yearning for peace. Great masses of the people were at the end of their
strength from starvation. The inevitable inequality of misery made it
the bitterer to bear. In time of war, and especially when war is going
ill, the injustices of this world loom up in their most cruel form before
men's eyes.

The disillusionment was as sharp as the hunger. That very summer
of 1918 the people had been promised Belgium, Poland, and the Baltic
lands. As late as August Ludendorff had insisted upon these war aims.
Thus the armistice request, the raising of the white flag, took the masses
of the people by surprise. The spirit of the masses, subject as it is to
waves of emotion, reacted with blind despair and with fiery hatred
for the deceivers. Were not the propertied classes, the "bigwigs," the
ones who had preached these expansive aims and thereby prolonged
the war? If Germany's position had been half as good as they represented
it, was it not obvious that she could have obtained a compromise peace
at any time? Now the people were determined to have their peace at
any price. The revolution was a peace movement more than an attempt
to overthrow a ruling class. "Let them have their stinking Alsace-
Lorraine," the soldiers cried.

Into this soil deeply plowed by misery and bitterness, three kinds
of seed were planted. The first was scattered by the Communists. They
were headed by Dr. Karl Liebknecht, who had once helped to build the
Social Democratic Party. When speaking from a street-corner platform,
he would wrench open his jacket and shout, "Brothers, shoot me down
on the spot if what I say is not true." He inflamed the minds of the

masses in a manner peculiar to pathological characters. Bolshevistic ideas had already been carried to Germany by returning prisoners of war. After the Peace of Brest-Litovsk Soviet Ambassador Joffe distributed money and agitational literature in quantity in order to stimulate revolution in Germany as the Germans had stimulated it in Russia. Foreign Secretary Scheidemann, the shrewd Social Democrat, at last hit upon the idea of having one of Joffe's boxes of diplomatic mail dropped down a shaft at the Berlin railroad stations so that it broke open and the leaflets were scattered around for all to see. Only then did the government have the evidence needed to expel Joffe from Germany.

In 1917 the Social Democrats split into two groups: the Majority Socialists who rejected revolution, and the Independents who wanted it. The Independents were driven more and more to the Left for a strange reason: they had faith in Ludendorff's generalship. His brutal ruthlessness was the sort of thing they understood, and they consequently believed, at the beginning of 1918, that a German victory was certain. This victory they wanted to prevent.

The second seed was planted by Wilson's idealistic hand. In attacking Germany's "autocrats" in his notes, he was expressing only his desire for a democratic republic along American lines. It did not occur to this professional innocent that so shaken a government could not undergo mere reforms, that the pendulum might swing over to the extreme of Bolshevism, that in a topsy-turvy postwar Europe the Hohenzollern and Hapsburg dynasties, in spite of the shortcomings of their present representatives, Wilhelm and Karl, would form a bulwark against chaos. Wilson sowed the wind and reaped the whirlwind.

The third element was the sailors' mutiny, which was set off by the unfortunate order for the fleet to sail to its death. Had Scheer not issued that order, the revolution would hardly have broken out.

II

On the night of November 7, the Supreme Command at last sent word that it intended to suppress the sailors' rebellion by sending in some front-line divisions. The government sighed with relief; it was still in control of the situation in the east, south and west. But it was already too late. A few hours later General Gröner, Ludendorff's successor, telephoned that he would have to employ his troops to put down a new revolt in Cologne. Worse news followed: the supposedly reliable division which was sent against Cologne refused to attack, and dispersed.

At one o'clock that night word reached Berlin that the Wittelsbacher dynasty of Bavaria, the most conservative state in Germany, had been overthrown. At the end of October the Bavarian prime minister had strongly urged the state prosecutor to release Kurt Eisner, the Munich theatrical critic who was in jail on charges of high treason. His efforts had been successful. Eisner, a gifted columnist, had recently gone over to the right wing of the Majority Socialists. With his straggly beard, his shabby dress, and his distaste for soap and water, he embodied in the eyes of Bavarians the worst type of bohemian. Eisner had called a demonstration for November 7. The government could have forbidden it, dispersed it by a false air raid alarm, or fetched home the troops on the Tyrolese border to keep order. But in spite of warning examples in the north the Bavarian government decided to do nothing. Eisner marched his demonstrators to a beer hall and there founded the Munich Workers' and Soldiers' Soviet; a round of machine-gun fire would have sufficed to scatter the demonstration to the four winds. A small mob gathered in front of the palace, and the war minister had to face the fact that he had no troops who would be willing to fire upon the rioters. That evening the King fled to the mountains; toward midnight Kurt Eisner declared that the thousand-year-old Wittelsbacher dynasty was deposed. Next morning, unwashed and collarless, he appeared at the government offices and appointed himself premier.

III

Prince Max of Baden was still chancellor in Berlin on November 8. With a roll of drums the palace guard still took up its posts. But it presented arms to an empty palace, for at the end of October the Kaiser had fled to general headquarters. When the chancellor had demurred at his leaving, he had replied with base deceitfulness that he had to induct Gröner into his new duties as Ludendorff's successor. When Max asked for an audience, the Kaiser put him off on the grounds that there was danger of infection; Prince Max had just recovered from the grippe. The truth was that Wilhelm was trying to escape from the pressure of the men who were urging his abdication; at the same time he feared revolution. The idea of abdication was something he could never grasp; it did not fit in with his conception that he reigned by divine right—a medieval notion that his associates had let him hold for thirty years.

Ebert and the Social Democratic deputy Südekum—the latter with tears in his eyes—asked General Gröner to see to it that the Kaiser saved the throne by abdicating. Ebert assured Prince Max that he hated revolution, but that the masses were deserting his party in droves; he could persuade them to support the government only if Wilhelm stepped down and let either one of his sons or Prince Max take over as regent for his grandson. The Crown Prince would not do as a successor, having thoroughly discredited himself by his nationalistic speeches and his affairs with women.

Prince Max persistently called on the Kaiser to abdicate in favor of his grandson in order to save the Hohenzollern dynasty. The Kaiser was adamant. Prussian Minister of the Interior Drews rushed to headquarters and implored Wilhelm to make this sacrifice for his country. In vain. The Kaiser first took him to task for breaking his oath of allegiance, then asked him to stay for dinner. He ordered part of the army to turn about and march home to suppress rebellion. Late in the afternoon of November 8, Hindenburg and Gröner came to the conclusion that this order was ill-advised; the army would not obey. But they put off telling the Kaiser until the following morning.

Their delay was fatal. That evening Prince Max had a long telephone conversation with Wilhelm, who was his cousin as well as his emperor. He informed the Kaiser that almost all of Germany was in the hands of soviets of soldiers, that the Bavarian king had been overthrown, Wilhelm's son-in-law in Braunschweig deposed, and that there were no longer any reliable troops available. In Berlin the workers were planning to go out in a general strike the next day and the Socialists to withdraw from the Cabinet unless Wilhelm abdicated.

"Nonsense," Wilhelm retorted. "I have ordered the field marshal to work out an operation against the rebels at home. We are marching tomorrow." In despair, Prince Max hung up. His advisers recommended a coup d'état; let him announce that he had demanded Wilhelm's abdication and that the abdication would go through on the day after the signing of the armistice. But Prince Max was not forceful enough to take such a step. Had he done so, and at the same time proceeded vigorously against the rebels, he might have saved the monarchy and nipped the revolution in the bud. But this was something he recognized only after the war.

By the evening of November 8, however, the big cities of the Rhineland and of North and Central Germany were all, except for Stuttgart and Munich, in the hands of revolutionary soldiers. Berlin was an island in a red sea.

On the morning of November 9, a leader of the Independents issued a call for a general strike and an overthrow of the government. The Majority Socialists urged the workers to stay at their jobs, but they could no longer control their own followers. On November 9, endless columns of soldiers and workers marched through the streets of Berlin. Von Linsingen, the army commander in Brandenburg, had prepared battalions composed of officers, but he lacked the resolution to send them into battle. The reserve troop detachments refused to obey orders. General von Linsingen had the impression that the uprising could no longer be suppressed by force of arms, and issued orders to his soldiers not to fire on the crowds. Prince Max instructed him to have the troops use their weapons only to protect property and the government buildings. Linsingen informed the Prince that the men would probably not shoot even in such a juncture. While the endless processions surged up to the very steps of the government buildings, Prince Max waited in fear and trembling for the telephone call from general headquarters in Spa. Scheidemann declared that Berlin had become a madhouse, and resigned. The only step that might halt a catastrophe was the Kaiser's abdication, and perhaps even that would no longer save the monarchy.

IV

On the morning of November 9 Hindenburg and Gröner called upon the Kaiser. Field Marshal Hindenburg began by saying that he could not utter the words he had to speak; therefore he must resign. The Kaiser interrupted, and ordered Deputy Chief of Staff General Gröner to report.

In the past twenty-four hours Gröner had given up all hope of suppressing the uprising. The news from the front was that the Americans had crossed the Meuse. The revolutionaries were cutting off supplies to the army at the front; existing stocks would last only for five days. After the armistice, which was expected any day now, the army would march home in good order, but not under the banner of Kaiser Wilhelm.

The Kaiser swayed unsteadily as these words were pronounced. His son arrived. The Crown Prince leaped from his car exclaiming: "Hasn't that bunch of sailors been put up against the wall yet?"

The Crown Prince's staff chief, Count Schulenburg, took issue with Gröner. The soldiers must be reminded of their oath to the flag. Gröner shook his head. "The oath is only an idea." His judgment was quickly confirmed. Fifty regimental commanders were called to headquarters and asked whether their men would follow the Kaiser back to Germany to reconquer the homeland from the revolutionaries. Only one man said yes; the majority said no; a few could not say. Apparently, the army was not going to back the Kaiser in a civil war.

The Kaiser thereupon made a decision as weird as his entire life. He would abdicate as Emperor, but remain King of Prussia. Otherwise, he explained, the army officers would resign their commissions and the army would fall apart. This argument revealed Wilhelm's utter ignorance of what was going on in the world. If he abdicated as Emperor and King, and a regent for his grandson was appointed by the government, the officers corps would have no reason to desert the flag. For the masses the Kaiser was the symbol of all their suffering during the past years; they were demanding that he atone by stepping down and leaving the way open to new and better elements. There was no longer any room in the Germany of November 9, 1918 for legalistic subtleties.

Foreign Secretary Hintze, who was at general headquarters, telephoned to Berlin that the Kaiser intended to abdicate; the chancellor must wait for the proclamation. The chancellor replied that there was no time; the abdication must be announced at once. Prince Max therefore took it upon himself to publish the news that Wilhelm had renounced his throne as Emperor of Germany and King of Prussia; he himself would remain in office as chancellor until a regent was installed. He intended to propose Ebert as the new chancellor and to hold elections for a National Constitutional Assembly. Prince Max would not accept the post of regent for himself, although this was urged upon him by South German representatives.

The proclamation had no sooner been issued than Ebert and Scheidemann called upon Prince Max. In a calm and gentle tone Ebert delivered what was in effect an ultimatum: the Social Democrats must take over the government.

"Do you intend to run the government on the basis of the Constitution?" the chancellor asked.

"Within the framework of the monarchic Constitution?" Ebert replied. "Yesterday I would have said yes to this question. Today I must first consult with my friends."

Scheidemann assured Prince Max that all the troops had gone over to the new government. The Prince need only go to the various barracks, or send a deputy, to convince himself of this.

Prince Max resigned, and Scheidemann went before the *Reichstag*. A tremendous crowd was gathered in front of the building. Most of the deputies, including President of the *Reichstag* Fehrenbach, had fled. Philipp Scheidemann was not a man of sober and deliberate temper like Ebert. Carried away by the situation, he stepped out on the balcony and cried: "The German people have won all along the line. The Emperor has abdicated. Germany is a Republic."

Ebert was indignant. "You had no right to do this!" he exclaimed. "That is a matter for the National Assembly." But what was done could not be undone.

In Spa, meanwhile, the Kaiser was dining while in the adjoining room his proclamation was being drawn up. When it was finished, Hintze telephoned the chancellery and began dictating the text: Wilhelm II hereby abdicated as Emperor of Germany and remained as King of Prussia. Privy Councillor Simons at the chancellery replied that the abdication had already been announced, and that no one had foreseen that Wilhelm would choose to remain as King of Prussia. In any case, he said, it did not matter; it would have been out of the question to put through so half-hearted an abdication.

Back at headquarters there was great indignation. "Treason, shameless treason," the Kaiser exclaimed. "A Prince of Baden has overthrown the King of Prussia." The ability to grasp reality was not given to the

Kaiser even at this moment. He covered telegraph blank upon telegraph blank with protests.

They were never sent out, for an hour later events had tempestuously overridden even the abdication. Field Marshal Hindenburg reported to the Kaiser that the situation had grown even worse. "The troops will no longer stand by Your Majesty. There are no longer any loyal troops. Would to God things were different." He feared that the Kaiser might be seized by mutinous troops and carried to Berlin or turned over to the enemy, and he recommended that Wilhelm go to Holland. The Kaiser wavered. At six o'clock in the afternoon he consented to depart, changed his mind at nine, and at ten finally decided to go. Next morning he rode to Holland in the imperial train. To his son he wrote that he had had to leave the field since, with the army shattered, Hindenburg could no longer guarantee his safety.

V

During the war Wilhelm II had scarcely governed his country. How zestfully, before the war, he had spoken time and again of the spirit of battle. But when in wartime it became necessary to make decisions which events could prove right or wrong within a matter of hours, he had left the responsibility to others. The sterling intelligence he periodically displayed had upon occasion operated during the war. At times he was inclined toward a compromise peace, but never pushed the matter. In a highly unautocratic manner he complained that the Supreme Command and the *Reichstag* were ignoring him. His associates took care to shield him from the truth. The clique of aides around him warned all those who wanted to make him face the facts that His Majesty would suffer a nervous collapse. And Wilhelm himself cooperated with them by hiding from reality. When a naval attaché fresh from Constantinople wanted to tell him about the battles for the Dardanelles, the Kaiser did not give him a chance to speak; instead he lectured the man for hours on the Hittites. Toward the end of the war he was an isolated shadow emperor.

One wonders whether on that November 9 he recalled the sentence Bismarck had written to him long ago, when he was still young Crown Prince Wilhelm: that in times of stress the King of Prussia must be prepared to die sword in hand at the foot of his throne. A number of Pomeranian junkers declared their readiness to die with him in a cavalry charge against the enemy lines. Certainly such a heroic death would have saved the dynasty. In justice to Wilhelm it must be admitted that such a last battle would have been difficult to carry out. The Kaiser was almost sixty; and a charge over rough ground might very well have ended in a ludicrous fall from a horse. And if he attempted an assault on foot against the enemy advance guards, he could not be certain that the fatal bullet would strike him. But whatever the outcome, it would have formed a noble climax to the tragedy for several hundred officers, with the Kaiser, Field Marshal Hindenburg and the generals of the court at their head, to have sought death in storming an enemy battery. If he were taken prisoner, he could follow the example of Frederick the Great, who always carried poison in his pocket. Many officers, including Gröner, mentioned this solution to the Kaiser and offered to join him. Wilhelm did not want such an end.

VI

On the night of November 9, while Wilhelm was dining in his special train—thoroughly composed, according to the testimony of his aides— Prince Max bade farewell to Ebert. The new chancellor asked the Prince to remain as regent. But Prince Max refused. He knew that Ebert intended to take the Independents into his government, and he felt he could not work with them. At the door he turned to say: "Herr Ebert, I commit the German Empire to your safekeeping." Ebert replied: "I have lost two sons for this Empire."

Prince Max had entrusted the Reich to a real statesman. Friedrich Ebert, once a saddler, later an editor and secretary of the Social Democratic Party, concealed behind a nondescript exterior a sure instinct for essentials. He was a great personality. During the first three hours of his rule he made two crucial decisions, and both were right. Hardly another man in Germany would have done so.

The revolution was still proceeding along lines consistent with the German love for order. There were no acts of revenge against the erstwhile rulers, no violence; private property was scarcely touched. The representatives of the bourgeois parties had simply vanished. Glee Clubber Fehrenbach, the President of the *Reichstag*, said to Vice Chancellor Payer, "I have been greatly disappointed in Providence," and abandoned the field.

But how long could the masses be kept quiet? Ebert took a bold step: he declared his readiness to form a government consisting of six representatives of the Majority Socialists and the Independents. With great perspicacity he recognized that the radicals could be restrained only if they were inside the government, and then only if he carried out a particular plan he had in mind. The Independents hesitated. As things stood, to remain in the Opposition was a more grateful task than to enter the government. They cunningly asked whether Ebert would also accept Liebknecht in his government. Ebert replied that he would not wreck national unity over the question of personalities; if they wanted

Liebknecht they should have him. Thereupon three Independents agreed to enter the Council of Deputies; they really did not want Liebknecht at all. But they proposed a radical program: political power was to remain in the hands of the workers' and soldiers' soviets. Scheidemann replied in a paternal manner that this was of course impossible. Ebert was wiser. He knew how little programs meant, and he had his plan. He agreed, and let the others go on with their debates.

Back in his room, however, he picked up the telephone and called General Gröner. Ebert knew that the government needed no programs or speeches, but reliable troops; otherwise how in the world could it command respect? And only Hindenburg and Gröner had some reliable troops. In this madhouse that was Germany there was only one stable force: the officers corps. Ebert had to ally himself with the officers.

On this point he found himself in agreement with the new deputy chief of staff. The steady-nerved Gröner had persuaded Hindenburg to stay at his post and lead the army back home. In one brief conversation Ebert and Gröner formed their alliance. The government would assure the supply of food to the army and would support the authority of the officers. The officers corps would defend the government and fight Bolshevism. "Kindly transmit to Field Marshal Hindenburg the gratitude of the government," Ebert said to Gröner. By that act Friedrich Ebert saved Germany from Bolshevism.

VII

At the end of October the Allies had sat down together to confer on armistice conditions. British Field Marshal Haig proposed asking only that the Germans evacuate the occupied territories and Alsace-Lorraine. They were fighting bravely as they retreated, he argued; it was unwise to make stipulations which could not be enforced. The British army was ready to fight, but weary; the French army was scarcely inclined to attack; and the American army was untrained. He did not, of course, mention that England had no desire to see France become too strong.

Pétain favored the surrender of all guns; the Germans must not be in a position to resume the struggle, he insisted, although he recognized that such a condition would scarcely be accepted. Objectively General Pershing should have been most interested in making sure the Germans were not rendered defenseless. For President Wilson's position as arbiter of the world would exist only so long as the Allies needed him to hold down the Germans. But this obvious consideration did not occur to the American general; he sided with Pétain. Clemenceau thought that if the Germans broke off the negotiations now, Germany might succumb to Bolshevism. Lloyd George, too, held that the principal enemy now was not Germany but Bolshevism. Foch, when asked for a military opinion, replied that if the war went on it could last another three to five months. Sonnino, the Italian, emphasized that no armistice with the Germans must be concluded until one had been made with the Austrians. "Otherwise Germans disguised as Austrians might turn up on our front." Clemenceau was royally amused at this timorousness. "We will conduct the negotiations simultaneously," he said. "Will that satisfy you?" "I should like to have that in writing." "We shall be glad to oblige you."

The conditions finally agreed upon amounted to a capitulation: retreat beyond the Rhine; evacuation of three bridgeheads on the right bank of the Rhine; surrender of numerous guns; unilateral release of prisoners of war; continuance of the blockade; surrender of part of the navy; cancellation of the Treaties of Brest-Litovsk and Bucharest; evacuation of occupied territories in the east.

Not until November 5 was a German armistice commission given permission to cross the Allied lines. Prince Max had chosen Erzberger to head it. This was a mistake; the commission should have been headed by a military man, perhaps accompanied by a political adviser. That the grotesque figure of Mathias Erzberger should stride forward out of the November mists at Compiègne to meet Marshal Foch only capped the sorry farce with which the war ended. Erzberger knew no more of the French language than he did of social forms. He himself had not wanted the assignment; he had consented to go out of patriotism or out of vanity.

Foch received the commission with a curt: "What do you want?"

"We have come here," Erzberger replied, "to negotiate on the proposals for an armistice of the Allied Powers."

"I have no proposals to make or negotiations to conduct," Foch answered, and rose to go. Erzberger was at his wits' end. The diplomat on the commission, Count Oberndorff, came to his rescue. "The hour is too grave to quarrel over words, Marshal. How would you like us to put it? The words do not matter to us."

"You gentlemen must know yourselves what you want."

"We have come here on the basis of a note from the President of the United States. With your permission I will read it." Oberndorff read the note aloud; only then did Foch condescend to name the conditions. Erzberger said that they were hard, not to say intolerable; he would have to transmit them to the chancellor and to general headquarters. Foch insisted that this be done by courier. He gave them seventy-two hours to reply. A cavalry captain left at once, crossed the front lines with German bullets whistling around his ears, and reached General Gröner on the evening of November 9. The general had on that same day suffered through the Kaiser's abdication, the proclamation of the republic, and the alliance with Ebert; on top of everything else came these armistice conditions.

But the Supreme Command was no longer in a position to turn down any conditions whatsoever. With revolution in the rear, with supplies for only five days, with open roads to the southern border of Germany, Gröner's only choice was to sign or watch one division after another capitulate for lack of food and munitions. When the supply officer of a corps asked for shells, the staff of the First Army replied: "Throw stones; we have no shells."

Gröner sent the armistice commission a coded radio message asking modifications in regard to the blockade and the prisoners of war. The army officers on the commission negotiated. While Colonel Winterfeld was talking with Foch's chief of staff, Weygand, Foch entered the room and said: "If you are not finished in a quarter of an hour, I shall return, and I guarantee that then we will be finished in five minutes." He showed the German envoys the newspapers; Germany was in the grip of revolutionary chaos, the papers proclaimed. There could no longer be any question of resistance; the Allies therefore had no reason to make concessions.

A new radio message from the Supreme Command arrived uncoded through an oversight. It empowered the members of the commission to sign the armistice even if they could not obtain any amendments. Gröner had sent the telegram in the name of the chancellor; who the chancellor was at the moment, he did not know. Therefore the telegram ended: "Chancellor *Schluss*" (i.e., "end of message"). "Who is this new Chancellor Schluss?" the French asked warily.

On the night of November 10-11 the armistice was signed. Winterfeld turned his face to the wall. But Erzberger rose and delivered a speech, talking so fluently that the interpreter could scarcely keep up with him. The Germans would honestly endeavor to meet the conditions, he said, although some of them were impossible. The British and French looked aside; they were embarrassed to see a man making a speech in this hour of profound humiliation. Erzberger concluded: "A nation of seventy million suffers, but it does not die." "Very well," Foch said, and left the room. Erzberger gave a low bow.

The guns fell silent. More than nine million dead lay upon the battlefields. Of thirteen million German soldiers, about one seventh had fallen. One fourth of the active officers were dead.

VIII

Seven months after the armistice, peace was concluded. For the first time in the history of nations the statesmen of the victorious powers were forced to keep their eyes more upon their electorates than upon the future. At the Congress of Vienna in 1815 Castlereagh had stated that the task was not the easy one of taking vengeance, but the difficult one of establishing a lasting peace. Wilson, Lloyd George, Clemenceau and Orlando could not afford the luxury of the long view. The peoples were deciding now, and the peoples wanted revenge and spoils. The masses are immoderate. Consequently, the Treaty of Versailles became the worst peace in modern history. It violated the agreements the Allies had made with the Germans before the armistice. And what was worse, it violated good sense and the great tradition of the European balance of power. In the heart of the Continent it created a power vacuum, thereby throwing the structure of Europe out of joint for good and all. Europe never again regained her lost position in the world.

CHAPTER THIRTY

Why Germany Lost the First World War

Against greatly superior forces it is possible to win a battle, but hardly a war.

—NAPOLEON

The struggle was beyond our strength.

—HINDENBURG

I

The four Central Powers were opposed by twenty-nine countries comprising four-fifths of the population of the earth. To be sure, some of those countries entered the war only to the extent of confiscating German property and supplying the combatant Allies with goods. But even the Allies who took a direct part in the war commanded at the end a fourfold superiority in population and productive resources. It followed that they were enormously the richer in war equipment. For example, by the end of the war the Allies had some 200,000 trucks at their disposal; the Germans 40,000. The armies these Allies were able to place in the field averaged, throughout the war, twice the manpower of their enemies; if the war had continued into 1919, the proportion would have risen to four to one. The Allied navy was about five times the size of the combined fleets of the Central Powers. It was able to cut the Central Powers off from the world and establish a blockade which by sheer starvation seriously undermined their resistance. The Central Powers' two principal foes, England and America, were protected by their geographical situation from an attack upon their home grounds.

Germany, supported by inadequate allies, stood against the entire world. Even before the first cavalry patrolmen swung foot into stirrup in August 1914, German diplomacy had lost the war.

Confronted with such vast superiority, Germany was never in a position to force all her enemies to their knees and carve huge provinces out of their lands. Even a compromise peace in which Germany retained what had been hers would have been a victory; after Russia's downfall, Germany's position would have been stronger than at the start of the struggle. And such a compromise peace Germany could have obtained if she had refrained from the crucial error of unrestricted submarine warfare. A few months later Russia collapsed. Had the Allies not known, at the time of the Russian breakdown, that America was behind them, they would almost certainly have made peace.

As late as the beginning of 1918 Germany could still, in all probability, have obtained a tolerable peace—that is, one in which large parts of Alsace-Lorraine were exchanged for French colonies. Lloyd George once remarked that the war would probably have turned out differently if Germany had been led by Bismarck and the elder Moltke.

II

The great British prime minister went on to say that the mistakes of the Germans had saved the Allies from the consequences of their own errors. He dwelt fondly upon the inadequacies of British generals. "Our war administration," he said, "have committed every blunder that the enemy could wish them to be guilty of." It was the fault of the British generals that the flower of English youth was slaughtered in the mud of Flanders. The generals had failed completely in supplying munitions because they did not realize in time that hand grenades and machine-guns were replacing the rifle, high-explosive shells the shrapnel shells. They had left it to outsiders to invent the tank and see that it was used. They had never achieved unified command among all the Allies. In short: "It became increasingly evident to the rawest amateur mind that the military were fumbling badly with their job. We have been let down so often that it is criminal folly on our part to depend any longer for the safety of the Empire on our present military organization." In a similar vein Clemenceau said: "War is far too difficult a matter to be left to the generals."

Even if we take the temperamental outbursts of the great Welsh demagogue with a grain of salt, it may still be said that the Allies probably could have won the war much sooner. In their strategy they did not fully exploit their command of the seas and their material superiority.

The German blunders have been listed many times by military commentators on both sides. The Battle of the Marne; the awkward Austrian deployment in 1914; the commitment of new regiments at Ypres; the failure to support Hindenburg's army in November 1914; the refusal to attempt a pincers movement in the east in 1915; the assault upon Verdun in 1916; the failure to advance from Tyrol in the fall of 1917; leaving too many troops in the east in 1918; failing to build rear positions in France; the offensive in the west in 1918; and above all the two most frightful follies: unrestricted submarine warfare and the request for an armistice. Nor were these tactics deplored purely in hindsight. Most of the measures referred to were condemned with good reason by intelligent military and non-military experts before they were undertaken.

British Prime Minister Asquith once remarked to Field Marshal Wilson that it was strange the war had not produced any great generals. "Nor has it produced a statesman," Wilson replied. His retort was just. None of the statesmen of the First World War even remotely compares with men like Talleyrand, Stein, Metternich, Castlereagh, Gladstone, Cavour, Bismarck or Salisbury. The German statesmen demonstrated their inadequacy above all by clinging to war aims which sensible Germans recognized from the very beginning to be unattainable. In the making of the peace the Allies showed that they lacked the most important trait of the statesman: the capacity for putting over what is reasonable as against what is popular. All together opened the gates to the inordinate evils which burst upon the world during the subsequent years of the twentieth century. The guilt for present world conditions is shared by the statesmen, monarchs, parliaments and peoples of all countries.

Why did Germany lose the war? Because wars against such vastly superior forces cannot be won. At best Germany could have had a draw. She lost the chance for that by grave strategic and political errors.

III

There is a theory once popular in Germany that the German defeat cannot have been due to the superiority of the enemy and the blunders of German leadership. Rather, the story has it, the victorious army was stabbed in the back by traitors at home. This stab-in-the-back theory appears in two forms. According to the one, the German army's morale had been undermined by subversive forces long before the collapse. According to the other, the peace would not have turned out so badly if the November uprising had not knocked all the weapons out of the hands of the German leaders.

Let us examine the first charge. There is no denying that considerable pacifistic and revolutionary propaganda was being disseminated in Germany—as it was among all the belligerents. How effective was this agitation? Undoubtedly morale had sagged in the army and at home in 1918; between July and November the Germans lost 350,000 prisoners. But many forces were operating: the offensive had failed; the hopes for peace had vanished; rations were bad; the enemy's technical and manpower superiority was steadily growing. How are we to determine the influence of radical agitation upon the flagging fighting spirit of the men?

The men who were officially charged with guarding the morale of the army are perhaps our best witnesses. At the end of June 1918, Colonel Nicolai, the German Chief of Counter-Intelligence, told a meeting of officers in charge of patriotic indoctrination: "From all that has been said by you gentlemen, who have your fingers upon the pulse of the army, I conclude that the army's spirit is sound." At the end of September, when Ludendorff admitted defeat, he did not so much as mention radical agitation as one of the causes, although at the time he was eagerly seeking scapegoats. In the secret report of the general staff to the military Cabinet, dated October 31, 1918, there is not a word about propagandistic subversion of the troops. At the end of October Ludendorff also mentioned that the divisions which had folded during Haig's great August offensive had again done their duty in the middle of October; influenza and the shortage of potatoes had weakened them earlier, he said. He did not mention agitation.

In short, right down to the end of the war no member of the Supreme Command ever held that systematic subversion at the front had greatly contributed to the military defeat. There was a plethora of other causes for defeat.

IV

There is something to the argument in its second form: that without the revolution Germany would have been able to obtain better armistice and peace conditions.

Even without the mutiny of the sailors and the revolution, the Allies would have insisted on capitulation, for the armistice conditions had been drafted before these events. And regardless of circumstances the Allies would have refused concessions which would have allowed Germany to resume the struggle after a breathing spell; no victorious army gives its enemy a breathing spell. In any case, after retreating from France Germany would have been incapable of any *protracted* resistance. Enemy superiority was too overwhelming; not a gun was left in the fortresses of Metz and Strassburg—they had all been used for the field army. And brief resistance would only have meant useless sacrifices.

But if there had been no revolution Prince Max might have had a free hand, and to judge by his stated intentions he would have used it to some effect. When he received the text of the armistice agreement, he might have announced publicly: "Since we are being asked to surrender unconditionally, two questions about President Wilson's Fourteen Points must first be clarified. We will sign the armistice only if we receive two assurances:

"First: No territory will be detached from Germany without the holding of a plebiscite under neutral supervision; the German-speaking inhabitants of Austria must also be permitted to determine their own destiny by plebiscite. We will forgo a plebiscite in Alsace-Lorraine.

"Second: The peace treaty must not contain clauses which violate Germany's honor or which will destroy her economy. In disputed cases a neutral tribunal will decide."

Would the Allies have extended such assurances? Undoubtedly France would have held out for harshness. But for Lloyd George and Woodrow Wilson it would have been difficult to refuse concessions which corresponded so completely with the ideas of their voters. And would the soldiers of the Allied Powers really have been tempted to run head-on into the Antwerp-Meuse line or fight their way across the Rhine in order to win more territory for the Poles and Czechs? At such a moment London might well have recalled her traditional concern with the balance of power, might well have wanted to dampen French ambitions. We know that the Allies had a high estimate of German fighting power at the end of October. They themselves were having the hardest time bringing up their supplies. A grand offensive in Lorraine was being planned, but Foch himself said later that it would not have been an annihilating blow. The Italians were terrified at the thought of fighting German troops. The Salonika army would have had to organize an extensive new supply system before it could advance to the southern border of Germany. Lloyd George did not like the idea of spilling more blood and had expressly warned Haig against incurring heavy casualties. Foch was opposed to risks. The Allies were, of course, absolutely confident of victory at this point. But if they could win the chief fruits of victory without more fighting, would they really have presumed to sacrifice more tens of thousands of human lives? They feared above all providing a tremendous opportunity for their principal enemy, the Bolshevists. They feared the possibility of an alliance between a desperate German government and revolutionary Russia.

It seems therefore highly probable that the Allies would have made and kept both assurances—or at least the first. That would have been enormously important. It would have prevented the detachment of some of the Polish provinces of Prussia; it would have united German Austria, the Sudetenland and South Tyrol with Germany; there would have been no bickering over reparations. All things considered, it must be said that had the German revolution not taken place, the Treaty of Versailles would have turned out differently and the entire postwar history of Europe would have been a good deal happier.

In this war, as so often in history, embittered fanaticism plunged Germany into ruin. First the fantastic war aims of the Right, and the unrestricted submarine warfare which sprang from those aims, robbed

Germany of her chances for a compromise. The revolution at the worst possible moment cost her the opportunity for a rational peace in which she would lose something but not everything.

V

Winston Churchill concluded his memoirs of the First World War with the words: "For four years Germany fought and defied the five continents of the world by land and sea and air. The German Armies upheld her tottering confederates, intervened in every theatre with success, stood everywhere on conquered territory, and inflicted on their enemies more than twice the bloodshed they suffered themselves. To break their strength and science and curb their fury, it was necessary to bring all the greatest nations of mankind into the field against them. Overwhelming populations, unlimited resources, measureless sacrifice, the Sea Blockade, could not prevail for fifty months. Small states were trampled down in the struggle; a mighty Empire was battered into unrecognizable fragments; and nearly twenty million men perished or shed their blood before the sword was wrested from that terrible hand. Surely, Germans, for history it is enough!"

CHRONOLOGICAL TABLE

1888	Accession of Kaiser Wilhelm II.
1890	Dismissal of Bismarck. Caprivi chancellor. Reinsurance Treaty with Russia not renewed.
1894	Caprivi dismissed. Hohenlohe chancellor. Beginning of the Berlin-to-Bagdad Railroad.
1898	Kiaochow occupied. First Navy Law. Spanish-American War.
1898–1901	British overtures to Germany.
1899–1901	Boer War.
1900	Hohenlohe dismissed. Bülow chancellor. New Navy Law.
1904	Anglo-French entente.
1904–05	Russo-Japanese War.
1905	Russo-German Treaty of Björkö.
1906	First Morocco Crisis. Landing in Tangier. Algeciras Conference.
1907	Anglo-Russian pact.
1908	*Daily Telegraph* interview. Annexation of Bosnia.
1909	Dismissal of Bülow. Bethmann chancellor.
1911	Second Morocco Crisis. *Panther's* spring to Agadir.
1912–13	Balkan Wars.
1914	Assassination of Franz Ferdinand (June 28). Austria's ultimatum (July 23). Outbreak of War (August 1). German advance in west. Retreat on the Marne (September 10). Battle of Tannenberg (August 26–30).
1915	Positional warfare in the west. Struggle for Gallipoli. Breakthrough at Gorlice (May 1), followed by advance in the east. Conquest of Serbia (after October 6).
1916	Offensive at Verdun (February 22). Battle of the Somme (July 1 to November 26). Brussilov offensive (June 1). Rumanian declaration of war (August 28). Hindenburg and Ludendorff take command (August 29). Proclamation of Polish state (November 5). Peace feeler of Central Powers (December 12).
1917	Unrestricted submarine warfare (February 1). Russian Revolution (after March 8). Siegfried withdrawal in the west. American declaration of war (April 6). Bethmann's fall; Michaelis chancellor. Peace resolution (July 14). Papal mediation (August 1). Fall of Michaelis; Hertling chancellor (October 30). Bolshevist Revolution (November 6). Armistice in the east (December 13).

1918   Treaty of Brest-Litovsk (March 3). Beginning of German
            offensive (March 21). Beginning of counteroffensive (July
            18). Collapse of Bulgaria (October 24). Ludendorff asks
            for an armistice (September 29). Resignation of Hertling;
            Prince Max of Baden chancellor (October 5). Sailors'
            mutiny (November 3). Victory of the Revolution; abdica-
            tion and flight of the Kaiser (November 9). Armistice
            (November 11).

1919   Treaty of Versailles (July 26).

SELECTIVE BIBLIOGRAPHY

Source material for the period from 1890 to 1918 is extensive. Many excellent bibliographies are available in such works as:

Frauenholz, E. v., *Führer in die Weltkriegsliteratur*. Berlin, 1932.
Langer, William L., *European Alliances and Alignments 1871–1890*. New York, 1950.
———, *The Diplomacy of Imperialism 1890–1902*. New York, 1950.
Salis, J. R. von, *Weltgeschichte der neuesten Zeit*, Vol. I. Zürich, 1951.

The most valuable material is to be found in the collections of documents:

British Documents on the Origins of the War 1898–1914. Edited by G. P. Gooch and H. Temperley, 14 vols. London, 1925 *et seq.*
Die deutschen Dokumente zum Kriegsausbruch. Collected by K. Kautsky. Edited by M. Montgelas and W. Schücking, 2nd ed., 4 vols. Berlin, 1927.
Die grosse Politik der europäischen Kabinette, 1871–1914. Edited by A. Lepsius, A. Mendelssohn-Bartholdy, and F. Thimme, 52 vols. Berlin, 1922–26.
Documents diplomatiques français 1871–1914. Edited by a committee under the chairmanship of S. Charléty. Paris, 1929 *et seq.*

For the War, there is data published by the various general staffs. In addition, extremely valuable material is contained in the 21 volumes published by the Investigating Committee of the German *Reichstag* on World War I.

Memoirs, posthumous papers or letters of most of the participants in the events have been published. There are such works by:
Asquith, Bernstorff, Bethmann, Bismarck, Brussilov, Bülow, Burian, Cadorna, Caillaux, Churchill, Clemenceau, Conrad, Czernin, Erzberger, Eulenburg, Falkenhayn, Fisher, Giolitti, Grey, Giessl, Haig, Helfferich, Hindenburg, Hoffmann, Hohenlohe, Jagow, Jellicoe, Joffe, Kerensky, Kiderlen, Kluck, Kühlmann, Liman, Lloyd George, Ludendorff, Prince Max of Baden, Michaelis, Moltke, Musulin, Paléologue, Payer, Pétain, Poincaré, Pourtalès, Sazonov, Scheer, Scheidemann, Schoen, Schweinitz, Sukhomlinov, Tirpitz, Waldersee, Wilhelm II, Wilson, Witte.
The titles of such memoirs can be found in the above-mentioned bibliographies, which also list the most important biographies of these personages.

The number of major histories on our period is likewise very large. In addition to the works already mentioned, the following are particularly noteworthy:

Brandenburg, Erich, *Von Bismarck zum Weltkrieg. Die deutsche Politik in den Jahrzehnten vor dem Krieg.* 2nd ed. Berlin, 1925.

Croce, Benedetto, *History of Italy 1871–1915.*

———, *History of Europe in the Nineteenth Century.*

Dawson, W. A. and G. P. Gooch, *The Cambridge History of British Foreign Policy, 1773–1919.* Vol. III. London, 1923.

Fay, Sidney B., *The Origins of the World War.* 2 vols. New York, 1928.

Friedjung, H., *Das Zeitalter des Imperialismus, 1884–1914,* 3 vols. Berlin, 1919–22.

Gooch, G. P., *History of Modern Europe, 1878–1919,* 4th ed. London, 1928.

———, *Recent Revelations of European Diplomacy,* 4th ed. London, 1930.

Hartung, Fr., *Deutsche Geschichte (1871–1919),* 2nd ed. Bonn, 1924.

Oncken, Hermann, *Das Deutsche Reich und die Vorgeschichte des Weltkrieges,* 2 vols. Leipzig, 1922.

Rachfahl, F., *Deutschland und die Weltpolitik, 1871–1914.* Vol. I: *Die Bismarcksche Ära.* Stuttgart, 1923. Vol. II: *Die deutsche Aussenpolitik in der wilhelminischen Ära.* Berlin, 1924.

Renouvin, Pierre, in the "Clio" collection: *L'Epoque contemporaine* II, "La Paix armée et la grande guerre." Paris, 1939. (Reprinted 1949.)

Wahl, Adalbert, *Deutsche Geschichte von der Reichsgründung bis zum Ausbruch des Weltkrieges (1871–1914),* 4 vols. Stuttgart, 1926–36.

Wegerer, Alfred von, *Der Ausbruch des Weltkrieges 1914.* Hamburg, 1939.

Studies of special problems of the period are also listed in the bibliographies. Among the more recent publications which are not included in these bibliographies, the following may be mentioned:

Breucker, Wilhelm, *Die Tragik Ludendorffs.* Stollham, 1953.

Foerster, Wolfgang, *Der Feldherr Ludendorff im Unglück.* Wiesbaden, 1953.

Selective Index of Names